POETIC CRAFT IN THE EARLY
GREEK ELEGISTS

POETIC CRAFT IN THE EARLY GREEK ELEGISTS

A. W. H. ADKINS

THE UNIVERSITY OF CHICAGO PRESS · CHICAGO AND LONDON

A. W. H. ADKINS is the Edward Olson Professor of Greek, professor of philosophy and early Christian literature, and Chairman of the Committee on the Ancient Mediterranean World at the University of Chicago. He is the author of *Merit and Responsibility*, also published by the University of Chicago Press.

The University of Chicago Press, Chicago 60637
The University of Chicago Press, Ltd., London
© 1985 by The University of Chicago
All rights reserved. Published 1985
Printed in the United States of America

94 93 92 91 90 89 88 87 86 85   5 4 3 2 1

Library of Congress Cataloging in Publication Data

Adkins, A. W. H. (Arthur W. H.)
  Poetic craft in the early Greek elegists.

  Bibliography: p.
  Includes index.
  1. Elegiac poetry, Greek—History and criticism.
2. Greek language—Metrics and rhythmics.   I. Title.
PA3113.A3   1985   884′.01′09   84-16203
ISBN 0-226-00725-1

CONTENTS

Poems Analyzed in This Book vi
List of Tables vii
Preface ix
Acknowledgments xi
1 Introduction 1
2 Archilochus 33
3 Callinus 55
4 Tyrtaeus 67
5 Mimnermus 93
6 Solon 107
7 "Theognis" 133
8 Simonides 161
9 Xenophanes 174
10 Retrospect and Prospect 199
Appendix: Solon 4W. 12–13 207
Notes 209
Bibliography 231
General Index 241
Greek Index 247

POEMS ANALYZED
IN THIS BOOK

ARCHILOCHUS
3W 44
4W 47
5W 50
13W 35

CALLINUS
1W 55

MIMNERMUS
1W 95
5W 101

SIMONIDES
6W 162
8W 166

SOLON
4W 108
27W 125

THEOGNIDEA
31–38W 15
133–42W 15
183–92W 134
237–54W 142
731–52W 153

TYRTAEUS
4W 68
5W. 5–8 28
11W 75

XENOPHANES
1W 175
2W 186

LIST OF TABLES

1. Position of Punctuation: Hexameters   8
2. Percentages of Punctuation: Hexameters   12
3. Position and Percentages of Punctuation: Pentameters   12
4. Position and Percentages of Major Caesurae   13
5. Percentages of Punctuation at Major Caesurae   13
6. Length of Final Words in Hexameters   16
7. Length of Final Words in Pentameters of the Eight Elegists   17

PREFACE

In this book I study what the ancient Greeks themselves, who did not distinguish art from craft, would have termed the τέχνη of the early Greek elegists. My goal is to establish the resources of language, culture, and meter that were available to the early elegists of Greece and to discuss the extent to which each poet made use of his opportunities. It is my hope that the discussions that follow will enhance my readers' appreciation of the early Greek elegists as poets. Though few of my earlier publications address questions of the kind raised in this book, my concern with them is not a recent aberration. The second course of lectures of my career, delivered to the Honours Class of the Humanity (Latin) Department of the University of Glasgow in 1955/56, had Virgil's *Eclogues* as its theme, and much of my time was devoted to topics analogous to those discussed in the present work: the characteristics of the Latin and Greek hexameter and Virgil's use of his borrowings from Theocritus. My interest in the rhythmic qualities of Greek and Latin meters began earlier, at the period when I first composed botched copies of verses in the meters, if not in the manners, of the Greek and Roman poets. My interest in the rhythmic qualities of English meters began earlier still. I find it difficult to understand why I did not write a book of this kind long ago.

The present book has not been quickly brought to birth. It was conceived in the fall of 1974, and I write these words in September 1983—a period of gestation that would have pleased Horace but ill suits these less leisurely times. (I hope that any siblings may see the light of day more promptly.) Completion of the work has been delayed by other intellectual pursuits and also by five rather grim years spent as chairman of Classics at the University of Chicago. However, the study leave in the Winter and Spring quarters of 1982, which was the reward for my unfruitful labors, furnished both the stimulus and the opportunity to complete the manuscript. For this relief my sincerest thanks are due to all concerned.

I wish to thank also Joanne Mencius—a paleographer *manquée*—for producing an elegant typescript from my ever more illegible longhand, and Jacqueline Trussell for typing assistance in the final stages of the work.

ACKNOWLEDGMENTS

The text of the early Greek elegists used throughout this book is that of M. L. West, *Iambi et Elegi Graeci ante Alexandrum Cantati*, 2 vols., copyright © 1971, 1972, by Oxford University Press. Reprinted by permission of Oxford University Press. I have printed the letter W after each poem or fragment number and have referred to the work itself throughout as West 1972.

The third chapter of this book consists of an adapted version of pages 61–75 of my article "Callinus 1 and Tyrtaeus 10 as Poetry," published in *Harvard Studies in Classical Philology* 81 (1977): 59–97. In addition, parts of my first chapter are elaborated from pages 62, 68–69, 87, and 88–89 of that article. The material is reprinted here by permission of the President and Fellows of Harvard College.

Five stanzas from Rudyard Kipling's "The Exiles' Line" are reprinted here from *The Definitive Edition of Rudyard Kipling's Verse* (London: Hodder & Stoughton, 1948) by permission of The National Trust.

The fifth stanza of Ogden Nash's "Exit, Pursued by a Bear," copyright © 1954 by Ogden Nash, which first appeared in *The New Yorker*, is reprinted from Ogden Nash, *Verses from 1929 On* (Boston: Little, Brown, 1959), by permission of Little, Brown and Company. In Great Britain this poem is published in Ogden Nash, *I Wouldn't Have Missed It* (London: Andre Deutsch, 1983) and is reprinted here by permission of Andre Deutsch, Ltd.

1
INTRODUCTION

If not impossible, it is certainly very unlikely that a modern reader will immediately respond to poetry written in ancient Greek, the dead language of a remote culture, precisely as the poet intended or as the original audience did respond. The modern reader lacks not merely particular items of factual information, which, when available, can be neatly presented to him in learned footnotes. He lacks many things, most of which can now be acquired, if at all, only by sustained effort, though they were immediately accessible to those who lived in the culture and spoke the language.

Consider first the language. A sensitivity to the connotation of words, imperceptibly acquired in one's own language as one uses it from earliest years, is difficult to develop in a second language even where native speakers are readily available, and it is many times more difficult in a dead language, where documents are few and native speakers no longer exist.[1] There are also cultural differences in the manner in which the poems are presented. The modern reader, silently perusing the page, does not experience Greek poems in the same way as the audience for whom the Greek poets composed them; for Greek poetry was written not to be read but to be heard in performance. The modern reader does not experience the sounds of the words or the tensions and relaxations of the meter and so may well overlook the manner in which the poet has more or less skillfully composed his poem to take advantage of the characteristics of his meter. Lastly, the modern reader does not participate in the culture as the ancient poet and his audience participated in it, as it pervaded every aspect of their lives and created poetic possibilities which may be unique. Much of the cultural horizon of the early elegists and their audiences was bounded by the Homeric poems. This situation furnished a potential resource for the early elegists. I shall argue that a number of them drew upon it.

We cannot now hope to stand precisely where the archaic, or even the classical, Greeks stood and appreciate ancient poetry precisely as they did. But every step in that direction which can be taken is worth taking. The goal of the chapters that follow is to take one or two steps toward the appreciation of a number of archaic Greek poets. The goal furnishes the sole justification for the methods employed. To know, for example, the distribution of punctuation or caesurae in early elegy is relevant insofar as it enhances the appreciation of particular poems. The methods are not the only possible methods of studying poetry; but they seem compatible with most others, since their aim is to exhibit the complexity of the works studied, and they are in principle applicable to any ancient Greek poetry.

This book will discuss works of eight writers: Archilochus, Callinus, Tyrtaeus, Mimnermus, Theognis—or, rather, the *Theognidea*—Solon, Simonides, and Xenophanes. Since the most obvious common characteristic of the works selected is that all are composed in elegiac couplets, it will be best to begin with a discussion of the elegiac meter.

The Elegiac Couplet

Formally, the elegiac meter is composed of repeated couplets: a longer line, known as a dactylic hexameter catalectic, followed by a shorter line, known as a dactylic pentameter. If $\smile\smile$ signifies the possibility of replacing two short syllables with a long syllable, and × a syllable which may be either long or short, the elegiac couplet may be represented as follows:

$$-\smile\smile-\smile\smile-\smile\smile-\smile\smile-\smile\smile-\times$$
$$-\smile\smile-\smile\smile--\smile\smile-\smile\smile\times$$

Modern scholarship treats the couplet as consisting essentially of four dactylic hemiepe. In the notation of Paul Maas (1962) and West (1982), the dactylic hemiepes, $-\smile\smile-\smile\smile-$, is represented by D, and the couplet is represented thus:

$$D\smile\smile D\times$$
$$DD$$

For my purposes, this analysis of the pentameter presents no problems. It is mandatory that the end of a word coincide with the end of the first hemiepes of the pentameter. There is colon diaeresis at this point. The pentameter in performance is heard as two dactylic hemiepe.

In the hexameter, however, D is a metrician's abstraction. In performance, the hexameter too consists of two units. It may be phrased in three ways to give units of six different lengths, only one of which is D. To use a notation which suggests that the line is experienced as two hemiepe with a number of extra syllables may be seriously misleading.

Introduction

I shall accordingly use the former method of representing the couplet here. Since it will frequently be necessary to refer to particular syllables in the line, I shall number the syllables, using the prefixes H and P to refer to the hexameter and pentameter:

H $-\underset{2\ 3}{\smile\smile}-\underset{5\ 6}{\smile\smile}-\underset{8\ 9}{\smile\smile}-\underset{11\ 12}{\smile\smile}-\underset{14\ 15}{\smile\smile}-\underset{17}{\text{x}}$

P $-\underset{2\ 3}{\smile\smile}-\underset{5\ 6}{\smile\smile}--\underset{8\ 9}{\smile\smile}-\underset{11\ 12}{\smile\smile}\underset{14}{\text{x}}$

In the hexameter, one or more of the first five dactyls may be replaced by spondees; in the pentameter, either or both of the dactyls in the first hemiepes may be replaced by spondees, but the second hemiepes must always be dactylic.

The meter is flexible. In a system where any of a number of units may have one of two values, the number of possible states of the system is 2^n where n is the number of units. Since five of the dactyls in the hexameter and two in the pentameter may be replaced by spondees, here $n = 7$, and the number of possible states is 2^7, or 128. The limits of variation for the hexameter are represented by a completely dactylic line, such as Callinus 1W. 10 (for "W," see above, p. xi):

ἔγχος ἀνασχόμενος καὶ ὑπ' ἀσπίδος ἄλκιμον ἦτορ

and by the completely spondaic *Odyssey* 21. 15 (a rare phenomenon):

τὼ δ' ἐν Μεσσήνῃ ξυμβλήτην ἀλλήλοιϊν

The pentameter may vary between the completely dactylic, as in Callinus 1W. 17:

τὸν δ' ὀλίγος στενάχει καὶ μέγας ἤν τι πάθῃ

and the line with spondaic first hemiepes, as in Callinus 1W. 19:

θνήσκοντος, ζώων δ' ἄξιος ἡμιθέων.

For the poets' audiences, variations in the form of the couplet were immediate acoustic data. Performed aloud, the completely dactylic Callinus 1W. 10 has an effect completely different from the completely spondaic *Odyssey* 21. 15; and between these extremes a complex and subtle counterpoint of dactyl against spondee is accessible to all who have ears to hear.

The hexameter has other mandatory features. There must be word end at H7, H8, or H10. There is a mandatory caesura in each hexameter. In many discussions, "major caesura" is synonymous with "mandatory caesura," but for my purposes it may be necessary to distinguish between the two.

In the majority of dactylic hexameters, caesura occurs after either H7 (penthemimeral) or H8 (trochaic). The first line of the *Iliad*,

$$\text{Μῆνιν ἄειδε, θεά, | Πηληϊάδεω Ἀχιλῆος}$$

exemplifies the first. The first line of the *Odyssey*,

$$\text{Ἄνδρα μοι ἔννεπε, Μοῦσα, | πολύτροπον, ὃς μάλα πολλά}$$

exemplifies the second.

Some lines have no word end at these points. Such lines always have caesura at H10 (hephthemimeral). An example is *Iliad* 1. 307:

$$\text{ἤϊε σύν τε Μενοιτιάδῃ | καὶ οἷς ἑτάροισιν.}$$

Lines of this type are comparatively rare. Those with caesura at H10 usually have caesura also at H7 or H8, as do the seventh and eighth lines of *Iliad* 1:

$$\text{Ἀτρεΐδης τε ἄναξ ἀνδρῶν καὶ δῖος Ἀχιλλεύς.}$$
$$\text{τίς δ' ἄρ σφωε θεῶν ἔριδι ξυνέηκε μάχεσθαι;}$$

It seems to be customary to treat the third-foot caesura, where there is one, as the major caesura of the line,[2] so that each of these lines has major caesura at H7. But the demand for caesura in the hexameter, diaeresis in the pentameter, is an acoustic demand: the lines are phrased in smaller units in performance. Lines such as *Iliad* 1. 307 indicate that a phrasing which divides the line at H10 is acceptable.

Consider *Iliad* 1. 7–8. To phrase 8 in two units divided at H7 enhances the sense; but to phrase 7 similarly separates ἄναξ from its dependent genitive, which has no grammatical relationship with any word in the speech unit in which it is now included. Where caesura occurs in both the third foot and at H10, I take into account the sense of the lines in determining the major caesura. It is prima facie implausible that sense did not affect the phrasing of the lines in performance, and the implausibility becomes even more apparent when the elegists' methods of composition are studied in detail.

My percentages of caesurae occurring at H7, H8, and H10 differ greatly from those of other scholars. Maas, evidently reckoning any third-foot caesura as the major caesura, estimates that there is only 1 percent of fourth-foot caesurae in Homeric hexameters, and West (1974, 112) lists only eight lines of this type in the elegists studied in this book, all in the *Theognidea* and Xenophanes. Since not all hexameters in Homer and elegy have caesura at H7 or H8, these caesurae cannot be termed mandatory; but since all hexameters in six of the poets discussed here have caesurae at H7 or H8, sometimes accompanied by caesura at H10, it might be argued that for these poets caesura at H7 or H8 is mandatory. Some caution is desirable: only 1 percent of Homeric lines are of this form, and of the six elegists in question only Solon furnishes more than one hundred extant hexameters. But even if for these elegists a caesura at H7 or H8 was mandatory, there are numerous lines of their poetry in which that caesura is not the major caesura in the sense described above.

Since diaeresis occurs wherever word end coincides with the end of the metrical foot or colon and caesura occurs at the end of all other words,[3] an elegiac couplet contains many caesurae and many diaereses. In the following discussions, where the sense is clear I shall sometimes use "caesura" for "major caesura" and "diaeresis" for "colon diaeresis."

Line end in both hexameter and pentameter marks the most important divisions of the elegiac couplet: syllaba anceps and hiatus are common in both positions, and elision between lines does not occur. Syllaba anceps and hiatus are very rare at caesura and diaeresis, and elision is allowed (Xenophanes 1W. 17, Callinus 1W. 2). Nevertheless, each line is not one unit but two, in both composition and performance, so that the two lines of the couplet present themselves as four units to the ear. (How the divisions are marked acoustically will be discussed later.) The pentameter is always divided into two units of equal length, 2½:2½; the hexameter, on the contrary, is always divided into two units of unequal length, 3½:2½ or 2½:3½. The hexameter's divisions may occur at three points, of which one (at H8) is confined to lines whose third foot is dactylic. Of the 128 forms of the elegiac couplet, half have a dactyl, and half have a spondee, in the third foot of the hexameter. With dactylic third foot, 192 (64 times 3) forms of couplet are possible; with spondaic third foot, there are 128 (64 times 2). The number of possible forms of couplet is accordingly 320.

The elegiac couplet, then, consists of three units of comparable length and one longer unit, and the longer unit may occur in first or second position of the four. Since the second unit of the hexameter is the only one of the four which does not begin at the beginning of a foot, that unit cannot closely resemble the others in rhythm: after hephthemimeral caesura, it resembles the units of the pentameter merely in length. But the unit which precedes the penthemimeral caesura in the hexameter is a hemiepes. The elegiac couplet may contain three hemiepe—indeed, three hemiepe of the same rhythm (which must be entirely dactylic, since the second hemiepes of the pentameter must have this rhythm), as in Tyrtaeus 11W. 31–32:

$$\text{καὶ πόδα πὰρ ποδὶ θεὶς} \mid \text{καὶ ἐπ' ἀσπίδος ἀσπίδ' ἐρείσας}$$
$$\text{ἐν δὲ λόφον τε λόφῳ} \mid \text{καὶ κυνέην κυνέῃ.}$$

On the other hand, the couplet may contain only two hemiepe, and the first hemiepes of the pentameter may be completely spondaic, producing a couplet with four units each of quite different rhythm, as in *Theognidea* 123–24W:

$$\text{τοῦτο θεὸς κιβδηλότατον} \mid \text{ποίησε βροτοῖσὶν}$$
$$\text{καὶ γνῶναι πάντων} \mid \text{τοῦτ' ἀνιηρότατον.}$$

Such variations in the couplet could not be missed by any ear of average sensitivity.

That the hexameter is longer than the pentameter already gives a certain character to the verse, but the manner in which it is longer is also important. The hexameter is catalectic: its final dactyl lacks the second short syllable. The hemiepe of the pentameter, of which the second is more important here, are brachycatalectic: each lacks both short syllables of its final dactyl. The hexameter characteristically ends –⏑⏑–x, the pentameter –⏑⏑x. The pentameter is more than one syllable shorter than the hexameter; but the missing final syllable is the most significant, since the shorter of two lines related as is the pentameter to the hexameter is frequently used as a clausula to one or more of the longer lines. The Pherecratean xx–⏑⏑–x is thus related to the Glyconic xx–⏑⏑–⏑–, as in Aeschylus, *Supplices* 641–42,

$$\mathrm{α\breve{ι}δο\bar{ῦ}ντα\bar{ι}\ δ'\ \bar{ἱ}κ\acute{ε}τ\breve{α}ς\ Δῐ\acute{ο}ς}$$
$$\mathrm{π\bar{ο}\acute{ι}μν\bar{α}ν\ τ\bar{ά}νδ'\ \breve{ἀ}μ\acute{ε}γ\breve{α}ρτ\acute{ο}ν.}$$

The paroemiac ⏑⏑–⏑⏑–⏑⏑–x is similarly related to the anapaestic dimeter ⏑⏑–⏑⏑–⏑⏑–⏑⏑–, as in Aeschylus, *Persae* 27–28,

$$\mathrm{φο\breve{β}ερο\bar{ὶ}\ μ\breve{ὲ}ν\ \bar{ἰ}δε\bar{ῖ}ν,\ δ\bar{ε}ινο\bar{ὶ}\ δ\breve{ὲ}\ μ\acute{α}χ\bar{η}ν}$$
$$\mathrm{ψ\bar{υ}χ\bar{ῆ}ς\ \bar{ε}ὐτλ\bar{ή}μο\breve{ν}\breve{ι}\ δ\acute{ο}ξ\bar{η}.}$$

where the paroemiac line 28 closes a run of four anapaestic dimeters. The elegiac pentameter seems well suited for the role of clausula, and indeed it is virtually always the second line of the couplet.[4]

It is also important that the second element of the hexameter does not begin at the beginning of the dactylic foot; for to the ear the rhythmical effect is anapaestic rather than dactylic, particularly when the line has a caesura (penthemimeral or hephthemimeral) which falls after the long syllable of the dactyl. (Consider, as an example, Tyrtaeus 11W. 31, quoted above.) A counterrhythm is thus established in the second unit of the hexameter, which contrasts with the other three units of the couplet, and especially with the second unit of the pentameter. The counterrhythm of the second units of the hexameter and the pentameter seems likely to enhance the clausulaic effect of brachycatalexis.

The composer of elegiac verse has a four-unit repeating structure into which to fit the words, phrases, clauses, and sentences of his poem. The later chapters of this book will study the varying ways in which the early elegiac poets employ the resources of the couplet. Here I suggest a few general considerations.

While paying attention to caesura, a poet might compose one clause for each line of verse. Some early Greek elegiac poets tend to compose thus: of the first twelve lines of Tyrtaeus 12W, ten contain one clause, while the other two lines (1–2) contain a clause of couplet length. Alternatively, a poet might treat the couplet as a unit and always have a period or other heavy stop at the end of the pentameter. The Roman elegiac poet Ovid always composed in this manner; but in extant early Greek elegy only Solon 27W seems purposely to aim at this form, and Solon's motive for using it there is evident from the subject matter (see below, chapter six).

Poets who do not invariably compose in the manner of Tyrtaeus 12W. 1–12 will evidently sometimes compose enjambed lines, hexameters or pentameters. Poets who compose in the manner of Solon 27 may compose enjambed hexameters: only three of the nine hexameters of Solon 27 (3, 11, 17) have a mark of punctuation at the end of the line in West 1972.

Three types of enjambment may be distinguished. In the first, the end of the clause has not been reached, but the words in the line are comprehensible and contain the finite verb of the sentence, as in Tyrtaeus 10W. 31–32:[5]

ἀλλά τις εὖ διαβὰς μενέτω ποσὶν ἀμφοτέροισι
στηριχθεὶς ἐπὶ γῆς, χεῖλος ὀδοῦσι δακών.

(ποσὶν ἀμφοτέροισι can be construed with either διαβάς or στηριχθείς.) In the second type of enjambment, the end of the line coincides with the end of a sense group in the clause, but the finite verb of the clause, or its equivalent, has not yet been reached. Tyrtaeus 10W. 21–22, furnishes an example:

αἰσχρὸν γὰρ δὴ τοῦτο, μετὰ προμάχοισι πεσόντα
κεῖσθαι πρόσθε νέων ἄνδρα παλαιότερον.

Here πεσόντα completes the participial phrase, and κεῖσθαι is the equivalent of a finite verb in the accusative and infinitive construction depending on αἰσχρόν . . . τοῦτο. In the third type of enjambment, line end divides a sense group, as in Callinus 1W. 9–11:

ἀλλά τις ἰθὺς ἴτω
ἔγχος ἀνασχόμενος καὶ ὑπ᾽ ἀσπίδος ἄλκιμον ἦτορ
ἔλσας, τὸ πρῶτον μειγνυμένου πολέμου.

Here the second participial phrase of 10 ends at ἔλσας in 11.

The elegiac poet need not compose by the line or by the couplet. As the last example indicates, the pentameter too may be enjambed; and all three examples of enjambment have marks of punctuation, and therefore of pauses, demarcating clauses and phrases, within the line. We may now inquire into the relationship of these pauses to the mandatory caesurae and diaeresis, already discussed.

From the schema of the elegiac couplet printed on page 3 it is apparent that punctuation, which represents a pause in delivery, might in principle occur within the line at sixteen positions within the hexameter, at thirteen in the pentameter. No punctuation is canonical, for the ancient Greeks used none;

TABLE 1. POSITION OF PUNCTUATION: HEXAMETERS

| | Elegy | | | | Homer | | | |
| | All Lines | | Without Vocatives | | All Lines | | Without Vocatives | |
Position	Incidence	%	Incidence	%	Incidence	%	Incidence	%
1	6	1.17	1	0.21	2	0.36	2	0.43
2	12	2.33	1	0.21	20	3.56	15	3.25
3	38	7.38	29	6.18	77	13.70	43	9.31
4	37	7.18	36	7.68	65	11.57	52	11.26
5	3	0.58	3	0.64	5	0.89	3	0.65
6	0	0.00	0	0.00	0	0.00	0	0.00
7	45	8.74	40	8.52	121	21.53	110	23.81
8	137	26.60	132	28.14	106	18.86	89	19.26
9	0	0.00	0	0.00	0	0.00	0	0.00
10	39	7.57	38	8.10	40	7.12	31	6.71
11	0	0.00	0	0.00	0	0.00	0	0.00
12	195	37.86	186	39.66	122	21.71	116	25.11
13	2	0.39	2	0.43	2	0.36	1	0.22
14	1	0.19	1	0.21	1	0.18	0	0.00
15	0	0.00	0	0.00	1	0.18	0	0.00
16	0	0.00	0	0.00	0	0.00	0	0.00
	515	99.99*	469	99.98	562	99.96	462	100.01

*Percentages have been rounded in all the tables in this chapter.

but the punctuation of modern editors is indicative of pauses which are necessary if the audience is to understand what is said.

Table 1 analyzes the position of marks of punctuation in the 1,017 extant hexameters of the poets discussed in this book, and it then presents comparative figures for the first 1,017 lines of Homer's *Iliad* (1. 1–2. 406). West 1972 was used for the elegiac writers, Monro 1890 for the *Iliad*. Since epic poetry contains more vocatives than does elegy, and since West is very sparing of commas before and after such vocatives as do occur in elegy, I present also the results which are obtained by excluding punctuation marks set round vocatives and apostrophes.

Consider the hexameter first. In the sample material there are no examples of punctuation in positions 6, 9, 11, or 16 and very few in 5, 13, and 14.[6] Punctuation near to the end of the line is likely to be infrequent in most meters, and little explanation is needed. Positions 6, 9, and 11 immediately precede or follow the mandatory (or major) caesurae. The significance of these figures should be emphasized. It is not merely that punctuation and pause do not occur next to the caesura in a particular line, so that punctuation at H6 does not accompany caesura at H7. Punctuation at H6 does not accompany caesura at H8 or H10 either.

Word end is permitted at H6, H9, and H11. It occurs at H6, for example, with spondaic second foot at *Theognidea* 1W:

ὦ ἄνα Λητοῦς ⁝ υἱέ, Διὸς τέκος, οὔποτε σεῖο

and at *Iliad* 1. 127:

ἀλλὰ σὺ μὲν νῦν ⁝ τήνδε θεῷ πρόες· αὐτὰρ Ἀχαιοὶ

and with dactylic second foot at *Theognidea* 35W:

ἐσθλῶν μὲν γὰρ ἄπ' ⁝ ἐσθλὰ μαθήσεαι· ἢν δὲ κακοῖσι

and at *Iliad* 1. 5:

οἰωνοῖσί τε ⁝ πᾶσι, Διὸς δ' ἐτελείετο βουλή.

In both dactylic examples the word end at H6 receives some emphasis: the postpositive ἄπ' and the enclitic τε are phrased with what precedes.

Examples of word end at H9 are lines with dactylic third foot, such as Solon 4W. 26:

οὕτω δημόσιον κακὸν ⁝ ἔρχεται οἴκαδ' ἑκάστῳ

and *Iliad* 1. 49:

δεινὴ δὲ κλαγγὴ γένετ' ⁝ ἀργυρέοιο βιοῖο

Most examples of such word end in fact include proclitic or enclitic words, as in *Iliad* 1. 40–41:

ἦ εἰ δή ποτέ τοι κατὰ ⁝ πίονα μηρί' ἔκηα
ταύρων ἠδ' αἰγῶν, τόδε ⁝ μοι κρήηνον ἐέλδωρ.

There is word end at H9 in both lines, but the proclitic preposition κατὰ would be spoken closely with the following word in 40, while the enclitic μοι would be spoken closely with the preceding τόδε in 41, thus weakening the effect; but in other lines nouns and adjectives without following enclitic stand in this position, and in some, as in the Solon example given above, the natural phrasing of the line would favor a pause after the third dactyl.[7]

Word end at H9 with the third foot spondaic seems much rarer. Most involve proclitics or enclitics; but there are a few like *Theognidea* 1009W:

τῶν αὐτοῦ κτεάνων εὖ ⁝ πασχέμεν· οὐ γὰρ ἀνηβᾶν.

Even here it should be noted that εὖ πασχέμεν is a closely knit phrase. Occasionally lines occur in which the natural phrasing would link the word which ends at H9 with the words preceding it, as in *Iliad* 1. 154:

οὐ γὰρ πώ ποτ' ἐμὰς βοῦς ⁝ ἤλασαν οὐδὲ μὲν ἵππους.

But generally poets seem more reluctant to allow word end at H9 when the third foot is spondaic.

Word end at H11 must occur at the trochee in a dactylic fourth foot. Most examples are blurred by enclitics or proclitics, but a few lines like Xenophanes 1W. 17 occur:

οὐχ ὕβρεις· πίνειν δ' ὁποσόν κεν ⁞ ἔχων ἀφίκοιο.

Here the enclitic κε emphasizes the word end. *Iliad* 1. 168 is similar:

ἔρχομ' ἔχων ἐπὶ νῆας, ἐπεί κε ⁞ κάμω πολεμίζων.

It must be remembered that the results of this analysis do not reveal mere statistical quirks of poets for whom the hexameter line is no more than a series of long and short syllables. Nor do they mechanically follow rules laid down by a theoretical metrician. There were no theoretical metricians in archaic Greece; and even in cultures where they exist, poets rarely allow themselves to be dictated to by metrical theorists.[8]

The analysis reveals which of the sixteen positions for pause that are in principle possible in a dactylic hexameter are in practice acceptable to the Greek ear in a verse destined for oral performance. It remains to inquire why these preferences should exist and to make any possible inferences about the sound of the verse in performance.

We have seen that punctuation does not occur at H6, H9, or H11. More accurately, pauses of the duration indicated even by a comma do not occur at these positions. Such pauses are avoided in any line no matter which caesura occurs in that line. This fact suggests that the absence of punctuation at H6, H9, and H11 and its virtual absence at H5 are to be accounted for not so much by the desire to avoid juxtaposing such pauses with the syllable followed or preceded by caesura as by a desire to avoid emphasizing certain rhythms in the line.

Now punctuation at H6 gives a rhythm before the pause of either (*a*) $-\cup\cup-\cup\cup$ or (*b*) $-\cup\cup--$. The latter gives a rhythm characteristic of the end of the hexameter, which might well be felt undesirable elsewhere in the line; but it is less clear why *Theognidea* 53W,

Κύρνε, πόλις μὲν ἔθ' ⁞ ἥδε πόλις, λαοὶ δὲ δὴ ἄλλοι

is evidently acceptable, while

Κύρνε, πόλις μένει· ἔστι πόλις, λαοὶ δὲ δὴ ἄλλοι

is apparently not acceptable metrically, even though the stop is four syllables from the fourth-foot caesura at H10.

Both possibilities at H9 are easier to explain. For it is evident that part of the rhythmic effect of the hexameter depends on its being divided into two unequal parts by the caesura. The rhythm (*a*) $-\cup\cup-\cup\cup-\cup\cup$ divides the line at the halfway point, while (*b*) $-\cup\cup-\cup\cup--$ in addition gives a similar clausula to both parts. This effect is evidently undesirable in stichic hexameters and even more so in elegiacs; for one of the many contrasts on which the elegiac couplet depends for its flexibility and variety is the contrast between the unequally divided hexameter and the equally divided pentameter.

The undesirability of pause at H11 $-\cup\cup-\cup\cup-\cup\cup-\cup$ again presumably derives from the rhythm of the hexameter clausula $-\cup\cup-\cup$ thus emphasized before the end of the line.

It seems likely that avoidance of punctuation at H5 also is to be explained by avoidance of the rhythm $-\cup\cup-\cup$, which is that of the end of the hexameter.

Some further conclusions seem possible. Consider once again *Iliad* 1. 154:

οὐ γάρ πώ ποτ' ἐμὰς | βοῦς ⋮ ἤλασαν οὐδὲ μὲν ἵππους

and *Iliad* 1. 53:

ἐννῆμαρ μὲν ἀνὰ | στρατὸν ⋮ ᾤχετο κῆλα θεοῖο.

The placing of a stop after βοῦς or στρατόν would apparently render the lines rhythmically unacceptable, though the lines have one of the mandatory caesurae. Accordingly, the pause at the caesura is weaker than that marked even by a comma. On the other hand, if the caesura *qua* caesura were marked by no pause or by a pause weaker than that at phrase end, these lines would surely be unacceptable; for the phrasing of the line suggested by the sense would produce a pause of greater duration or intensity than that at the caesura,[9] which would then become the dominant feature of the line and produce the same objectionable effect as a comma. It therefore seems reasonable to grade word divisions on a scale, weakest first, as follows: (*a*) division between proclitic and the following word or between enclitic and the preceding word (the point on the scale may well be zero for enclitics, since caesura followed by an enclitic is avoided; caesura after a proclitic does occur, as in *Iliad* 1. 53 above, but is not common); (*b*) division between words not so related; (*c*) division at caesura; (*d*) division followed by a comma; (*e*) division followed by a heavier stop (this last is a mere presumption but a likely one).

We may now consider the effect of punctuation at the positions where it does occur. In the following chapters I shall consider effects in particular lines; in this chapter the discussion must be more general.

Punctuation at H7, H8, and H10, the major caesurae, accounts for 42.91 percent of all punctuation within the line in the elegists discussed in this book and 47.59 percent of those in the Homer sample; but punctuation at these points occurs in only 21.73 percent of all extant hexameters in these poets and in 26.25 percent of the hexameters in the Homer sample. The percentages of all hexameters which have marks of punctuation at the end of the sixteen positions are shown in Table 2.

Before commenting on these data, I shall consider the figures for the 1,010 pentameters of the poets discussed in this book, which are tabulated in Table 3. Here, too, certain positions in the line are avoided. There are no occurrences of punctuation at P8, P12, and P13 and only one at P6. Punctuation

TABLE 2. PERCENTAGES OF PUNCTUATION: HEXAMETERS

Position	ELEGY %	HOMER %
1	0.59	0.20
2	1.18	1.97
3	3.74	7.57
4	3.64	6.39
5	0.29	0.49
6	0.00	0.00
7	4.42	11.90
8	13.47	10.42
9	0.00	0.00
10	3.83	3.93
11	0.00	0.00
12	19.17	12.00
13	0.20	0.20
14	0.10	0.10
15	0.00	0.10
16	0.00	0.00
	50.63	55.27

TABLE 3. POSITION AND PERCENTAGES OF PUNCTUATION: PENTAMETERS

Position	Incidence	Percentage of Punctuated Lines	Percentage of All Pentameters
1	8	2.71	0.79
2	31	10.51	3.10
3	83	28.14	8.22
4	76	25.76	7.52
5	7	2.37	0.69
6	1	0.34	0.10
7	75	25.42	7.42
8	0	0.00	0.00
9	4	1.36	0.40
10	9	3.05	0.90
11	1	0.34	0.10
12	0	0.00	0.00
13	0	0.00	0.00
	295	100.00	29.24

is unlikely close to the end of the line. Punctuation at P8 would give $-\cup\cup-\cup\cup--$, the hexameter clausula, and also disrupt the balanced rhythm which is the characteristic feature of the pentameter in contrast with the hexameter. The single example of punctuation at P6 (*Theognidea* 800W) may well be for deliberate effect:

ἀλλ' ὡς λώιον, | εἰ | μὴ πλεόνεσσι μέλοι.

The unusual rhythm highlights and, as it were, italicizes εἰ, and the effect is relevant to the sense. In general, punctuation at P6, as at H6, would produce

Introduction 13

hexameter clausula (with $-\cup\cup--$) or would unbalance the line intended to pivot at P7 (with $-\cup\cup-\cup\cup$). Punctuation at P5 $-\cup\cup-\cup$ may be avoided for the same reason as at H5.

Fewer pentameters than hexameters are punctuated at all. A pentameter is twice as likely to be punctuated at one of the first four positions as at any of the next nine, and it is twice as likely to be punctuated at P3 or P4 as at P7, the only mandatory word end in the line.

The data for hexameter and pentameter should be considered together, for it is the rhythm of the couplet as a whole which seems to produce certain poetic preferences; and the data for elegiac hexameters should be compared with those for epic.

The incidence of caesura at H7, H8, and H10 in the two specimens of 1,017 lines from the elegists and from Homer is remarkably similar, as Table 4 shows. The differences are certainly not statistically significant. In particular, the elegist does not avoid caesura at H7 to a greater extent than Homer.[10] But the elegist does avoid punctuation at H7 to a greater extent: only 8.74 percent of all punctuation occurs there in elegy compared to 21.53 percent in the Homer sample. Since punctuation indicates pause, and pause emphasizes the rhythm of the unit marked off by the pause, punctuation at H7 emphasizes the hemiepes rhythm $-\cup\cup-\cup\cup-$, which is mandatory in the pentameter, in the first half of the hexameter. The figures suggest that elegiac poets usually wish to avoid this effect: it occurs in only 4.42 percent of all hexameters in the elegiac sample (Table 2). The percentage in the epic sample is 11.90: the epic poet has no inducement to avoid emphasizing this rhythm in stichic hexameters. Indeed, if we confine our attention to punctuation occurring at major caesurae, the percentage of such punctuation occurring at H7 is, for epic, higher than the percentage of major caesurae occurring at H7 (Tables 4 and 5).

Another striking difference between the epic and elegiac hexameters occurs at H12, the bucolic diaeresis. Word end is very common at this point; but the

TABLE 4. POSITION AND PERCENTAGES OF MAJOR CAESURAE

Position	Elegy		Homer	
	Incidence	%	Incidence	%
H7	357	35.10	366	35.99
H8	518	50.93	503	49.46
H10	142	13.96	148	14.55
	1,017	99.99	1,017	100.00

TABLE 5. PERCENTAGES OF PUNCTUATION AT MAJOR CAESURAE

Position	Elegy		Homer	
	Incidence	%	Incidence	%
H7	45	20.36	121	45.32
H8	137	62.00	106	39.70
H10	39	17.65	40	14.98
	221	100.01	267	100.00

bucolic diaeresis cannot substitute for the major caesurae, one of which must also occur in the line. In the epic sample, punctuation at H12 is one of the two most common positions, accounting for 21.71 percent of all punctuation; in the elegiac sample, it is by far the most common, accounting for 37.86 percent of all punctuation (Table 1).

Like the relative avoidance of punctuation at H7, the greater incidence of punctuation at H12 reflects the difference between elegiac hexameters and stichic hexameters. It has already been noted that the relationship of pentameter to hexameter in elegiac couplets resembles that of the clausulae in some lyric stanzas ("In the hexameter rises the fountain's silvery column / In the pentameter falling slowly in melody back"). Consequently, the pentameter ending is a perfect cadence, the hexameter an imperfect cadence, in this meter. (In stichic hexameters the hexameter ending is the cadence of every line, and it cannot produce a similar effect.) When, as frequently happens in elegiac verse, a new sentence or clause begins at H12, the syntax is usually incomplete at the end of the line; and the sense of incompleteness is enhanced by the imperfect cadence, which increases the alertness of the ear, in its desire for resolution, to what is being said.

The perfect cadence of the pentameter does not lend itself to this effect. Though pentameters are not infrequently enjambed,[11] punctuation is very rare in the second half of the line (1.4% of the sample, as shown in Table 3). The pentameter, as has been noted, is more than twice as likely to be punctuated at P3 or P4 as at P7, the only mandatory word end within the line. Of the elegiac hexameters which are punctuated within the line, many (though not all of the 19.17% shown in Table 2) of those which have some stop at the bucolic diaeresis begin a new sentence there, with the effect already discussed; of the pentameters which are punctuated within the line, many (though not all of the approximately 27% shown in Table 3) end a sentence in the first half of the line, when the ear is awaiting the resolution of the imperfect cadence, before the point at which the rhythm of the verse itself would supply a perfect cadence. The many artistic possibilities of these devices will be discussed in subsequent chapters.

It should be noted here, however, that the mere infrequency of occurrence of punctuation within the line will produce some effect when it does occur, whether or not the poet displays skill and whether or not the effect is appropriate. No position of punctuation within the line is so common as to dull the ear.

Punctuation within the line, as a percentage of the extant lines of the poet, varies from 20.28 (Tyrtaeus) to 61 (Archilochus); but if punctuation at line end is added, the variation is much smaller, from an average of 0.897 marks of punctuation per line (Xenophanes) to 1.084 marks per line (*Theognidea*). These figures suggest that the average phrase length approximates to one line. Poems which maintain this average and have most of their punctuation at line end will strike the ear very differently from poems which exceed or fall short of it, particularly if their punctuation is for the most part not at line end. Contrast *Theognidea* 133–42W:

> οὐδεὶς Κύρν' ἄτης καὶ κέρδεος αἴτιος αὐτός,
> ἀλλὰ θεοὶ τούτων δώτορες ἀμφοτέρων·
> 135 οὐδέ τις ἀνθρώπων ἐργάζεται ἐν φρεσὶν εἰδὼς
> ἐς τέλος εἴτ' ἀγαθὸν γίνεται εἴτε κακόν.
> πολλάκι γὰρ δοκέων θήσειν κακὸν ἐσθλὸν ἔθηκεν,
> καί τε δοκῶν θήσειν ἐσθλὸν ἔθηκε κακόν.
> οὐδέ τῳ ἀνθρώπων παραγίνεται ὅσσ' ἐθέλῃσιν·
> 140 ἴσχει γὰρ χαλεπῆς πείρατ' ἀμηχανίης.
> ἄνθρωποι δὲ μάταια νομίζομεν, εἰδότες οὐδέν·
> θεοὶ δὲ κατὰ σφέτερον πάντα τελοῦσι νόον.

and *Theognidea* 31–38W:

> ταῦτα μὲν οὕτως ἴσθι· κακοῖυι δὲ μὴ προσομίλει
> ἀνδράσιν, ἀλλ' αἰεὶ τῶν ἀγαθῶν ἔχεο·
> καὶ μετὰ τοῖσιν πῖνε καὶ ἔσθιε, καὶ μετὰ τοῖσιν
> ἵζε, καὶ ἅνδανε τοῖς, ὧν μεγάλη δύναμις.
> 35 ἐσθλῶν μὲν γαρ ἄπ' ἐσθλὰ μαθήσεαι· ἢν δὲ κακοῖσι
> συμμίσγῃς, ἀπολεῖς καὶ τὸν ἐόντα νόον.
> ταῦτα μαθὼν ἀγαθοῖσιν ὁμίλει, καί ποτε φήσεις
> εὖ συμβουλεύειν τοῖσι φίλοισιν ἐμέ.

West (1972) regards both poems as authentic Theognis. Such variations give no reason to doubt the attribution: a good poet varies the design of his poem to suit his subject matter. Both of these poems are well composed.

Turn now to individual words. Native speakers testify to the effect of the number, syllabic length, and syllabic quantity of words in the line.[12] These can be properly evaluated only in their context, but some general remarks may be made about the syllabic length of the final word of the line. Since ancient Greek was accented by pitch, not stress,[13] the constraints of the Latin hexameter are absent.[14] A brief comparison of a few lines of Ovid with any Greek elegist will reveal the greater freedom of the Greeks. However, the results for our elegists and some sample Greek epic are worth tabulating. In the hexameter, the last two feet play an important part in giving the verse its characteristic rhythm. The sixth foot is always catalectic, the fifth almost always dactylic; and words placed at the end of the line gain some prominence from their position, so that all of their characteristics receive notice.

The following overall percentages, like those for individual poets in the chapters which follow, pay no regard to the grouping of words in phrases. No attempt is made to prove that any word length up to pentesyllable in the hexameter and heptasyllable in the pentameter is debarred. In fact, all occur. Refinements of analysis would complicate the exposition or multiply the endnotes unnecessarily, and they would do little to advance my argument, which concerns aesthetic effects; for, as subsequent chapters will show, aesthetic effects can be adequately discussed only in their individual context. These figures are intended as a rough indication of the comparative frequency of words of different lengths, and they indicate merely the length of the last word, without taking account of accompanying articles, prepositions, or other proclitics. Only where the last word is itself enclitic have I reckoned it with the preceding word as one unit.

In Table 6 I show the percentages of different word lengths in hexameters with dactylic fifth foot and the percentages of molossus and dispondee in lines with spondaic fifth foot in the 1,017 extant lines of the eight elegists and in the first 1,017 lines of the *Odyssey* (1. 1–3. 139). Figures for "others" in the Homer columns refer to final words which occupy more than the last two feet of the line.[15]

The percentages are remarkably similar. The complete absence from these elegiac hexameters of final words occupying more than the last two feet presumably reflects an aesthetic preference, possibly allied to the frequency of punctuation at H12: where a pentameter is to follow, H12 is felt as an important pivotal point in the line. Again, the spondaic and longer dactylic final words (molossus, dispondee, pentesyllable, and "others") appear more than twice as frequently in epic hexameters (10.52% : 4.32%). This fact gives some confirmation of the subjective impression that the elegiac hexameter is "lighter" than its epic counterpart. If this result is added to those for punctuation at H7 and H12, some general qualitative differences become apparent.

The second hemiepes of the pentameter is metrically invariant. Little variety is introduced by the pauses denoted by punctuation, for punctuation is rare (1.40% of all pentameters in the poets studied). The subtler effects

TABLE 6. LENGTH OF FINAL WORDS IN HEXAMETERS

	ELEGY		HOMER	
	Incidence	%	Incidence	%
Dactylic fifth foot				
Monosyllable	20	1.97	22	2.16
Disyllable	375	36.87	314	30.87
Trisyllable	451	44.35	462	45.43
Quadrisyllable	127	12.49	112	11.01
Pentesyllable	35	3.44	59	5.80
Spondaic fifth foot				
Molossus	3	0.29	17	1.67
Dispondee	6	0.59	23	2.26
Others (dactylic or spondaic)	0	0.00	8	0.79
	1,017	100.00	1,017	99.99

TABLE 7. LENGTH OF FINAL WORDS
IN PENTAMETERS OF THE EIGHT ELEGISTS

	Incidence	%
Monosyllable	19	1.88
Disyllable	327	32.38
Trisyllable	330	32.67
Quadrisyllable	183	18.12
Pentesyllable	123	12.18
Hexasyllable	25	2.48
Heptasyllable	3	0.30
	1,010	100.01

produced by phrasing can be discussed only in context,[16] and these, too, are rare in this part of the couplet. Apart from these, differences in the length of words, and of the final word of the couplet in particular, are the only variables. All possible word lengths occur in final position (see Table 7).

We are assured by a native speaker that the number and length of words in a poetic line is a noticeable acoustic phenomenon. Even if no Greek ever used word length as an artistic device—which the same native speaker would vigorously deny[17]—the chance occurrence of monosyllabic, pentesyllabic, molossus, and dispondaic endings in elegiac hexameters, and of monosyllabic, hexasyllabic, heptasyllabic, and possibly pentesyllabic endings in pentameters, is sufficiently uncommon to attract attention. If a positive aesthetic effect is produced in a particular case, it is worth debating whether it is deliberate.

Poetical Composition

Thus far we have treated words merely as objects with metrical qualities (or quantities), available to a poet who wishes to produce some utterance with a regular rhythm. Few poets, however, or even humble versifiers, are content merely to produce a form of words without metrical faults. We have discovered certain constraints on punctuation and therefore on the metrical form of phrase or clause that is acceptable in elegiac poetry; but few writers will aspire no higher than to observe these rules.

Any poem, and most evidently any poem in a regular, definable meter, may be viewed as a hierarchy of interacting systems. The most fundamental is the meter itself. There are 320 possible forms of the elegiac couplet if caesura is taken into account. A sequence of words which does not conform to one of the 320 has been produced by a composer who either was not attempting to produce an elegiac couplet or failed to do so. But only the most inept of writers will simply juggle his words until one of the 320 forms occurs. Even a versifier of comparatively small ability may judge that a spondaic rather than a dactylic rhythm better suits what he is trying to say, and this decision will affect his choice both of words and of form of line, and it may determine the word order he can use. Alternatively, he may judge that a particular word order will be most effective, and this decision may restrict and determine his choice of words and dictate a particular rhythm from the 320. Ideally, of course, meter, word choice, word order, phrase and clause length, and the position of word, phrase, and clause in relation to the mandatory units and the tensions and resolutions of the elegiac couplet will all fulfill exactly the poet's desires and intentions. It is a fortunate poet who can always achieve such success. Few early elegists are treated as poets at all; but a study of the different aspects of composition just mentioned may serve both to indicate what they—sometimes—achieve and to distinguish one poet from another.

Dactyls and Spondees

There are 128 different permissible arrangements of long and short syllables in the elegiac meter, and a sensitive ear will soon come to appreciate this abundant variety. But all 128 result from a choice, at seven different positions in the couplet, between writing a long syllable or two short syllables. The choice is between dactyls and spondees; the variety results from permutations and combinations. It follows that the choice will be made for different reasons at different times; there is no single purpose or effect to be sought.

Variety itself may be the poet's goal: the cool spot on the pillow is always pleasant to the ear. But the inclusion of even one spondee in a sequence of dactyls is immediately noticeable: it emphasizes the spondaic word. The effect of the sentence may be much enhanced, as in Solon 13W. 27–31, where the occurrence of πάντως in the otherwise dactylic lines 28 and 31—and in a largely dactylic passage—greatly and appropriately highlights the repeated word.

The pronunciation of only two syllables in the same time as the three syllables of the dactyl endows the spondee with the effect of slowness; gloom, despondency, and seriousness seem suitable subjects for spondaic lines, to be contrasted with cheerful dactyls. This effect occurs quite frequently; Callinus 1W. 18–19 and Tyrtaeus 10W. 3–4 will serve as examples. But poems rarely interchange the themes of life and death, gloom and despondency, after every line, and the ear craves relief quite quickly. As a result, frequently—and in the two examples cited—a part of the gloomy sentence will be dactylic, highlighting the spondaic words. Nor should an easy correspondence between spondees and gloom be posited. Poets may have other priorities in composition: the first ten lines of Mimnermus 2W, a fine poem by a fine poet, are almost entirely dactylic.

In fact, in a general introductory discussion, little more definite can be said than that a change of rhythm from dactylic to spondaic gives prominence to

Introduction

the spondaic words. (The meter is predominantly dactylic: spondees are the unusual features.) Particular effects can be evaluated only in their context.

Word Order; Phrase, Clause, Sentence; Position in Verse

An inflected language affords greater freedom of word order than does a non-inflected language. Greek has proved notoriously intractable to any attempt to demonstrate the existence of generally applicable rules of word order, and the conclusion is sometimes drawn that Greek word order is " 'free,' 'arbitrary,' or 'indeterminate' " (Dover 1960, 2, though this is not Dover's own conclusion).

The general question is irrelevant to the present discussion. The absence of general rules governing the word order of all Greek sentences, or even all sentences written by any one Greek writer, does not entail that it is impossible to judge the effects of a particular word order in a particular sentence, even though we must acknowledge that our ability to do so falls far short of that of the writer's contemporaries. No general rules exist governing the composition of all music, paintings, or sculpture; nevertheless, it remains possible, with proper care, to judge the compositional effects discernible in a particular piece of music, painting, or statue.

Sensitive readers of Greek will perceive the greater freedom of Greek word order not as randomness but as a flexibility permitted by a more subtle and complex set of rules or tendencies of order, whose goal, in each individual sentence, is to communicate as clearly and hence as effectively as possible what is intended, with each nuance given its proper weight. Good word order provides comprehensibility by demarcating one sense group from another, and it indicates nuances by emphasizing particular words. Even when the author is playing on words, as Solon does in 4W (below, chapter 6), word order has much to contribute. Indeed, the more complex and nuanced the message, the more important it becomes to render as clearly as possible the structure and emphases of the sentences by which it is expressed.

To take a simple example: ἀνδρεῖος ὁ στρατηγός and ὁ στρατηγὸς ἀνδρεῖος are syntactically equivalent, but the different word order affects the emphasis; and if we add τοὺς πολεμίους νικᾷ, the possibilities of varying nuance are greatly increased. ἀνδρεῖος, ὁ στρατηγός, τοὺς πολεμίους, and νικᾷ constitute four units which, while preserving the same syntactical links, may be arranged in any of 24 (4!) orders. (In more complex clauses, some orders might be ruled out on the grounds of lack of clarity.)

A short example of Greek rhetorical prose will serve as an illustration. Demosthenes, in the *First Philippic* (4.2), writes:

πρῶτον μὲν οὐκ ἀθυμητέον, ὦ ἄνδρες Ἀθηναῖοι, τοῖς παρoῦσι πράγμασιν, οὐδ᾽ εἰ πάνυ φαύλως ἔχειν δοκεῖ· ὃ γὰρ

ἐστι χείριστον ἐκ τοῦ παρεληλυθότος χρόνου, τοῦτο πρὸς
τὰ μέλλοντα βέλτιστον ὑπάρχει. τί οὖν ἐστι τοῦτο;

The first word or phrase in a Greek sentence stands in a prominent position, particularly when, as here, it is divided from the rest of the sentence by a pause. Accordingly, οὐκ ἀθυμητέον . . . τοῖς παροῦσι πράγμασιν emphasizes οὐκ ἀθυμητέον rather than τοῖς . . . πράγμασιν. The words τοῖς . . . πράγμασιν could easily have been emphasized by reversing the order of the phrases; but it was appropriate to emphasize οὐκ ἀθυμητέον, since Demosthenes was exhorting the Athenians to courage, not making the point that ἀθυμία would have been appropriate in the past but is so no longer. (Demosthenes would not have wished to concede the point explicitly, though it is perhaps implied by ὃ γάρ . . . ὑπάρχει.) In many sentences δοκεῖ would not be placed last, since that position, too, is a prominent one, and "seems" or "is thought" is frequently not the most important idea in its clause. Here, however, the sense is "Do not despair, even if things *seem* to be going badly." Again, the word order of one sentence is affected by the purposes of the writer in the next sentence, or the whole paragraph, or some even wider context. The final position of δοκεῖ closely juxtaposes that word with ἐστι and thus highlights the contrast between the apparent badness of the present situation, resulting from what was done or not done in the past, and the real advantages which, according to Demosthenes, the Athenians now enjoy. Not only ἐστι at the beginning of the sentence, but ὑπάρχει at the end, in the same position as δοκεῖ, draws this contrast. To ensure that the ear does not miss the parallel when the speech is delivered, Demosthenes sets ἐστι and ὑπάρχει in prominent positions at opposite ends of his sentence; and since what ἐστι and what ὑπάρχει are both opposed not merely to what δοκεῖ but to one another, he sets them at opposite ends of a chiasmus, a device which explicitly aligns each element in the first part with a corresponding element occurring in reverse order in the second part. The alignment points the contrast, here between χείριστον and βέλτιστον and ἐκ . . . χρόνου and πρὸς τὰ μέλλοντα. The positioning of ἐστι χείριστον and βέλτιστον ὑπάρχει gives somewhat greater prominence to them than to the temporal phrases, as indeed the question τί οὖν ἐστι τοῦτο; also indicates.[18]

Effective expression is the concern of the poet too. The sentences of Greek poetry for the most part differ from those of developed Greek prose in being characteristically[19] shorter, simpler, and more paratactic; but here, also, word order serves to demarcate sense groups and to indicate emphases.

The poet, however, has not merely the resource of word order, of position in the syntactical unit: position in the metrical unit is a further resource at his disposal. As an example, consider the clause ἐν εἰρήνῃ δὲ δοκεῖτε ἧσθαι. The clause has an excellent prose order, on the assumption that the author wishes to emphasize ἐν εἰρήνῃ and ἧσθαι rather more than δοκεῖτε: the clause is clearly demarcated, since ἐν εἰρήνῃ and ἧσθαι must be construed together, so that the intervening words must be part of the same clause. When Callinus (1W. 3–4) writes

... ἐν εἰρήνῃ δὲ δοκεῖτε
ἧσθαι, ἀτὰρ πόλεμος γαῖαν ἅπασαν ἔχει,

the clause loses none of its prose excellence and is much enhanced by its position in the verse. A new sentence begins at ἐν εἰρήνῃ. In prose, the phrase would possess great prominence in that position. In Callinus' verse the phrase does not merely begin a sentence. It stands immediately after the trochaic caesura and thus at the beginning of a new verse unit. The syntax is incomplete at the end of the line, so that the effect of imperfect cadence produced by the meter is intensified by the sense. The mind is rendered more alert and pays attention both to δοκεῖτε and to whatever will complete the syntax. ἧσθαι does so, and ends its clause. But in verse it gains additional prominence, for it stands also at the beginning of its line and is followed by a pause in a very unexpected position, which occurs in little more than 3 percent of the pentameters under discussion (see Table 3). The clause is also suited to its wider context, which will be discussed later.

To claim that all three elements of the clause have prominence may appear absurd, since the prominence of anything must be reckoned by its relationship to what is less prominent. To make the claim for a poem much longer than an epigram might be absurd; and the discussion of Callinus 1W will show that Callinus is aware of the need to vary intensity. But poets are characteristically less verbose than prose writers and demand more work from the words they use: ἐν εἰρήνῃ, δοκεῖτε, and ἧσθαι are all pulling their weight and deserve their prominence.

The Elegists and Homer

In attempting to understand and evaluate any literary figure, it is advisable to take into account those of his predecessors who can be shown to have influenced him. The earliest elegiac poets extant, Archilochus, Callinus, and Tyrtaeus, have one important ascertainable influence: the Homeric poems.[20] They presumably also had a now indeterminable number of elegiac predecessors, for the sophistication with which Callinus and Archilochus handle the meter suggests that they are not pioneers, even if they were the first to compose elegies in writing; but the contribution of earlier elegiac poetry can be merely acknowledged, not evaluated.

The Homeric poems, extant and no longer extant,[21] constituted the towering peak of literary achievement for the earliest elegiac poets. The supremacy of Homer was indeed rarely challenged in antiquity; but later centuries had at least more possible challengers to offer, in a variety of genres. It was inevitable that the earlier elegists should be greatly affected by the Homeric poems; and it will be useful to note the similarities and differences between Homeric epic and early Greek elegy before studying in detail how these poets—who, with the exception of Hesiod, were the first to write down their own poems and to develop distinguishable poetic methods and personalities—use, learn from, reject, and define themselves against the Homeric poems.

The elegiac poets share one line of their meter with Greek epic, and we have already observed subtle modifications in the hexameter to render it rhythmically more suitable for its use in the elegiac couplet. An adequate account of the manner in which Homer composes sentences in hexameters would require another book; but a few words here may help to indicate some features that the elegiac poets might have borrowed from epic and also some which, as they replaced the methods of oral composition with those of literacy, they would be likely to eliminate.

Consider, as an example, *Iliad* 6. 29–36:

Ἀστύαλον δ᾽ ἄρ᾽ ἔπεφνε μενεπτόλεμος Πολυποίτης·	29
Πιδύτην δ᾽ Ὀδυσεὺς Περκώσιον ἐξενάριξεν	30
ἔγχεϊ χαλκείῳ, Τεῦκρος δ᾽ Ἀρετάονα δῖον.	31
Ἀντίλοχος δ᾽ Ἄβληρον ἐνήρατο δουρὶ φαεινῷ	32
Νεστορίδης, Ἔλατον δὲ ἄναξ ἀνδρῶν Ἀγαμέμνων·	33
ναῖε δὲ Σατνιόεντος ἐυρρείταο παρ᾽ ὄχθας	34
Πήδασον αἰπεινήν. Φύλακον δ᾽ ἕλε Λήιτος ἥρως	35
φεύγοντ᾽· Εὐρύπυλος δὲ Μελάνθιον ἐξενάριξεν.	36

These lines, constructed from common Homeric formulae, narrate a run-of-the-mill description of battle, little more than a tabulation of casualties. Yet great skill in variation of phrase length is used to avoid monotony. Line 29 is end-stopped: the sense is complete in itself. 30 is overrun to the caesura at H7 in 31, which is subsequently end-stopped. 32 is overrun, but this time the pause is at H4 of 33; and 33 too is end-stopped. 34 runs on to the caesura at H7 in 35, but, in contrast with 31, 35 continues to a pause at H3 in 36, after a spondaic first foot. With the exception of 30–31(H7) and 34–35(H7), all the clauses in these eight lines are of different metrical length. Greek epic diction is subtle and sophisticated.

On the other hand, the enjambment is for the most part of the continuative type commonly found in Homer (Kirk 1966) and to be expected in formulaic oral poetry. To ensure their usefulness for the oral bard, as many lines as possible must be freely transferable from one context to another; and lines whose sense is complete in itself but can be extended—by apposition, by a dependent phrase, or some similar means—satisfy this requirement. Here the sense of 30 and 32 is complete at the end of the line. No feeling of anticipation is aroused, to be satisfied by the enjambed words; and no excitement is engendered by the—not unexpected—information that it was with a brazen spear that Odysseus killed Pidytes, or by the—well known—fact that Antilochus was the son of Nestor. The sense of 34 is completed by the enjambed "lofty Pedasus"; but here we have a different, incomplete, type of formula; and it is the formulaic 34 which decrees that the object of the verb should be enjambed, even though it does not decree the length of the enjambed phrase.[22] We should not be surprised to find some continuative enjambment in early elegy: Homer is a powerful influence.

But 35–36 are quite different. True, the sense is complete at the end of 35, so that the effect is less striking than when an emphatic word appears in enjambment and the sense of the previous line is incomplete. But a heavy spondaic disyllable followed by a heavy stop at H3 derives great emphasis from position, pause, and the comparative rarity of the phenomenon,[23] and φεύγοντ' fully merits its prominence, for it describes the greatest shame that a Homeric warrior can suffer: death while in flight from the enemy. Even continuative enjambment affects the ear and the mind to some extent. Doubtless the effect was soon noticed by the bards of the oral tradition. The constraints of oral composition required that most enjambment should be continuative; but when opportunity offered, the Homeric poems, even in routine battle poetry, could produce effects by enjambment that even Virgil might not have disdained. Freed from oral constraints, the elegiac may be expected to develop the latter type of enjambment and—quickly or gradually—to eliminate the continuative kind.

The earlier of the elegiac poets to be discussed here employ a vocabulary[24] which is exclusively, or almost exclusively, Homeric. This fact is in itself of minor significance: one might deliberately employ the vocabulary of Burns, Milton, or Shakespeare to produce poetry which bore no resemblance to theirs and was not intended to recall theirs. Apollonius Rhodius' *Argonautica*, though much criticized since its composition, is not usually reprehended for its use of Homeric vocabulary, which the poet uses in ways that the bards did not, and would not have been able to, employ. The elegiac poet's use of Homeric language does not demonstrably constitute a defect in itself: one may use a preexisting poetic language creatively.

However, these poets do not merely compose poems out of individual Homeric words; they use phrases drawn from Homer. This practice is usually either recorded without comment or made the basis of a pejorative judgment; and in the twentieth century, in which novelty is the goal of every artist and borrowing or imitation is readily equated with plagiarism, the elegists' use of Homeric phrases is likely to appear at best inept, at worst underhand. But the case for these poets should not go by default. At the least, an earlier poet's phrases might be employed more or less artistically; and, in fact, I shall argue, they might be used to produce a novel and otherwise unattainable poetic effect. For where a phrase is well known to the writer and his readers or audience, the two or three words might serve to recall an entire character or episode, together with its appropriate aesthetic and emotional coloring, and counterpoint it against the form and content of the poet's own work.

My contention is not that any later writer will always use his borrowed phrases in this manner; I am saying merely that the resource is available in suitable cultural conditions, where the author drawn upon is sufficiently well known. Instances in which the resource has not been used can readily be produced. Macbeth's speech (Shakespeare, *Macbeth* 5. 5),

> Tomorrow, and tomorrow, and tomorrow
> Creeps in this petty pace from day to day,
> To the last syllable of recorded time;
> And all our yesterdays have lighted fools
> The way to dusty death. Out, out, brief candle!
> Life's but a walking shadow, a poor player,
> That struts and frets his hour upon the stage,
> And then is heard no more: it is a tale
> Told by an idiot, full of sound and fury,
> Signifying nothing

has been quarried for play and novel titles to a greater extent than any other passage of English literature known to me. By using the borrowed phrases as titles, the authors gave Shakespeare's words great prominence: the reader's eye could not lightly pass over them. The quotations were drawn from a well-known speech in a well-known play: they were not accidental reminiscences of a mind steeped in Shakespeare's works. The authors of the plays and novels knew the source of their quotations, knew that many of their readers would recognize the Shakespearean references, and presumably expected that some would be able to place them in context. Yet those authors made no use of the original context; it is irrelevant to the works to which they gave Shakespearean titles that the words were first uttered by Macbeth, regicide, murderer of his guest, usurper of his royal power, at the time when he realized that the fruits of his crimes were slipping from his hands.

Allusion may be a mere cultural gesture in the direction of a generally admired predecessor: a Shakespearean title for one's play or novel may be thought to lend a *cachet* to the work.[25] Even so much is more than readers of the early elegists would be prepared to grant: all, or almost all, their use of Homeric phrases is held to be the result of accidental reminiscence or mechanical borrowing by minds steeped, or submerged, in the Homeric poems. Discussion of this question must be left to later chapters. Here I wish to point out that much more than cultural gesture is possible. Where the predecessor is well known to the intended readership or audience of the later work, allusion may be used in a purposive and aesthetically enriching manner.

Some modern parallels may make my point clearer. It is not necessary that the method of allusion be exactly the same; my goal is to show how, if a trigger of some kind is available, the aesthetic enrichment may occur. However, the examples must be selected with care. Among writers of the twentieth century, Joyce, Pound, and Eliot have made notable use of allusion; but since they were deliberately writing for a small, learned readership and selected their allusions with such readers in mind, the parallel is not close. An example from more popular poetry is needed.

Edward Fitzgerald published the first version of his translation of *The Rubaiyat of Omar Khayyam* in 1859. Its remarkable immediate and sustained popularity enabled Rudyard Kipling, who was not writing for a small, learned readership, to write, in 1890,[26]

> Now the New Year reviving old desires,
> The restless soul to open sea aspires
>   Where the Blue Peter flickers from the fore,
> And the grimed stoker feeds the engine-fires,

and be confident that his readers would recall Fitzgerald's

> Now the New Year reviving old desires,
> The thoughtful soul to solitude aspires,
>   Where the White Hand of Moses on the bough
> Puts forth, and Jesus from the ground suspires.

Whatever may be said of the early elegists, few will claim that Kipling wrote his poem in this form because he could think of no other way to write it or that he has simply plagiarized Fitzgerald. Nor is his poem a parody[27] or even that kind of imitation which is said to be the sincerest form of flattery. The allusions are purposive, and the result is much more than an imitation.

Kipling begins with an exact quotation from Fitzgerald, the only one in the poem. Not even one such quotation was needed to establish allusion: the characteristic form of stanza would have sufficed. The exact quotation, and the choice of quotation, may indicate that more than parody is the goal. For in this stanza, having proclaimed that his theme is in some sense Khayyam's (or Fitzgerald's), Kipling immediately creates a set of oppositions and contrasts. Some of these serve to establish the complex mood of his poem: restless soul/thoughtful soul, open sea (and the close juxtapositions of shipboard)/solitude (inland in Persia), grimed stoker/Jesus. Others (Blue Peter/White Hand, fore-[mast]/bough) seem designed to render the formal correspondence as close as possible, though fore(mast)/bough also opposes sea to land once more.

The first stanza sets the tone for the whole poem, which alludes to Fitzgerald's work throughout, even though some stanzas contain of Fitzgerald no more than Khayyam's meter and rhyme scheme and the translator's general tone of voice. Others approach Fitzgerald more closely. So the first two lines of Kipling's sixth stanza

> The shadow of the rigging to and fro
> Sways, shifts and flickers on the spar-deck's snow

are surely meant to recall Fitzgerald's [28]

> For in and out, above, about, below
> 'Tis nothing but a Magic shadow-show
>   Played in a Box whose Candle is the Sun
> Round which we Phantom Figures come and go.

This is a vaguer allusion; but note Kipling's choice of the same rhyme as the one Fitzgerald used for the first, second, and fourth lines of his stanza. Compare also, again noting the similar rhymes, Kipling's eighth stanza:

> For the same wave that meets our stem in spray
> Bore Smith of Asia eastward yesterday,
>   And Delhi Jones and Brown of Midnapore
> Tomorrow follow on the self-same way

with Fitzgerald's [29]

> Each Morn a thousand Roses brings, you say:
> Yes, but where leaves the Rose of Yesterday?
>   And this first summer month that brings the Rose
> Shall take Jamshyd and Kaikobad away.

The allusions in this stanza are not emphasized. It is the first line of Kipling's poem, identical with a line of Fitzgerald, the close parallelism of the first stanza, the verse form, and the significant echoes of particular lines that create the general climate of allusion in which these vaguer allusions can be taken. The harmony and counterpoint between the two poems, made possible by this general climate, give Kipling's poem its emotional and aesthetic complexity.

Kipling's eighth stanza in itself counterpoints the commonest English names against place names of an East at that time more remote, romantic, and unknown. His soldiers and civil servants may nonetheless be seen in one light as humdrum, chained to a round of duties; but the Fitzgerald stanza echoed by Kipling's eighth, and the general evocation of Khayyam's world aroused by Kipling's allusions, link Smith, Jones, and Brown with Jamshyd and Kaikobad. Smith, Jones, and Brown do not possess the meditative wisdom of Khayyam, though they may occasionally attempt to change their ways. (Kipling, in one of his closer allusions,[30] associates his travelers' fruitless resolve to abandon service in India with Khayyam's equally fruitless resolve to give up his dependence on the grape.) Nevertheless, Smith, Jones, and Brown are associated in their active lives with the mighty dead heroes of Persia.

The poem as a whole, as the first stanza promises, contrasts the busy life of the servants of Queen Victoria's Raj with the meditative hedonism of

Khayyam. But read as a whole, the poem does much more than that. The echoes and close imitations of Fitzgerald/Khayyam also endow the busy life described with the romantic, sentimental, fatalistic overtones of the earlier poem. Furthermore, the Magic shadow-show in Khayyam's world includes both Jamshyd and Khayyam, and meditative poet and busy functionary are alike phantoms. So that when Kipling writes, not in imitation of any particular thought of Khayyam,

> Bound in the wheel of Empire, one by one,
> The chain-gangs of the East from sire to son,
>   The Exiles' Line takes out the exiles' line
> And ships them homeward when their work is done,

a sensitive reader will not merely associate the lines with the fatalism of Khayyam but will recall his insistence on the fleeting insubstantiality of all things human. (One should remember the likelihood of an early death in Kipling's India.) The coexistence of the two poems in the mind, like the coexistence of two pictures before the eyes in a stereoscope, gives Kipling's poem an emotional and aesthetic depth and complexity which he could not have attained by other means.

It would be difficult, having read both Fitzgerald's poem and Kipling's, to deny that allusion is present in the latter, for several triggers are used. Most of these are not available to the elegist if he wishes to allude to Homer. He cannot imitate Homer's verse form: as an elegist, he uses a meter one of whose lines must, like Homer's, be a dactylic hexameter, so that its coincidence with Homer in form is unremarkable, while the other must be a dactylic pentameter, so that coincidence in form is impossible. The elegist can merely borrow phrases.

However, in favorable circumstances a borrowed phrase can carry a purposive allusion. Decades after Kipling, Ogden Nash wrote[31]

> The lion and the lizard
> No heavenly harmonies hear
> From the high fidelity speaker
> Concealed behind the Vermeer.

Though the phrase is only five words long, there is evidently allusion here. ("They say the lion and the lizard keep / The courts where Jamshyd gloried and drank deep.")[32] The only other explanation would be to suppose that the poet had gone out of his mind, since the lines are nonsense if there is no allusion. (Mr. Nash obligingly mentions Jamshyd in the next stanza.) Furthermore, the allusion is purposive. The Nash poem, like the verses of Khayyam alluded to, has the theme of transience, decay, and disaster. The allusion should evoke memories of Khayyam's fatalistic hedonism, or rather Fitzgerald's version of it, and juxtapose them with the very different verses of the urbane and witty Mr. Nash, counterpointing the spare against the full-blown, the dry against the lush, and the contemporary with the remote. The allusion, by economically suggesting to the reader two very different emotional responses to the situation, produces that density and complexity of communication which is one poetic goal.

One may use allusion, then, to enrich's one's own work. The skillful employment of allusion indicates considerable poetic talent: if any of the elegists could use allusion in this way, it is greatly to their credit. Whether they did so or not can be discussed only in the detailed analyses of poems.

A brief example of possible allusion must suffice here. Tyrtaeus writes of the warriors who fought in the earlier Messenian War (5W. 5–8):

νωλεμέως αἰεὶ ταλασίφρονα θυμὸν ἔχοντες
αἰχμηταὶ πατέρων ἡμετέρων πατέρες·
εἰκοστῷ δ' οἱ μὲν κατὰ πίονα ἔργα λιπόντες
φεῦγον Ἰθωμαίων ἐκ μεγάλων ὀρέων.

νωλεμέως is very common in Homer in the sense of "steadfastly, relentlessly." ταλασίφρων is much less common. (The phrase ταλασίφρονα θυμόν occurs here first in extant Greek.) It occurs twice in the *Iliad*, eleven times in the *Odyssey*. Of these thirteen examples, one (*Iliad* 4. 421) has general reference; the other twelve, including the *Iliad* passage, *all refer to Odysseus*, who likewise endured many hardships and triumphed *in the twentieth year*. An audience sensitive—or sensitized—to purposive allusion could interpret Tyrtaeus as saying allusively, "Our grandfathers suffered hardships like Odysseus but triumphed in the end, like Odysseus, because they had a spirit like that of Odysseus."

I shall test the hypothesis that there are purposive allusions to Homer, of which this is one, in the poems of the early elegists. The hypothesis may be entertained without positing a similarity in culture between the elegists' audiences and the readers of Mr. Nash. (It seems unlikely that his allusion would be as widely comprehensible as Kipling's.) Epic poetry in the seventh century B.C. enjoyed a cultural supremacy certainly not shared by Fitzgerald in the nineteenth and twentieth centuries A.D.;[33] both absolutely and in comparison with our own day, there was little competing poetry of any kind, and the members of nonliterate, or recently and still largely nonliterate, cultures of necessity place much more reliance on their memories than we do.

The very possibility of establishing such hypotheses raises difficult critical questions of authorial intention. They can be established, if at all, only by combining the careful study of individual passages of particular poems with a study of general characteristics and probabilities. If it can be argued that a word at a certain position in the elegiac couplet and at a certain position in its phrase will have great prominence, and if a poet frequently places important words in that position, there must be some frequency above which the hypothesis of chance becomes the less plausible one.

Again, since there are 320 metrically different forms of the elegiac couplet, the odds are quite long against a poet's composing by fortunate chance even one couplet in which the meter seems well adapted to the sense; and if meter and sense frequently are in harmony, the odds against chance rapidly become astronomical. (Nor does the existence of inept lines prove lack of attention to the goal claimed. If art is a matter of aiming at a target, the target is not clearly in view. One may always miss a target even when it is patently before one's eyes; and particularly in the development of an art, where the working of an effect and the manner in which it is to be attained are not clearly understood, and where some difficulty may be experienced in handling the material at all, some failures or partial successes are to be expected.)

Similarly, one "allusion" of the type claimed in Tyrtaeus 5W. 5–8 may well be a coincidence, but more than a certain number of instances will render coincidence a less likely explanation than intent. There will be dispute over the appropriate frequency, but it cannot be denied that there is one.

It should also be noted that even the hypothesis that these poets are deliberately composing in elegiac verse rests finally on a judgment of statistical probability. One could produce the rhythmic sequence in any of these poems, or all of them, by chance. Those monkeys with typewriters could produce the sonnets of Shakespeare. The universe has not yet existed long enough for them to have produced all of the possible variant sequences of letters, but it is not necessary, or even probable, that the *Sonnets* should be produced only after all the other possible sequences. The sequence of letters which constitutes the *Sonnets* is no more and no less likely to occur at the first, or any subsequent, attempt. Nevertheless, I believe that these poets were deliberately writing elegiac verse and that each had some other ascertainable poetic goals. Assuming that the hypothesis concerning their meter may be taken as established, I shall argue in the later chapters for the others.

Poetry and Rhetoric in the Early Elegists

The elegists discussed in this book enjoy differing reputations as poets. Archilochus, Simonides, and Mimnermus are the best regarded; but Archilochus' poetic fame does not rest primarily on his elegies, and Simonides' esteem is not derived from the two poems discussed here or from any included by West in his edition (1972) of the elegists. My purpose in writing this book is not to argue that the poems I have selected for discussion are the finest of extant Greek poetry. The best elegies of the best poets are very fine; but I wish to argue merely that the genre is underestimated by most readers and that seven of the poets show clearly distinct poetic personalities and styles, so that their poems afford distinguishable kinds of poetic satisfaction. The eighth, "Theognis," is an anthology, which furnishes an indefinitely large number of additional poets, most of them probably unknown to us even by name.

Such evaluations must depend on the detailed study of individual poems, but a more general question requires immediate discussion. It is widely supposed that early Greek elegy consists essentially of hortatory poetry. West has argued cogently that the scope of the genre is much wider (West 1974, 1–21); but it cannot be denied that much early elegy has a "message." I do not wish to deny that in such elegy the writers regarded the content of their writings, the message they wished to convey to their contemporaries, as of the first importance. Even if we distinguish the poet from his poetic persona, the point remains true of the latter. "Poetry for poetry's sake" is not characteristic of the elegists. (Nor can I discern any irony: the message is what it purports to be.[34] Those for whom the "real" Tyrtaeus is a pacifist, the "real" Solon an anarchist, and the "real" Mimnermus an optimistic gerontophile should read no further. There is nothing for them in this book.) Nor do I reject the time-honored judgment that some at least of these writers composed in verse because there was no developed prose ready to hand, and verse was the medium of formal and memorable utterance.

In this situation any attempt to treat the elegists as poets must elicit immediate doubts. The austere may hold that poetry with a message cannot be poetry at all. Others may insist that "mere rhetoric" is in fact the best that our elegists can achieve. Yet others may suppose that even effective rhetoric is not to be expected from early moralists and lawgivers.

What our elegists can in fact achieve must await detailed analysis. But in a culture in which verse is the customary medium of memorable and polished diction, a concern for effective expression in verse is likely to be widespread among those who suppose themselves to have something of importance to convey: possession of a message is not necessarily accompanied by a lack of interest in the skills required to deliver it effectively. An innovator in ideas may display creativity also in the handling of his verse, and the man who exhorts to battle has an evident interest in stirring the hearts of his audience by every possible means. Neither may prove to possess any talent for handling words and meter; but the assumption that a moralist, a lawgiver, or a composer of military exhortation must be innocent of such talents is sometimes too readily made.

Here, however, some preliminary distinctions will be useful. Where compositions are intended to persuade, there is an inducement to treat all effective use of language as rhetoric. It certainly serves a rhetorical purpose, but the distinction between poetry and rhetoric is worth drawing, nevertheless. For the same lines could occur in more than one genre. Lorenzo's speech to Jessica at Belmont (Shakespeare, *Merchant of Venice*, 5. 1. 1–6) will serve as an example:

> The moon shines bright. In such a night as this,
> When the sweet wind did gently kiss the trees
> And they did make no noise, in such a night
> Troilus methinks mounted the Trojan walls,
> And sighed his soul towards the Grecian tents
> Where Cressid lay that night.

This is a speech from a play and therefore dramatic poetry. The lines could, however, occur without change in a "pure" lyric poem which had no further intent than to express the poet's response to a moonlit night. Or, again without change, they could constitute part of a poem with the hortatory intent of persuading the recipient to pursue a particular course of action: to emulate Cressida, perhaps. (If the lines existed only on a scrap of papyrus, without context, could anyone with confidence assign them to a genre?)

The characteristics of these lines which all critics would term "poetic" if the lines formed part of a lyric poem are those which I shall denote by "poetic" and "poetry" in subsequent chapters. I shall use "rhetoric" and "rhetorical" to denote language which, were it not expressed in meter, would be taken to be simply effective prose: contrast Solon 4W. 5–8 with Solon 4W. 34–35. I shall also use the adjective of rhetorical figures and devices. That the last of the poets discussed in this book laid down his pen more than a generation before the appearance of the first rhetorical handbook is irrelevant to the existence in their works either of general rhetorical skills or of particular rhetorical figures. There are rhetorical figures in Homer.[35] As an example from the elegists, consider Tyrtaeus 10W. 9–10, an excellent rhetorical tricolon:

> αἰσχύνει τε γένος, κατὰ δ' ἀγλαὸν εἶδος ἐλέγχει,
> πᾶσα δ' ἀτιμίη καὶ κακότης ἕπεται.

Rhetorical figures antedate rhetorical theorists as grammar antedates grammarians.

Procedure

In each of the eight following chapters I follow the same procedure. I begin with a few lines of biography or, in the case of "Theognis," explain why a biography would be inappropriate. I merely locate the poet in space and time: not from any doctrinal belief that a poet's biography is necessarily irrelevant to our understanding of his work but from a skepticism over the existence of a biographical tradition independent of the poems themselves.[36] There follow some numerical analyses of the extant lines of the poet. The analyses are intended solely to sharpen the reader's perception of those lines as poetry. It is possible that if we possessed all the elegiacs of Callinus and Tyrtaeus, Callinus would prove to have written enjambed pentameters no more frequently than Tyrtaeus; but to note that enjambed pentameters are three times more frequent in extant Callinus than in extant Tyrtaeus is to draw attention to one of a number of real differences, immediately noticeable in performance, between the Callinus and the Tyrtaeus that have come down to us. In the remainder of the chapter, one or more poems is discussed in detail. In each case a text is printed, followed by a translation. As explained above (p. xi), the text is that of M. L. West (Oxford, 1972), which is by far the best available.[37] The few points at which I dissent from West's reading or punctuation are noted in the individual discussions. The translation serves no purpose beyond that of a construe; the subsequent discussion indicates my understanding of the lines. My argument throughout is that poetry is untranslatable. The translations are interspersed with a question mark in parentheses at points where the English should be treated with even greater caution than usual. Next, I give a "static" analysis of the text, pointing out certain features which seem to me to be uncontroversially present. There follows a "dynamic" analysis, in which I discuss these and other features of the poem, viewed as the product of a poet with certain, possibly ascertainable, goals. Where relevant, I also discuss possible allusions to Homer, Hesiod, or other early poets.

The commentary is many times longer than the text. Some of it is abstract and schematic. But all is intended to enhance the aesthetic experience of reading these poems and to encourage the reader, now become an audience, even if only of his own performance, to approach other Greek and Roman poetry in the same way.

2
ARCHILOCHUS

Archilochus, Callinus, and Tyrtaeus are the earliest elegiac poets of whose work anything survives. Archilochus may be the earliest by a few years.[1] It is certainly convenient to discuss him first, since his more numerous fragments, mostly not elegiac, supply an appropriate occasion for discussing some questions that are relevant to all three.

That Archilochus was born on Paros in the Cyclades and subsequently migrated to Thasos in the north Aegean seems certain (Herodotus 1. 12; Clement, *Stromateis* 1335; Horace, *Epistles* 1. 19. 23, etc.). That he was alive during the period 680–640 B.C. is widely accepted (Jacoby 1941, 97). Unless his poetical persona or personae bear no relation at all to the poet himself, that he was a man of action and violent emotions would be difficult to deny.[2] That on at least one occasion he fought and ran away is an inference, as is the ascription to Archilochus' own career of virtually any other particular event in the poems. For, as Dover has cogently argued (in Hardt 1964, 183–222), in no case can we be certain that the "I" of the poem, or the person whose sentiments are being expressed, is Archilochus. In some cases the poem as a whole might have clearly established that the speaker was not Archilochus. But we rarely, if ever, possess a complete poem;[3] and even if complete poems were available, comparative material from other nonliterate or recently nonliterate[4] cultures readily furnishes first-person poetry whose content is not, and at the time of composition was known not to be, autobiographical, even though the poem itself gives no indication. Archilochus may have used many different poetical personae.

Complete skepticism is not necessarily the only tenable position;[5] and reliable biographical information, demonstrably derived from no poem, might be very illuminating, for it is difficult to believe that Archilochus' poetry is not the fruit of a life intensely lived. But for my present purpose it is more relevant to try to establish the relationship between Archilochus' practice and that of

Homer in matters of language and poetic technique, in the hope of more adequately understanding Archilochus' achievement as a poet.

Here too there are problems. We can readily establish which words used by Archilochus occur also in the *Iliad*, *Odyssey*, and *Homeric Hymns*[6] and are in that sense "Homeric." But if individual words are to be "Homeric" in an aesthetically significant sense, more is needed: the words must belong solely to the Homeric poems, for only so will their use impart the "flavor" of Homer to Archilochus' poetry. We may retain the aesthetic significance while changing the terminology if we suppose that the words used by both Homer and Archilochus belonged to a vocabulary confined earlier to epic poetry or—on the reasonable assumption that Archilochus had predecessors in elegiac verse (see Dover, in Hardt 1964; Nagy 1974)—to dactylic poetry or, when meter would permit, to poetry as such. "Epic" or "poetic" will then represent the situation; but if a word which appears in Homer and Archilochus was used also in everyday speech, to term it "epic" or "poetic" is likely to be confusing.

Consider two passages of Shakespeare which I have already quoted: Macbeth's soliloquy (*Macbeth*, 5. 5.) and Lorenzo's speech to Jessica (*Merchant of Venice*, 5. 1. 1–6). Both are unmistakably Shakespearean poetry, but even now, almost four centuries later, there is hardly a word used there which is not used now in everyday speech. None in use recalls poetry or Shakespeare. Contrast two lines from Chatterton: "The trees enleaféd unto heaven straught" and "Methinks my hartys joy is steynced with some care." At least four of these words were not used in ordinary speech in Chatterton's own day. The aesthetic effect is quite different.[7]

Archilochus' vernacular was that of Paros: Ionic. It has been noted that, in his imitations of the dialectally mixed "art language" of Homer, Archilochus favored the Ionic elements (Treu, in Hardt 1964, 167). This fact might suggest vernacular influence; but our knowledge of seventh-century vernacular Ionic is much too scanty to confirm or refute the hypothesis. It seems improbable that there was no overlap between vernacular and poetic vocabulary; but some words would be excluded from poetry by meter.[8] The art language of Homer resulted in part from the need to find forms that would scan in dactylic hexameters. But the proportion of vernacular,[9] and hence the overall "flavor" of Archilochus' elegiacs, is impossible to estimate.[10]

We may, however, try to evaluate the manner in which Archilochus employed his vocabulary. Take an extreme case. Even if no word in Homer belonged to any contemporary vernacular and Archilochus used only words which occurred in Homer, our estimation of an Archilochus who always used Homeric words in Homeric phrases would be very different from that of an Archilochus who always used Homeric words in phrases of his own.

Even "using Homeric words in Homeric phrases" has been blurred in scholarly controversy; but it will be more convenient to discuss the question in the context of the individual poems.

First a few general remarks. We possess 36 complete elegiac lines of Archilochus,[11] 20 hexameters and 16 pentameters. (Four of the hexameters occur as one-line fragments and might be from stichic hexameters, but there is no certain evidence to demonstrate that Archilochus used this meter.)[12] The longest continuous passage of elegiacs is the ten lines of 13W. There is one passage of four and a half continuous lines (3W), and there are two of four lines each (4W, 5W).

This is a very small sample, but it is large enough to enable the reader to form some judgment of Archilochus as an elegiac poet, to regret that not more of his elegiacs are preserved, and to compare him with other early elegists.

Where so few lines are preserved, no statistically significant data can be compiled, but enumerating what occurs in the surviving lines may draw attention to qualitative features of Archilochus' elegiacs. Of the 20 hexameters, 5 have caesura at H7 (25%), 14 have trochaic caesura at H8 (70%), and 1 has caesura at H10 (5%): a much higher preference for H8 than in the early elegists in general.[13]

The line endings of his 20 hexameters comprise 7 disyllabic, 11 trisyllabic, and 2 quadrisyllabic: percentages (35, 55, 10) quite close to the overall figures for elegiac and for the Homer sample (see Table 6). Of the 16 pentameters, 4 end in disyllables, 6 in trisyllables, 1 in a quadrisyllable, and 5 in pentesyllables. The percentage of pentesyllables (31.25) is much higher than the overall figure for elegiac (12.18). It need not be representative of Archilochus' elegiac poetry, of which we doubtless possess only a small fraction; but the figure draws attention to a feature of the verses we possess. Whether aesthetic goals ever guided Archilochus' choice of line endings can be discussed only in particular contexts.

If we discard 15, 16, and 17W, which, as one-line fragments, are printed end-stopped, the remaining nine poems have 13 end-stopped lines out of a total of 33, and there are 22 stops within the line: figures which already suggest some fluency in composing elegiacs.

I shall discuss 13W first. As the longest extant passage of Archilochan elegiacs, it offers the opportunity of observing the poet's technique on a somewhat larger canvas. It will be convenient to discuss the shorter passages against this background.

ARCHILOCHUS 13W

κήδεα μὲν στονόεντα Περίκλεες οὔτέ τις ἀστῶν
μεμφόμενος θαλίης τέρψεται οὐδὲ πόλις·
τοίους γὰρ κατὰ κῦμα πολυφλοίσβοιο θαλάσσης
ἔκλυσεν, οἰδαλέους δ' ἀμφ' ὀδύνης ἔχομεν

```
5       πνεύμονας. ἀλλὰ θεοὶ γὰρ ἀνηκέστοισι κακοῖσιν
        ὦ φίλ' ἐπὶ κρατερὴν τλημοσύνην ἔθεσαν
        φάρμακον. ἄλλοτε ἄλλος ἔχει τόδε· νῦν μὲν ἐς ἡμέας
        ἐτράπεθ', αἱματόεν δ' ἕλκος ἀναστένομεν,
        ἐξαῦτις δ' ἑτέρους ἐπαμείψεται. ἀλλὰ τάχιστα
10      τλῆτε, γυναικεῖον πένθος ἀπωσάμενοι.
```

Pericles, neither will any of the citizens, finding fault with our grievous woes, take pleasure in festivities, nor yet will the polis. Such men has the wave of the much-resounding sea drowned, and we have our lungs swollen because of our sorrows. But the gods, my friend, to our woes without cure have applied firm endurance as a remedy. Now one, now another has this woe. Now it has come to us, and we are lamenting a bloody wound, but on another occasion it will visit others in turn. But swiftly ⟨begin to⟩ endure, having thrust away womanly grief.

This poem, or fragment, of consolation and exhortation to endurance is quoted by Stobaeus (4. 56. 30) and referred to by Philostratus (*Vita Apollonii* 7. 26). Plutarch (*Quomodo aud. poet.* 12, p. 33a–b) quotes an elegiac couplet (11W) from Archilochus' poem on the death by drowning of his brother-in-law. Some scholars have thought it possible that 11W and 13W are parts of the same poem.[14] Nothing, however, links Archilochus' brother-in-law with 13W. Neither Stobaeus nor Philostratus mentions him in quoting or referring to 13W, and Longinus (*De sublimitate* 10) refers so vaguely to Archilochus' "poem on the shipwreck" that it is impossible to identify the poem.[15] Again, as Campbell (1967, 146) says, if 13W is part of the poem on the brother-in-law's death, it seems strange that the poet should address Pericles rather than his own sister. Possibly the fact that more than one drowned person is mentioned (τοίους, 3) points in the same direction: even if the whole complement of the ship was lost, in a poem to console his sister Archilochus might well have written exclusively of her husband. Nor can one readily reconstruct a poem including both 13W and 11W, the latter of which may be rendered "I shall remedy nothing by weeping, nor make matters worse by rejoicing and feasting (τερπωλὰς καὶ θαλίας ἐφέπων)." These words accord very ill with 13W. 1–2. Are we to suppose that Archilochus in one and the same poem stated that none of the (other?) citizens would take pleasure in feasting at this time (θαλίης τέρψεται) and also that he might as well feast, since it would not make matters worse? 11W could certainly not stand earlier in the complete poem than 13W, and it could hardly stand later, after the grim τλῆτε. Moreover, I agree with Campbell (1967, 145) in finding that the lines we have in 13W "have the air of a complete poem."[16] My reasons will become apparent in the course of the discussion.

I begin with a static analysis. Of the ten lines of this poem only three (2, 8, 10) are end-stopped. All five hexameters are enjambed. 1 is overrun to the end of 2. (West [1972] prints no stop within this couplet, in accordance with his general policy on vocatives; but in performance there must have been a pause on each side of Περίκλεες.) 3 is overrun to a comma at P3, with dactylic first foot in 4, which is itself overrun to a full stop at P3 in 5, again with dactylic first foot. There is then no mark of punctuation until the full stop after φάρμακον at H3 in 7, after yet another dactylic first foot. (A pause before and after ὦ φίλ' in 6 is demanded by the sense.) 7 itself contains an unusual phenomenon: a complete sentence in the middle of a hexameter (from H4 to H12). From the bucolic diaeresis H12, 7 is overrun to H3 in 8, so that for the fourth time in five lines a mark of punctuation occurs after a dactylic first foot. 8 is then end-stopped with a comma, while 9 has a full stop at the bucolic diaeresis H12. 9 is then overrun to a comma at P2 in 10, and the poem—or the lines we possess—closes at the end of 10.

The composition within the structure of the elegiac couplet is fluent. True, four of the pauses occur at H3 or P3, all with a dactylic first foot, in contrast to the variety of Callinus 1W; but such facts can be evaluated only in terms of their effect in the poem in which they occur. Two pauses marked by punctuation occur at the bucolic diaeresis, and there must have been a pause both there and at the trochaic caesura in 1.

Little attempt is made to match meter to mood.[17] In a poem of grief followed by grim resolution, six lines (1, 2, 4, 6, 7, 8) are entirely dactylic, three (5, 9, 10) contain one spondee each, and one (3) contains two spondees: five spondaic feet in ten lines.[18] Though the trochaic caesura at H8 is presumably lighter in effect than the penthemimeral caesura at H7, Archilochus maintains the usual[19] preference for the trochaic (4:1 here) found in both epic and elegiac writers. But Archilochus has other weapons in his poetic armory.

1–2. The poem begins strongly.[20] Followed by the pause demanded by the vocative, κήδεα μὲν στονόεντα,[21] set first and in isolation, states with appropriate emphasis a theme of the poem: the woes, their cause, and the correct attitude for a warrior to adopt to them in the world as it is constitute Archilochus' subject. After the vocative, οὔτέ τις ἀστῶν completes the line but not the sense. It is indeed impossible to guess even what general sense the verb will have; and οὔτε indicates that the verb, whatever it is, will have an additional subject, whose identity it is equally impossible to guess. To the imperfect cadence of the hexameter in the elegiac couplet is added the effect of a particularly marked incompleteness of sense. (Contrast line 3, where only a verb is needed to complete the sense, and there is little doubt what kind of meaning the verb will have.) The mind is accordingly awaiting the verb in 2 with unusual alertness, and the verb gains emphasis additional to that which it derives from its position as first word in the pentameter. Again, μεμφόμενος is not exactly the verb one might have expected with κήδεα, so that the mind still awaits both an explanation and the finite verb of the sentence. θαλίης τέρψεται supplies the verb; but a second subject is needed after οὔτέ τις ἀστῶν, so that the mind remains expectant to the end of the line. Archilochus indicates that the second subject, πόλις, is the more important by preceding it, not by a second οὔτε, but by οὐδέ (Denniston 1954, 193).

Whether πόλις is sufficiently important to deserve the emphasis and sustain interest to the end of the sentence and couplet depends on the interpretation of πόλις, which is not immediately clear. The word might be simply shorthand for πάντες οἱ πολῖται; but "neither any of the citizens will grieve, nor all of them" seems bathetic in any word order and in any position in the verse, and particularly so in weak position at the end of the pentameter. In usages of this kind one can be certain that the citizens are not collectively denoted only where such an interpretation would be nonsense, as in *Theognidea* 39: Κύρνε, κύει πόλις ἥδε. Here metaphor is undeniable; but metaphor is not the only alternative. An action of the *polis* need not be the sum of the actions of its citizens; it might be an official action taken on behalf of all the citizens by the proper authorities. The sense here would then be equivalent to "there will not be any private feasts nor any public, civic festivities either"; whereupon πόλις expresses an unusual manifestation of mourning,[22] there is no bathos, οὐδέ is justified, and the sense compensates at least to some extent for the weak position of πόλις.

3–4(P3). τοίους deserves its first position: it is the quality of the men drowned that justifies the intensity of the grief. The meter adds to the effect: τοίους is one of the poem's five spondees. κῦμα πολυφλοίσβοιο θαλάσσης is a Homeric formula, whose function I shall discuss later.[23] ἔκλυσεν is given prominence by enjambment. There can be no doubt at the end of 3, as there was in 1, about the general meaning of the word to be enjambed. But ἔκλυσεν is vivid—"washed away," not merely "submerged"; and position and pause at P3, together with the contrast of the long subject and its pentesyllabic ornamental epithet, whose rhythm suggests the rolling of the sea,[24] with the brief ἔκλυσεν, well convey a feeling of finality.

4(P4)–5(H3). The remaining clause of the sentence is enclosed by οἰδαλέους . . . πνεύμονας, noun and adjective in agreement. In both prose and poetry, such a word order is frequently used to mark the beginning and end of sense groups. Words so placed derive emphasis from their position. To emphasize the effects of grief is appropriate here. (ἀμφ' ὀδύνης needs less prominence: the grief was emphasized in 1.) The clause is also skillfully placed in the elegiac couplets. οἰδαλέους, set between the pauses after ἔκλυσεν and at the diaeresis at P7, is at the beginning of its clause; πνεύμονας is at the end of its clause but at the beginning of its line, followed by a strong pause. (The comparatively rare enjambment of the pentameter[25] draws added attention to the fact that πνεύμονας is at once a beginning and an end.) There is a pleasing symmetry-in-asymmetry.

οἰδαλέους is a striking word, very rare and here first in extant Greek. The related verbs οἰδέω and οἰδάνω are themselves not common in early Greek; but ᾤδεε δὲ χρόα πάντα is used of Odysseus' body when he crawls ashore on Phaeacia after his long swim from his shipwrecked raft (*Odyssey* 5. 455), and οἶδμα is used literally of the sea in *Iliad* 23. 230. On hearing οἰδαλέους in this context, a Greek of Archilochus' day might have thought of swelling waves in a stormy sea or of bodies swollen from exposure to water. By the end of the line it is clear that οἰδαλέους refers to the living; but πνεύμονας is a surprising word with such an adjective. If the thought of swelling waves and swollen bodies has already been evoked by οἰδαλέους, the swollen lungs of the living gain added pathos from the association.

5(H4)-7(H3). This sentence is the pivot of Archilochus' poem. In the earlier lines, the theme has been overwhelming grief at disaster; from this point on, a more positive attitude will be urged. The change of theme may furnish an additional motive for the overrun of πνεύμονας to 5(H3), for some early elegists seem to avoid a major change of theme at the beginning of the hexameter. Their goal is doubtless in part to avoid emphasizing that the elegiac meter is composed of repeated couplets: counterpoint of speech rhythms against the regularities of the meter gives variety and interest. Another example of this practice occurs in Callinus 1W. 6-8(H4); others will be observed in other poets.[26] Any additional effects will be noted in context.

In this sentence, the gods and their remedy—the important ideas—are duly given pride of place. Set between ἀλλά and γάρ, in isolation at the beginning of its clause, θεοί is emphatic.[27] There follows ἀνηκέστοισι, whose juxtaposition with θεοί reminds Archilochus' audience that there are some disasters which not even the gods are able to prevent or remedy.[28] At the end of 5 the sense is still unclear: "the gods . . . for ? by means of ? woes incurable . . . have . . . done something positive? plagued mankind?" Once again, the mind is alert for what is to come. In 6, ὦ φίλ' contributes little to the sense but heightens suspense yet further. The remainder of 6 makes matters clearer, but the sense is not quite complete at the end of the line. φάρμακον is needed even though, as Campbell (1967) points out, ἐπιτιθέναι seems to be the appropriate term for applying remedies, so that there may already be a connotation of φάρμακα. However, the great emphasis which φάρμακον derives from position and pause is merited: as κήδεα set the keynote for the earlier lines, φάρμακον sets the keynote for the remainder. There is some resemblance in effect also to the similarly placed δυσμενέσιν in Callinus 1W. 8.

In general sense, Archilochus' words resemble *Iliad* 24. 49: τλητὸν γὰρ μοῖραι θυμὸν θέσαν ἀνθρώποισιν. But Archilochus has greatly strengthened the Homeric expression by combining κρατερήν with τλημοσύνην. κρατερός is for the most part used of bodily strength in Homer, whether of the whole body (*Iliad* 16. 624) or a part (*Odyssey* 4. 288); but it is also used of feelings, states of mind, or emotions. When anything that is passively experienced (πένθος, *Iliad* 11. 249; ἄλγεα, *Odyssey* 15. 232) is characterized as κρατερός, the adjective brings to mind the intensity of the experience and consequently the power of whatever is inflicting the grief or pain. But when the adjective is used of an active state of mind (κρατερὸν μένος, *Iliad* 7. 38),[29] as when it is used of a strong active body, κρατερός characterizes the endowments, psychological and physical, respectively, of the Homeric hero. τλημοσύνη is an active state of mind in the sense that, unlike grief or pain, one has to resolve to manifest it, and the adjective κρατερήν has similar connotations of heroism in this context. If we remember the ancient Greek opinion of women, it is evident that κρατερὴν τλημοσύνην is directly opposed to γυναικεῖον πένθος in 10, an opposition pointed up by the placing of the phrases in their pentameters, astride the diaeresis at P7.[30]

The oxymoronic contrast between ἀνηκέστοισι and φάρμακον is evidently deliberate. It is heightened by the position of the words both in their own lines and in relation to 6, as well as by an incompleteness of sense sustained over two enjambments; and the three long syllables of ἀνηκέστοισι have their part to play. The dynamic of the language is skillful: it builds up to "remedy," suggesting that a remedy for the κακά has been found. The remedy, however, is not for the deaths, which are irremediable, but for the κήδεα, the griefs, of 1.

7(H4)–9(H12). From ἄλλοτε onward, Archilochus furnishes not an example of τλημοσύνη but an aid to displaying it: the wheel of fortune turns, and one will not have to endure forever. ἄλλοτε ἄλλος ἔχει τόδε,[31] an independent clause from H4 to H12, creates a conversational tone, which extends to ἐτράπεθ' in 8(P3). νῦν μὲν ἐς ἡμέας again combines imperfect cadence with incomplete sense: not only is it unclear precisely what type of verb is to follow, but μέν indicates that the sentence is to contain an opposition. (Compare lines 1–2. The meaning of the following verb is less predictable in 1 than in 7, but the effect of οὔτε is very similar to that of μέν.) νῦν μέν, ἐς ἡμέας, and ἐτράπεθ' are all, in different ways, given prominence:[32] a prominence which is deserved, despite the relative colorlessness of the words and the conversational tone. αἱματόεν δ' ἕλκος ἀναστένομεν—whose word order is good, with the emphatic words at beginning and end—heightens the emotional pitch again and in itself gives no hope of an end to woe; but the ideas in the preceding phrase—"now, on the one hand," "to us," and "turned"—quietly insist on life's changes and prepare for the assurance of ἐξαῦτις δ' ἑτέρους ἐπαμείψεται. In these circumstances, the molossus ἐξαῦτις fully merits its metrical weight and its position in the line.³³

9(H13)–10. The preceding clause was without emotional coloring and received no amplification to parallel αἱματόεν . . . ἀναστένομεν: Archilochus has no concern with those who will be suffering woes at some future time. The tone suits its own sentence and also furnishes a strong contrast with what follows.

ἀλλὰ τάχιστα τλῆτε would be a powerful exhortation in prose, particularly after what has preceded it. In Archilochus' poem, the strong adversative particle and the superlative adverb are reinforced by the effect of imperfect cadence and incomplete sense at line end, and the imperative is reinforced by its position and the unusual pause at P2.

Lines 7–9 have suggested thoughts which may aid the mourners to display the τλημοσύνη of 6. τλῆτε takes up τλημοσύνη; but Archilochus also changes his stance. The poem is addressed to an individual, Pericles; but the first-person plurals ἔχομεν (4) and ἀναστένομεν (8) associate Archilochus with the grief. He now distances himself from Pericles and his fellow mourners, addressing them in the second-person plural, and the poem ends with a contrast which, for an ancient Greek, is scornfully pointed. γυναικεῖον πένθος—the adjective emphasized by its spondee—is opposed immediately to τλῆτε, more remotely to κρατερὴν τλημοσύνην, and also serves to echo κήδεα μὲν στονόεντα (1), thus furnishing an elegant example of ring composition. Ring compositions demarcate the boundaries not only of whole poems but also of parts of poems; but I find it difficult to imagine a larger poem of which these lines could have formed a part.

It remains to discuss the possibility of Homeric allusion in this poem. Most of the words are found in Homer;³⁴ but few Homeric phrases occur. Of these, ἐπὶ κρατερὴν τλημοσύνην ἔθεσαν / φάρμακον is probably not a conscious echo of *Iliad* 4. 190–91, ἐπιθήσει / φάρμαχ'. The enjambment is similar, but φάρμαχ' is the direct object, and the usage is literal. The metaphorical use of φάρμακον is new and striking and would be likely to deflect the mind from seeking particular literal precedents. (The metaphor is sustained in αἱματόεν δ' ἕλκος.)

Other Homeric phrases are confined to the first three lines, and here allusion seems more likely. In *Odyssey* 9. 12 we find σοὶ δ' ἐμὰ κήδεα θυμὸς ἐπετράπετο στονόεντα / εἴρεσθ' and, in *Odyssey* 11. 603, τέρπεται ἐν θαλίῃς, which θαλίῃς τέρψεται closely resembles. Neither phrase occurs anywhere else in Homer. The one in 9. 12 occurs in Odysseus' speech in reply to Alcinous' questions about him, eight lines before he finally discloses his identity—a passage which must have been well known. The one in 11. 603 refers to Heracles: Odysseus saw his ghost in Hades, but Heracles himself τέρπεται ἐν θαλίης among the immortal gods. τέρπονт' ἐν θαλίῃσι occurs once in Hesiod, at *Works and Days* 115. There the line ends κακῶν ἔκτοσθεν ἁπάντων, and the reference is to the Golden Race, who "lived like gods, with a heart free from κῆδος (ἀκηδέα θυμὸν ἔχοντες)," and are now δαίμονες (120).

Acceptance of the hypothesis of allusion must depend largely on the number of plausible instances that can be adduced, but instances where the text is puzzling without the allusion greatly strengthen the case: remember the lion, the lizard, and the high-fidelity speaker (above, p. 27).

The first two lines of this poem, read without allusion, are rather strange:[35] why, out of all the sentiments Archilochus might have expressed, should he choose to assure Pericles that neither any of the citizens nor the whole city will find fault with the griefs of the bereaved and take pleasure in festivities? But if "griefs" and "festivities" are triggers for allusion, the use of the phrases is explicable; for if the allusions are taken, a poetic and consolatory goal is attained: the dead men are linked with Odysseus, the most storm-tossed warrior of them all, and their deaths by drowning gain in pathos and grandeur. (Note the initial position of κήδεα στονόεντα, before there is any context to restrict the free play of association, and indeed—though it is far from uncommon in Greek poetry—the absence of such words as "our" from the first couplet. τοίους [3] is the first word which explicitly refers to the particular situation.) If it is recollected also that τέρπεται ἐν θαλίης was used of Heracles in *Odyssey* 11. 603 *in contrast with* the shades of the dead—those who are not so fortunate as to be immortal—then text and allusion together communicate "The men who have drowned resemble Odysseus in their κήδεα στονόεντα, their storm-tossed sufferings (and, if any have survived, they have suffered hardships comparable with those of Odysseus). To grieve at such disasters is natural, inevitable, and no one will find fault: no citizen is in the fortunate position of Heracles, who, not subject to death, τέρπεται ἐν θαλίης and so is beyond feeling the griefs associated with it."

The hardships and griefs gain in grandeur; but possibly Archilochus, like other poets to be discussed later, is not expressing unalloyed admiration for Homeric values and behavior. Despite its first two couplets, the poem as a whole does find fault with sorrow and weeping and commends fortitude. Archilochus himself directly reprehends grief in line 10. (The movement of thought and feeling is made more evident by the ring composition, noted above.) In Homer, the heroes weep quite unself-consciously: in *Odyssey* 8. 521–31 Odysseus weeps like a woman bewailing her lost husband, who has died defending his city. There is a shift in the poem at 5–7: Archilochus, having conjured up the ethos of Homer and endowed the dead with heroic attributes, may now be demanding more fortitude from the living than Homer does.[36]

The most unmistakable Homeric phrase in the poem is κῦμα πολυφλοίσβοιο θαλάσσης. There can be no allusion to any of the passages in Homer in which the phrase occurs,[37] but it need not be dismissed as a formula used because Archilochus could think of nothing else. Metrically it suits the poet's purposes, as we have seen; but it also marks as Homeric the sea that has drowned these men, who are fit to be linked with the heroes of Homer, and it may also indicate retrospectively to the audience that the earlier allusions were indeed purposive.

One more possible echo of Hesiod may be noted.[38] In *Theogony* 612 we find καὶ ἀνήκεστον κακόν ἐστιν. In Hesiod the phrase refers to having a bad wife, which might appear somewhat bathetic in the context; but the immediately following lines in our text of the *Theogony* insist on the impossibility of escaping the intentions of Zeus, and they cite the fate of Prometheus as an example.

If the existence of these allusions is granted, Archilochus' lines gain grandeur and an added dimension. But even without allusion, this is a fine poem. Archilochus fluently composes in a manner which exploits the resources of his meter; the whole and the parts are well structured; there are variations in emotional intensity; and, far from being a slavish echo of Homeric formulae, the poem has (unless we are to count phrases which occur only once in Homer) only one Homeric formula, and that one has point. οἰδαλέους . . . πνεύμονας, κρατερὴν τλημοσύνην, and the metaphorical use of φάρμακον and αἱματόεν ἕλκος are not merely avoidances of Homeric formulae but striking new uses of language.

Page evaluates Archilochus' poetry very differently, and this poem furnishes a suitable occasion to discuss his evaluation. Of 13W Page says, "in structure, in sentiment, and in phrasing these lines are wholly within the limits of the traditional oral Epic. The facts that the subject-matter is actual and that the metre has taken on a new form make no difference whatsoever either to the matter or to the manner of what is said." Of οἰδαλέους . . . πνεύμονας he says, "The phrase which follows is new to us and may be the poet's invention, '*We have our lungs swollen through sorrows*;' but it is merely a variation on a common theme, exemplified in *Il.* 9. 553 χόλος οἰδάνει ἐν στήθεσσι, 646 οἰδάνεται κραδίη χόλῳ. The transition from 'heart swelling with rage' to 'lungs swelling with grief' is such as might have been made at any time; Archilochus is doing what was constantly done during the creative period of the Epic—adapting an old formula, creating a new one" (in Hardt 1964, 126–28).

To write thus is to use the phrase "wholly within the limits of the traditional oral Epic" so broadly as to leave it with very little meaning. Archilochus' phrase contains none of the words which occur in the passages cited; one of

Archilochus' words may be a new coinage; the syntax is completely different; and the location of the clause in the elegiac couplet is skillful and purposive. In the context of drowning, οἰδαλέους may have particular overtones. Whether it has or not, "my heart swells with anger" records a direct experience in the Homeric manner, as "lungs swollen with grief" does not. The angry man feels that something is swelling within, but it requires thought to conclude that weeping might swell the lungs, which do not feel swollen, and the audience would perceive the phrase as novel. If all this does not constitute creativity in the use of language, many other poets, including many who are not archaic Greeks, will fail to meet Page's criteria.

The general position represented here seems to derive from an attitude to Homeric epic which is compatible with, but certainly not necessitated by, the work of Milman Parry and his followers. To compose dactylic hexameters *ex tempore* is a very difficult technique, even with all the formulaic aids which have been so carefully studied during the past fifty years. This fact, however, does not entail that the better bards regarded their craft as merely that of producing hexameters that would scan and carry on the line of narrative that their story required. Still less does it entail that the audience did not discriminate between a tale well told and a tale less well told or that this discrimination was unrelated to the use of language in a context. Such use of language occurs in Homer; that it is invariably accidental and that the audience were totally unresponsive to it seem implausible hypotheses.

ARCHILOCHUS 3W

> οὔτοι πόλλ' ἐπὶ τόξα τανύσσεται, οὐδὲ θαμειαὶ
> σφενδόναι, εὖτ' ἂν δὴ μῶλον Ἄρης συνάγῃ
> ἐν πεδίῳ· ξιφέων δὲ πολύστονον ἔσσεται ἔργον·
> ταύτης γὰρ κεῖνοι δάμονές εἰσι μάχης
> 5 δεσπόται Εὐβοίης δουρικλυτοί.

Not many bows will be strung, nor numerous slings, when Ares brings together the melee of war in the(?) plain. There will be the grievous work of swords: for in this fighting the spear-famed lords of Euboea are expert(?).

Plutarch (*Theseus* 5. 2–3) quotes this fragment as evidence for the warlike prowess of the Abantes of Euboea, having just remarked that they cut short the hair on the front of their heads so that their enemies should not grasp it in close combat,[39] but Archilochus does not mention this custom.

No one is directly addressed in the fragment; but the future tenses of 1 and 3 suggest that information and, in the poem as a whole, possibly exhortation were being given to soldiers about to join battle: an appropriate theme for an elegiac poem.

◫

Of the few complete lines, only 3 is end-stopped; and unless 5 was completed by a brief phrase or clause in agreement with δουρικλυτοί, which seems unlikely, 5 can hardly have been punctuated at the end of the line.[40] Both pentameters are overrun. None of the stops coincides with caesura or colon diaeresis, and there is great variation in their position: at H12, bucolic diaeresis, in 1 and 5;[41] at P3 in 2, after dactylic first foot; after H4 in 3; and at line end in 3. Once again Archilochus is skillfully varying the manner in which his sentences fit into the patterns of the elegiac couplet. The meter is a little more spondaic: six spondees in five lines. So much for static analysis.

◫

1–3(H4). The arrangement of words and clauses serves dynamic purposes also. Some may not be immediately apparent. Position gives emphasis, which may seem unwarranted, to σφενδόναι (2) and ἐν πεδίῳ (3). After "not many bows nor many . . ." another weapon must follow, so that σφενδόναι is hardly surprising. ἐν πεδίῳ, standing at the end of its sentence and in enjambment from a pentameter, may appear no better: prepositional phrases so placed will rarely be effective, since in most cases the sentence will be comprehensible without the phrase, and the mind will not be alert for it. But here the sentence is incomplete at the end of 2: since bows and slings were frequently used in warfare, Archilochus' original audience would be puzzled to hear that such weapons would not be used in the coming battle, until ἐν πεδίῳ was added. Again, σφενδόναι, followed by pause at P3, has point if the emphatic position of the spondaic negative οὔτοι is taken into account also: "*not* . . . (bows or) . . . slings . . . in a (or 'the') *plain.*"

3(H5)–5(H12). ξιφέων is emphasized by its position at the beginning of its clause and (with δέ) by being set between a heavy pause and the pause for H8 caesura. Note how the word order of πολύστονον . . . ἔργον demarcates those three words as a unit of sense and combines with the position of ξιφέων δέ to highlight the latter and present it as a separate idea, duly contrasted with "bows" and "slings." The effect of ταύτης at the beginning of 4 is similar: "of *swords* there will be the grievous work; for in *this* warfare are skilled those spear-famed lords of Euboea." The spondees of ταύτης γὰρ κεῖνοι emphasize the type of warfare and the identity of the enemy, in contrast with the dactyls of πολύστονον ἔσσεται ἔργον: an appropriate distribution of emphasis in lines whose function is to contrast types of warfare. The heavy stop at the end of the hexameter (3), combined with the enjambment of the following pentameter, reverses the usual movement of the elegiac couplet and gives great prominence to the opening words of the next hexameter, here to the identity of the foe. Compare Callinus 1W. 16–17, discussed in chapter three.

The goal of hoplite warfare and the need for hoplites to fight on level ground are discussed in chapter 4. Archilochus' poem reflects the strategic and tactical requirements that were developing in his own day.

Two words merit particular comment. In 4, most manuscripts have δαήμονες; two recent manuscripts have δαίμονες. West prints Fick's δάμονες, a word not otherwise attested. δαήμων occurs in Homer (*Iliad* 15. 411; 23. 671), on one occasion with an objective genitive (*Odyssey* 8. 159), as here.[42] But in Homer δαήμων is trisyllabic; here synizesis is necessary to produce acceptable meter. Synizesis occurs in elegiacs and might be invoked here.[43] If Archilochus wrote δαίμονες, δαήμονες must have been a gloss or a deliberate textual correction. (δαίμονες in late manuscripts is presumably an emendation.) It is unusual to gloss a common with a less common word; but δαίμονες, though common, is a *hapax legomenon* in the sense of "knowing." Modern scholars indeed derive δαίμων not from δαῆναι, "know," but from δαίω, "distribute"; but Plato (*Cratylus* 398B) treats "knowing, expert" as the original sense of δαίμονες and glosses it with δαήμονες. Some of Plato's etymologies are evidently produced *ad hoc* and *ad hominem*;[44] but if for Archilochus and other early Greeks δαίμων had even a faint connotation of "knower," the stage is set for a possible play on words.

After κεῖνοι in 4 a word meaning "skilled, expert" is needed. Any such connotation in δαίμων would be activated by the context. δαίμων is employed so frequently as "god, spirit" that the usage could not be excluded from the mind. But there is no need to exclude it: the poetry is enhanced if δαίμων is understood in both senses. To suggest that the warriors of Euboea are not merely skilled in battle but warlike spirits would be a powerful trope in any poetry. In early Greece it is more, for deities were believed sometimes to take part in battles.[45] Ares is given a function in battle in 2, in a usage not entirely metaphorical at this period.

δαίμονες thus understood combines with other features of these lines to present the coming battle in impersonal, nonhuman terms. Bows, slings, and swords are handled, but no handler is mentioned. Ares is a god, or war; at all events, he is not merely human. μῶλος does not mention human fighters and so depersonalizes the idea of battle; and δαίμονες would raise the enemy to the level of the superhuman.

This interpretation postulates the existence of a three-syllable *sound* which could be interpreted in this manner by Archilochus' audience. Even if δαίμων and δαήμων were in most circumstances clearly distinguished, the poetical effect is available if δαήμων with synizesis approximated in sound to δαίμων. How Archilochus represented this sound in writing we do not know. It is the existence of the sound that is important. This is written poetry, but written poetry primarily intended to be heard, not read.

The second word that merits comment is δουρικλυτοί. At first sight it may seem strange to refer to swordsmen as "famed with the spear." The word occurs some twenty times in Homer and might be supposed a thoughtless borrowing. But the sentence is not tautological or otiose, as would be a sentence which proclaimed that δουρικλυτοί were expert at fighting with the spear.[46] Archilochus tells his audience that these δουρικλυτοί are good at fighting with the sword: a new piece of information of practical value to those about to fight with them.[47]

The language of Archilochus 3W is generally Homeric,[48] but no phrase found in Homer is employed here. In fact, Archilochus seems to avoid Homeric phraseology deliberately: he writes μῶλον Ἄρης συνάγει where Homer has μῶλον Ἄρηος (as in *Iliad* 2. 401); ἔριδα ξυνάγοντες Ἄρηος (*Iliad* 5. 861); ξυνάγωμεν Ἄρηα (*Iliad* 2. 381; 19. 275); and σύναγον κρατερὴν ὑσμίνην (*Iliad* 14.448). In Homer, human agents are the subject of ξυνάγειν; here, for the first time in extant Greek, Ares is the agent who ξυνάγει the moil and toil of war. To our ears, and to later Greek ears, trained to expect of poets some strikingly novel phrase, such innovation may seem tame; but to an age accustomed to the formula, the novelty may have been immediately apparent and appreciated.[49] Whether or not it was appreciated as a novelty, giving ξυνάγειν a nonhuman subject has poetical effect, as we have seen. Archilochus, not meter or inherited vocabulary, is the master in this poem. Though not quoted for its poetical qualities by Plutarch, it is poetry nonetheless.[50]

ARCHILOCHUS 4W

.(.)].(.)[
φρα[
  ξεῖνοι̣.[
δεῖπνον δ' οὐ[
5 οὔτ' ἐμοὶ ὡσαῖ[
ἀλλ' ἄγε σὺν κώ⌊θωνι θοῆς διὰ σέλματα νηὸς
φοίτα καὶ κοίλ⌊ων πώματ' ἄφελκε κάδων,

48   Chapter Two

ἄγρει δ' οἶνον ⌊ἐρυθρὸν ἀπὸ τρυγός· οὐδὲ γὰρ ἡμεῖς
νηφέμεν ⌊ἐν φυλακῇ τῇδε δυνησόμεθα.

But come, with your cup go to and fro over the benches of the
swift ship and tear off the stoppers from the hollow jars and drain
the red wine to the dregs; for we shall not be able to be sober on
this watch.

The four complete lines of this poem were quoted by Athenaeus (11. 483d) for the use of κώθων to mean "cup" in the general sense of κύλιξ, in opposition to Critias, who claimed in his *Constitution of the Lacedaemonians* (cited 11. 483b) that κώθων was applied particularly to a Lacedaemonian cup used on expeditions. The motive for the quotation is philological. If the fragment proves to have poetic qualities, that is our good fortune.

There is a fit with a papyrus (*Oxy.* 854) which preserves the beginning of five earlier lines, together with those quoted by Athenaeus. A paragraphus after the first (of which nothing can be read) indicates that our poem began at the second line of the papyrus. Athenaeus therefore began with line 5 of Archilochus' poem. West (1972) numbers the lines of the papyrus, so that the first fully extant line of the poem, Archilochus' line 5, is West's line 6.

The sense of the first four lines cannot be established with certainty, for the papyrus preserves little of them. But ξεῖνοι seem to be mentioned, and West's "cena ne[c tibi in promptu est] nec mihi" plausibly accounts for what can be read and gives coherent sense. Archilochus—or the speaker—and some guest-friends have (unexpectedly?) met. Neither has food for entertaining, but Archilochus evidently possesses an abundance of wine. (It seems to be Archilochus' wine from the tone in which he dispatches someone to fetch it.) Such an explanation suits the lines we possess and explains τῇδε in 9: the occasion is a special one.

Both hexameters are overrun, the first to φοίτα at P3 with spondaic first foot. (West prints no mark of punctuation after φοίτα, and none is needed; but some pause there in performance seems inevitable.) The second hexameter is overrun to the end of the fragment. The first sentence continues to H12 in the second hexameter, but the preceding pentameter is not enjambed. The second pentameter completes the sense and is naturally punctuated at the end with a full stop. Indeed, the poem may have ended there. There are four spondees in the four lines. The contrast of dactyls and spondees contributes little to the poem.

The content of the fully preserved lines of 4W is much simpler than that of 3W, and this simplicity is reflected in a much simpler clause structure and arrangement of words. 6–8 contain three imperatives. (ἄγε is an interjection.)

But the lines are not artless. 6 contains merely two prepositional phrases, one before and one after the caesura at H8.⁵¹ The sense demands a verb of motion; a verb of motion, not surprisingly, follows. But φοίτα is not bathetic; meaning "go to and fro, backwards and forwards, with repeated motion" (*LSJ*, 1968, s.v.),⁵² it is the appropriate word to express repeated recourse to the wine store, and it merits its prominence; for, together with the present tense of all three imperatives, which indicates that the command is not restricted to one occasion, it well leads up to the rejection of sobriety in 8–9, which is the climax of the lines we possess. (The change of rhythm to spondaic with φοίτα also emphasizes the word; but the spondaic rhythm of κοίλων seems to contribute little.) Again, the three imperatival clauses are of different lengths, with the verbs in contrasted positions: φοίτα at the end of its clause and the beginning of its line, ἄφελκε in the middle, and ἄγρει at the beginning of clause and line. (Such positional variety, unlike variations in rhythm, may not be consciously noted in performance; but it may make an impression nonetheless.) Furthermore, as Page notes (in Hardt 1964), ἄφελκε and ἄγρει are violent words: "wrench off," "seize." The word order of θοῆς . . . νηός and κοίλων . . . κάδων demarcates the boundaries of the phrase and clause in which they occur.

Archilochus ends the third imperatival clause at H12 in 8. οὐδὲ γὰρ ἡμεῖς possess the prominence derived from being the first words of a new sentence which begins at this position in the line, with the audience's attention alerted by the combination of incomplete sense and imperfect cadence;⁵³ and νηφέμεν⁵⁴ is emphasized by enjambment and first position in its line. But sense forbids a pause at νηφέμεν; the mandatory word break at diaeresis (P7), with its slight pause, gives the line its phrasing. This phrasing contributes to the effect, for it gives prominence to the whole of "not . . . we . . . be sober on guard." Slightly separated from φυλακῇ by pause, τῇδε receives emphasis, which is appropriate: presumably Greek soldiers of Archilochus' day did not always become drunk on watch. Lastly, the meaning and metrical weight of the pentesyllabic δυνησόμεθα end the lines strongly: "shall not be able to be sober" in the circumstances is a much stronger expression than "shall not be sober."

As Page notes (in Hardt 1964, 131), ἀφέλκειν, κάδος, κώθων, νήφειν, σέλμα, and τρύξ are not found in Homer. But though he entertains the possibility that ἄγρει and ἄφελκε may be "selected words; they add colour to the picture of carousal," he then says, of the un-Homeric words: "but there is nothing which the Epic might not have admitted at need." Given this definition of epic diction, it would be difficult for Archilochus' diction to be anything but epic.

There are two Homeric phrases in the poem. Homer has θοὰς ἐπὶ νῆας

(*Iliad* 1. 12), θοῆς ἐπὶ νηός (*Odyssey* 1. 260), and οἶνον ἐρυθρόν (*Odyssey* 5. 165). The adjectives are routine, formulaic, unmemorable; and κοίλων with the (un-Homeric) κάδων seems little more vivid. There is nothing here to compare with the use of adjectives in 13W.[55]

But "unmemorable" need not mean "chosen without purpose." The routine adjectives highlight the vivid and violent imperatives. The emphasis is upon going to get the wine with speed and vigor, not on the particular qualities of the ship or the wine. (Contrast the Ismaric wine of Archilochus 2W. 2.)

The unmemorable adjectives also render the language of 6–9 more diffuse: more words are used than are strictly necessary, since the adjectives add little. There may be aesthetic purpose here too. 4W has not the emotional intensity of 13W; but just as Archilochus lowers the emotional intensity of 13W from 7(H4) to 9(H12) to prepare for the powerful exhortation of 9(H13)–10, so he may be using the unmemorable adjectives of 4W. 6–8(H12) as a foil for the vigorous closing sentence, in which no word is wasted and all are effectively placed. If this comment is justified, the comparison of 4W. 6–9 with 13W. 7–10 reveals some traces of Archilochus' methods of composition. In a different sense, 13W and 4W may be contrasted: 4W emphasizes verbs and action; in 13W most of the emphasis is on other parts of speech, and the adjectives add great intensity. But the contribution of a word to a poem can be evaluated only in its context, and intensity is not the only poetic effect: one should not assume that Archilochus includes in his poems even the most routine of Homeric phrases in response to a conditioned reflex.

Archilochus 5W

ἀσπίδι μὲν Σαίων τις ἀγάλλεται, ἣν παρὰ θάμνῳ,
ἔντος ἀμώμητον, κάλλιπον οὐκ ἐθέλων·
αὐτὸν δ' ἐξεσάωσα. τί μοι μέλει ἀσπὶς ἐκείνη;
ἐρρέτω· ἐξαῦτις κτήσομαι οὐ κακίω.

In my shield some Saian is taking delight, a blameless weapon which I left by a bush against my will. But I saved myself. Of what concern to me is that shield? Let it go hang! Another day I shall get one that is no worse.

Before this notorious quatrain can be discussed as poetry, some words on text and background are necessary.

Many ancient writers quote from this poem or allude to it, but none preserves all four lines. Plutarch (*Instituta Laconica* 34, p. 239b) has 1, 2, and

4 complete, but 3 is lost to H12. Sextus Empiricus (*Outlines of Pyrrhonism* 3. 216) quotes 1, 2, and a version of 3 to H12: αὐτὸς δ' ἐξέφυγον θανάτου τέλος. Aristophanes (*Peace* 1298–99, 1301) quotes 1, 2, and ψυχὴν δ' ἐξεσάωσα as the first part of 3. The first two lines appear again, with minor variants,[56] in Strabo (10. 2. 17, p. 457, and 12. 3. 20, p. 549) and in the *Life of Aratus* (p. 77. 1 Maass). Olympiodorus, in his commentary on Plato's *Gorgias* (p. 141. 1 Westerink), quotes 1, 2, 3, and ἐρρέτω; and other Neoplatonists echo him. In 3, Olympiodorus has αὐτὸν μέν μ' ἐσάωσα, Elias has αὐτόν μ' ἐξεσάωσα. The poetically significant variants are confined to 3; I shall discuss them later.

The tone of the poem makes it clear that Archilochus has done something shocking to his contemporaries: he is flying in the face of their values—and Homer's. The Homeric hero may sometimes judiciously avoid combat with a more powerful foe in the melee of battle (*Iliad* 15. 583–91), and, if he receives a disabling but not immediately fatal blow, he may withdraw from the fighting (*Iliad* 11. 822–48); but he should not retreat from a combat, once joined, with another hero, and he certainly should not jettison his weapons and flee. In Homer, these are the values of attacking Greeks and defending Trojans alike.

In the world whose material conditions are reflected in the Homeric poems, the shame of abandoning one's weapons and thus conceding defeat must have been compounded by practical considerations: metal is scarce. In the *Iliad*, even Achilles has no spare armor when his own is lost at the death of Patroclus. The first action after slaying one's enemy is to try to strip him of his armor, so that (ἐξ)εναρίζειν may be used for "kill"[57] (*Iliad* 5. 151, 155; 6. 20; etc.).

In Archilochus' world of the mid-seventh century, metal was presumably becoming somewhat more plentiful.[58] Weapons could be replaced more easily. Again, Archilochus was evidently in the attacking force: maybe the Saians had to fight to the death to avoid annihilation or slavery, but Archilochus could run and fight another day—or so one would suppose. But Archilochus' attitude remained shocking, for both attackers and defenders, in later Greece.[59]

The reason—or a reason—is clear. Unlike the defenders, the attackers were not fighting for crops, homes, and liberty; but the hoplite phalanx, the heavy-infantry formation, depended for its success on no one's breaking ranks, for the weapons which rendered the hoplite phalanx the most effective land force for over two centuries were much less effective when wielded by an individual out of formation.[60]

It will be appropriate to consider this question when discussing the poems of Tyrtaeus, the hoplite's poet. Archilochus' attitude suggests that either the tactics or the values of hoplite fighting are not yet fully developed. Tyrtaeus' poems are concerned with both values and tactics, and his arguments gain added point if one supposes them addressed to potential Archilochuses.

I shall discuss West's text of the poem (poetically significant variants are discussed in the endnotes).

Each line is end-stopped and contains one stop within the line. At no point do more than five words elapse without a punctuating pause. Archilochus 5W is a poem of short utterances. There is great variation in the position of the stops within the lines, so that phrases and clauses are of different lengths: 1 is stopped at H12, the bucolic diaeresis; 2 at colon diaeresis (P7); 3 at H8, the trochaic caesura; and 4 at P3 with dactylic first foot.

To produce such variety, even for its own sake, in so short a poem is an indication of considerable skill. The indication is confirmed by the manner in which Archilochus has marshaled not merely words and phrases but clauses and sentences within this structure: the effect before H8 in 3 is quite different from that in the remainder of the poem.

The meter is predominantly dactylic. 13W indicates that Archilochus may employ dactyls even in poetry of sorrow and grim resolve. Here a desire to keep the tone of the meter light is readily explicable. As in 13W, the spondees serve to highlight appropriate words: ἀμώμητον (2), αὐτόν (3), and ἐξαῦτις (4).

1. ἀσπίδι, the subject of the poem, appears as its first word, in emphatic position. But we should note the manner in which Archilochus doles out his information. We know the subject of the poem before we read it, and we will translate "my shield." But Archilochus simply writes ἀσπίδι. When he adds Σαίων τις ἀγάλλεται, the suspicion arises that Archilochus—or the speaker—has lost his shield and is still alive; for, in poetic Greek, ἀσπίδι may readily mean "my shield." But if we had only the five words out of context—and in performance, that is what the audience possesses so far—the words could express the delight of a Saian in his own shield. ἣν παρὰ θάμνῳ leaves the hearer or reader in suspense, the sense incomplete at the imperfect cadence. But the suspicions increase: why was the shield beside a bush? The audience may begin to entertain the hypothesis that the shield belonged to the speaker.

2. ἔντος ἀμώμητον heightens the suspense and aggravates the shame if Archilochus has indeed done this thing: if to part with any weapon is shameful, presumably it is even more shameful to part with a "blameless" weapon, one with whose quality no fault can be found. (Linguistically, too, ἔντος would be somewhat surprising: the singular occurs only here and in a papyrus fragment of another Archilochan poem.)[61] The adjective also sets up an implied opposition between the shield and the poet, who, in the values of his day, cannot be blameless if he has really acted as he appears to have done. There follows κάλλιπον; and even now the admission is not certain, for κάλλιπον might be the third-person plural. Lastly, οὐκ ἐθέλων makes all clear even as it attempts to offer an extenuating circumstance.[62] In poems of military exhortation the end of the pentameter poses a problem for the poet (Adkins 1977a, 77); in this line the dying fall well suits the sense.

3. In 1, ἀσπίδι was accompanied by μέν. A δέ-clause is to be expected.[63] αὐτὸν δ' ἐξεσάωσα—with αὐτόν (in the sense of ἐμαυτόν)[64] emphatic, and corresponding in position, while it contrasts in sense, with ἀσπίδι—is abrupt and shocking. The first couplet might have been expressing contrition. Now the tone abruptly changes and, with the tone, the sentence structure. Whether one prints a raised stop (Diehl) or a comma (West) after ἐθέλων, the μέν . . . δέ ensures that the train of thought continues to H8 in 3: this part of the poem contains three clauses, with the words of the first two arranged in the manner already discussed, in a series of gradual admissions. The last clause, beginning a new couplet, sets a new tone for the rest of the poem.

Archilochus proclaims his new value with defiance. The tone of the staccato αὐτὸν δ' ἐξεσάωσα[65] is enhanced by its position in the first half of the hexameter, in contrast with the dying fall of κάλλιπον οὐκ ἐθέλων. There follows a short, equally defiant question, ending, as does the line, with ἐκείνη. ἐκεῖνος is fairly uncommon in verse,[66] since a mere demonstrative pronoun is not usually worth the weight of three syllables. Here, however, the pronoun is effective: "that shield" by implication presents others to the mind. However blameless it may have been, there are plenty more where that one came from, and Archilochus values himself more highly than any shield. ἐκείνη prepares for the last line of the poem.

4. ἐρρέτω, occupying the first dactyl of the line, preceded and followed by a heavy pause, is staccato, forceful, and contemptuous. ἐξαῦτις, emphasized by position at the beginning of its sentence, and οὐ κακίω, the end of its line and possibly the end of the poem, are well set round κτήσομαι, a necessary but less emphatic word. οὐ κακίω well ends the line, summing up the theme that one's life is irreplaceable, but the world contains more good shields.

Note also how the first clause of the first hexameter is contrasted in sense with the second clause of the second hexameter (the two longest clauses), and the first half of the first pentameter with the second half of the second pentameter.

▣

The language is generally Homeric,[67] but the only phrase which occurs also in Homer is οὐκ ἐθέλων (2), and a poet of Archilochus' quality hardly needs assistance to invent such a phrase.[68] Some of the individual words are uncommon in Homer and therefore more available for allusion, though one-word allusions are difficult to take unless the word is striking and notably restricted to one person, place, or activity. ἐξεσάωσα(ε) occurs twice (*Iliad* 4. 12, *Odyssey* 4. 501),[69] ἀμώμητον only once, of Polydamas (*Iliad* 12. 109). Homer elsewhere prefers ἀμύμων.[70] ἐρρέτω occurs at the beginning of a line three times (*Iliad* 9. 377 and 20. 349; *Odyssey* 5. 139). In the second of the last two *Iliad* passages the word is both preceded and followed by a heavy stop, as here; but in no case is there any question of an allusion.

ἀγάλλεται perhaps merits a little more consideration, since the third-person singular of the present indicative passive of ἀγάλλω occurs only twice in Homer, and both contexts are memorable. In *Iliad* 17. 472–73 the sentence runs τεύχεα δ' Ἕκτωρ / αὐτὸς ἔχων ὤμοισιν ἀγάλλεται Αἰακίδαο; and 18. 131–32 is a variant, also referring to Hector and the armor of Achilles. The word occurs in the same position in the lines[71] as in Archilochus, all are concerned with rejoicing in the possession of armor acquired in battle, and the importance to the plot of Hector's taking and wearing this armor renders the Homeric lines memorable.

However, it is doubtful whether this one-word allusion could be taken, and its purpose as an allusion is debatable. Archilochus can hardly be hinting that some mightier Greek than he will slay the Saian and avenge him, particularly as Archilochus is not dead; but he might be implicitly contrasting the fate of Patroclus, who stood his ground and died, with Archilochus' running to fight again another day.

The latter would enrich the poem; but, as we have seen, Archilochus directs his audience's attention primarily to the loss of his shield, his consequent situation, and his attitude to it. (The joy of the Saian is mentioned merely to point to Archilochus' shame; presumably he did not wait to see whether anyone picked up the shield.) The trigger is very flimsy, and in this poem a word with the emphasis of ἀμώμητον or οὐκ ἐθέλων seems a more likely choice for allusion.

It seems more likely that ἀγάλλεται is at most an unconscious reminiscence of the *Iliad* passages or of similar epic contexts now lost. Unconscious reminiscence is far removed from the slavish imitation of formulae, a practice found nowhere in Archilochus' elegiacs. This beautifully crafted little poem is excellent poetry in its own right.[72]

3
CALLINUS

Callinus lived in Ephesus in the mid-seventh century. He is datable by his reference to the Cimmerian invasions of Ionia. Strabo (14. 647) quotes Callinus 5aW and adds that he mentioned the fall of Sardis elsewhere in the poem. The fall of Sardis is datable to 652 B.C. by the records of Asshurbanipal. We possess only one substantial fragment of his poetry, preserved by the anthologist Stobaeus among poems in praise of daring. Strabo (14. 647) also informs us that "Callinus refers to the Magnesians as still flourishing and successful in their war against the Ephesians." Callinus may have been rousing the youth of Ephesus against the Magnesians, but the enemy may be the Cimmerians or some other foe unmentioned by our sources.

CALLINUS 1W

μέχρις τέο κατάκεισθε; κότ' ἄλκιμον ἕξετε θυμόν,
 ὦ νέοι; οὐδ' αἰδεῖσθ' ἀμφιπερικτίονας
ὧδε λίην μεθιέντες; ἐν εἰρήνῃ δὲ δοκεῖτε
 ἧσθαι, ἀτὰρ πόλεμος γαῖαν ἅπασαν ἔχει

. . . .

5   καί τις ἀποθνῄσκων ὕστατ' ἀκοντισάτω.
τιμῆέν τε γάρ ἐστι καὶ ἀγλαὸν ἀνδρὶ μάχεσθαι
 γῆς πέρι καὶ παίδων κουριδίης τ' ἀλόχου
δυσμενέσιν· θάνατος δὲ τότ' ἔσσεται, ὁππότε κεν δὴ
 Μοῖραι ἐπικλώσωσ'. ἀλλά τις ἰθὺς ἴτω
10   ἔγχος ἀνασχόμενος καὶ ὑπ' ἀσπίδος ἄλκιμον ἦτορ
 ἔλσας, τὸ πρῶτον μειγνυμένου πολέμου.

οὐ γάρ κως θάνατόν γε φυγεῖν εἱμαρμένον ἐστὶν
ἄνδρ', οὐδ' εἰ προγόνων ᾖ γένος ἀθανάτων.
πολλάκι δηϊοτῆτα φυγὼν καὶ δοῦπον ἀκόντων
15 ἔρχεται, ἐν δ' οἴκῳ μοῖρα κίχεν θανάτου,
ἀλλ' ὁ μὲν οὐκ ἔμπης δήμῳ φίλος οὐδὲ ποθεινός·
τὸν δ' ὀλίγος στενάχει καὶ μέγας ἤν τι πάθῃ·
λαῷ γὰρ σύμπαντι πόθος κρατερόφρονος ἀνδρὸς
θνῄσκοντος, ζώων δ' ἄξιος ἡμιθέων·
20 ὥσπερ γάρ μιν πύργον ἐν ὀφθαλμοῖσιν ὁρῶσιν·
ἔρδει γὰρ πολλῶν ἄξια μοῦνος ἐών.

How long [will] you lie idle? When will you have a brave spirit, young men? Do you not even feel shame before those who dwell round about, thus slothful as you are? You suppose that you are sitting there in peace, whereas war possesses the whole land . . . . Let a man as he dies hurl a javelin for the last time. For it is a glorious and splendid act for a man to fight for his land, his children, and his wedded wife against the foe. Only then shall death come, when the Moirai spin it for him. When battle is being "blended," let him grasp his spear, gather his brave heart behind his shield, and march straight forward. For it is no man's lot to escape death at all events, even if he be sprung from immortal ancestors. Often having fled war and the thud of spears a man returns home, and the lot of death comes upon him in his house; but in any case he is not dear to the people or missed by them. But the humble and the great lament the brave man if he suffers anything [i.e., death in battle]. For all the people feel regretful longing for a stout-hearted man who is killed, and while he lives he has the worth of demigods. For in their eyes they see him as a tower: for he does deeds worthy of many men, single-handed as he is.

Callinus 1W is the only substantial extant fragment of Callinus' poetry. We possess 23 complete elegiac lines—11 hexameters and 12 pentameters. Of these, 10 hexameters and 11 pentameters constitute the first fragment. In all, 11 lines are end-stopped, and there are 13 stops within the line.

Callinus, like Homer, Archilochus, and the eight elegists as a group,[1] shows a preference for the trochaic H8 caesura (7 examples) over those at H7 (3 examples) and H10 (2 examples)[2] in his hexameters. The 11 complete examples furnish 4 disyllabic, 5 trisyllabic, 1 monosyllabic, and 1 pentesyllabic ending: proportions quite close to those for the eight elegists as a group.[3] His pentameters have endings of all available word lengths save the monosyllable and the hexasyllable: 6 disyllables, 3 trisyllables, 2 quadrisyllables, 1 pentesyllable, and 1 heptasyllable—five word lengths in thirteen lines.[4] In Callinus 1W, no consecutive couplets end the pentameter with a word of the same length, and the heptasyllabic is followed by a disyllabic ending. This may be chance, but it suggests that Callinus is consciously seeking variation.[5] Variation may be a poetical effect in its own right; I defer the question whether it here subserves a further purpose.

If we next consider the position of the major marks of punctuation, the impression of variation consciously sought is reinforced. The brief opening question runs to the H8 caesura of line 1; the second runs to the end of the dactylic first foot of 2 (P3); the third question, like the first, ends at the H8 caesura but is much longer. The next sentence that we can confidently punctuate ends at the end of 5; but there must have been a major mark of punctuation in the lacuna, and the comma after the first trochee of 4 (P2) is worth noting. The next sentence occupies more than a couplet, ending after the long syllable in the second dactylic foot of 8 (P4); the next runs to the diaeresis of the pentameter in 9; the next to the end of 11, with a significant pause after the first (spondaic) foot of 11 (P3). From 12 onward the heaviest stops are at the ends of the lines (13, 16, 17, 19, 20, 21); but variety is derived from the positioning of the lesser stops—the comma after the first syllable of 13, after the first (dactylic) foot of 15 (P3), and after a word of molossus length at the beginning of 19 (P4)—while the run-on of the sentence past the end of the couplet in 15 to the end of the hexameter in 16 gives an unusual effect. At least three of the pentameters of this poem are not end-stopped: 2, 7, and 9. (Whether the end of 4 constituted the end of the sentence is unclear, and West wisely prints no mark of punctuation there.)

So much for static analysis. Callinus is evidently varying lengths of clause and sentence as a conscious effect. Such variation is a pleasing effect in itself and would be a positive quality even if Callinus had no further goal in using it.

As soon as we examine Callinus' words from a dynamic point of view, it becomes apparent that much more was in his mind. This is a poem of impassioned appeal in a crisis: Callinus was not seeking the approbation of the literary critic but a vigorous response from the allegedly slothful young warriors. Nevertheless, the resources of poetry—and rhetoric—are not irrelevant to his purposes.

1–2(P3). The poem begins with a short, stabbing question. (In discussing early elegiac poetry, it is always more prudent to write "the poem as we have it begins . . ."; but the absence of a connecting particle, and the effectiveness of such an opening, make it likely that this is the first line of the poem.)[6] Callinus follows it with another, similar, question: κότ' ἄλκιμον ἕξετε θυμόν; So far as concerns syntax, the sentence could end there. If a weak word followed, the effect of placing it in a strong position at the beginning of 2 would be bathetic. The vocative ὦ νέοι fully deserves its emphasis. The young are the first line of defense and attack. If for some reason they are ineffective, their elders too must fight; and the emphasis on ὦ νέοι here suggests that, as in Tyrtaeus' Sparta,[7] there may be some expressed conflict of interest.

2(P4)–3(H8). Line 2 is enjambed, but the enjambment is of the first type discussed above (p. 7). The syntax is complete at the end of the line, and ἀμφιπερικτίονας—syllabically the longest word in the poem and a very rare example of a heptasyllabic word occupying the second hemiepes of the pentameter—lends great weight to the important motive for action which the line contains (see below, p. 62). Once again, a weak beginning to the next line would produce bathos; but the contemptuous ὧδε λίην μεθιέντες is a strong phrase, which benefits from the prominence it receives at the beginning of a hexameter following the comparatively rare enjambed pentameter (9.31% in the eight elegists).

3(H9)–5. The next sentence (or rather two sentences, for there must surely have been a heavy stop in the lacuna) cannot be adequately discussed, since the lacuna has destroyed Callinus' poetic effect. It seems more probable to suppose, with Bergk (1882 ad loc.), a lacuna of at least three lines rather than Gesner's one (cited by Bergk) and to surmise that 4 was not end-stopped. If we print a heavy stop at the end of 4 and posit a lacuna of one line, we produce a couplet in which presumably an exhortation one line in length in the hexameter is paralleled by a one-line exhortation in the pentameter. Such parallelism is common enough in elegiac couplets and is indeed a snare before the feet of the elegiac poet; but Callinus avoids it elsewhere in this carefully wrought poem. Furthermore, one line seems quite inadequate as a passage from the general statement of 4 to the vivid particularity of 5.[8] So striking a picture demands a better frame than could be supplied in half a dozen words.

In the lines as we have them, we may note the effective placing of the emphatic ἧσθαι at the beginning of its line, followed by a pause at P2: effective in itself, and here a culmination of the effects produced by the similarly strongly positioned κατάκεισθε and μεθιέντες. I have already discussed ἐν εἰρήνῃ δὲ δοκεῖτε / ἧσθαι (above, p. 21). ἐν εἰρήνῃ is preceded by the mandatory pause at H8, and πόλεμος is followed by the mandatory pause at P7. The pause demanded by sense at ἧσθαι (P2) is stronger, but in performance those before ἐν εἰρήνῃ and after πόλεμος would serve to give added contrast to the ideas.[9] Note also the contrast in sense between the line endings δοκεῖτε, at imperfect cadence, and ἔχει, which has the greater finality of the perfect cadence. Whether it ended its sentence or not, the quieter plain statement γαῖαν ἅπασαν ἔχει provides the necessary lowering of tension after Callinus' three impassioned rhetorical questions. Callinus well understands the need for variations in emotional intensity.[10]

6-8(H4). Line 6 continues with another sentence which proceeds in a continuous rush, ending only with an overrun of one word into the next couplet. To overrun δυσμενέσιν might appear bathetic: Callinus and his audience both know that it is the foe who is to be fought. But the effect is deliberate. Yet again, the word is syntactically unnecessary: "fight on behalf of one's native land, children, and wedded wife" would have sufficed. Callinus has chosen to include it, not merely as an overrun word, but in hyperbaton after the whole pentameter. Now δυσμενέσιν denotes a group opposed in every sense to those mentioned in the pentameter, and the whole couplet is emotionally opposed—since it is concerned with what is dear and desirable—to the hostile and unpleasant expressed by δυσμενέσιν and by the *next* sentence, down to ἐπικλώσωσ'. The function of the overrun δυσμενέσιν is to carry the sentence, over the boundary of the couplet, from the glories of defense to the realities of defense.[11] To the end of 15, the poem continues to be concerned with the realities of life and battle. The overrun also avoids the dangers of the dying fall: contrast Tyrtaeus 10W. 5-6, which ends the line with a similar, though longer, sequence of prepositional phrases but without the heightening of tension which δυσμενέσιν provides.

8(H5)-13. In 8, θάνατος is placed prominently at the beginning of its clause, juxtaposed with δυσμενέσιν. The effect of positioning θάνατος δέ . . . ἐπικλώσωσ' so that it is framed within its couplet by words from other sentences is that of a parenthetic statement, a point conceded: "Granted, death will be your lot when the Moirai spin it for you." But the strongest positions in the couplet are reserved for δυσμενέσιν and ἀλλά τις ἰθὺς ἴτω, the beginning of Callinus' positive exhortation,[12] which is run on to ἔλσας, first-foot spondaic word followed by a pause, admirably expressing the firm resolution of the warrior, particularly after the wholly dactylic preceding line.[13] A similar effect is produced by ἄνδρ', a most unusual pause after the first syllable of the pentameter. The word and its positioning are each chosen with care. That no human being can escape death was, of course, a platitude even in Callinus' day,[14] though a platitude that can be employed effectively in such exhortations as these. But Callinus raises his sentence suddenly above the level of platitude by writing not ἄνθρωπον, a human being, but ἄνδρ', a warrior, a Man,[15] and placing it, in monosyllabic form, in the strongest possible position: "For in no way—to escape death at all events—is it *moira* for a / Warrior, even if he be sprung from forebears who are immortal." The run of the couplet, while conceding the inevitability of death, reminds the νέοι that they are not merely human beings but warriors, and it links them in their warriorhood with such heroes as Achilles, who, sprung from deities though they were, nevertheless died in battle. Nor should we think only of legendary heroes as having divine ancestry: many noble Greek families in historical times traced their lineage back to a deity. The reasoning is that all, even those sprung from deities, must die; but you are warriors, like Achilles and others of divine parentage. Emulate them; you can suffer no worse than they did.

14–16. The next couplet, 14–15, continues to state the realities of life and is not complete in itself. The logic of Callinus' exposition demands that φυγών here must mean "having shunned, fled from, deliberately avoided," [16] not "having (fought and) escaped death." [17] Callinus is not saying that it is preferable to fight and die rather than to fight and live; he is opposing the view that it is better to be a live mouse than a dead lion, but this does not require him to hold that it is better to be a dead lion than a live one. It is the coward, not the living hero, who is οὐκ ἔμπης δήμῳ φίλος οὐδὲ ποθεινός; and ἤν τι πάθῃ (17),[18] used of the man contrasted with the φυγών, makes it clear that the citizens, great and small, hope that he will *not* παθεῖν τι. The emphatic (and appropriately positioned) word is ἔρχεται, on which I shall have further comment later.[19]

Most editors print a raised stop at the end of 15, a comma at the end of 16;[20] but West's comma at the end of 15, raised stop at the end of 16, is preferable, for there is a continuous sweep of thought from πολλάκι to ποθεινός, the whole of which is contrasted with 17. Callinus is saying that the coward is nonetheless overtaken by death; but there is no word for "coward" in 14–15. The transition from 13 to 14 is awkward with any punctuation; but with a full stop after θανάτου (15), 14–15 can refer only to ἄνδρες in general, the subject of the previous couplet. In fact, as West's punctuation indicates, the subject of thought in Callinus' mind in 14–15 is "the one, the coward," but it is not expressed until 16. Then τὸν δ' (17), otherwise rather unclear (since ὁ μέν also is unclear), becomes easier as "the other"—the one who, not earlier mentioned, is evidently, in contrast with the whole of 14–16, "he who does not shrink from war."

If it is accepted that there is a continuous movement of thought from πολλάκι to ποθεινός, two further points can be made. Line 16, in overrunning the couplet 14–15, performs much the same function as does δυσμενέσιν in 8: it is pendant to its sentence and introduces a new consideration, which is forthwith elaborated. As δυσμενέσιν introduced the grim realities of war, so 16 introduces the evaluation of different forms of death. Like δυσμενέσιν, it is used by Callinus as a means of preventing his poem from being a mere series of couplets (always a danger with elegiac verse). The drawbacks, to a poet in Callinus' situation, are not merely aesthetic: it is urgent that the νέοι be induced to fight, and to fight bravely; and such means as these of binding together his poem and his thought have great practical, as well as artistic, value. Two of the major transitions of thought in the poem are thus made rhetorically and poetically more effective by very similar devices.

Furthermore, to overrun an elegiac couplet to the end of the next hexameter, and there, as in this case, to have a strong pause, is to produce a movement which the ear does not expect. Not only is the strong pause expected at the end of the pentameter absent; it occurs at the end of the hexameter, where it is not expected. In elegiac couplets, the hexameter ending gives imperfect, the pentameter ending perfect, cadence (above, p. 14). In such couplets as these, the perfect cadence is overrun and the sentence ends on the imperfect cadence, heightening the usual effect. The ear, more eager even than usual for the resolution, becomes especially alert for what is to follow.

17. What follows here (17, elaborated in 18–21) is the heart of Callinus' message: all must die, but the warrior can so live as to enjoy the esteem of a demigod while he lives and be remembered and sorely missed after his death. The message is important practically, and Callinus uses all his art to ensure that it receives attention.

18–21. Lines 18–19 contain another overrun, the molossus θνήσκοντος,[21] whose heavy weight and position admirably suit its importance and meaning; and it is neatly juxtaposed with the contrasted ζώων. The four lines contain an elaborate set of contrasts, highlighted by position. λαῷ at the beginning of 18 is well contrasted both with κρατερόφρονος ἀνδρός at the end of 18 and with ἡμιθέων at the end of 19: the stout-hearted warrior is both contrasted with the mass of the inhabitants and raised to the status of a demigod. ὁρῶσιν at the end of 20 is set against ἔρδει in 21: the people look on, the warrior acts. Finally, μοῦνος ἐών at the end of 21 is contrasted both with πολλῶν in the same line and with the whole phrase λαῷ . . . σύμπαντι at the beginning of 18. In addition, there is an effective repetition. Since the second hemiepes of the pentameter is metrically invariant, elegiac poets are sometimes constrained to repeat themselves; but here the repetition ἄξιος . . . ἄξια emphasizes the message of Callinus' lines. Whether or not 21 was the last line of Callinus' poem, 18–21 are a powerful conclusion to the lines which we possess.

I now turn to consider the manner in which Callinus uses the Homeric element in this poem. That every word in Callinus 1W, with the exception of ἀμφιπερικτίονας and ποθεινός, is found in the Homeric poems is not in dispute.[22] But that fact in itself tells us little of aesthetic significance about Callinus' poem. I have argued that there is a limited amount of purposive allusion to Homer in Archilochus 13W and more in Tyrtaeus 10W (Adkins 1977a, 84–94). I now inquire whether Callinus uses such allusion in this poem.

1–2. κατακεῖσθαι is Homeric and not common. (Uncommon words and phrases furnish better triggers for allusion.) It occurs nine times, including three in the *Hymn to Hermes*.²³ Callinus uses it of reclining in sloth when stern action is needed. Homer does not; he uses it of writhing in a torment of grief, of a hare cowering in a thicket, of a boar in its lair, and of a child in its cradle.²⁴ There is no allusion, and the word has no definite connotation: it denotes merely a recumbent posture. ἄλκιμος and θυμός are both common Homeric words, but ἄλκιμον . . . θυμόν is not in extant Homeric poetry, ἄλκιμον ἦτορ being the formula.²⁵ ἦτορ is unsuitable here, since it begins with a vowel. This is not a vividly creative use of language, but it already indicates a poet not slavishly bound to the Homeric formula. ἀμφιπερικτίονας is not Homeric.²⁶

3–4. μεθιέναι is used intransitively some twenty-five times in Homer. If the audience remembered Hector's rebuke to Paris (*Iliad* 6. 523), Callinus' point would be reinforced, for it would place them in the position of Paris, Callinus in that of Hector. But the word is too common, and the hearers were unlikely to remember this passage in particular. The line is strong in itself: μάχης μεθιέναι is always αἰσχρόν in early Greek.²⁷ The sentiment in the lines resembles the words of Iris (*Iliad* 2. 796–97), but not closely enough for reminiscence.

5. All the words are Homeric, but they are used to paint so novel and vivid a picture that it is difficult to imagine what pejorative value judgment could be based on this fact.

6–7. Callinus uses τιμῆεν and ἀγλαόν in a creative rhetorical and poetical manner. τιμήεις is used in Homer of persons, to denote one who possesses or gains status-enhancing material goods, as when Telemachus responds to Antinous' scoffing suggestion that Telemachus may become king (*Odyssey* 1. 392–93):

οὐ μὲν γάρ τι κακὸν βασιλευέμεν· αἶψά τέ οἱ δῶ
ἀφνειὸν πέλεται καὶ τιμηέστερος αὐτός.

It is also used of gold (e.g., *Iliad* 18. 475, *Odyssey* 8. 393, 11. 327); and we find the phrase δῶρον τιμῆεν, μάλα καλόν (*Odyssey* 1. 312). A gift may also be ἀγλαόν, as in *Iliad* 11. 124. Indeed, ἀγλαὰ δῶρα occurs twelve times²⁸ to denote gifts; in Ebeling's words, "qualia a regibus atque diis dantur" (Ebeling 1885, s.v. ἀγλαόν). ἀγλαόν is also used of pure water (*Iliad* 2. 307), fine garments (*Odyssey* 10. 223), admirable children (*Iliad* 18. 337, etc.), and in the common patronymic phrase ἀγλαὸν υἱόν with an appropriate genitive of the father.

In Homer these adjectives are applied to what is desirable because it enhances one's status, glory, or material well-being, or—in phrases like ἀγλαὸν ὕδωρ—to what is shining and beautiful (and pleasant to drink?). Each is used in the context of fighting, but in a significantly different manner from Callinus' usage. When Phoenix (*Iliad* 9. 605) said to Achilles that if he delayed his return to the fray until the enemy reached the ships, οὐκέθ' ὁμῶς τιμῆς ἔσεαι πόλεμόν περ ἀλαλκών, he meant that, if Achilles returned now, when Agamemnon was promising gifts, he would receive τιμή—the said gifts—and therefore become more τιμήεις (see Adkins 1960b); but if he fought later, because he had to do so in order to save his own ship along with the others, the Greeks would not give him τιμή, so that he would be less τιμήεις than he might have been. Similarly, a ransom or recompense, ἄποινα, may be ἀγλαά. The only aspect of fighting of which ἀγλαόν is used is that of raising a victory shout (e.g., *Iliad* 7. 203).[29] There is no suggestion that fighting is, in itself, ἀγλαόν.

The Greeks before Troy were fighting for τιμή—for status-enhancing material goods. Defenders of a city are likely to gain little material τιμή. They are more concerned with avoiding material loss, the loss of all their τιμή, if the city is captured. The desire to avoid such loss might appear to be sufficient motive; but both Callinus and Tyrtaeus find the warriors of their respective cities insufficiently active and effective.[30] In this situation Callinus employs a strikingly novel usage: to the act of fighting for one's land and one's family he applies two adjectives—ἀγλαόν and τιμῆεν—which have not been used before to denote fighting but which have very desirable connotations and a high emotive charge, derived from what they have customarily been used to denote. His intention is to endow such fighting with all the desirable connotations and emotive charge possessed by the adjectives.

This is a creative use of language, a creative extension of Homeric language, if indeed we should still speak of Homeric language when merely the words, not the manner of their employment, are found in Homer. With an effort of the historical imagination we can recapture the original freshness of the line. Callinus, of course, was not primarily concerned with literary success but with practical effects. He might well hope for such effects: the language is not only fine poetry but excellent military rhetoric, and in both roles it does not tamely echo Homeric usage but employs the resources supplied by that usage for a creative, un-Homeric effect.

In 7, κουριδίης τ' ἀλόχου is a Homeric formula. No particular Homeric reminiscence can be intended: the phrase is too common.[31]

8–9. In these two lines the realities of warfare are described in Homeric language, but it is the general sentiment, not the phrases, that reminds the reader of Homer:[32] no one acquainted with the *Iliad* could fail to remember Hector's reflections on the inevitability of *moira* and the demand that the warrior should fight (*Iliad* 6. 486 ff.).

9(P8)–11. Line 9 ends with a strong exhortation, which runs over into the largely formulaic 10, which in turn runs over to the spondaic ἔλσας. The remainder of line 11, however, consists of a metaphor which is un-Homeric and doubtless Callinus' own. μείγνυμι is common enough in Homer. It is used literally of mixing wine (e.g., *Odyssey* 1. 110) or φάρμακα (*Odyssey* 4. 230), or of the mingling of winds (*Odyssey* 5. 317). It is used with a personal subject of men fighting (e.g., *Iliad* 4. 456), προμάχοισι μιγέντα, or closely similar phrases, being frequent (e.g., *Iliad* 4. 354). The closest usage to that of Callinus occurs at *Iliad* 20. 374, where we have τῶν δ' ἄμυδις μίχθη μένος, ὦρτο δ' ἀϋτή. Elsewhere in Homer, in passages concerned with fighting, μείγνυμι has a personal subject. Even here the persons are not far away: "their μένος" is not far from "they with μένος."[33] In Callinus, however, it is πόλεμος that is being mixed, and this is a new metaphor, employing, as metaphors do, the wide range of usage of the word. It seems likely to be a metaphor from the mixing of wine, when the dark wine and the clear water are mingled confusedly, not yet fully mixed,[34] with the liquid turbulent from the action of the ladle. κρατήρ is used later as a metaphor, as in Aeschylus' τοσῶνδε κρατῆρ' ἐν δόμοις κακῶν . . . πλήσας (*Agamemnon* 1397). The effect is enriched by awareness of the use of μείγνυσθαι with personal subjects, which must have been recalled to the minds of the Greek audience. Once again, this is a new use of language—one which draws new resources from Homeric forms of expression rather than merely reflecting them.

12–13. Lines 12 and 13, though not formulaic in the strict sense, contain not merely Homeric but very common Homeric words. Any enrichment derived from Homer must be drawn from memory not of words but of events and persons: of Achilles, sprung from a goddess but doomed to an early death, or of Zeus's own son Sarpedon, whom he unavailingly tries to save (*Iliad* 16. 433 ff.).

14–15. Lines 14 and 15 contain only Homeric words and one formula (δοῦπον ἀκόντων). In 15, however, a readily available Homeric formula is avoided: κατὰ μοῖρ' ἔλαβεν μέλανος θανάτοιο (*Odyssey* 17. 326). μοῖρ' ἔλαβεν θανάτου or μοῖρα λάβεν θανάτου would scan here; but Callinus writes κίχεν. Once again the hexameter is overrun, this time to ἔρχεται in 15.

Thus in three successive couplets the hexameter contains only common, familiar Homeric words and is overrun by one word into the pentameter. The effect, as already said, is to highlight ἔλσας, ἄνδρ', and ἔρχεται. But there is more to be said. Variations of tempo, phrase length, and emotional intensity are important resources of poet and orator alike; and here Callinus writes three hexameters of low poetic intensity, judged in terms of the language employed, and he highlights his sentence in each case by one word, of a different syllabic length on each occasion, overrun into the pentameter. Those parts of a speech or poem which are written at a lower degree of intensity contribute much to the total effect; for it is by contrast that the more intense parts of the work produce their impact. I do not suggest that Callinus could have expressed what he has to say in these hexameters with great power and originality and chose not to. Like other early elegiac poets, he is engaged in a difficult struggle to evolve an individual style. However, art is a matter of making the most effective use of the medium in which one is working, which has always its own limitations or recalcitrance; and the device of counterpointing the familiar Homeric language—the medium in which Callinus must work— of the hexameters against the three highlighted words produces a total effect which is good poetry and good rhetoric.

16–17. In 16, all the words except ποθεινός are Homeric, but δήμῳ φίλος does not occur as a phrase. In 17, though all the words are Homeric, μέγας and ὀλίγος are used in quite un-Homeric senses. ὀλίγος is used of human beings only in a literal sense, to denote size, in Homer. It is used of gods in passages in which we, and later Greeks, would interpret it as meaning "powerful" but which earlier Greeks may have taken in a more literal sense.[35] ὀλίγος is rarely used of human beings in Homer but is used of Ajax son of Oileus in a literal sense in *Iliad* 2. 529. In Callinus both ὀλίγος and μέγας are evidently status terms, denoting poor and rich or members of the lower and upper class, respectively.[36] It is a reasonable surmise that this is an Ephesian usage, and, once again, little seems to be gained by terming the language Homeric.

18–19. The form of the couplet is similar to that of 10–11, 12–13, and 14–15, save that the overrun word is a molossus. All the words are Homeric, and κρατερόφρονος ἀνδρός is a formula.[37] The word κρατερόφρων is not common in Homer and is used only of Odysseus, Heracles, Castor, and Pollux. There is no specific allusion, but a word so restricted in its usage must have connotations of great strength and endurance. To use it is powerful commendation, and the choice of the word, good rhetoric. ἡμίθεος occurs only once in Homer (*Iliad* 12. 23), in a passage in which the poet is reminiscing about the Greek warriors before Troy from the point of view of a later age (Leaf and Bayfield 1895, ad loc.). Callinus desires a similar effect. The brave warrior of his own day will have the worth of a Homeric hero, now viewed as a veritable demigod. Powerful rhetoric indeed!

20–21. These lines may display a different method of using Homeric resources. Callinus says that the people look on the steadfast warrior as if he were a πύργος. In Homer, πύργος is used metaphorically of an individual only once.[38] In *Odyssey* 11. 555–58 Odysseus, encountering the shade of Ajax, assures him

τὰ δὲ πῆμα θεοὶ θέσαν Ἀργείοισι·
τοῖος γάρ σφιν πύργος ἀπώλεο· σεῖο δ' Ἀχαιοὶ
ἶσον Ἀχιλλῆος κεφαλῇ Πηληιάδαο
ἀχνύμεθα φθιμένοιο διαμπερές.

Now if Callinus meant his audience, on reading πύργος in 20, to remember this passage, he was using association to increase the power of his line by allusion to a particular Homeric warrior. *Odyssey* 11. 555–58 must have been a well-known passage, and the repeated portrayal of Ajax with a shield ἠΰτε πύργον[39] might be expected to make the association of πύργος and Ajax easier. (It may have suggested the metaphor to the author of *Odyssey* 11.) Furthermore, the resemblance between the two passages is stronger than I have so far suggested: in both, the death, actual or possible, of the warrior is emphasized, along with the great grief of those whom he defended in life. True, we must not remember how and why Ajax died, and Ajax is in general not the most attractive of Homeric warriors. But (*a*) an allusion may be more or less complete,[40] (*b*) in the passage to which allusion is made Odysseus does not refer precisely to the manner of Ajax's death, and (*c*) since Odysseus is trying to placate the shade of Ajax, he emphasizes (550–51 and the lines quoted) that Ajax was inferior to Achilles alone. If the allusion were taken, then, Callinus would be in a position to imply that the warriors of 20 and 21 are worthy of comparison with Ajax in beauty and valor.

In this poem Callinus shows himself a fluent composer in elegiac paragraphs—a master in the art of organizing sentences in a meter which has a double movement and of making creative use of Homeric language to express his thoughts and emotions. Possibly, like Archilochus, he also employed purposive allusion to the Homeric poems to enrich his work. To judge from his meager remains, he—or his poetic persona—was less complex than Archilochus, and he evidently lacked the metrical versatility of Archilochus, who was credited with the invention of many meters[41] and certainly used many; but his one substantial fragment gives Callinus a claim to be judged similar in quality to Archilochus as an elegiac poet.

Our roster of eight elegists begins with two of the finest: poets who fully understand the resources of their meter and can exploit them. It seems very unlikely that the elegiac couplet was invented or first used in their day.

4
TYRTAEUS

Tyrtaeus is preeminently the poet of the Second Messenian War, which ended with the final subjugation and helotization of Sparta's western neighbors. He may be assigned a *floruit* a little after 650 B.C. (The war itself is commonly dated *c.* 640–620.) Plato (*Laws* 629A) claims that Tyrtaeus was an Athenian by birth who became a Spartan citizen. Even so Laconophile an Athenian as Plato seems reluctant to allow the Spartans any talent for the arts.[1] The scholiast on the *Laws* passage and Strabo (4. 15. 6) add further touches: Tyrtaeus was a lame Athenian schoolmaster of little intelligence, who was lent to the Spartans by the Athenians when the Spartans asked for help. There is in fact no reason to doubt that Tyrtaeus was a Spartan, even though the item of linguistic evidence adduced to clinch the matter will not bear the weight often placed upon it.[2]

Tyrtaeus employs a dialect in the poems which for the most part is evidently not Doric; any Doricisms would be inadvertent lapses. Dover (in Hardt 1964, 190) terms it a language "derived not primarily from epic but from the Ionic vernacular"[3]—not because Ionic was Tyrtaeus' native dialect but because Ionic was the dialect of the genre: it was borrowed with the meter from Ionia, where elegiac poetry had been invented.

We possess 143 complete elegiac lines of Tyrtaeus: 71 hexameters and 72 pentameters.[4] Of the relevant 141 lines,[5] 101 are end-stopped, and there are only 29 stops within the line. The proportion of end-stopped lines is much higher, that of stops within the line much lower, than in Archilochus or Callinus. In their case the total number of extant lines is too small to furnish statistically significant results, but a detailed examination of individual poems will reveal a qualitative inferiority in Tyrtaeus' skill in composing freely within the structure of the elegiac couplet. If, as Dover maintains (in Hardt 1964, 193), there was indeed a long tradition of oral elegiac in Ionia before Archilochus and Callinus, and if the meter was borrowed from Ionia only by or in the lifetime of Tyrtaeus, Tyrtaeus' relative clumsiness might be explained thereby. But no explanation beyond limitation of talent is needed: the Ionian Xenophanes of Colophon, a century later than Tyrtaeus, handles the meter no more fluently.

Of Tyrtaeus' 71 extant hexameters, 16 (22.54%) have caesura at H7, 39 (54.93%) at H8, and 14 (19.72%) at H10, and 2 (2.82%) could be read with caesura at either H7 or H10. The percentage at H7 compares with 35.99 for the Homer sample and 35.10 for the elegists studied. (For the overall figures, see Table 4.) There is a corresponding increase in the percentages of caesurae at H8 (Homer 49.46, elegists 50.93) and H10 (Homer 14.55, elegists 13.96). The increase is fairly equally distributed between H8 and H10; but an increase from 14 percent to 19 percent is much more noticeable than an increase from 50 percent to 55 percent. The much greater proportional difference at H10 gives an audibly different movement to Tyrtaeus' hexameters in performance in comparison with the extant hexameters of Solon (12.96% at H10).

The 71 hexameters have 23 final disyllables (32.39%), 32 trisyllables (45.07%), 10 quadrisyllables (14.08%), and 6 pentesyllables (8.45%). The percentage of pentesyllables is more than double that for the elegists as a group, as shown in Table 6, and this fact, though it has no statistical significance, endows extant Tyrtaeus with another difference from extant Archilochus, whose few extant hexameters contain no pentesyllabic final word. The 72 extant pentameters furnish 22 disyllabic endings (30.56%), 28 trisyllables (38.89%), 13 quadrisyllables (18.06%), 7 pentesyllables (9.70%), 1 hexasyllable (1.39%), and 1 heptasyllable (1.39%). The overall percentages for Tyrtaeus are sufficiently close to the figures shown in Table 7 for elegy as a whole to be unremarkable. The effect of any particular choice of word must be evaluated in its context.

Tyrtaeus 4W

Φοίβου ἀκούσαντες Πυθωνόθεν οἴκαδ᾽ ἔνεικαν
μαντείας τε θεοῦ καὶ τελέεντ᾽ ἔπεα·
ἄρχειν μὲν βουλῆς θεοτιμήτους βασιλῆας,
οἷσι μέλει Σπάρτης ἱμερόεσσα πόλις,
5 πρεσβυγενέας τε γέροντας· ἔπειτα δὲ δημότας ἄνδρας
εὐθείαις ῥήτραις ἀνταπαμειβομένους
μυθεῖσθαί τε τὰ καλὰ καὶ ἔρδειν πάντα δίκαια,
μηδέ τι βουλεύειν τῇδε πόλει ⟨σκολιόν⟩·
δήμου τε πλήθει νίκην καὶ κάρτος ἕπεσθαι.
10 Φοῖβος γὰρ περὶ τῶν ὧδ᾽ ἀνέφηνε πόλει.

Having heard Phoebus, they brought home from Pytho the god's oracles and words that carry fulfillment: that the kings, whose *time* is from the gods, the kings, whose concern is the lovely polis of Sparta, and the elder old men should begin(?) the counsel; that then the men of the people, answering with [or "obeying"] correct ordinances, should say what is honorable and do all things just, and not give any ⟨crooked⟩ counsel to this polis; and that victory and might should accompany the mass of the people. For Phoebus thus made revelation about these matters to the city.

The ten lines printed by West are derived from two sources: Plutarch, *Life of Lycurgus* 6, and Diodorus 7. 12. 6. Plutarch quotes the first six lines, Diodorus all ten, but his first two are quite different from Plutarch's; in Diodorus they read: ⟨ὧ⟩δε γὰρ ἀργυρότοξος ἄναξ ἑκάεργος ᾿Απόλλων / χρυσοκόμης ἔχρη πίονος ἐξ ἀδύτου. Diodorus' lines have been suspected, the first two justifiably (Wade-Gery, 1944).[6] But Plutarch's first line and Diodorus' last line produce an effect of ring composition (Φοίβου / Φοῖβος) which is too apposite to be the result of mere chance. I shall accordingly discuss West's text, which consists of the Plutarchan version of 1–2, Plutarch's and Diodorus' 3–6, and Diodorus' 7–10.

This book is not a history of archaic Greece; but the composition of Tyrtaeus 4W was a significant historical act in archaic Sparta, and, if we are to appreciate the poem, the historical situation must be briefly discussed.

Before quoting his six lines, Plutarch quotes from a document in prose, the relevant portion of which is (in West's text): "[the kings and the gerousia] are to introduce business to the assembly and to dismiss it (ἀφίστασθαι), and the *demos* is to have the right to speak against the proposal, and the power (κράτος)." Plutarch then says that when "the many" exercised this power and made alterations in the proposals brought before them, Polydorus and Theopompus, the kings, made the following addition: "But if the *demos* should say a crooked (σκολιάν) thing, the elders and leaders should be dismissers (ἀποστατῆρας)."

Plutarch terms this document, the *rhetra*, an oracle (μαντείαν), which it plainly is not. It is a provision of the Spartan constitution: not *the* foundation document, since the technical terms in the lines which precede those that I have quoted are not defined or explained and therefore refer to institutions that already exist or at least were defined elsewhere in what must have been a much larger document (Wade-Gery 1944). Plutarch's quotation defines "certain things *about the composition and powers of the gerousia*" (Wade-Gery 1944, 116); and Plutarch's own words reflect a tradition that the Spartan *demos* once had the right to introduce and pass amendments to proposals initiated by the kings and gerousia but subsequently lost that right.

Tyrtaeus' poem may be dated to the second half of the seventh century. The text of the *rhetra* cannot be dated, and its traditional dates are very unlikely to be correct. It purports to be Lycurgan, with an alleged addition by Polydorus and Theopompus. Lycurgus probably never lived. If he did, the latest date assigned to him is that of Aristotle (*Politics* 1271b): 776 B.C.[7] King Theopompus is assigned by Tyrtaeus himself to two generations before Tyrtaeus' own time. Consequently, Theopompus was king about 700 B.C., with Polydorus' reign overlapping his at some point.

Scholars have frequently discussed the date of the introduction of alphabetic writing into Greece. For a time, the first half of the eighth century was favored, but there now seems to be more support for a date in the second half of the century. If the latter date is correct, evidently there can have been no written *rhetra* in 776 B.C. But even if alphabetic writing was available in 776, it may not have been used to record political documents. Where the law and constitution have been orally transmitted, those who administer them are likely to have a vested interest in their remaining unrecorded. Even if writing had been available for two generations by 700 B.C., there may still have been no written *rhetra* at that time. Historians in ancient Greece seem to have experienced difficulty in discovering authentic prose documents from this period. If we accept that Sparta in the later seventh century was as advanced as Athens[8] and that Draco published a written Athenian legal code and constitution at this period, a written *rhetra* was possible in the later seventh century. But, written or not, a constitution of some kind existed in Sparta before Tyrtaeus' day, and Tyrtaeus 4W evidently is related to constitutional provisions similar to those of the *rhetra*.

If there was no written *rhetra* before 700, Polydorus and Theopompus cannot have amended an already existing text; and if, as is likely, there was no written *rhetra* before Tyrtaeus' day, there was no written amendment either. Nor was there ever any contemporary written evidence of Spartan motives and actions in the eighth and early seventh centuries. Plutarch and Diodorus mention the kings and Lycurgus, but their versions of 4W do not. If the lines existed in a wider context which mentioned the kings and Lycurgus, presumably Plutarch and Diodorus—or their sources—would have quoted those lines too. It seems reasonable to infer that the story preserved in Plutarch is of later date and that it has probably affected the transmitted text of the poem.[9]

Aristotle, however, tells us (*Politics* 1306b36 = Tyrtaeus 1W) that there was political unrest in Sparta as a result of distress caused by the Messenian War, and he cites Tyrtaeus as evidence. True, Aristotle says that the unrest was motivated by a desire for redistribution of the land, not by a dispute over political rights; but if economically hard-pressed Spartans desired land redistribution, their ability to gain their ends by political means would be significantly affected by their ability to amend proposals of the kings and gerousia, who would be unlikely themselves to propose a redistribution.

Whatever the date of the *rhetra*, then, Tyrtaeus' poem may be presenting an interpretation of the Spartan constitution at a time of crisis. I shall consider later whether any inferences can be drawn from the manner in which Tyrtaeus carries out his task.

◻

Two hexameters (1, 5) are enjambed, and one pentameter (6). There is only one stop within the line, at the caesura of 5. These are not unlikely figures for Tyrtaeus;[10] but if 3, 5, 7, and 9 are actually quoted from the oracle (see below, p. 74), their poetry and rhythm are the responsibility of Delphi, not Tyrtaeus.[11] The meter is more spondaic than that of the Archilochus and Callinus poems discussed. Archilochus has 18 spondees in 23 lines (0.78 per line); Callinus, 25 in 21 (1.19 per line). Tyrtaeus 4W has 17 in 10 lines (1.70 per line). The proportion in Tyrtaeus' extant work as a whole is 181 spondees in 143 lines (1.27 per line). If one treats 3, 5, 7, and 9 of Tyrtaeus 4W as a Delphic composition, the remainder contains 8 spondees in 6 lines (1.33 per line). Though the last figure is close to that for extant Tyrtaeus as a whole, the samples are of course too small to be statistically significant.

◻

1–2. That Tyrtaeus has only one stop within the line in the ten lines of 4W suggests little ability or interest here in composing his sentence flexibly within the pattern of the elegiac couplet in the manner of Archilochus and Callinus. We may reflect that versified propaganda is unlikely to call forth the highest poetic skills even from those who possess them. But nothing suggests that Tyrtaeus was a reluctant partisan, and the first couplet at all events is effectively composed. Φοίβου and Πυθωνόθεν, the one beginning its participial phrase in first position in the line, the other beginning the main clause after the H7 caesura, receive—appropriately—greater emphasis than ἀκούσαντες. It is the source of the information, not its being received by ear, that is important: the sanction of Apollo at Delphi for political arrangements remained important at much later dates (Plato, *Laws* 738c, 759d, 914a, 947d). The two spondees add suitable weight. The incompleteness of the main clause at line end produces the usual effect.

What is enjambed is syntactically simple: merely the object of the verb. The line is characteristically Tyrtaean, for it contains two parallel phrases (Adkins 1977a, 76). Such writing may become wearisome by repetition, but here both phrases, and the word order, have point. μαντείας, set first, is the most important word in the line, for it expresses the sanction of what is to follow in 3–9. (Even when Tyrtaeus aspires no higher, he tends to begin his lines with emphatic words.) Its molossus rhythm enhances the effect. θεοῦ, in weaker position, apparently contributes little, since we have already been told that they heard the words of Apollo. However, if some doubted whether "they" had transmitted the words correctly, the assurance that they brought home the words of the god rather than others is not without relevance. τελέεντ' ἔπεα, "words that carry fulfillment," makes explicit what is merely implicit in μαντείας: effective rhetoric, at least.

3–5(H8). ἄρχειν appropriately begins 3, for it is the most important word of its sentence. The line of thought is continued by ἔπειτα δέ in 5. To translate ἄρχειν by "begin," however, suggests that πρῶτον μέν would have been equally effective. But ἄρχειν followed by a genitive case may mean "rule" as well as "begin"; and, until ἔπειτα, the verb might have this sense. (μέλει, in 4, rather suggests this interpretation.) Since the original audience were thinking in Greek, they would receive both messages. If the oracle clearly said "begin," Tyrtaeus is displaying more verbal skill than most would grant him; for the Spartan government evidently wished to transmit the stronger message. (This is merely one example of the difference between receiving a sentence as a sequence of aural stimuli and perceiving it as a set of marks on papyrus or paper. The eye of the puzzled reader leaps ahead; the ear of the puzzled hearer cannot do so; and virtually all ancient literature is composed for the ear.) θεοτιμήτους expresses the close link with the gods enjoyed by kings in early Greek belief[12] and serves to enhance their status. 1–2 emphasized the divine origin of the *rhetra*. 3 reminds the Spartans that kings are specially favored by deity, and the three spondees of the line—more than in any extant hexameter of Archilochus or Callinus—give a suitably grand effect.

In 4, μέλει suggests "is exclusively (or especially) the concern." There is no question of allusion, but the flavor of the word is illustrated by Hector's words to Andromache (*Iliad* 6. 492) or by Telemachus' to Penelope (*Odyssey* 1. 358; 21. 352). Tyrtaeus does not use their bluntness and say to the rest, on the kings' behalf, "Busy yourselves with your own concerns; these matters have nothing to do with you," but there is more than a hint of it. In 5, if one assumed that the intention was to accord equality of status to kings and gerousia, one would judge πρεσβυγενέας τε γέροντας bathetic: the sentence is complete at the end of 4, and the mind is not on the alert for a second subject for ἄρχειν. (In addition, the kings have a more honorific adjective and a relative clause that increases their claims.) But if the intention is to give prestige to the kings at the expense of the gerousia, to present the members of that council as an afterthought is skillful rhetoric. (Note also the dactylic rhythm, in contrast with the spondees of 3.)

Line 4 contains an effect of a quite different order: ἱμερόεσσα πόλις. In a poem generally read as a historical document, the adjective may pass almost unnoticed; but in Homer it is used of the breasts of Aphrodite (*Iliad* 3. 397); of the skin of Hera when she is setting off to charm Zeus (*Iliad* 14. 170); of the functions of Aphrodite contrasted with those of Ares and Athena (*Iliad* 5. 428–30); of dancing, in the city at peace on Achilles' shield (*Iliad* 18. 603);

and of singing (*Odyssey* 1. 421). In Homer the word is always applied to objects or activities already charged with desire. The choice of an adjective with such connotations to characterize a city, and Sparta in particular, gives us an unusual insight into the attitude of a Spartan citizen to his city—or into the attitude which Tyrtaeus hoped to inspire. (Homer uses neither ἱμερόεις nor ἱμερτός of cities; but other elegiac poets do so, and the idea is eloquently expressed in Pericles' Funeral Speech.)[13] The adjective strikes a note quite different from anything else in these lines. There is no reason to suppose that it was cynically chosen; but even if its use did not come from the heart, it evidently spoke to the heart of Tyrtaeus' audience.

5(H9)–8. That the new sentence begins at H9 enhances, as usual, the effect of imperfect cadence and incomplete sense, and the previous sentence increases the intensity. The kings and the gerousia seem to have acquired the lion's share. Now the people are introduced: what is left for them? Tyrtaeus expresses their role in the most stately form of pentameter, three words only, with a spondaic first hemiepes (beginning with a molossus word) and a heptasyllabic second hemiepes,[14] at the end of which the sense is still incomplete, and the sentence continues to the end of 7 without a stop. The reversal of the customary movement of the couplet produces the usual effect:[15] the following pentameter is highlighted. Metrically, the stateliness of 6 is increased by contrast with the dactylic 5, and the three infinitives of 7–8 gain prominence—appropriate, since the *behavior* of the common people is the subject of the lines—from their spondaic rhythm.

The common people have a grandeur of form rather than substance. They may have stately rhythm, but they have no adjective to compare with the kings' or even with that of the gerousia. Unlike the gerousia and like the kings, their infinitival activity is qualified; but whereas the kings have a relative clause, with a finite verb, to express their role as guardians, the people have a participial—that is, adjectival—phrase of doubtful meaning. ἀνταπαμειβομένους might mean either "answering *with* ordinances" (Edmonds, 1931)[16] or "obeying the decrees of the kings or the provisions of the Lycurgan rhetra" (*LSJ*, 1968). In either case, there is great emphasis on εὐθείαις, which evidently means "correct in the eyes of higher authority." The kings and gerousia would clearly prefer the interpretation "obeying." Possibly the ambiguous Greek reflects another Tyrtaean effort to blur and change the sense of Delphi's words in the interests of authority. Note how ἀνταπαμειβομένους at the end of 6 balances the similarly ambiguous ἄρχειν at the beginning of 3, and note also how the supplement σκολιόν at the end of 8 balances εὐθείαις at the beginning of 6. (σκολιόν is the appropriate contrary of εὐθείαις. If the *rhetra* was already in existence when Tyrtaeus composed 4W, the reading is guaranteed by the wording of the alleged amendment as recorded by Plutarch. Even without the *rhetra*, the supplement is virtually certain.) 7 expresses in generally laudatory terms what the people are to do, and the highlighted pen-

74   Chapter Four

tameter particularizes what they are not to do: give advice that is [deemed by those in authority to be] σκολιόν for this city. (Note how the mention of τῇδε πόλει serves to counterpoint the position of the people in 8 against that of the kings in 4.)

9–10. 8 is end-stopped, and the sentence has come to its conclusion; but the report of Apollo's words continues to the end of 9, a line given great weight by its four spondees, more than in any other extant line of Tyrtaeus. But again the grandeur seems to be of form, not of substance. Those who have read Tyrtaeus' lines as a versified *description* of the Spartan constitution have held that Tyrtaeus is here simply asserting the right of ἀνταγορία of the *demos* (below, p. 75); but if we bear in mind the skillful rhetoric of the preceding lines, we may well conclude that, once the kings had ἄρχειν in the stronger sense and the *demos* had ἀνταπαμείβεσθαι in the weaker, and once εὐθείαις, καλά, δίκαια, and σκολιόν had been interpreted by the kings and gerousia in their own interest, 9 would leave the *demos* no other function than to vote in favor of the proposal put before them. In other words, whether the *rhetra* yet existed in writing or not, Tyrtaeus is expressing in skillful rhetoric the same message as that set out in plain blunt prose in the *rhetra*.

Since Apollo's seven lines of instructions end at the imperfect cadence of 9, 10 receives prominence: the ring composition is highlighted, and the lines reach a quick but firm ending. West suggests μέν for γάρ in 10, implying that the poem continued. He may be correct in that supposition, but I should nonetheless prefer γάρ in the interests of the ring effect; and Dover's observations on the subject of oral poetry and occasional poetry in Archilochus (in Hardt 1964, 199–212), the implications of which have yet to be fully worked out, apply to any occasional poetry of this period: if the circumstances of composition supplied the context, Tyrtaeus 4W could be a complete poem.

Bergk (1882) supposed that lines 3, 5, 7, and 9 constituted the original hexameter oracle given by Delphi, on two grounds: that the pentameters contribute nothing to the sense and that Tyrtaeus does not usually write in this manner. West (1972) agrees. The conclusion may be sound, but neither premise seems justified. Any poet with a tendency to compose by the line, as Tyrtaeus does, may produce elegiacs whose pentameters are dispensable, so far as syntax is concerned. (Consider the priamel of 12W. 1–10.) And it is only the syntax which is dispensable in 4, 6, and 8 of 4W, for much of the rhetorical effect is produced by these lines. If Tyrtaeus was adapting an existing oracle in this manner, one can only admire his rhetorical skill.

Historical Note.—The *rhetra* gives the *demos* a right in one clause and makes it ineffective in the next. Interpreted as I have interpreted it, Tyrtaeus' poem does the same. This state of affairs may throw light on a historical problem. Tyrtaeus appears to say that the *demos* had the right of ἀνταγορία. Aristotle (*Politics* 1273a6–16) denies it. Wade-Gery (1943) emended the text of the *Politics* to make Aristotle agree with Tyrtaeus. But on the present interpretation both are right. Take a modern parallel. Under the British Constitution, the monarch's signature to all legislation passed by the Houses of Parliament is the necessary final step, and it is solemnly reported to Parliament that the signature has been applied to the document. In theory, the monarch could refuse to sign; but I know of no one who holds that the monarch could refuse in practice or, at all events, could do so on more than one occasion, for the right would be withdrawn. If Aristotle were describing the British Constitution, would he say that the monarch had or had not the right to refuse to sign legislation duly passed by the Houses of Parliament? Similarly, the Spartan *demos* has the right of ἀνταγορία; but the right is held under such conditions that it can be exercised only by acquiescing in the will of the kings and gerousia.

🔲🔲🔲

Tyrtaeus 11W

ἀλλ', Ἡρακλῆος γὰρ ἀνικήτου γένος ἐστέ,
θαρσεῖτ'· οὔπω Ζεὺς αὐχένα λοξὸν ἔχει·
μηδ' ἀνδρῶν πληθὺν δειμαίνετε, μηδὲ φοβεῖσθε,
ἰθὺς δ' ἐς προμάχους ἀσπίδ' ἀνὴρ ἐχέτω,
5   ἐχθρὴν μὲν ψυχὴν θέμενος, θανάτου δὲ μελαίνας
κῆρας ⟨ὁμῶς⟩ αὐγαῖς ἠελίοιο φίλας.
ἴστε γὰρ ὡς Ἄρεος πολυδακρύου ἔργ' ἀΐδηλα,
εὖ δ' ὀργὴν ἐδάητ' ἀργαλέου πολέμου,
καὶ μετὰ φευγόντων τε διωκόντων τ' ἐγέ⟨νε⟩σθε
10 ὦ νέοι, ἀμφοτέρων δ' ἐς κόρον ἠλάσατε.
οἳ μὲν γὰρ τολμῶσι παρ' ἀλλήλοισι μένοντες
ἔς τ' αὐτοσχεδίην καὶ προμάχους ἰέναι,
παυρότεροι θνήσκουσι, σαοῦσι δὲ λαὸν ὀπίσσω·
τρεσσάντων δ' ἀνδρῶν πᾶσ' ἀπόλωλ' ἀρετή.
15 οὐδεὶς ἄν ποτε ταῦτα λέγων ἀνύσειεν ἕκαστα,
ὅσσ', ἢν αἰσχρὰ μάθῃ, γίνεται ἀνδρὶ κακά·
ἀργαλέον γὰρ ὄπισθε μετάφρενόν ἐστι δαΐζειν
ἀνδρὸς φεύγοντος δηΐῳ ἐν πολέμῳ·
αἰσχρὸς δ' ἐστὶ νέκυς κατακείμενος ἐν κονίῃσι
20 νῶτον ὄπισθ' αἰχμῇ δουρὸς ἐληλάμενος.
ἀλλά τις εὖ διαβὰς μενέτω ποσὶν ἀμφοτέροισι
στηριχθεὶς ἐπὶ γῆς, χεῖλος ὀδοῦσι δακών,

μηρούς τε κνήμας τε κάτω καὶ στέρνα καὶ ὤμους
ἀσπίδος εὐρείης γαστρὶ καλυψάμενος·
25 δεξιτερῇ δ' ἐν χειρὶ τινασσέτω ὄβριμον ἔγχος,
κινείτω δὲ λόφον δεινὸν ὑπὲρ κεφαλῆς·
ἔρδων δ' ὄβριμα ἔργα διδασκέσθω πολεμίζειν,
μηδ' ἐκτὸς βελέων ἑστάτω ἀσπίδ' ἔχων,
ἀλλά τις ἐγγὺς ἰὼν αὐτοσχεδὸν ἔγχεϊ μακρῷ
30 ἢ ξίφει οὐτάζων δήϊον ἄνδρ' ἑλέτω,
καὶ πόδα πὰρ ποδὶ θεὶς καὶ ἐπ' ἀσπίδος ἀσπίδ' ἐρείσας,
ἐν δὲ λόφον τε λόφῳ καὶ κυνέην κυνέῃ
καὶ στέρνον στέρνῳ πεπλημένος ἀνδρὶ μαχέσθω,
ἢ ξίφεος κώπην ἢ δόρυ μακρὸν ἔχων.
35 ὑμεῖς δ', ὦ γυμνῆτες, ὑπ' ἀσπίδος ἄλλοθεν ἄλλος
πτώσσοντες μεγάλοις βάλλετε χερμαδίοις
δούρασί τε ξεστοῖσιν ἀκοντίζοντες ἐς αὐτούς,
τοῖσι πανόπλοισιν πλησίον ἱστάμενοι.

But since you are of the race of unconquered Heracles, be of good cheer. Zeus is not yet turning his neck away. Do not fear the mass of men, nor flee(?), but let a man hold his shield directly against the foremost fighters, treating his life as his foe and the black spirits of death dear as the rays of the sun. For you know the destructive deeds of Ares, who causes many tears, and are well acquainted with the temper of grievous war and have been with those who pursued and those who fled, young men, and reached satiation with both. For those who, remaining by their comrades' sides, have the courage to go into the melee and the foremost fighters—they die in smaller numbers and preserve the people behind them; but of men who have fled in terror all the valor is gone. No one could ever complete the full tally of all the woes which come upon a man if he learns(?) to do what is shameful. For it is grievous(?) to cleave the back of a fleeing man from behind in fierce battle, and shameful-and-ugly is a corpse lying in the dust with the point of a spear driven through its back from behind. No; let a man take a firm stance and stand fast, with both feet planted upon the ground, biting his lip with his teeth, having hidden his thighs and calves below and chest and shoulders with the belly of his broad shield. In his right hand let him brandish his mighty spear and make his crest wave, terrible over his head. By doing mighty deeds let him teach himself to fight, and let him not stand beyond the range of the weapons, for he has a shield. Rather let him go near and, wounding at close quarters with long spear or sword, let him slay his foe, and, having set foot by foot and thrust shield against shield, and having drawn near, crest to crest, helmet to helmet, let him fight his man, holding either the hilt of his sword or a long spear. And you, you light-armed, crouching on this side and that beneath the shield, have at them with great handstones and with polished spears as you cast your javelins at them(?), standing close to the warriors in full armor.

Tyrtaeus 11W is the whole or a part of a hortatory war poem. We owe our possession of it to Stobaeus (4. 9. 16), who quotes it as an example of poems περὶ πολέμου. As in 10W and 12W, Tyrtaeus is endeavoring to arouse the valor of Spartan warriors in their struggle against the Messenians in the Second Messenian War.

My primary concern here is with the poetic qualities of early elegy, but our understanding of the poetry may depend on the discussion of other topics. To appreciate Tyrtaeus 11W, some knowledge of the history of Greek arms and warfare is needed.

In the *Iliad*, the effective fighters are a small number[17] of well-armed soldiers who usually fight as individuals, only occasionally assembling in small groups to protect the body of a dead comrade (as in 17. 120–39). Passages such as 13. 125–35 and 16. 210–17, where larger organized groups are in combat, are usually held to reflect the mode of fighting of a later age. The well-armed soldiers of the Homeric poems are equipped with throwing spears, usually two in number, a large neck-to-ankle shield, body armor, including helmet and greaves, and a sword, to which they resort after the spears have been thrown. They travel to and from the battle in chariots—doubtless because such armor was very heavy[18]—but characteristically they fight on foot.

In the classical Greek *polis*, by contrast, the most effective fighting force was the phalanx of hoplites, the heavy-armed infantry. Large bodies of troops[19] armed with metal helmet, corslet, round shield, thrusting spear, and sword fought in close formation, several ranks deep. To pass from Homeric to classical fighting methods required time;[20] neither the new armor nor the new tactics can have been invented overnight. To understand Tyrtaeus' poem, it is necessary to know what point in the transition from Homeric to classical fighting has been reached.[21]

Tyrtaeus' words give some indications of hoplite fighting in the classical manner but also present some incongruities. The mention of sword and thrusting spear as alternative weapons of attack (in 30 and 34) is classical, as is the assumption that only the light-armed will throw missiles (35–38). (The Homeric hero might throw stones, as in *Iliad* 5. 302: Diomedes hurled a mighty stone, "which two mortal men of the present day could not carry," and almost killed Aeneas with it.) The huge shield of 23–24, "which covers chest, shoulders, and shins," is held by a recent authority to be certainly a hoplite shield (Snodgrass 1964, 181). On the other hand, line 28 exhorts the heavy-armed warrior not to hang back out of range of the missiles: behavior which seems impossible in the well-disciplined classical phalanx. The presence of light-armed troops lurking behind the hoplites' shields also seems incompatible with classical practice.

It seems best to conclude that in Tyrtaeus we find a rudimentary form of the hoplite phalanx. The weapons have been invented but not yet perfected,[22] and the best tactics, and the strict order and discipline needed for the most successful use of the phalanx formation, have not yet been fully evolved.

The transitional position of the Tyrtaean hoplite gives added point to Tyrtaeus' exhortations. The classical hoplite did not need more courage than the Homeric hero; he needed courage of a different kind. In Homer it is shameful—αἰσχρόν—and the mark of a κακός to run away before a stronger or more numerous foe, as Odysseus reflects (*Iliad* 11. 401–10); nevertheless, Homeric fighting has a great degree of fluidity. Individuals sometimes retreat, as do Odysseus and Ajax (*Iliad* 8. 92–98; 16. 114–22), and there is no close-knit battle formation which they disrupt by so doing. In the classical phalanx, on the other hand, to break ranks disrupted the whole structure and might precipitate a rout. Figures of casualties suffered by the armies of victors and vanquished in hoplite battles indicate that lines 11–13 of this poem state no more than the truth.[23]

The classical hoplite, then, fought a similarly armed foe face to face at a distance of a few feet. He could not retreat; he could barely sidestep.[24] Courage in war always ranked as the highest manifestation of courage in ancient Greece,[25] but its particular mode of expression was adapted to suit different types of warfare. Hoplite warfare demands courage of a singularly dour, cold-blooded, and enduring kind. If we think of Tyrtaeus in this poem, together with 10W and 12W, as endeavoring to create a new mode of manifesting courage in war, in a situation of crisis for the city, the emotional immediacy of the poem is greatly enhanced.[26]

Even a static analysis suggests that Tyrtaeus has little skill or interest in composing sentences which derive some of their effect from the manner in which they are set in the elegiac couplet. Twenty-seven of the thirty-eight lines are printed end-stopped by West (1972).[27] There are only eleven stops within the lines (1, 2, 3, 5, 10, 13, 16 *bis*, 22, 35 *bis*.) Of these, four (3, 5, 13, 22) demarcate parallel phrases or clauses, three (10, 35 *bis*) are set round vocatives, and two round the protasis of a conditional clause (16). Three of the stops (5, 13, 35) occur at the caesura (H10, H8, H8), two (16, 22) at colon diaeresis (P7), and one (3) at bucolic diaeresis (H12). These figures indicate that, even on the few occasions when Tyrtaeus' clauses do not coincide in length with the line, his major pauses at the end of clause or phrase tend to fall at the major divisions of the hexameter and pentameter. That many pauses within the line should do so is to be expected; but Archilochus and Callinus exhibit much greater variety (above, chapters 2 and 3).

Tyrtaeus is also the most spondaic of the poets so far studied.[28] Whether he uses spondees purposively will become apparent in the course of the discussion.

1–2. Whether or not Tyrtaeus' poem began here,[29] line 1 is a powerful beginning to the lines which we possess. That Heracles was the progenitor of the Spartan kings is the ground of Tyrtaeus' exhortation to be of good cheer, and Ἡρακλῆος is duly emphasized: it is set strongly between ἀλλά and γάρ;[30] the H8 caesura after γάρ gives some additional prominence to the only word in the group which is not a particle; and Ἡρακλῆος is the first word in its clause and the first word in its line, apart from the particle ἀλλά. ἀνικήτου and γένος also contribute to the sense: Heracles was invincible, and some of his might may reasonably be supposed to have been transmitted to his descendants. Though the end of 1 needs its comma, the sense is incomplete: the mind wishes to know what will follow such a strong reason and is alert for θαρσεῖτ', which derives great prominence from position also, and from the heavy pause at P3. The meter of the couplet is very spondaic: 1 has three spondees, more than any extant hexameter of Archilochus or Callinus, and the first hemiepes of 2 is completely spondaic. The spondees produce an effect of seriousness, solemnity, and grandeur here. (Note also in 2 how the diaeresis at P7 brings the ideas of confidence and Zeus closer to each other.)

The idea of γένος has more to contribute. Heracles was not merely invincible but the son of Zeus, and descent via Heracles from Zeus is here ascribed, by a rhetorical extension, not merely to the kings of Sparta but to Spartan warriors in general. In a persistent strand of Greek belief, to be a god's blood descendant gives one a great advantage, in obtaining divine help, over those who are not: one is "part of the family," and the gods have human motivations and values (Adkins 1972b, 1975, 1982a, 1982b). I interpret line 2 in the light of this belief.[31] "Zeus has not yet turned his head away," whether through disfavor (*LSJ* 1968, s.v. λοξός) or mere inadvertence.[32] Since at this time Greek gods were not believed to be omniscient and were believed to be irascible, possibly both connotations are present. In either case, the Spartans' descent from Zeus is offered as a reason for Zeus's favor and active attention to their needs; and to reject both reasons why Zeus might fail to help strengthens the argument. Possibly, though it would be poor rhetoric to mention it explicitly, the long duration of Heracles' Labors is hinted at in the couplet: the Spartans should not repine if the war is long.

3–4. ἀνδρῶν and ἀνήρ are rhetorically effective and are well placed. ἀνήρ is a warrior, a Man. By setting ἀνδρῶν at the beginning of his couplet, Tyrtaeus emphasizes the warrior status of the foe but adjures the Spartans neither to fear them nor to flee.[33] He then sets ἰθὺς δ' ἐς προμάχους in a strong position at the beginning of the pentameter, sharply contrasted in sense with the verbs of the hexameter. ἀσπίδ' may appear strange, for one might have expected Tyrtaeus to emphasize an offensive weapon; but the possession of a shield seems to define the hoplite in Greek eyes.[34] ἀνήρ and ἀνδρῶν frame the couplet and emphasize parallelism: the foe are Men, but so are the Spartans, and can meet them in battle face to face. There is an implied argument: the Spartans have not merely the expectation of divine favor in addition to mighty ancestors; they can rely on their own qualities too. The seven long syllables at the beginning of 2 give due awesomeness to the "throng of warriors," and they are counterpointed against the largely dactylic rhythm of the remainder of the couplet. ἰθύς too receives appropriate emphasis from its position as first-foot spondaic word in an otherwise dactylic line.

5–6. The preceding couplet was framed by two cases of the same powerful noun. 3–4 is framed by adjectives contrasted in sense: ἐχθρήν and φίλας. In addition, ψυχήν is contrasted with κῆρας; and κῆρας is elaborated by the addition of θανάτου . . . μελαίνας, φίλας by the contrasting ⟨ὁμῶς⟩ αὐγαῖς ἠελίοιο. The rhetoric is skillful. Tyrtaeus must reserve his elaboration of wording for the second phrase. What he is saying would be startling at any time and is quite new in seventh-century Greece. Homer's language is quite different (see below, p. 87). To add "as the gates of Hades" to ἐχθρήν, in the manner of *Iliad* 9. 312 and *Odyssey* 14. 156, would be bizarre and unlikely to persuade when the noun is ψυχήν: so strange a notion as ἐχθρήν . . . ψυχήν is best left unelaborated. Furthermore, a rhetorical dicolon is usually more effective when the second element is longer. θανάτου δὲ μελαίνας / κῆρας, which, like αὐγαῖς ἠελίοιο, closely resembles a common Homeric formula (below, p. 88), adds rhetorical fullness and vividness and also furnishes a contrast between darkness and light. The order as a whole enables Tyrtaeus to begin—briefly—with ἐχθρήν and to end with the most attractive—and longest—phrase of the couplet. The careful composition may help to conceal the fact that the second participial phrase is as bizarre as the first—as it must be, since it is the mirror image of the first. The meter, which gives a heavy spondaic rhythm to "life," a largely dactylic rhythm to "death," reinforces the effect of the unusual advice. The new and enjambed phrase beginning at H10 caesura combines imperfect cadence with incomplete sense. The immediately enjambed word κῆρας is unsurprising after θανάτου δὲ μελαίνας, but the pentameter is unpunctuated, and the enjambment carries the thought on to the end of 6, emphasizing the unity of the phrase and highlighting the contrast between ἐχθρήν and φίλας.

7–10. Tyrtaeus has already emphasized the Spartan warriors' divine descent and human valor. He now turns to their experience. νέοι they may be;[35] but—in emphatic positions—they *know* the deeds of Ares and have *well* learned the temper of grievous war. Knowledge and skill are the subjects of the first halves of 7 and 8, the grim nature of war that of the second halves.

Tyrtaeus is modulating from the qualities of the warriors to the nature of war and from the nature of war to the main theme of his poem (11 ff.): the behavior most likely to ensure one's well-being in war. 8 seems superfluous, for it is virtually a repetition of 7. Tyrtaeus is given to repeating himself, and repetition is not necessarily a fault; but this repetition is not so differently expressed as to act as a reinforcement. 9 elaborates the theme of the warriors' experience and certainly does not merely repeat 7–8; but one might wonder why Tyrtaeus mentions that the νέοι have fled in the past when he is exhorting them not to flee now (3). 10 adds a good deal to the sentence, but does it add what is needed? "You are fed up with fleeing and pursuing" may seem merely inept. There may be Homeric allusion here (below, p. 88). The intransitive use of ἐλαύνειν occurs here first in extant Greek and may be a Tyrtaean invention;[36] but whether driving on to satiation is the most appropriate idea after the literal fleeing and pursuing of 9 is a moot point: the image seems too similar.

The meter of 7–10, if purposively contrived, is chosen for different reasons from that of 1–6. One might suppose that 7–8, which contain one spondee, continue the transvaluation of values of 5–6 and that, despite πολυδακρύου, ἀΐδηλα, and ἀργαλέου, the rhythm is intended to express cheerfulness. But it is difficult to see why Tyrtaeus should be cheerful about the situation of 10; and the completely dactylic rhythm of 10, combined with ἠλάσατε, might seem to suggest—inappropriately—that the young warriors had arrived at satiation with war rapidly, at full gallop. However, one should always remember that the poet's choice between dactyls and spondees has to serve many purposes, including variety; and the first six lines of 11W contained twelve of the poem's fifty spondees, so that the ear may welcome a respite. (The ten lines of Archilochus 13W, a poem of sadness and grim resolution, contain only four spondees.) But to write ἐς κόρον ἠλάσατε in the second hemiepes of the pentameter, at the end of a four-line sentence where the sense is emphasized by the dying fall of the verse, must appear unfortunate in a poem of military exhortation; for the poet does not overtly follow this line with a vigorous call to new efforts. Here too, however, there may be Homeric allusion (below, p. 88).

11–14. Line 11 begins with a problem: what is contributed by γάρ? 11 is not an explanation of 7–10, and none of the other uses of γάρ seems appropriate.[37] Indeed, there appears to be no clear connection of thought between 7–10 and 11. Tyrtaeus has been concerned with a surfeit of fleeing and pursuing; he now turns abruptly to a more grim, static, unflinching kind of warfare. The abruptness too may be indicative of allusion (below, p. 88).

11–14, however, are excellent lines in themselves. The two couplets form a diptych, of which 11–13 and 14 are the asymmetrical panels. In 12, αὐτοσχεδίην and προμάχους are sufficiently different in sense to reinforce one another and indeed might be regarded as a hendiadys. τολμῶσι, the first non-structural word in its clause, is appropriately emphasized by its position and is effectively contrasted with τρεσσάντων, similarly placed in 14, the other panel of the diptych. παρ' ἀλλήλοισι μένοντες is a strong phrase (Adkins, 1977a, 79, 90). Though the couplet is end-stopped with a comma, the main clauses have not yet been reached, and the sense is incomplete. The dying fall of the pentameter is thereby obviated, the mind remains alert, and the main clauses receive an emphasis which their content well merits, for the line expresses two of the themes of Tyrtaeus' message: if one stands one's ground, one is less likely to be killed and one also protects others. Reversal of the usual movement of the couplet by continuing a sentence to the end of the hexameter after an overrun pentameter always gives prominence to the following pentameter. Tyrtaeus makes full use of the opportunity thus created: every word of 14 is powerful and damning. In 13, παυρότεροι, the first word of the first main clause, receives appropriate emphasis. Tyrtaeus cannot pretend that nobody dies in battle, but fewer die when they stand bravely shoulder to shoulder with their fellows. Tyrtaeus is much less skilled than Archilochus or Callinus at organizing his composition within the structure of the elegiac couplet, but the handling of the sentence in 13 is effective. All brave hoplites help to save the λαός behind them,[38] and Tyrtaeus' sentence, duly analyzed, has this meaning; but the juxtaposition within one hexameter, with a pause at beginning and end, of the two contrasted main clauses, and of θνήσκουσι and σαοῦσι in particular, emphasizes the contribution of those who fight bravely and die. Since Tyrtaeus is urging that even death is choiceworthy in the achievement of the larger good, to emphasize the contribution of those who die is good rhetoric; and to do so in the very words which claim that of those who fight bravely fewer die is very economical writing and even better rhetoric. The fate of the coward, prepared for by the μέν of 11, which is answered by the δ' of 14, receives a mere line; and here the dying fall of the pentameter is appropriate.[39] The quantitative πᾶσ' of 14 may resonate with the quantitative παυρότεροι of 13. Metrically, the largely dactylic rhythm of the optimistic 13 well contrasts with the five long syllables of the first hemiepes of 14 and helps to suggest that flight is worse than the risk of death.

15–20. There are problems of reading in 15–20. I read πάθη in 16 with the manuscripts (μάθη, West 1972) and ἁρπαλέον with Ahrens (1841) in 17 for the ἀργαλέον of the manuscripts.[40]

15–16. Line 15 in itself may seem a flabby line: ποτε and ταῦτα add little to warrant the expenditure of four syllables, and ταῦτα is vague. No sense is produced by taking it to refer to 14, 11–14, or even 1–14. The alternative, to take it with ἕκαστα, is pleonastic. The word appears to be a mere "filler." (Note also the absence of any connecting particle in 15.) On the other hand, the solitary spondee οὐδείς, together with its position, gives appropriate emphasis to that word; and the dactylic rhythm of the remainder of the line suits the idea of much speech and well contrasts with the stopping rhythm of 16, whose two stops within the line include the very unusual pause after P1 (for comparative figures, see Table 3). 16 effectively juxtaposes in chiastic order the two grim aspects of defeat: its disgrace and its disasters.

17-20. Even with ἁρπαλέον for ἀργαλέον, the development of thought from 15 to 20 may appear strange. Despite the introductory γάρ, 17-18 do not explain 15-16. But poetry always tends to be simpler and more paratactic than prose, and the periodic sentence of later elegant prose is unknown to the seventh century. If 17-18 are understood as the μέν-clause balancing the δέ-clause of 19-20, γάρ makes sense: "for though it is pleasant to . . . , yet a corpse lying in the dust is αἰσχρός." It is not clear whether the subject of thought in 17-20 is the same throughout or whether 17-18 present Spartan defeat from the Messenian, 19-20 from the Spartan, point of view. The rhetorical point remains the same and well leads up to the sustained exhortation which continues to the end of 11W.

In 17-20, as is his wont, Tyrtaeus places important words and phrases at the beginning of the lines for emphasis (Adkins, 1977a, 76): ἁρπαλέον, ἀνδρὸς φεύγοντος, αἰσχρός, and νῶτον. The word ἁρπαλέον, from ἁρπάζω, means both "snatching, eager" and "attractive, pleasant." Both usages are relevant here, and the audience might well activate all the connotations of the word. The sense is almost complete at the end of 17, but something seems needed to qualify μετάφρενον, so that ἀνδρὸς φεύγοντος receives some emphasis from enjambment as well as position.[41] The disgrace of flight is further highlighted by juxtaposition with "Man," "warrior." αἰσχρός spans both "shameful" and "ugly" and is the most powerful word available to decry an action or state of affairs. Both senses are relevant here: the Greek does not distinguish the two (Adkins 1960a, 163-64; 1977a, 95-96). In 20, νῶτον is the emphatic word: the wound is in a shameful position for a warrior. The enjambment of 19-20 may be less effective than that of 17-18. In 10W, Tyrtaeus seems to be arguing against the view that a corpse in the dust is αἰσχρός per se, at least in the sense of "ugly" (Adkins 1977a, 95-96). If Tyrtaeus found it necessary to argue thus, the view was presumably prevalent. Consequently, there is no feeling of incompleteness at the end of line 19 of this poem. Metrically, 17-18 furnish an effect similar to 13-14, with the dactyls of 17 reflecting the cheerful words, and the five long syllables of the first hemiepes of 18 expressing the shame of the fleeing warrior. The dactyls of 19 evidently express neither the shame nor the immobility of a corpse with a spear wound in its back; but the solitary first-foot spondee αἰσχρός merits its emphasis, unlike the sole spondee αἰχμῇ in 20: the shame is the same, be the weapon spear, sword, arrow, javelin, or handstone.[42]

21–22. This couplet is identical with Tyrtaeus 10W. 31–32, and scholars have debated which is the interpolation; but Tyrtaeus might have used the couplet twice. 10W and 11W are presumably different poems: it would be difficult to imagine a poem of which both could form a part, other than a work much longer than is likely for a work of exhortation. The lines were doubtless originally performed at different times; and if a poet can quote Homer, why should he not quote himself?[43] For 21–22 is an excellent couplet. In performance, μενέτω could be phrased with either the preceding or following words to produce sense, and it is set between the H7 and H10 caesurae. To perform the line with the usual indication of caesura in both places would give μενέτω a pivotal role, and it is the most important word in the line, echoing μένοντες in 11. εὖ διαβάς is vigorous. ποσὶν ἀμφοτέροισι, a descriptive touch, slackens the tension and prepares for στηριχθείς, a word of vivid meaning intensified by position, enjambment, and molossus rhythm. (If the performer indicates caesura after μενέτω, there will be less inducement for the audience to understand ποσὶν ἀμφοτέροισι with what precedes, and the mind will be more alert for the pentameter.) The wholly dactylic rhythm of 21 does not reflect the sense, but it contrasts well with στηριχθείς. I shall discuss χεῖλος ὀδοῦσι δακών later (below, p. 89).

23–28. In reading 23–38, it is essential to remember that Tyrtaeus is giving urgent practical advice in a crisis; he is not composing poetry to be savored at one's leisure in the study. Otherwise, the detailed military instructions must appear prolix and superfluous. The poem will not itself serve as a drill manual for those who know nothing of hoplite weapons and tactics; Tyrtaeus is reminding the warriors of what they already know, producing a detailed self-image of themselves in battle. (There is, however, a suggestion in 27 that some of these soldiers may be less experienced than those addressed in 7–10.) At all events, production of a self-image in such detail displays good psychology and effective rhetoric.

23–24. Nevertheless, 23–24 are not among Tyrtaeus' most successful lines. 21–22 is a fine couplet, but it consists essentially of three participial phrases. In 10W it stands, if not at the end of the poem, at the end of the lines we possess. To append to it, as Tyrtaeus does here, another participial phrase which occupies a whole couplet, whose hexameter is a mere list of nouns, allows the sentence to trickle away into the sand. However, soldiers about to fight the enemy might evaluate differently a couplet which reassured them, with details, that their shields were large and protected most of their bodies.[44] Furthermore, 24 is an excellent line in itself, consisting of four effective words well arranged, and its excellence may compensate to some extent for the unwinding syntax of the sentence. γαστήρ for the "belly" of the shield seems to be a Tyrtaean novelty; it is probably a new word for a new shape of shield. If new, the metaphor cannot be dead; and perhaps at first sight it appears quaint to characterize the shield with a metaphor from part of the body in a context in which so many parts of the warrior's body are mentioned. However, ἀσπίς is feminine and γαστήρ is used of the womb (as in *Iliad* 6. 58); combined with καλύπτεσθαι, the words may have had a certain psychological resonance which the customary translations fail to bring out. The spondaic rhythm of εὐρείης appropriately highlights the word.

25–26. The soldier knows that he holds his spear in his right hand and that his crest is over his head, but mention of these facts is not otiose: all contribute to the detailed self-image. The meter of 25 emphasizes the initial molossus κινείτω, a word which I shall discuss later (below, p. 90).

27–28. In 27, the present tense of participle and imperative are important: "By doing mighty deeds let him teach himself how to fight." Throughout this passage the relationship of Tyrtaeus' Greek to Homer, whether echo or counterpoint, may be significant. The advice seems to be given to a tyro rather than to the seasoned warriors of 7–10. Tyrtaeus must reach as much of his audience as possible. ἀσπίδ' ἔχων is not a weak ending to the line: ἔχων is not merely "while holding," nor is ἀσπίς unemphatic in the context. The sense is "inasmuch as you have a shield," and are a hoplite, and can make light of the enemy's missiles.[45] The use of ὄβριμος twice in three lines would be avoided by modern poets; but Greek poets much more admired than Tyrtaeus freely repeat words in this way, evidently without offending contemporary taste,[46] and any warrior would be pleased to be assured that both his deeds and his spear were ὄβριμα.

29–34. Construction of the self-image continues. The juxtaposition of similar words in different cases (πόδα, ποδί; ἀσπίδος, ἀσπίδα) in 31 effectively expresses reciprocity and proximity; but to use the device twice more in 32 ("crest to crest, helmet to helmet") must appear artistically inept and probably less efficacious than a better rhetoric would be, even if we remember Tyrtaeus' practical goal. However, the emotional effect of the lines upon those who had fought in this manner, and expected to do so again, cannot be gauged by the critic at his desk.

The enjambments of 29–30 and 32–33 are inept. The incomplete sense of 29 creates the usual expectations and emphasizes the beginning of 30. The mind is alert for some vivid word expressing action with the spear. ἢ ξίφει does not merit its emphasis: it seems almost an afterthought. Similarly, 32 is one of only two enjambed pentameters in this poem. Any such enjambment emphasizes what follows; and if the sense is continued without pause to the end of the hexameter, as it is in 33, the movement of the couplet is reversed and the following pentameter is highlighted.[47] Here Tyrtaeus uses none of these resources; he seems simply to be fitting his sentence into the couplet as best he can.

In 34, West (1972) reads ἔχων for the manuscripts' ἑλών.⁴⁸ Either reading is possible in general, but the manuscript tradition gives the better sense here. West regards ἑλών as an error caused by ἑλέτω in 30; but ἔχων itself occurred as recently as 28, where it is appropriate. Here ἔχων, combined with the absence of definite articles, is vague, for its sense can be as weak as "having" either a sword or a spear, suggesting that these warriors were armed with one or the other.⁴⁹ κώπην may suggest "holding"; but the aorist ἑλών, suggesting the act of grasping one of the two offensive weapons possessed by the hoplite, is much more vivid.

35–38. The last four lines of 11W are devoted to the light-armed troops, who are addressed directly. There was no formal address to the hoplites; it merely became apparent that they were the subject of the earlier part of the poem. This might suggest that 1 is not the first line of Tyrtaeus' poem; but even in 1 the identity of those addressed is in no doubt, since the light-armed were socially too insignificant to have claimed descent from Heracles. In addition, the original context of performance will have furnished its own frame of reference, as may be indicated by 37, where αὐτούς must refer to the enemy but is very vague. If the enemy were actually or imminently present, "them" would need no explanation: compare "Up, Guards, and at 'em" or "Don't fire until you see the whites of their eyes." But the present imperatives⁵⁰ rather suggest advice generally relevant to the crisis. (If Tyrtaeus were deliberately writing the poems to be used as the fourth-century Attic orator Lycurgus says they were used in his day, when they were declaimed to the army before any battle, the immediacy suggested by αὐτούς and the generality of the imperative would both be explained.)

35–38 are in other respects awkward. 36–37 can be understood in two ways, neither satisfactory. If τε (37) links the two dative phrases, both depend on βάλλετε, and πτώσσοντες and ἀκοντίζοντες are parallel but grammatically unlinked: (*a*) "cowering, hurl at them with great handstones and polished spears as you ἀκοντίζετε at them." If τε links the whole of 37 as a participial phrase with πτώσσοντες, the result is (*b*) "hurl at them with great handstones as you cower and ἀκοντίζετε at them with polished spears," which grammatically subordinates one act of throwing to another. Again, the whole of the last couplet (with *b*) or the last one and a half lines (with *a*) consists of two participial phrases, and the syntax unwinds in a manner similar to that observed earlier in this poem. πτώσσοντες,⁵¹ "cowering," is a pejorative term when used of fighting men, and it leaves no doubt of the inferiority of the light-armed to the hoplites.⁵²

It is impossible to be certain whether Tyrtaeus 11W ended here, for there are very few early Greek elegies in which we can be sure that the last extant line is the last line of the poem.⁵³ Four lines may seem a meager allocation to the light-armed; but it may have appeared appropriate in Tyrtaeus' Sparta, and it is not impossible that the whole poem consisted of direct exhortation.

◫

Most of the words in Tyrtaeus 11W are also found in the Homeric poems. There are also Homeric phrases, some of which may constitute echoes and allusions or other purposive rehandling of Homer's language.

1–2. Neither ἀνίκητος nor λοξός is Homeric. λοξός occurs first here, but it does not have the ring of a poetical coinage. ἀνίκητος occurs first in Hesiod, *Theogony* 489, of Zeus himself.

3–4. δειμαίνειν does not occur in the *Iliad* or *Odyssey*, but it does appear in *Hymn to Apollo* 404 (which may be later than this poem).⁵⁴ The use of πληθύς and πρόμαχοι is novel. In Homer, πληθύς may denote the enemy taken together as a mass—a terrifying sight, which arouses fear in Odysseus (*Iliad* 11. 405)—but it may also be contrasted with the πρόμαχοι, as in *Iliad* 20. 376, where Apollo advises Hector not to fight as a πρόμαχος against Achilles but to withdraw into the πληθύς. Traditionally, then, when πληθύς and πρόμαχοι appeared in the same context, the πρόμαχοι would be the more terrifying. Here, however, the Spartan warrior is urged not to fear the πληθύς but to go straight forward against the πρόμαχοι.⁵⁵ The solution is presumably related to the change in arms and armor and possibly to Tyrtaeus' rhetorical goals. In the rudimentary hoplite phalanx there are many more fully armed men (πανόπλοισιν, 38) than in a Homeric battle. There is a πληθύς of well-armed, in fact, of whom already more disciplined fighting is required than from Homer's well-armed; there seems little or no role for the individualistic Homeric πρόμαχοι, the few well-armed warriors available (see above, p. 77). Tyrtaeus seems to have taken a Homeric term and reapplied it to the front rank of the phalanx (in which, as presumably the most dangerous position, the doughtiest fighters might well be stationed). In a culture imbued with epic terminology and values, so to reapply important and emotive Homeric terms would be excellent rhetoric: it sets the Spartan front-ranker alongside Ajax, Achilles, and Diomedes.

5–6. In 10W. 14 and 18 Tyrtaeus adjured the warrior not to be sparing of ψυχή and not to φιλοψυχεῖν (probably a Tyrtaean coinage). In 5–6 he greatly elaborates, in a manner which suggests that 11W may be a later composition than 10W. Tyrtaeus' words would be startling at any time, but the Homeric phrases in 5–6 evoke an implicit contrast with the very different evaluation of life and death found in Homer. "Hateful as the gates of Hades to me" is an

88   Chapter Four

extreme expression of enmity in Homer, as in *Iliad* 9. 312, *Odyssey* 14. 156; and here Tyrtaeus uses the same adjective of one's life. "Baneful (κακός) death and black κήρ" is a Homeric formula, as in *Iliad* 21. 66, where Lycaon not surprisingly greatly longed to avoid such a fate. Tyrtaeus asks the Spartan warrior to regard black κήρ as equally dear as the rays of the sun—and "to see the rays of the sun" is a Homeric formula for "being alive," a condition always regarded as preferable to death in Homer.[56] There is no allusion to particular passages, but the transvaluation of Homeric values would be unmistakable. (Tyrtaeus does not rest his case on such rhetorical hyperbole: 11-14, his prudential argument, is much more likely to be persuasive at any time and certainly so in the context of early Greek values and beliefs.)

7-8. These lines may contain an allusion. ἔργ' ἀΐδηλα occurs twice in our *Iliad* manuscripts (5. 757, 872), but Aristarchus preferred τάδε κάρτερα ἔργα, and most modern editors follow him. However, Tyrtaeus' use of the phrase with Ares may suggest that he knew it from the *Iliad*, for in 5. 757 Hera is complaining that Ares is killing many Greeks, while in 5. 872 Ares is bellowing loudly when wounded by Diomedes. The formula πολύδακρυν Ἄρηα (*Iliad* 3. 132; 8. 516; 19. 318) is not used in either of the *Iliad* 5 passages; but remembrance of those passages would give a double significance to πολύδακρυς in 7, with respect to death and wounds inflicted and received, and would well introduce the contrasts of pursuit and flight, victory and defeat, slayer and slain, which are Tyrtaeus' theme until 20. ἀργαλέου πολέμου in 8 is another Homeric/Hesiodic formula (*Iliad* 14. 87, Hesiod *Works and Days* 229), but there are no significant echoes.

ὀργή (8) is un-Homeric,[57] except for a doubtful reading in *Hymn to Demeter* 205 (which may be later than Tyrtaeus). Its use implies that πόλεμος is personalized here. It is inappropriate to speak of metaphor: in early Greek, any external force which impinges upon one may readily be viewed in personal terms, and a personal deity like Ares may be used to signify "war" with no feeling that logical categories are thereby transgressed. Here we find both phenomena in two lines.[58]

10-11. So far, general or particular memories of Homer would enrich Tyrtaeus' lines for his audience. Now, however, the comprehensibility of the argument may depend on taking an allusion. As stated above (p. 81), the link in thought between 10 and 11 is unclear. An allusion using κόρος may supply the key. Satiation in Homer may be not only with food or wine (*Odyssey* 14. 28, 46), but with weeping (*Iliad* 22. 427; *Odyssey* 4. 103, 541; 10. 499; 20. 59) or war, sleep, love, song, and dance (*Iliad* 13. 633-39). Satiation with war occurs also in a well-known passage, *Iliad* 19. 221-37, remembrance of which would clarify Tyrtaeus' poem. In *Iliad* 19 Achilles in his anguish at the death of Patroclus wished to fight on an empty stomach. Odysseus replies by saying that satiation with war comes quickly and that the Achaeans should eat first so that they may fight more relentlessly. He ends (235–37):

ἥδε γὰρ ὀτρυντύς· κακὸν ἔσσεται, ὅς κε λίπηται
νηυσὶν ἐπ' Ἀργείων· ἀλλ' ἀθρόοι ὁρμηθέντες
Τρωσὶν ἐφ' ἱπποδάμοισιν ἐγείρομεν ὀξὺν Ἄρηα.

In Tyrtaeus 11W, lines 10–14 do not well follow line 9; they do, however, appropriately continue Odysseus' speech in *Iliad* 19, of which the quoted lines are the last. Odysseus says it will go hard with the shirkers,[59] and he adjures the Greeks in a body (ἀθρόοι: compare παρ' ἀλλήλοισι μένοντες in Tyrtaeus 11W. 11) to stir up war against the Trojans; to this Tyrtaeus adds the inducement that those who fight bravely in close order are less likely to be killed. It would not be essential to remember Odysseus' words in detail: the general tenor of the speech—the recollection that, despite talk of satiation with war, Odysseus ends with an urgent admonition to fight bravely—would suffice. (Compare Ogden Nash's use of Khayyam/Fitzgerald's lion and lizard, above, p. 27: the "trigger" may recall the precise words of Fitzgerald, but the general subject and emotional tone would be sufficient to enable the reader to take Nash's point.) Odysseus' exhortation supplies the necessary link between satiation with war and Tyrtaeus' next words. The allusion is the more likely to be taken in view of the inappropriateness, already discussed, of Tyrtacus introducing the thought of satiation with war into his vigorous lines. The mind, surprised, will seek an explanation; and if, as is argued here, allusion to Homer is not uncommon in early elegy, the correct explanation may well be found.

11. παρ' ἀλλήλοισι μένοντες is a Homeric phrase.[60] Tyrtaeus in fact needs to give the phrase greater intensity than does Homer, since the demand that the ranks not be broken is far more urgent (Adkins 1977a, 79–80, 90–91).

13–14. In *Iliad* 14. 520–22 we find "But Ajax slew most, for there was no one like him in pursuit when warriors fled (ἀνδρῶν τρεσσάντων)." The aorist participle of this verb occurs only here in Homer. Homer uses it in the genitive plural, with ἀνδρῶν, as the first half of a line. So does Tyrtaeus. Tyrtaeus' line is good in its own right; but the Homeric reminiscence enriches it, and the sentence from which the allusion is taken leads on to the subject matter of 17–18. If Tyrtaeus' audience had been reminded of Ajax in 14, they would realize that they had been placed in the position of that mighty warrior in 17–18. Powerful rhetoric indeed, and surely not unworthy poetry.[61]

21–22. I have discussed this couplet elsewhere (Adkins 1977a, 83–84, 94). Though στηρίζειν is used only twice in Homer, and on each occasion with the dative plural of πούς, as here, the contexts in Homer are irrelevant to Tyrtaeus' poem. χεῖλος ὀδοῦσι δακών is a Tyrtaean coinage. A formulaic Homeric couplet evidently supplied the inspiration:

ὣς ἔφαθ'· οἱ δ' ἄρα πάντες ὀδὰξ ἐν χείλεσι φύντες
Τηλέμαχον θαύμαζον, ὃ θαρσαλέως ἀγόρευε.

When these lines are used in the *Odyssey* (1. 381; 18. 410; 20. 268), they describe the suitors' surprise at Telemachus' new-found willingness to speak out and their suppression of a reply, apparently from fear. Tyrtaeus, however, is adjuring the young men of Sparta to bite the bullet and show steadfast courage. In this couplet he seems to be engaged in original composition without allusion; and if he used the lines twice, we may infer that he was pleased with the result.

25–26. Line 25 ends with a common Homeric formula (ὄβριμον ἔγχος, 13 times in the *Iliad*; also Hesiod, *Scutum* 135). δεξιτερῇ δ' ἐν χειρί, the opening phrase, recalls a number of Homeric expressions which employ the same noun and adjective (e.g., *Iliad* 7. 108; 14. 137; 21. 166–67); but they are the first noun and adjective likely to occur to the mind to express the thought. τινάσσειν is Homeric and occurs with ἔγχος as object (*Iliad* 20. 163).[62] Formulaic or not, the line is full of Homeric ethos. The next line might recall a common Homeric couplet (*Iliad* 3. 336; 15. 480; 16. 137):

κρατὶ δ' ἐπ' ἰφθίμῳ κυνέην εὔτυκτον ἔθηκεν
ἵππουριν· δεινὸν δὲ λόφος καθύπερθεν ἔνευεν.

Tyrtaeus uses δεινόν and λόφος, but in place of ἔνευεν, "nodded (of its own accord)," he uses κινείτω, "cause to wave," emphasized by position and meter. Having created his Homeric ambience, is Tyrtaeus urging his audience, by a significantly varied allusion, to be more positively terrible in appearance than the Homeric hero? There would be purpose in so doing, and Tyrtaeus appears to act similarly elsewhere.[63]

27–28. ὄβριμα ἔργα is not found in Homer, but ὀβριμόεργος occurs twice: in *Iliad* 5. 403, where Dione says of Heracles σχέτλιος, ὀβριμόεργος, ὃς οὐκ ὄθετ' αἴσυλα ῥέζων, and in *Iliad* 22. 418, where Priam, after the death of Hector, says of Achilles: λίσσωμ' ἀνέρα τοῦτον, ἀτάσθαλον, ὀβριμόεργον, / ἤν πως ἡλικίην αἰδέσσεται, ἠδ' ἐλεήσῃ. There is disapproval in both speeches; but (*a*) the disapproval may be carried by αἴσυλα and ἀτάσθαλον rather than by ὀβριμόεργος,[64] (*b*) the words are spoken from the point of view of the victims, and (*c*) Heracles and Achilles were not generally disapproved of in early Greece. Tyrtaeus is certainly encouraging the Spartans to perform ὄβριμα ἔργα and is evaluating them from the Spartan point of view. What is important is that the word is not used of the merely average. If the Spartans remembered the Homeric lines and likened themselves to Heracles and Achilles, they would do so with pride.

Line 27 may contain another purposive allusion to Homer. διδασκέσθω πολεμίζειν does not occur in Homer; but in *Iliad* 16. 811, and only there, we find διδασκόμενος πολέμοιο, which seems close enough to be reminiscent. The reference is to Euphorbus son of Panthus, "who excelled all his coevals in swordsmanship, in handling a chariot, and in fleetness of foot; for on that occasion he knocked twenty men from their chariots, having come to battle for the first time, διδασκόμενος πολέμοιο." *LSJ* render the last phrase "skilled in war," but the tense surely requires "being taught" or, better, "teaching himself." The lines portray Euphorbus' dramatic debut in the *Iliad*, and he next delivers the first of the wounds which end Patroclus' *aristeia* with his death. Once again the passage must have been a famous one, and remembrance of it could only serve to hearten any comparatively inexperienced hoplite in the Spartan army.

31–33. These lines furnish the last notable Homeric echo of the poem. *Iliad* 13. 130–33 (compare 16. 214–17) present this picture of the massed Greeks:

φράξαντες δόρυ δουρί, σάκος σάκεϊ προθελύμνῳ·
ἀσπὶς ἄρ' ἀσπίδ' ἔρειδε, κόρυς κόρυν, ἀνέρα δ' ἀνήρ·
ψαῦον δ' ἱππόκομοι κόρυθες λαμπροῖσι φάλοισι
νευόντων, ὡς πυκνοὶ ἐφέστασαν ἀλλήλοισιν·

As Snell observes (1969, 47), in Homer the weapons are most important—they furnish two of the three subjects of ἔρειδε and the subject of ψαῦον; but in Tyrtaeus the warriors are the subject. (The contrast is not so sharp if *Iliad* 13. 130 is included in the quotation, as Snell does not; but it is present nonetheless.) Snell also notes that Homer portrays the massed ranks of the Achaeans, while Tyrtaeus' lines urge the Spartan warrior in his phalanx to bring himself and his weapons into close contact with his foe. At all events, that seems the more likely interpretation; but even if the lines were read in a sense closer to Homer's, Tyrtaeus is emphasizing the role of the human agent to a much greater extent than does Homer. Here, as in 10W. 23–27 (Adkins 1977a, 91–92), there can be no doubt that Tyrtaeus' reminiscence of Homer is conscious and deliberate. His variation on Homer portrays his warriors in a manner more fiercely combative than Homer's—a fact which favors my interpretation of 25–26 here. (Archilochus 13W may take a similar attitude to Homer; see p. 42, above.)

Recall the arguments of Tyrtaeus' poem. He says to the warriors (*a*) "You have reason to expect special treatment from the greatest of the gods; and he is paying attention." (*b*) "Reverse your evaluations of life and death." (*c*) "Fight bravely, and you are much less likely to be killed. To be defeated, to run away, is not only αἰσχρόν but κακόν. War is delightful (reading ἁρπαλέον) when one is winning; and you are experienced in war." (*d*) "Grit your teeth, and teach yourself to fight by fighting." (*e*) "Follow my detailed military advice."

Of these, (*b*) is likely to be the least convincing as rhetoric: the dank and unpleasant Homeric Hades resists such reevaluation. It is not surprising that Tyrtaeus makes this point early in his poem, to startle his audience into attention, rather than resting his argument upon it. (*c*) and (*d*) contain one apparent, and one real, contradiction: it is not inconsistent to say both that pursuing one's routed foe is delightful and that one must grit one's teeth grimly before the foe is routed; but it is inconsistent to portray one's audience both as seasoned warriors and as tyros.

The inconsistency is readily explicable. Tyrtaeus wishes to hearten every member of his audience, from the most to the least experienced; and he includes reflections which will reach as many soldiers as possible.

Tyrtaeus 11W, as I have shown, also exhibits in its fine details much skilled rhetorical use of language; while Tyrtaeus 4W achieves its—much more subtle—goal by plays on words, impressive if the ten lines were all free composition, much more impressive if the poet is adapting an already existing hexameter oracle. His rhetorical talents seem undeniable.

Tyrtaeus lacks a number of Archilochus' and Callinus' poetic gifts. His elegiacs are halting, awkward. He cannot compose a paragraph flexibly within the constraints of his meter. Had a developed formal prose been available to him, he would doubtless have found it more congenial. Striking new images are not entirely absent, but they occur less frequently in his extant lines than in those of Archilochus or Callinus. But an artist, to succeed, needs to make the best use of his talents, whatever these may be, and also of the material with which he has to work; and Tyrtaeus' use of Homeric allusion to give poetic, rhetorical, and emotional supplementation to his own limited poetic resources shows a remarkable realization of the possibilities residing in an unusual cultural situation.

5
MIMNERMUS

Mimnermus' place of birth is disputed, and only vague information is available about the date of his poetical activity. Strabo (14. 643) and Photius (*Bibliotheca* 319b11) state without qualification that he was born in Colophon; but the *Suda* lists three birthplaces, Colophon, Smyrna, and Astypalaea, a Dorian island near Cos. Herodotus tells us (1. 150) that the Colophonians captured Smyrna, apparently about 800 B.C., and it has been suggested that the confusion about Mimnermus' birthplace reflects this fact. It is possible that Colophonians living in Smyrna continued to be known as Colophonians; but unless Colophonians continued to migrate, Mimnermus, if correctly dated, must on this hypothesis have been born in Smyrna. The ascription to him of a poem entitled *Smyrneïs* also associates him with the city (Mimnermus 13aW).

The *Suda* informs us that Mimnermus was alive in the 37th Olympiad (B.C. 632–629). Pausanias 9. 29. 4 (which West prints as Mimnermus 13W) refers to Mimnermus' poem on the fight of the Smyrnaeans against Gyges and the Lydians, and Mimnermus 14W praises a warrior who fought in the plain of the Hermus. Since in the latter poem he says (14. 2) that he heard the exploit from his elders, it seems likely that it is to be dated to the time of Gyges and that Mimnermus' prime is to be dated at least a generation later. Solon 20W comments on Mimnermus 6W, but this fact is compatible with any possible dating of either poet. It seems reasonable to conclude that Mimnermus flourished in the second half of the seventh century, probably a little later than Archilochus, Callinus, and Tyrtaeus.

The precise nature and extent of his published work is also unclear. Porphyrio, commenting on Horace, *Epistles* 2. 2. 1, writes: "Mimnermus duos libros luculent⟨is vers⟩ibus scripsit"; the *Suda* (s.v. Μίμνερμος) seems to ascribe "many books" to him. Callimachus at the beginning of his *Aitia* employs the work of Mimnermus to support his preference for short poems. His words suggest that one of the books was a collection of short poems, while the other, "the big woman," was not. Hermesianax of Colophon, a fourth-century elegist, tells us that Mimnermus loved a girl called Nanno. Five of the extant fragments (4W, 5W, 8W, 9W, 12W) are cited from the *Nanno*. Callimachus' distaste for the poem he cites suggests that it was a long work on a single subject, and one might expect the subject to be Nanno. But the five fragments of the *Nanno* are on different subjects, and it is difficult to discover a unifying theme. The supposition that Callimachus is contrasting the styles of the two books is equally unhelpful: 1W and 2W, not cited as from the *Nanno*, seem indistinguishable in style from 5W, which is ascribed to that poem. If we suppose 1W and 2W in fact to be from *Nanno*, and *Nanno* to be a single long poem, the problem becomes more difficult still: how could paragraphs on the themes of 1W, 2W, and 5W all occur in the same poem? As individual poems, they are acceptable as different treatments of the same theme. And if there are only two books—an untitled collection of short pieces and the *Nanno*—in which are we to place the *Smyrneïs*? For the *Smyrneïs* is hardly a short poem itself, and its theme is surely unsuitable to Nanno.

Callimachus writes of ἡ μεγάλη γυνή with disfavor. Possibly the adjective in attributive position contrasts "the big woman" with "the little woman." *Smyrneïs* too is feminine, and indeed a possible form of woman's name in Greece. Can it be that ἡ Σμυρνηῖς is "the big woman," while Nanno, possibly named in the first poem of the collection, gave her name to the collection of short poems?

In later antiquity, Mimnermus' fame, like that of Archilochus, rested on only one aspect of his work. Archilochus' bitter invective is the subject of most references. Mimnermus is treated as almost exclusively a love poet obsessed by the fleetingness of youth. The first six fragments, which include those discussed here, have this theme; but in addition to the warlike and historical subjects already mentioned, he also wrote poems with mythological themes.

Of the life and times of Mimnermus little is known with certainty. It is a pleasure to turn to the poems, some of the most beautiful of extant early elegy.

Of the 84 lines of Mimnermus whose ending can be ascertained, 43 are hexameters, 41 are pentameters. Forty-nine are end-stopped; but 15 of these are the last lines of poems or fragments. Our text of Mimnermus, like that of all the poets in this book except the *Theognidea*, depends on quotations in other writers, and one can rarely be certain that the poem, or the sentence, ended with the last extant line. (In the case of Mimnermus 12W and 14W, it is certain that the poem did not end at the end of the quotation, since both fragments end with a hexameter; and in the case of 14W one can be certain that the sentence did not end at line 11.) Of the remaining lines, 34 are end-stopped, 35 not, and there are 39 stops at other positions: figures which in themselves suggest a considerable fluency of composition within the structure of the couplet.[1]

Once again, the number of lines preserved is too small to furnish significant statistics. The following figures merely quantify what appears in Mimnermus' extant lines and facilitate comparison with what may be read in the extant lines of the other early elegists.

Mimnermus' 43 hexameter endings comprise 1 monosyllabic final word (2.3%), 21 disyllabic (48.8%), 15 trisyllabic (34.9%), 4 quadrisyllabic (9.3%), and 2 pentesyllabic final words (4.7%). The proportion of disyllabic endings is unusually high in this small sample.[2] Mimnermus' 41 pentameters exhibit 13 disyllabic (31.7%), 7 trisyllabic (17.07%), 15 quadrisyllabic (36.59%), and 6 pentesyllabic endings (14.63%). There is a complete absence of heptasyllables and hexasyllables, but otherwise Mimnermus shows an apparent preference for longer final words in the pentameter than do the other poets so far studied.[3]

Mimnermus' hexameters furnish 13 penthemimeral caesurae at H7 (30.2%), 23 trochaic at H9 (53.5%), and 2 hephthemimeral at H10 (4.7%), in addition to five lines which could be read with the major caesura at either H7 or H10 (11.6%).[4] The last-mentioned type of line, in which the word between H7 and H10 occupies a pivotal position, seems characteristic of Mimnermus' style.

Mimnermus 1W

> τίς δὲ βίος, τί δὲ τερπνὸν ἄτερ χρυσῆς Ἀφροδίτης;
> τεθναίην, ὅτε μοι μηκέτι ταῦτα μέλοι,
> κρυπταδίη φιλότης καὶ μείλιχα δῶρα καὶ εὐνή,
> οἷ' ἥβης ἄνθεα γίνεται ἁρπαλέα
> 5 ἀνδράσιν ἠδὲ γυναιξίν· ἐπεὶ δ' ὀδυνηρὸν ἐπέλθῃ
> γῆρας, ὅ τ' αἰσχρὸν ὁμῶς καὶ κακὸν ἄνδρα τιθεῖ,
> αἰεί μιν φρένας ἀμφὶ κακαὶ τείρουσι μέριμναι,
> οὐδ' αὐγὰς προσορῶν τέρπεται ἠελίου,
> ἀλλ' ἐχθρὸς μὲν παισίν, ἀτίμαστος δὲ γυναιξίν·
> 10 οὕτως ἀργαλέον γῆρας ἔθηκε θεός.

What life is there, what is pleasant, without golden Aphrodite? May I die when these things are no longer of concern to me: secret love, and gentle gifts, and bed, such things as become pleasing flowers of youth for men and women; but when painful old age comes, which makes a man both ugly and inferior alike, ever do grievous worries distress the mind, and a man takes no delight in seeing the rays of the sun, but is hateful to boys, and of no account in women's eyes. So grievous has the god made old age.

These ten lines could stand as a satisfactory poem in themselves, but there is no scholarly agreement that they in fact constitute a complete poem.[5] The themes of youth and love, age and woe, are juxtaposed and contrasted. Broadly speaking, up to 5(H8) youth and love are the subject, with the remainder devoted to old age and woe; but 1 and 2 bring the alternative to youth and love vividly before the mind. 2 indicates either that Mimnermus was still young when he composed 1W or that he is still writing from the point of view of a young man. If one considered this poem in isolation, the absence of any attempt to match a slower rhythm to age and woe (particularly in 5 and 6) might suggest the argument that Mimnermus, despite the emotional language, was indeed young—that he was contemplating the horrors of old age from a distance and was not entirely involved emotionally. But we have already studied poems in which the combination of dactyls and woe can have no such explanation;[6] and the ear needs respite whether the subject matter changes or not.

Eight of the ten lines are end-stopped: a higher proportion than in some other Mimnerman poems or fragments, or in Callinus 1W or even in Tyrtaeus 11W;[7] but Mimnermus is a much more fluent composer of elegiacs than is Tyrtaeus. There are five stops within the line: at H4 in 1, where the comma separates the two questions, at P4 in 2, at H8 in 5, where the preceding pentameter is enjambed, at P2 in 6 after an enjambed hexameter, and at H8 in 9. There is variety here, and it is not sought merely for its own sake.

1–2. In 1, the two brief interrogative expressions, made more urgent by the omission of ἐστι, occupy the line up to the trochaic caesura. The slight pause there emphasizes the parallelism of the two four-syllable questions, each to be filled out by the contents of the second half of the line. In 2, τεθναίην is powerfully emphasized. The three long syllables contrast with the predominantly dactylic couplet; the metrically equivalent length (choriamb for molossus) and the similar position of τίς δὲ βίος and τεθναίην are combined with contrast of meter and sense; and the word is highlighted by the comparatively rare pause at P4 (7.52%, as shown in Table 3). The remainder of 2 is colorless, and the sense suits the dying fall of the second hemiepes. The lack of color serves a purpose: it lowers the tension, to contrast with the rush of vigorous words that will carry the poem on to the trochaic caesura of 5. The sense of 2 prepares for this effect: ταῦτα, which must refer forward, arouses curiosity in the mind. The couplet is not self-contained, despite the final comma. (One might contrast many similarly stopped Tyrtaean couplets.)[8]

3–5(H8). The sentence which began with τεθναίην is complete in sense at the end of 3. But when the movement of the elegiac couplet is thus reversed,[9] the imperfect cadence of the hexameter is intensified. The mind is alert for whatever follows, be it in the same sentence or a new one. But when 4 is enjambed, ἀνδράσιν ἠδὲ γυναιξίν may appear otiose and bathetic, for the sense is complete at the end of the hexameter: we know that Mimnermus is not concerned with the amatory exploits of sheep or pigeons. Mimnermus has an evident motive for the enjambment of 4. A new theme begins at 5(H9); and we have already noted the elegists' practice, which is particularly common in extant Mimnermus,[10] of beginning new themes elsewhere than at the beginning of a hexameter. Such composition produces a double effect, for in two ways it runs counter to the usual movement of the elegiac couplet: the absence of the customary pause at the end of the pentameter, closely followed by a heavy pause where it is less expected, gives to the end of the sentence an enhanced feeling of finality, appropriate to the end of one theme; and beginning a sentence close to the imperfect cadence of the end of the hexameter produces a particularly strong feeling that a fresh start is being made. Such a device well suits a change of theme.[11]

A poet determined to begin a new theme after the caesura of the hexameter may be constrained to compose a "filler" to produce a sufficiently long preceding sentence (Adkins 1977a, 82). But is ἀνδράσιν ἠδὲ γυναιξίν a mere "filler," and would a Greek of the period have found 4 complete in sense? Other early usages (*Odyssey* 8. 163–64, Tyrtaeus 11W. 17, *Theognidea* 1353W)[12] show that ἁρπαλέος can be used absolutely; but, like other adjectives which express similar qualities ("attractive," "repellent," "sweet," "bitter"), it readily takes an attendant dative. There would be a reasonable expectation that a dative might follow. Nor are the words in the dative necessarily otiose. Extant Mimnermus is not so evidently hortatory as are the extant remains of some other early elegists; but Mimnermus 1W may be not simply elegiac lamentation for the fleeting joys of youth but also an attempt either to win over some particular recipient of the poem by hinting that she, too, will grow old or to create a climate more generally favorable to Mimnermus' advances by the same warning. (Like more recent popular songs, the poem could also be used by others for the same purpose.)[13] "Gather ye rosebuds while ye may," in fact. If so, γυναιξίν is well placed for emphasis. The emphatic positioning of ἥβης (4) points the hint; and amorous persuasion may be present in the similar emphasis given to κρυπταδίη. A mere description of the joys of "golden Aphrodite" would not be confined to illicit love. Mimnermus' open generalization in 3–5 is an expression of his aspirations, not a mere statement of fact.

οἷ' ἥβης ἄνθεα (4) is emphasized also by its spondaic rhythm in a largely dactylic sentence. The occurrence of ἄνθεα and ἁρπαλέα in the same line (and the reading seems certain) must appear awkward; but we do not know precisely how the words were pronounced in Mimnermus' day and dialect.

5(H9)–6. With ἐπεὶ δ' ὀδυνηρόν the second theme of the poem begins. ὀδυνηρὸν ἐπέλθῃ γῆρας would be an excellent expression in prose, with the more vivid words, in agreement with one another, set at beginning and end to bind the phrase together. Its position in the elegiac couplet greatly enhances the effect: ὀδυνηρόν, the first nonstructural word in its clause, immediately and emphatically characterizes the second theme, while γῆρας, enjambed, the first word in its line and followed by a rare pause at P2 (3.1%, as shown in Table 3), identifies the theme with similar emphasis.[14] The remainder of 6 states in simple language that old age renders a man at once ugly and inferior,[15] a sentiment well suited to its position in the couplet.

7–9. The sense is incomplete at the end of 6. Lines 5–6 contain two subordinate clauses, and the mind awaits the main clause. In fact there are three main clauses (7, 8, 9) followed by an independent main clause (10). The remainder of the poem is entirely paratactic, each clause being allotted one line (9 introduces a minor variant, in that there are two phrases linked by μέν and δέ). Such composition may be reminiscent of Tyrtaeus; but Mimnermus displays more art than the preceding comments might suggest. Of the two subordinate clauses of 5–6, the first makes the point that old age is painful, the second, that it renders a man ugly and unvalued. Of the three main clauses, 7 and 8 expand the idea of painfulness and express two aspects of it, while 9 more briefly expresses the notion of being unvalued, again in two ways.[16] There is an elegance here which is not found in Tyrtaeus.

In 7, the spondaic word αἰεί derives emphasis both from meter, as the first spondee since the diaeresis of 4, and from position, as first word both of its line and of the first main clause. Its emphasis is merited: Mimnermus' generalizations in these lines have no exceptions. The sentence could end at the end of 7; but at the end of an elegiac hexameter the mind expects more to follow. The effect is similar to that in 3. At the end of 8, however, there is a feeling of finality, and the sentence seems complete. (I shall discuss the effect of 8 later.) But there is nothing bathetic or anticlimactic in 9, with two strong phrases balanced about the caesura and reflecting the structure of what is said. 9 is a rhetorically effective dicolon, with the longer phrase after the shorter, a quadrisyllabic adjective following a disyllabic adjective, and a trisyllabic noun following a disyllabic noun.

10. In evaluating 10, tastes differ. The last sentence ended at the imperfect cadence of 9: the mind is alert. If 10 was indeed the last line of the poem, a modern reader may expect a strong conclusion. Bowra indeed terms 10 "a short, damning summary" (1938a, 19); but even the most slow-witted of readers must have realized by the time 10 was reached that old age is grievous. However, much in early and classical Greek literature suggests that the Greeks found quiet endings to their taste in many literary genres.[17] But perhaps more can be said. The first line of the poem ends with the name of a goddess; the last word of the poem is θεός. One divine power gives all life's pleasures, another takes them away.[18] The effect is analogous to ring composition.[19] So viewed, it gives a satisfactory frame to what, with Campbell (1967, 224), I believe to be probably a complete poem.

To seek Homeric allusions in Mimnermus may appear absurd: his extant poetry is hardly heroic. However, discussion of Archilochus, Callinus, and Tyrtaeus has suggested that reinforcement of Homeric values, though one, is not necessarily the only use of such allusions. The vocabulary of Mimnermus 1W is certainly Homeric, with the exception of two or three adjectives: ὀδυνηρός and ἀτίμαστος are not found in Homer, and τερπνός has only one doubtful occurrence (*Odyssey* 8. 45).[20]

χρυσῆς Ἀφροδίτης is a Homeric formula (*Iliad* 3. 64, *Odyssey* 4. 14), and it is frequently supposed that adjectives in formulae make little impression on the mind. But "golden" is neither the only nor the most common adjective used of Aphrodite in Homer, and Mimnermus' adjectives rarely seem otiose or thoughtlessly chosen. Given its full value, the word evokes vivid visual images, contrasting sharply with those evoked by the gloomy adjectives of 5–6, and may resonate with "the rays of the sun" of 8 (which is itself a Homeric phrase): love is still bright and golden, the sun still shines, but the aged remain sunk in their woes. Again, the brightness of Aphrodite may be counterpointed against the secrecy of the love, with its suggestion of darkness, and "golden" might link the pleasures of Aphrodite with the giving of gifts (if this be the sense of μείλιχα δῶρα; but see below). Even though they are a formula, the words "golden Aphrodite" may have their full poetic value, and they may also trigger an allusion.

3. κρυπταδίη φιλότης, given great emphasis by position in this poem, occurs in Homer once only (*Iliad* 6. 161), in the well-known speech of Glaucus to Diomedes (6. 145–211), to the beginning of which Mimnermus certainly alludes in 2W. The Homeric context is Anteia's unsuccessful attempt to seduce Bellerophon. Mimnermus has no desire to emulate Bellerophon: Bellerophon almost died for refusing to engage in illicit love (6. 168–90), whereas Mimnermus prays for death when he can no longer do so. He cannot be resorting to allusion to reinforce attitudes; but, as the foregoing contrast may suggest, allusion may have other uses. μείλιχα δῶρα occurs in the tenth *Homeric Hymn*, a six-line hymn to Aphrodite which cannot be dated and might be later than Mimnermus 1W. However, the first three lines are

100   Chapter Five

> Κυπρογενῆ Κυθέρειαν ἀείσομαι, ἥ τε βροτοῖσι
> μείλιχα δῶρα δίδωσιν, ἐφ' ἱμερτῷ δὲ προσώπῳ
> αἰεὶ μειδιάει καὶ ἐφ' ἱμερτὸν θέει ἄνθος.

Here μείλιχα δῶρα are evidently the pleasures of sex; and ἄνθος, which occurs only four times in the Homeric corpus in a figurative sense, appears in the next line, as in Mimnermus' poem. Furthermore, one of the two occurrences of "golden Aphrodite" in Homer is *Iliad* 3. 64, μή μοι δῶρ' ἐρατὰ πρόφερε χρυσῆς Ἀφροδίτης. Paris is here adjuring Hector not to reproach him for possessing "the lovely gifts of golden Aphrodite," evidently (*Iliad* 3. 39, 44, 55–65) his physical beauty, which Hector contrasts with Paris' lack of warlike prowess. Paris adds that Aphrodite's gifts are not to be cast away but that no one would choose to possess them.

The use of δῶρα in *Iliad* 3. 64 and μείλιχα δῶρα itself may indicate the sense which the phrase had for Mimnermus and his original audience. μείλιχα δῶρα might be the gifts with which Mimnermus was wont to break down resistance in young women or boys. But if we take Mimnermus precisely at his word, both men and women received these gifts in youth; and by the time a boy was old enough to be termed ἀνήρ, he would not be likely to be the recipient,[21] though he would be far from the end of youth in Mimnermus' sense. Again, Mimnermus is unlikely to be characterizing youth solely from the point of view of the beloved, to the exclusion of the lover. True, Mimnermus might have taken pleasure, if not in the giving, in the hoped-for result; but the phrase so interpreted hardly seems to merit such prominence. In the light of the possible allusion—which at least illustrates early Greek linguistic usage—it seems likely that μείλιχα δῶρα in an erotic context referred to the pleasures[22] bestowed on mankind by Aphrodite. In that case, all three phrases[23] in 3 refer to erotic delights. The line is a rhetorical tricolon, unusual in that the units are arranged in descending order of length.

χρυσῆς Ἀφροδίτης, κρυπταδίη φιλότης, and (if the tenth *Homeric Hymn* is earlier) μείλιχα δῶρα seem to indicate a fairly complex process of reminiscence and possibly allusion. (Even if the tenth *Hymn* is later, the lines are routine and formulaic: it seems likely that the phrase was current in hexameter poetry concerned with Aphrodite.) The collocation of χρυσῆς Ἀφροδίτης and δῶρα in Mimnermus might in itself suffice to recall Paris' speech. If such was Mimnermus' intention, the values of the source are again rejected: Mimnermus wishes to lose his youthful beauty as little as he wishes to be a Bellerophon.

4. ἥβης ἄνθος occurs in *Iliad* 13. 484. Treated as an allusion, it reinforces the effect of the foregoing; for in Homer Idomeneus is expressing fear at the approach of Aeneas, who is a mightly slayer of men in battle, καὶ δ' ἔχει ἥβης ἄνθος, ὅτε κράτος ἐστὶ μέγιστον. For Mimnermus, the flower of youth is not the strength that renders a man a great warrior.[24] Remembering Bellerophon and Paris, one might begin to suspect that Mimnermus is doing it on purpose.

The sentiments of Mimnermus 1W are un-Homeric in their emphases. The Homeric hero enjoys sex when—indeed, whenever—he can get it; but his τιμή, his status and property, take precedence (Adkins 1960b). Achilles does not regard Briseis as merely animate τιμή (*Iliad* 9. 342); but it is as ἄτιμος (*Iliad* 1. 171; 9. 646–48) that he quarrels with Agamemnon. Again, Odysseus kills the suitors not only because they had wooed Penelope while he was—contrary to their belief (*Odyssey* 2. 96)—still alive, but because they had attacked his *oikos* and consumed his possessions (*Odyssey* 18. 143–44; 24. 454–60). However, one should not overemphasize the change: Mimnermus 1W is entirely concerned with amorous relationships and beauty and with the manner in which old age mars all and turns it sour;[25] but Mimnermus 2W. 11–12 shows that Mimnermus is lamenting not only the loss of beauty and sexual opportunity. Other aspects of life do matter to him, but amorous relationships have been thrust into the foreground. The allusions would serve to point the contrast, and their concentration in the first four lines of the poem enables each to reinforce the rest.[26]

Mimnermus 5W

αὐτίκα μοι κατὰ μὲν χροιὴν ῥέει ἄσπετος ἱδρώς,
πτοιῶμαι δ' ἐσορῶν ἄνθος ὁμηλικίης
τερπνὸν ὁμῶς καὶ καλόν· ἐπὶ πλέον ὤφελεν εἶναι·
ἀλλ' ὀλιγοχρόνιον γίνεται ὥσπερ ὄναρ
5   ἥβη τιμήεσσα· τὸ δ' ἀργαλέον καὶ ἄμορφον
γῆρας ὑπὲρ κεφαλῆς αὐτίχ' ὑπερκρέμαται,
ἐχθρὸν ὁμῶς καὶ ἄτιμον, ὅ τ' ἄγνωστον τιθεῖ ἄνδρα,
βλάπτει δ' ὀφθαλμοὺς καὶ νόον ἀμφιχυθέν.

All at once abundant sweat flows over my skin, and I tremble as I look upon the flower of my contemporaries, delightful and beautiful alike. Would that it lasted longer! But glorious youth is as fleeting as a dream. Over one's head forthwith is hanging old age, grievous and ugly, hateful and dishonored alike, which makes a man unknown and, poured around, hampers the eyes and the mind.

This poem poses an immediate problem similar to that of Tyrtaeus 4W. Lines 1–6 appear in Theognis manuscripts as 1017–22 of that poet. Lines 4–8 are quoted by Stobaeus (4. 50. 68) "from Mimnermus' *Nanno*"; but lines 1–3 are nowhere ascribed to Mimnermus, and his authorship has been doubted[27]— unjustifiably, as I shall argue below.

If *Nanno* was a single long poem, 5W cannot be a complete work; but the lines are at least a complete paragraph, and there is no connecting particle in 1. Of the eight lines, five are end-stopped by West; but those editors who place no stop at the end of 6 make the structure of the poem clearer. The lines consist of four flowing units, freely and fluently composed in the structure of the couplet, ending at εἶναι in 3, at τιμήεσσα in 5 (H8), at ἄτιμον in 7 (H8), and at ἀμφιχυθέν in 8. The three stops within the line all occur at the trochaic caesura of the hexameter; and if the comma at the end of 6 is deleted, all occur after enjambed pentameters. This fact may suggest monotony. But the rhythm of the half-line preceding the caesura is different in each case; three successive pentameters enjambed to the trochaic caesura are less monotonous than a series of end-stopped couplets; and the similarity of phrase length in two cases proves to be deliberate.

Once again, Mimnermus does not link dactyls with youth and joy, spondees with age and gloom. 4 and 6 are entirely dactylic; and while dactyls well portray the fleetingness of a dream, they have no obvious link with the picture of old age suspended over one's head in 6, a line also preceded and followed by dactylic half-lines. As usual, the choice between dactyls and spondees, where significant and not consequent on other aesthetic decisions, may have a variety of goals.

1–3. Little in 5W could be claimed as allusive, but the general Homeric associations of Mimnermus' language contribute much to the poem. Sweat in Homer flows as a result of exertions in battle or games, pain felt at wounds, or similar causes. ἄσπετος is defined by *LSJ* 1968 as "*unspeakable, unutterable*: mostly in the sense of *unspeakably great.*" It is used of the αἰθήρ (*Iliad* 8. 558), the stream of Ocean (*Iliad* 18. 403), the earth (*Iliad* 19. 61), the sea (*Odyssey* 5. 101). Menelaus' wealth, when termed ἄσπετα (*Odyssey* 4. 75), is compared with that of Zeus. When blood is termed ἄσπετον in *Odyssey* 22. 407, it is that of all the dead suitors; and the ἄσπετος ἀλκή of *Iliad* 16. 157 belongs to a number of wolves, indefinitely large but fit to be compared with the Myrmidons. ἄσπετος ἱδρώς is a prodigious amount of sweat for one individual, and we have not been told why he is sweating.

πτοιῶμαι occurs only once in Homer (*Odyssey* 22. 298): Athena held up her aegis, and the suitors' φρένες ἐπτοίηθεν.[28] The word expresses intense emotion. Something has affected Mimnermus as powerfully as the sight of the aegis affected the suitors and, since ἱδρώς in Homer is never ἄσπετος, perhaps more powerfully than any exertion described in the epics.

χροιή too occurs only once in Homer, referring to Hera's divinely soft and delicate skin when she is preparing for the deception of Zeus (*Iliad* 14. 164). χρώς too is used of women; but if χροιή were used exclusively of soft skin, Mimnermus would be hinting at his unwarlike nature[29] and possibly at the unwarlike reason for his sweating and alarm. However, χροιή is not so restricted in later Greek, at all events.[30]

Up to πτοιῶμαι, Mimnermus' readers are likely to be in suspense, and probably misled, over the reason for his excitement. The suspense is not resolved at the end of the pentameter. Simply "seeing the flower of one's contemporaries" does not explain the intensity of πτοιῶμαι. To feel an emotional bond with one's contemporaries is Homeric. Tros beseeches Achilles to spare him, ὁμηλικίην ἐλεήσας (*Iliad* 20. 465). The plea is unsuccessful but cannot be nonsensical, even when the contemporaries are fighting on opposite sides in a war. In *Odyssey* 3. 362–64 the disguised Athena says that among Telemachus' companions "he" alone is older: the rest are younger, all the ὁμηλικίη of Telemachus, who are following him out of φιλότης. Odysseus (*Odyssey* 22. 208–9) appeals to "Mentor" for help as a coeval: ὁμηλικίη δέ μοί ἐσσι. The bond is familiar: the excitement and alarm are most likely to be occasioned by some disaster threatening one's contemporaries, and ἄνθος ὁμηλικίης calls to mind their fighting strength (above, p. 100). (There is a disaster—old age; but Mimnermus does not yet reveal this.)

The sense is not yet complete; but the adjectives τερπνὸν ὁμῶς καὶ καλόν are neither what is expected nor self-explanatory. We have here novelty and enigma, sufficient to give poetic pleasure and to keep the mind eager to know the answer but not sufficient to obscure the development of Mimnermus' thought. The close of the hexameter is not a mere "filler" but a necessary resolution of the puzzle. (The full effect of τερπνὸν ὁμῶς καὶ καλόν is not apparent until line 7.)

The dynamics of the elegiac couplet enhance the effect. The lines are closely bound together: μέν in 1 points forward to δέ in 2, and 2, being incomplete in sense, carries the mind on to the next couplet, giving the usual emphasis to the enjambed adjectives. Imperfect cadence highlights ἄσπετος ἱδρώς in 1, position and molossus rhythm do the same for πτοιῶμαι in 2; and the two benefit from juxtaposition.

ἐπὶ πλέον ὤφελεν εἶναι derives its effect from contrast: it is the only simple expression in a poem loaded with vivid adjectives, nouns, and verbs. It draws attention to itself thereby and also gives a brief respite. (ἐπεί is the usual reading, but, as West points out [1974, 162], πλέον εἶναι is not Greek for "last longer." But his objection to ἐπεί on grounds of sense—that "it is not awareness of its impermanence that makes young beauty potent"—seems mistaken in the light of Homeric usage. Mimnermus' sweat and emotional disturbance are not the result simply of erotic ardor: anxiety and dread are intermingled. In general, early Greek words for emotions correlate badly with ours [Adkins 1969b].)

4–5(H8). ὀλιγοχρόνιος occurs here first in extant Greek. Mimnermus may well have coined it for this line, where the emphasis due to position is enhanced by its polysyllabic rhetorical weight. (Note again the contrast with ἐπὶ πλέον ὤφελεν εἶναι). The word merits its emphasis: it expresses the pivotal idea of the poem. ὄναρ is frequent in Homer; but the fleetingness of dreams is not singled out.[31]

τιμήεις is used in Homer of persons who gain, or already have, possessions which confer status, or it is used of the possessions themselves. We have already observed Callinus (1W. 6) transferring this glittering adjective to the action of fighting for one's country (above, p. 62). Mimnermus now applies it to youth, in an extension perhaps less startling but poetically effective. It is not that youth brings gifts but that youth itself is a status-conferring gift. To have youth is to have status and prestige. ἥβη τιμήεσσα receives great and appropriate emphasis from its position after the enjambed pentameter.

5(H9)–7(H8). After ἥβη τιμήεσσα, overrun to the third hexameter of this eight-line paragraph, Mimnermus embarks upon the second contrasted theme, which is carefully counterpointed against the first. Compare the manner in which he overruns the pentameter to the important ἀνδράσιν ἠδὲ γυναιξίν in 1W. 5 and the important οὔτ' ἀγαθόν in 2W. 5, on each occasion beginning the second, gloomy, theme of his poem immediately afterward. Though other elegiac poets produce similar effects,[32] this seems to be a favorite Mimnerman device. There can be little doubt that 4–8, at least, are by the same poet as Mimnermus 1W and 2W.

ἀργαλέον in 5 is Homeric. Mimnermus uses it with γῆρας also in 2W. 6. ἄμορφον and ὑπερκρέμαται occur here first in extant Greek. The latter, effective also as a weighty pentesyllabic ending, is a striking new metaphor; the picture of old age hanging over the heads of the young as they enjoy themselves curiously prefigures the condition of Damocles feasting with a sword suspended over his head by a single hair (Cicero, *Tusculan Disputations* 5. 21. 61). We are likely to be reminded of Tantalus too; but the stone suspended over his head seems to be attested first in Pindar, *Olympians* 1. 57. (There is no suggestion of it in *Odyssey* 11. 582–92.)

The verbal patterns and tensions of this poem are unusually complex. ἥβη, the first word of 5, well balances and contrasts with γῆρας at the beginning of 6. ἀργαλέον καὶ ἄμορφον, which introduce the second theme, are well counterpointed against τιμήεσσα in the same line and also against τερπνὸν . . . καὶ καλόν in 3. (ἄμορφον may have been coined to furnish a contrary for καλόν with appropriate metrical value.) The phrase ἐχθρὸν ὁμῶς καὶ ἄτιμον by its position in the poem (third line in the quatrain devoted to the theme in which they occur) and in its line (extending to the H8 caesura) exactly balances τερπνὸν ὁμῶς καὶ καλόν, a balance which is emphasized by the appearance of ὁμῶς in each phrase. (ἐχθρὸν ὁμῶς καὶ ἄτιμον is not merely structurally balanced with τερπνὸν ὁμῶς καὶ καλόν but is also opposed in meaning to τιμήεσσα in the intervening hexameter.)

It was presumably a desire for these contrasts and balances which induced Mimnermus to load γῆρας with four adjectives. The effect may seem excessive to some modern tastes; but we should remember that ποικιλία—complexity of surface texture[33]—was evidently admired in early Greek art.

Since τερπνὸν ὁμῶς καὶ καλόν is an essential part of 1–3, the fact that it can be linked in different ways with two phrases in 4–8 must indicate that 1–3 and 4–8 are part of the same poem; and the compositional resemblance of the theme change at 5W. 5 with those at 1W. 5 and 2W. 5 indicates that 5W is by the same author as 1W and 2W.

7(H9)–8. All the words are Homeric, but there are no Homeric allusions. Homeric usage, however, may throw some light on Mimnermus' meaning.

In the usual interpretation, 8 says that old age renders one blind and witless, "sans teeth, sans eyes, sans nose, sans everything." The change of subject is abrupt. In 1–3, Mimnermus is concerned with his own response to the youth of others. In 4–7 he is concerned almost exclusively[34] with the response of others to the aged. This poem, unlike 1W and 2W, has had little to say thus far about the sensations of being old or young oneself, and the first of the two parallel adjectival clauses which close these lines is similarly concerned with the attitude of others.

Mimnermus may simply have changed the point of view in 8. However, his language will bear a different interpretation. In Homeric Greek, βλάπτειν means not "to hurt" but "to hinder, hamper" (*LSJ* 1968, s.v., mng. I), and the phrase for "to render invisible" is "to pour air (or mist) around."[35] There are two occurrences of ἄγνωστος in Homer (*Odyssey* 2. 175 and 13. 189–91). The latter passage runs:

περὶ γὰρ θεὸς ἠέρα χεῦε
Παλλὰς Ἀθηναίη, κούρη Διός, ὄφρα μιν αὐτὸν
ἄγνωστον τεύξειε.

Athena poured air/mist round Odysseus to make him ἄγνωστος: she placed a tenuous material substance between him and any possible observer. There is nothing nonmaterial in the Homeric world: old age itself must be a tenuous material substance.[36]

Now consider 6–8. Old age hangs over the heads of those who are not yet old. It makes a man ἄγνωστος, and it hampers the eyes and the νόος—a word which in Homer combines the idea of vision with that of recognizing what is seen (von Fritz 1943)—when poured around. ἀμφιχυθέν could be construed with γῆρας either in both relative clauses or only in the second; *Odyssey* 13. 191 suggests that Mimnermus may well have intended it with both clauses and that the eyes and νόος are those of the observer, not of the old man.[37] In 5W Mimnermus' theme is loss of sexual attraction, which may well occur before one's dotage. In this case, there is no abrupt change of standpoint in 8, which becomes a vivid continuation in Homeric terms of the thought of 7.

Mimnermus composes with fluency and sensitivity, using all the resources of the elegiac couplet. His choice and positioning of words is skillful, and he draws on connotations established by the Homeric poems to produce new and striking effects. His poetry of love and youth, old age and woe, is in sharp contrast with the Homeric poems and expresses feelings which are novel in extant Greek poetry. If he used Homeric allusions in the manner suggested here to confront his world with Homer's, his apparently simple and emotionally direct poems sometimes possess a greater subtlety than has been supposed.

6
SOLON

Solon is the first Athenian poet of whom we know anything. (On the question of what we know, see Lefkowitz 1981, 40–48.) But it was probably not as a poet but as a statesman-lawgiver and moralist that he was primarily revered by the Athenians, and by other Greeks, of the fifth and fourth centuries, as is indicated by his—fictitious—confrontation with Croesus in Herodotus 1. 29–33. References to him in fourth-century Athenian oratory also point in this direction. He was archon at Athens in 594/3 B.C. and was later given full powers to revise the laws and constitution of Athens. Much of his poetry is related to the social, political, and economic crisis of his day, of which it was presumably the most important contemporary document: Aristotle in his *Constitution of Athens* (5–12) seems to have little other source material for the period. In consequence, later scholars, like Aristotle, have combed the extant works of Solon for factual information about the problems of the day, Solon's solutions, and sometimes Solon's political philosophy. Some of the poems do make statements about Solon's own actions; but poets, politicians, moralists, and lawgivers—and Solon was all of these—may use language for other purposes than the making of simple declarative utterances. Solon is a much more subtle user of language than is sometimes supposed, as I will argue in my discussion of poem 4W.

West (1972) ascribes to Solon twenty-nine elegiac poems or fragments of poems, ranging in length from one hexameter (17W, 28W) or pentameter (7W, 18W) to seventy-six lines (13W). Of these poems, two (15W and 24W) and part of a third (6W. 3–4), comprising eight couplets in all, are found also in the Theognid corpus. None of these poems is discussed in detail in this book; they are included in the general figures for both Solon and the *Theognidea*.

The twenty-nine poems include 218 lines, of which 108 are hexameters, 110 pentameters. The long fourth poem has three lacunae: the sixth and seventh hexameter and the fourteenth pentameter are missing (see below, p. 111). The twentieth poem begins with a pentameter supplied by West. Since the line is a quotation from Mimnermus (6W. 2) on which Solon is commenting, the supplement is certain. Though the line is a Mimnerman composition, it is here reckoned also with Solon's lines.

Since more than a hundred of his elegiac couplets are extant, the figures for Solon would furnish rather more reliable statistical conclusions than the figures for the other poets discussed so far; but I employ them here merely to draw attention to observable qualitative differences between Solon, other early elegists, and Homer.

Of Solon's 218 lines, 146 are end-stopped. Of these, 28 are last lines of poems (including one-line fragments). Poem 17W does not end at a stop. There are only 76 stops within the lines. These figures do not suggest a poet who composes elegiac paragraphs with the fluency of an Archilochus or Mimnermus.

Solon's 108 hexameters have 2 monosyllabic endings (1.85%), 38 disyllabic (35.19%), 48 trisyllabic (44.44%), 11 quadrisyllabic (10.19%), 8 pentesyllabic (7.41%), and 1 dispondaic word (0.93%). These figures are very close to the overall percentages for our elegists, as shown in Table 6, except that Solon, like Tyrtaeus, has more than twice the overall percentage (3.44) of pentesyllabic final words. Solon ends 2 of the 110 pentameters in monosyllables (1.81%), 28 in disyllables (25.45%), 29 in trisyllables (26.36%), 32 in quadrisyllables (29.09%), 15 in pentesyllables (13.64%), and 4 in hexasyllables (3.64%). The percentage of quadrisyllables is much higher than in the general elegiac sample (18.12%; see Table 7); a difference certainly perceptible in performance to a sensitive ear.

The hexameters have 38 caesurae at H7 (35.19%), 53 at H8 (49.07%), 14 at H10 (12.96%), and 3 which could be read with the major caesura at either H7 or H10 (2.78%): figures very close to the overall figures for elegy and Homer shown in Table 4.

Solon 4W

<blockquote>
ἡμετέρη δὲ πόλις κατὰ μὲν Διὸς οὔποτ' ὀλεῖται
αἶσαν καὶ μακάρων θεῶν φρένας ἀθανάτων·
τοίη γὰρ μεγάθυμος ἐπίσκοπος ὀβριμοπάτρη
Παλλὰς Ἀθηναίη χεῖρας ὕπερθεν ἔχει·
5 αὐτοὶ δὲ φθείρειν μεγάλην πόλιν ἀφραδίῃσιν
ἀστοὶ βούλονται χρήμασι πειθόμενοι,
δήμου θ' ἡγεμόνων ἄδικος νόος, οἷσιν ἑτοῖμον
ὕβριος ἐκ μεγάλης ἄλγεα πολλὰ παθεῖν·
</blockquote>

οὐ γὰρ ἐπίστανται κατέχειν κόρον οὐδὲ παρούσας
10   εὐφροσύνας κοσμεῖν δαιτὸς ἐν ἡσυχίῃ

. . . .

πλουτέουσιν δ' ἀδίκοις ἔργμασι πειθόμενοι

. . . .

οὔθ' ἱερῶν κτεάνων οὔτέ τι δημοσίων
φειδόμενοι κλέπτουσιν ἀφαρπαγῇ ἄλλοθεν ἄλλος,
οὐδὲ φυλάσσονται σεμνὰ Δίκης θέμεθλα,
15   ἣ σιγῶσα σύνοιδε τὰ γιγνόμενα πρό τ' ἐόντα,
τῷ δὲ χρόνῳ πάντως ἦλθ' ἀποτεισομένη,
τοῦτ' ἤδη πάσῃ πόλει ἔρχεται ἕλκος ἄφυκτον,
ἐς δὲ κακὴν ταχέως ἤλυθε δουλοσύνην,
ἣ στάσιν ἔμφυλον πόλεμόν θ' εὕδοντ' ἐπεγείρει,
20   ὃς πολλῶν ἐρατὴν ὤλεσεν ἡλικίην·
ἐκ γὰρ δυσμενέων ταχέως πολυήρατον ἄστυ
τρύχεται ἐν συνόδοις τοῖς ἀδικέουσι φίλους.
ταῦτα μὲν ἐν δήμῳ στρέφεται κακά· τῶν δὲ πενιχρῶν
ἱκνέονται πολλοὶ γαῖαν ἐς ἀλλοδαπὴν
25   πραθέντες δεσμοῖσί τ' ἀεικελίοισι δεθέντες

. . . .

οὕτω δημόσιον κακὸν ἔρχεται οἴκαδ' ἑκάστῳ,
αὔλειοι δ' ἔτ' ἔχειν οὐκ ἐθέλουσι θύραι,
ὑψηλὸν δ' ὑπὲρ ἕρκος ὑπέρθορεν, εὗρε δὲ πάντως,
εἰ καί τις φεύγων ἐν μυχῷ ᾖ θαλάμου.
30   ταῦτα διδάξαι θυμὸς Ἀθηναίους με κελεύει,
ὡς κακὰ πλεῖστα πόλει Δυσνομίη παρέχει·
Εὐνομίη δ' εὔκοσμα καὶ ἄρτια πάντ' ἀποφαίνει,
καὶ θαμὰ τοῖς ἀδίκοις ἀμφιτίθησι πέδας·
τραχέα λειαίνει, παύει κόρον, ὕβριν ἀμαυροῖ,
35   αὐαίνει δ' ἄτης ἄνθεα φυόμενα,
εὐθύνει δὲ δίκας σκολιάς, ὑπερήφανά τ' ἔργα
πραΰνει· παύει δ' ἔργα διχοστασίης,
παύει δ' ἀργαλέης ἔριδος χόλον, ἔστι δ' ὑπ' αὐτῆς
πάντα κατ' ἀνθρώπους ἄρτια καὶ πινυτά.

Our polis will never perish in accordance with the apportionment of Zeus and the intentions of the blessed immortal gods; for such a great-hearted guardian, she of the mighty father, Pallas Athena, holds her hands in protection over it. The citizens themselves, persuaded by wealth(?), are willing to destroy a mighty polis by their follies, and the mind of the leaders of the people is unjust. For the leaders it is prepared that they should suffer many griefs as a result of their great hubris. For they do not know how to restrain the excesses sprung from satiety or how to discipline in peaceful quiet the present merriments of the feast(?).... They grow wealthy, relying on unjust deeds.... Sparing neither sacred nor public property, they steal by snatching, one from one source, one from another, nor do they reverence the august abode where Justice is set(?), who in silence knows what is happening and what has occurred in the past, and who in time, at all events, comes to exact requital.

This is now coming(?) to the whole(?) polis as(?) an inescapable wound(?), and it comes(?) swiftly to grievous slavery(?), which(?) stirs up stasis among the people and sleeping (civil?) war, which destroys the lovely prime of many. For by the action of enemies a(?) much-beloved polis is swiftly brought to hardship in meetings(?) by those who wrong their friends. These woes go to and fro(?) in the land(?); and of the poor many come(?) to another land, sold and bound in unseemly fetters.... Thus a woe of the (common?) people comes home to each individual, and the courtyard gates are no longer willing to keep it out, but it leaps over the high fence and finds a man nonetheless, even if he is in flight in the recesses of his chamber.

These things my heart bids me tell the Athenians: that Dusnomia causes most woes to a polis. Eunomia shows forth everything orderly and appropriate and often puts shackles on the unjust; she makes the rough smooth, ends the insolence of satiety, dims hubris, and dries up the flourishing blossoms of infatuation, straightens crooked judgments, and tames proud deeds; she ends the deeds of civic conflict, ends the wrath of grievous strife; and all things are appropriate and prudent among men under her rule.

We owe our possession of this poem (which, after 13W, is the longest of Solon's extant poems) to Demosthenes (19. 254–56). It has been treated as evidence for Athenian history or early political theory, but Demosthenes quotes it as testimony for the attitude Solon would take to Aeschines. This book is not primarily concerned with Greek history or political theory; but if we are to see the poem clearly, it is necessary to discuss briefly the questions which have been raised.[1] Most historians now grant not merely that specific details of Solon's political program are absent from the extant fragments but that no poem of Solon contained such details; for otherwise Aristotle and Plutarch would have quoted them (so, for example, Woodhouse 1938, 10–16). But it is still assumed that in 4W Solon's goal was to expound all or part of his political philosophy with as much clarity as possible. Whether or not Solon had a political philosophy, he was a practicing politician; and even practicing politicians who possess political philosophies do not use language publicly solely to give dispassionate expositions of their theories.

In reading 4W, two things are particularly important: to recall that it was composed for performance (and that the ear of the hearer cannot leap ahead,

Solon 111

as can the eye on the written or printed page) and to establish the associations possessed by Solon's words in the sixth century rather than the associations that similar words may possess for us after two and a half millennia of political philosophy.

The manuscripts of Demosthenes[2] have three lacunae of at least one line each: two hexameters (after 10 and 11) and one pentameter (after 25). The extant lines have enjambment after the hexameter on nine occasions (1, 3, 5, 7, 9, 21, 23, 36, and 38) out of the nineteen possible. There can be no certainty about 25, but the sentence might well have ended at δεθέντες. With this possible exception, however, no hexameter ends with a heavier stop than a comma. Between the couplets there is enjambment after 12 and 24 (two out of eighteen possibilities);[3] comma after 6, 14, 16, 18, 27, 35, and 37 (seven out of eighteen); raised stop after 2, 4, 8, 20, 31, and 33 (six out of eighteen); and full stop after 22, 29, and at the end. As punctuated by West, the lines consist of three long sentences: 1–22, 23–29, and 30–39. West prints no stop at the end of 25, but some stop heavier than a comma must have occurred in the line or lines between the extant 25 and 26.

Marks of punctuation within the line occur only in 7, 23, 28, 34 (*bis*), 36, 37, and 38: eight in seven of the thirty-nine lines, five of them in a passage of five lines (34–38). Static analysis in itself suggests that Solon is composing differently in different parts of his poem. (Note also the clustering of the enjambed hexameters, enumerated above.) For most of the poem this analysis suggests composition by the couplet: nine of the nineteen hexameters have enjambment, but only one (36) is enjambed to a stop within the following line. Four (7, 23, 36, and 38) have the familiar punctuation at H12 bucolic diaeresis before the enjambment. Two other lines (28 and 34) have punctuation at H12 without a following enjambment, and two are punctuated at the major caesura: at H7 in 34 and at H10 in 36. In Solon 4W, with the exception of the raised stop at P4 in 37, all marks of punctuation within the line occur either at bucolic diaeresis or at major caesura.

1–2. Despite δέ, Solon's poem may have begun here.[4] However, ἡμετέρη, strongly emphasized in initial position, might well have served to contrast Athens with some less fortunate city or cities, which perished because their deities were unable or unwilling to defend them: Troy,[5] or any of the Mycenean Greek cities which no longer existed in Solon's day, might have been the subject of a preceding section of the poem.[6]

Line 1 begins strongly. ἡμετέρη πόλις was a powerfully emotive phrase for any polis-dweller of the archaic or classical periods. His freedom, status, and possessions, possibly his life itself, depended on the continued existence of his polis; and with that continued existence the actions of deities were believed to be closely linked. In 2, αἶσαν is emphasized by its position at the beginning of the line, by its spondaic rhythm in an otherwise dactylic couplet, and by the long hyperbaton from κατά: the hearer has been waiting for the word governed by the preposition for half a line. (φρένας may derive some prominence from its grammatical parallelism with αἶσαν, but it is in a weak position both in its phrase and in the couplet.) To emphasize αἶσα at the expense of Διός and to speak of the φρένες of the immortal gods is, at least rhetorically,[7] different from ascribing the cause to Zeus and the gods. The hearer will wonder why Solon has expressed himself thus and will be alert for his explanation.

3–4. When verse is spoken, position and meter may lend emphasis to short and otherwise inconspicuous words. Here the eye may pass lightly over τοίη γάρ, but the ear will not miss the initial sequence of three long syllables counterpointed against the three long dactylic words which complete the line. The grounds for the inference, and the quality of the protectress, are highlighted. μεγάθυμος is used of warriors and whole nations in Homer and Hesiod; and, of Athena herself, it is used twice in the *Odyssey* (8. 520; 13. 121). ἐπίσκοπος is used of the gods as "watchers over compacts" (*Iliad* 22. 255) and of tutelary deities in particular, but *LSJ* (1968) cite no earlier example than this passage. It is used of a human guardian of a city in *Iliad* 24. 729, in a passage which Solon evidently does not wish to recall, for it refers to the dead Hector. ὀβριμοπάτρη is always used of Athena in Homer and Hesiod (*Iliad* 5. 747, *Theogony* 587, etc.). Παλλὰς 'Αθηναίη is no surprise, but the name of their own polis-goddess could never be bathetic for an Athenian audience. The adjectives are strong, in effective contrast with the routine μακάρων and ἀθανάτων of 2; but ὀβριμοπάτρη may seem an odd choice. The daughter of a mighty sire is presumably herself powerful; but unless she is *more* powerful than Zeus (which even the most patriotic Athenian might be chary of asserting), Zeus's might seems *prima facie* an inappropriate theme at this point.

Solon now solves some of the problems he has set. Thus far the second couplet has vividly presented the power of Athena, which is great if not supreme, as one long subject phrase. After the pause at P7 the mind is eager to know what Athena will do. The next word, χεῖρας, derives prominence from the eagerness and explains the emphasis in αἶσαν. Athena, even if less powerful than Zeus, is offering actual physical help,[8] in contrast with what ought to happen and the mere intentions of other deities. Even human beings may go against αἶσα (*Iliad* 16. 780; 17. 321); and gods certainly may, though it seems that they ought not to (*Iliad* 16. 441–43; 22. 179–81; Adkins 1960a, 17–22). But the "ought" is weaker than the claims of ἀρετή, and it is the ἀρετή of the protector that Athena is to exercise on behalf of Athens.⁹ Solon does not say that it is αἶσα that Athens be destroyed or that other deities have hostile intent; but even if it were the case, Athena would effectively protect her city.

5–6. Though the second couplet resolved some perplexities, the hearer must still wonder why Solon is uttering these lines. Solon immediately makes his accusation and solves the enigma. In the first sequence of five long syllables in the poem, he says "selves (subject) . . . to destroy." In the context, "selves"—not "they themselves," for "we" or "you" could follow—must refer to the citizens. The pentameter drives the accusation home with five more long syllables: "citizens are willing." That the remainder of the couplet is dactylic both emphasizes the spondaic words and connects them in the mind as the most closely linked parts of the sentence. No word in the couplet is wasted, and the rather uncommon[10] pentesyllabic ending draws attention to ἀφραδίῃσι; but the spondaic words are the more prominent. The architecture of 1–6 is carefully designed.

The content of 6, however, may appear puzzling. How would a sixth-century audience have received βούλονται? Note the word order: "[they them]-selves–to destroy–a mighty polis–through their folly–the citizens–are willing." μέλλουσιν, of the same metrical value as βούλονται, might be expected; but βούλονται characterizes the results of the citizens' actions as not merely likely but voluntarily accepted. The word order suggests that βούλονται is surprising; but it is not so surprising in sixth-century Athens as it is to the modern reader, for in 26–29 Solon finds it necessary to argue that individual prosperity cannot survive civic disaster. The polis is a relatively new institution: powerful inhabitants might be willing to allow it to perish provided that their own *oikoi*, and those of their friends, were safe.[11] The rest of 6 is ambiguous: ἀστοί might denote the whole citizen body or a restricted group: "the nobles," "the prominent citizens."[12] Similarly, depending on the interpretation of ἀστοί, χρήμασι πειθόμενοι might mean "persuaded by (someone else's) great wealth" or "relying on, trusting in, being persuaded by (their own) great wealth." If 4W is a treatise in political theory, such ambiguity is a sign of inferior exposition; but if the poem is a political speech, designed to persuade, to strike two relevant targets with one expression is excellent rhetoric.

In denying divine responsibility for a particular occurrence, Solon is not innovating. Already in *Odyssey* 1. 33–34, Zeus complains that men wrongfully blame the gods (Jaeger 1926, 73):

ἐξ ἡμέων γάρ φασι κάκ᾽ ἔμμεναι· οἱ δὲ καὶ αὐτοὶ
σφῇσιν ἀτασθαλίῃσιν ὑπὲρ μόρον ἄλγε᾽ ἔχουσιν.

He instances Aegisthus, who seduced Clytemnestra and killed Agamemnon ὑπὲρ μόρον, though the gods sent Hermes to warn him that there would be τίσις from Orestes. It might have been Aegisthus' μόρος, a synonym for μοῖρα or αἶσα, to do what he did; but it was not. Later in the same book (*Odyssey* 1. 48–62) Athena asks why Odysseus is suffering on Calypso's island, though he always gave due sacrifice when at Troy; Zeus explains that Poseidon is angry with Odysseus because he blinded Poseidon's son Polyphemus. Here we have, closely juxtaposed, a woe resulting not from αἶσα but from the willfulness of a human being, and a woe caused by the intention of a particular deity. In *Odyssey* 1. 33–34, compare αὐτοί with αὐτοί in Solon 4W. 5, ἀτασθαλίῃσιν with ἀφραδίῃσιν in 4W. 5, and ὑπὲρ μόρον with κατὰ . . . Διὸς οὔποτ' . . . αἶσαν in 4W. 1–3. There are other similar passages in Homer.

Up to this point in the unfolding of his poem, Solon has said nothing novel. He has not created a world free from divine interference, in which laws or regularities of political science may function undistorted. In general, divine φρένες and αἶσα still have their role to play in the world. Nor has Solon made it clear that even Athens at that time was an area in which explanations invoking the supernatural were barred. Consistency in such matters is not to be expected in the sixth century, and the αἶσα of Zeus and the φρένες of the gods do not necessarily exhaust all possible sources of divine interference.

7–8. δήμου is emphasized, as the sole spondee in a dactylic couplet. After the vague but strong rhetoric of 6, δήμου θ' ἡγεμόνων had more precise reference for Solon's audience. The "leaders of the people" are presumably themselves prominent citizens, a subset of the ἀστοί, however understood, of 6.[13] The three sense groups of 7 are divided from each other by the H7 caesura and the bucolic diaeresis at H12. To begin a new clause at H12 draws attention to the words which complete the line, while enjambment and imperfect cadence keep the mind alert for the two powerful phrases, one to each hemiepes, of 8. ὕβρις hints strongly at offense given to deity, and οἷσιν ἕτοιμον means "for whom it is ready, prepared"; the closest earlier usage is *Iliad* 18. 96: αὐτίκα γάρ τοι ἔπειτα μεθ' Ἕκτορα πότμος ἑτοῖμος.

9–10. κατέχειν κόρον continues to evoke religious associations, for this is the κόρος which leads not to inaction but to ὕβρις:[14] the leaders of the people do not know how to restrain their κόρος and so will commit, or are committing, ὕβρις. Edmonds (1931) reads παρούσης for παρούσας in 9. The manuscript text makes sense and seems better poetry. With παρούσας, by the end of 9 Solon has said "the leaders of the people do not know how to restrain κόρος or the present _____." When παρούσας is reached, the hearer does not know how the sentence will develop. κόρον is evidently pejorative, and the accusative in οὐδὲ παρούσας suggests that a coordinate term, presumably another pejorative noun, governed by κατέχειν κόρον, is to follow.

εὐφροσύνας κοσμεῖν is unexpected in a rhetorically effective manner, and the phrase itself is poetically novel and creative. In Homer κοσμεῖν is used with persons and material objects: in the *Iliad*, solely of marshaling men and chariots (3. 1; 14. 379; etc.); in the *Odyssey* (7. 13), of arranging a meal—not a banquet, but a solitary meal for Nausicaa. The link with κόσμος was surely apparent; but overtones are derived from usage. Now εὐφροσύνη is used in the *Odyssey* in contexts where feasting takes place; but its etymological meaning is "merriment," not "feasting," and its Homeric and elegiac usages confirm that the Greeks so experienced the word (*Odyssey* 9. 6, Solon 26W. 2, Xenophanes 1W. 4). κοσμεῖν with such an object cannot mean merely "arranging," in a weak sense, as with Nausicaa's meal. The full sense of "order, rule, discipline" must be present. If the connotations of marshaling an army were present to the mind, the contrast with ἐν ἡσυχίῃ would give an additional piquancy to the phrase (Linforth 1919, 198–200). (Note that Solon does not highlight κοσμεῖν, as he could have done by simply transposing it and εὐφροσύνας.) For ἡσυχίη evidently does not suggest quiet disciplined behavior before battle is joined. It is indeed personalized, linked with justice and opposed implicitly to *stasis* by Pindar.[15] The unusual phrasing may be designed to highlight ἐν ἡσυχίῃ. The sense is complete at the colon diaeresis P7, and phrase end frequently occurs at P7 (at 4, 6, 8 already in this poem). The rhythm phrases δαιτός with ἐν ἡσυχίῃ; but the genitive with ἡσυχίη is usually that of separation, which makes no sense here.[16] δαιτός is preceded and followed by a pause. The prepositional phrase is highlighted by isolation, and the broken rhythm slows down the delivery of the—necessarily dactylic—second hemiepes of the pentameter. Since 10 is followed by a lacuna, it is possible that the line was enjambed and that ἐν ἡσυχίῃ was construed with a participle, perhaps elaborating the associations of κοσμεῖν, in the last hexameter. If so, the pause after δαιτός might have required a comma, and punctuation at P9 is rare indeed. (It occurs in 0.40% of all pentameters. See Table 3.)

11. The language is raised above the merely prosaic by πειθόμενοι. Solon used πειθόμενοι as recently as 6; but Greek poets seem little troubled by verbal repetitions. (There seems to be no purposive parallelism here.) πλουτέουσιν—initial molossus word in an otherwise dactylic line—has a somber emphasis. A completely dactylic preceding line would have enhanced the effect, but in the absence of context 11 cannot be adequately evaluated.

12–13. Line 12 is one of only two enjambed pentameters in this poem. The enjambment gives φειδόμενοι much greater emphasis than it would derive simply from its position as first word in 13. At first sight the emphasis seems unwarranted. The important verb in the couplet is not the negative participle but the affirmative κλέπτουσιν. The position of φειδόμενοι seems dictated by Solon's desire to write the carefully balanced 12, giving equal prominence to sacred and public property. Again, phrase end demands a pause at φειδόμενοι, and there must be some indication of line end after δημοσίων, a word whose choriambic rhythm exactly matches that of φειδόμενοι. The effect seems unpleasant to the ear, and it is virtually unparalleled in extant early elegiacs (see the Appendix).

But perhaps the effect should not be written off to Solon's ineptitude. The rhythm is so unusual that only a Greek deaf to such matters could have failed to notice it, and Solon has shown signs of metrical sensitivity already. Now 12–13 contain only one spondee; but the effect of dactyls varies with the position of word end. Three words in 12 end on a long syllable containing ω; another word is, after elision, a long monosyllable; and φειδόμενοι, in 13, maintains the pattern. After φειδόμενοι, all the words end on a short syllable. A skillful speaker, paying attention to word end, to the metrical pauses at P7 and line end, and to the sense pause after φειδόμενοι, could readily distinguish the solemn stopping rhythm, which prevails to φειδόμενοι, from the running rhythm, expressive of confused and bustling theft, of the remainder of 13. Here and in 10 we can perhaps glimpse some trace of Solon the skillful public speaker. Note that the pause after φειδόμενοι eliminates the usual effect of reversed rhythm which occurs when an enjambed pentameter is overrun without punctuation to the end of the following hexameter (above, p. 60).

14. Masaracchia (1958, 263) links θέμεθλα with θεσμός and θέσμιος and compares Aeschylus *Supplices* 708–9, τόδ' ἐν θεσμίοις Δίκας γέγραπται. θέμεθλα might suggest associations with θέμις, particularly after φυλάσσεσθαι, which is Hesiodic in the sense of "bear in mind" (*Works and Days* 263, 561—the former in a context in which a personified Dike also occurs). But θέμεθλα does not mean θεσμός: it is a metaphor here, and the literal sense of the word is unclear. *LSJ* (1968) give "the foundations, bottom, lowest part"; but in *Iliad* 14. 493 we find "he wounded him under the eyebrow through the θέμεθλα of the eye, and pushed out the eyeball; and the spear went through the eye and the muscle at the base of the neck." The phrase "pushed out the eyeball" suggests that the spear passed tangentially to the eye: "eye" in the next clause means "socket." In that case, the θέμεθλα are the muscles which hold the eye in place, here ("under the eyebrow") presumably those above the eye. Similarly, in *Iliad* 17. 47–50 a spear could hardly pass through the bottom of the trachea in delivering a neck wound;[17] and in Hesiod, *Theogony* 816 it is not clear that the Hundred-handers are at the bottom of Oceanus. In all these cases, the sense might be "what X is set in" (τίθημι): the muscles of the eye, the flesh of the neck surrounding the trachea, the surroundings of Ocean. Pindar's ἀμφὶ Παγγαίον θεμέθλοις ναιετάοντες ἔβαν (*Pythians* 4. 180) supports this interpretation: "foundations" are presumably under a mountain, and it would be difficult to live "round about them."

The metaphor is august, impressive, and, like all good metaphors, impossible to restate precisely in prosaic terms. "Foundations of justice," with or without a capital letter, besides being inaccurate as a literal rendering of θέμεθλα, introduces echoes of countless treatises on political philosophy. None had been written in the early sixth century, and Solon has offered his audience no political philosophy as yet. Still less should one render, with Linforth (1919, 200), "They have no fear of Dike, that august being upon whom, as on a rock, human society rests." He cites Pindar, *Olympians* 13. 6 ff., and Aeschylus, *Choephori* 646–47. But the sense of Aeschylus' Δίκας . . . πυθμήν is disputed, and πυθμήν is not necessarily the same metaphor as θέμεθλα; and Pindar has βάθρον πολίων ἀσφαλές, Δίκα—again a different phrase, with βάθρον, not θέμεθλα, and with πολίων, not Δίκας, as the dependent genitive. In addition, it is inappropriate to interpret an earlier text in the light of a later: the Homeric and Hesiodic examples indicate that Solon is speaking of the θέμεθλα of Justice, not of Justice as the θέμεθλα of the city.

15–16. Dike is now explicitly personalized (σιγῶσα σύνοιδε).[18] Were 1–6 intended to banish all divine activity from Athens, leaving Solon free to pursue an analysis in terms of proximate causes, 15–16 would be a contradiction. But 1–6 contained nothing novel and, as Masaracchia (1958, 258) points out, Solon is quite close to Hesiod in 15–16. In *Works and Days* 256–62 Hesiod presents the virgin goddess Dike, and in 217–18 he speaks of justice triumphing over *hubris* in the end. Hesiod's Dike complains to Zeus, whereas Solon's silently punishes on her own account; but we are in the same world of thought. (Jaeger [1926, 79] insists that Solon's language represents Justice as "die immanente Gerechtigkeit des Geschehens," but his argument rests on interpretation of later lines of the poem.) Note the prominence given to πάντως by its two long syllables in a largely dactylic couplet, and note also the rhetorical weight of the rare[19] hexasyllabic ending of the pentameter.

Thus far in 4W Solon has said little that is indubitably new, little that is precise, much that is emotive; and he has handled his meter with skill and care.

17–29. The interpretation of these lines has been much discussed: how much is general, how much particular to Athens? In the remainder of the poem, 1–14 refer to Athens, 15–16 characterize Dike generally, while 30–39 are general reflections on Dusnomia, Eunomia, and their effects. The generality of 30–39 is guaranteed by the present tenses with both Dusnomia and Eunomia: both cannot be exerting their influence on Athens at the same time, since the terms denote a prevailing state of affairs. (Dusnomia might be particular, Eunomia general; but discussion of this point depends on the interpretation of 17–29.)

In Greek poetry, the definite article need not be written: πόλις may mean "a city" or "the (this) city." In any Greek, the present tense may be either continuous and particular ("is now coming") or general ("is wont to come"), while the aorist indicative may be either a past tense or a generalizing, timeless present. In 16, ἦλθ' of Dike is certainly gnomic: to suppose that Dike had already exacted punishment would make nonsense of 1–14. The aorists of 20 and 28 seem equally gnomic, and those who (with Campbell) take ἤλυθε in 18 as "aorist with perfect sense" seem to have a particular view of Athenian events in mind. If we consider the lines not as translators but as speakers and thinkers in Greek, and if we remember the rhetorical nature of 1–16, we may come to a different view of Solon's goals here. (The question is relevant to the history of the period: if Solon is generalizing, one cannot infer that the events have occurred in Athens at this time.)

17–18. I assume that West's comma at the end of 16 is a misprint. The sequence of words in 17 could convey several messages to a Greek: "This is now coming to the whole city as an inescapable wound," "This inescapable wound is now coming upon the whole city," "This now comes to every city as an inescapable wound," "This inescapable wound now comes to every city." ἤδη is a sufficiently vague temporal adverb to permit any of these interpretations. A Greek who had heard only 1–16 would receive several messages at once. Similarly, in 18, ἤλυθε could mean either "comes" or "has come"; and, since δουλοσύνην is ambiguous, one cannot reply that the hearer would know whether slavery was present or not. "Slavery" could denote either those who had been literally sold into slavery overseas (as in Solon 36W. 8–9), or "sixth-parter" serfs (to whom there is no reference in extant Solon),[20] or the prominent citizens chafing under the rule of a tyrant (Solon 11W. 4). Different members of Solon's audience might interpret ἤλυθε and δουλοσύνην differently: as a particular description of the present or a generalized threat from which the appropriate hearers were to draw particular conclusions. Those who portray Solon as a political theorist render ἕλκος as "sore" or "sickness" resulting from the disease of injustice in the city.[21] But ἕλκος at this period is used of wounds inflicted from without by persons or animals (*Iliad* 2. 723; 4. 217; 5. 361; 11. 267; etc.). It never means "disease" or "sickness," and its first appearance in the sense of "sore" seems to be in Thucydides 2. 49. 5. Had Solon possessed such a novel theory, he would have had to explain it in detail to his contemporaries; for a sixth-century Athenian, after hearing of a personalized Justice coming to punish in 16, would have interpreted "comes" and "wound" in a familiar sense.

19–20. ἥ in 19 might agree with either πόλις or δουλοσύνην (Linforth [1919] records varied interpretations). It is usually taken with the latter: social injustice suffered by the poor stirs up—generally, or is doing so in the present case—sleeping stasis and (civil?) war. Historical parallels abound; but when the poor were dissatisfied with Solon's reforms, they did not resort to stasis. The threat remains an effective one; but the change of subject in 18 brings the idea of πόλις into the hearer's mind once again. Understand ἥ with πόλις, and the sense is "the city which stirs up stasis . . . swiftly comes to slavery (under a tyrant)": a fate suffered by Athens in Solon's lifetime, when Pisistratus apparently championed the cause of the poor in a conflict between himself and other powerful citizens.[22] The language enables Solon to express two relevant threats with one set of words. The sense of 20 is clear: ὤλεσεν must be gnomic. In 17–20, note the portentous weight of the five long syllables which begin 17, the dactyls of 18 which echo the gallop to slavery, and the emphasis given by their long syllables to ἔμφυλον and εὕδοντ' in 19.

21–22. The manuscript text of 22 gives no sense: τοῖς ἀδικοῦσι φίλοις. Bergk reads φίλαις, West φίλους, but without comment.[23] The other phrases in the lines are more important for the present interpretation. πόλεμον in 19 was ambiguous: civil or external war? Now Solon begins a new couplet with the vague and threatening ἐκ γὰρ δυσμενέων: civil or external enemies? Masaracchia (1958, 265) insists that ἐν συνόδοις (22) must mean "in associations," which limits the reference to civil war. This is the earliest extant occurrence of the word. It may not be a Solonian coinage, but it may have had no precise usage; and in fact σύνοδος is later used of the hostile meeting of armies (*LSJ* 1968, s.v., mng. I.5). More importantly, ἐν συνόδοις does not occur until 22. The general notion of "war" has been planted in the minds of the audience in 19; and 21 means "For by enemies (unspecified) swiftly a (our?) much-beloved city . . . ." Even if the message were clarified in 22, the emotive rhetorical effect of the broader, vaguer threats of 19 and 21 would not be canceled. Those who treat Solon 4W as political theory rest great weight on τρύχεται. Linforth (1919, 204) writes: "The figure of disease, which was first suggested by ἕλκος ἄφυκτον, is still in the poet's mind. τρύχεται is often used of a physical decline." Later, certainly; but, unlike σύνοδος, τρύχεσθαι has a well-established usage at this period. It denotes material hardship in Homer and Hesiod (*Odyssey* 10. 177 and 17. 387; *Works and Days*, 305); it is used several times of the effect that the suitors are having on the household of Odysseus (*Odyssey* 1. 248; 16. 125; etc.). Mimnermus (2W. 12) uses τρυχοῦσθαι similarly, and not with disease, which occurs a few lines later (2W. 15). After the ὕβρις, εὐφροσύνη, and banquets of 8–10, τρύχεσθαι might recall the suitors, but it would not recall disease. "A person τρύχεται by disease" would be comprehensible; but where the standard expression is "a household τρύχεται by the actions of a person," how could Solon's contemporaries interpret "a city τρύχεται by enemies" other than in the familiar sense?

23–25. Solon sums up the preceding six lines by ταῦτα μὲν ἐν δήμῳ στρέφεται κακά—a complete clause, followed by a heavy stop, ending at the bucolic diaeresis and neatly enclosed by ταῦτα and κακά in agreement. We may suppose that the sense is limpidly clear: δήμου in 7 apparently meant "the common people," and so we may take it here. But 17–22 delivered different messages to different hearers; and, since ἐν δήμῳ in early Greek may mean "in the land" (*Iliad* 16. 437; 20. 385; etc.), the clause is ambiguous. (Note how the long syllables of ἐν δήμῳ highlight the phrase.) The new clause beginning at H12 receives the usual benefits of enjambment and imperfect cadence: τῶν δὲ πενιχρῶν is emphasized, and attention is also focused on the following line, with its gloomy spondaic first hemiepes. 24 does not entirely resolve the ambiguity. If δέ is taken as a strong adversative, contrast requires that τῶν δὲ πενιχρῶν does not refer to the same group as ἐν δήμῳ, which is then contrasted with γαῖαν ἐς ἀλλοδαπήν, and the sense is "in the country." With a weak δέ—virtually "and" (Denniston 1954, 162)—τῶν δὲ πενιχρῶν might merely carry on the sense of ἐν δήμῳ; but ταῦτα (23) must refer to the confused messages of 17–22, some of which favor one sense of ἐν δήμῳ, some the other. Solon may also be contrasting στρέφεται, of motion within an area, the beloved land of Attica, with ἱκνέονται, motion to another place. ἱκνέονται personalizes the κακά (Linforth 1919, 204). The spondaic rhythm of ἱκνέονται πολλοί well suits the gloomy implications of the phrase. 25 shows that Solon can be direct when it suits his rhetorical purposes. After an enjambed pentameter the line has great emphasis; and the rare four-word[24] hexameter which follows, every word damning in a society in which freedom was a key value and slavery an ever-present possibility, takes every advantage of the situation: "sold–and in chains–shameful–bound." Again, as in 24, note the initial molossus word and the sequence of five long syllables.

There is a lacuna after 25. One manuscript (Cod. Matrit. 4562, f. 113) has παίκακα (presumably for πάγκακα) δουλοσύνης ζυγὰ φέρουσι βίᾳ: a line which, though not impossible, has endeared itself to few editors. The line makes a point which the audience must have taken by this time; but other elegiac poets similarly restate the obvious (compare Mimnermus 1W. 10), and δουλοσύνη, ζυγόν, and βία are all powerfully emotive words. If δημόσιον κακόν (26) is intended to refer unequivocally to ἐν δήμῳ κακά (23), to introduce another use of κακόν (or πάγκακον) here confuses the development of thought; but we have seen that 23, like much of 17–25, is itself not unequivocal.

26–29. δημόσιον κακόν may not be unequivocal either. The primary meaning is "public, common" as opposed to "personal, household"; but its overtones might echo any use of δῆμος in a suitable context, and, since 17 at least, Solon has been using language ambiguously. He begins 26 with οὕτω, another vague link (compare τοῦτ' in 17, ταῦτα in 23, ταῦτα in 30). Unless the lacuna is of several lines, the adjacent subject matter refers to the woes of the poor, and πάγκακα would emphasize the point. The audience then has the opportunity to understand δημόσιον κακόν as "a woe of the common people," and, despite ἑκάστῳ, Solon is really talking once again to the wealthy and prominent; for the poor are not likely to suppose that their households can withstand a civic disaster, and their houses are unlikely to have had courtyard gates, high fences, and remote recesses and even less likely to have had gates, fences, and recesses to which Homeric language could appropriately be applied.[25] Solon is not simply contrasting public and private good in a sense familiar to us. In 27, αὔλειοι and θύραι in agreement neatly enclose the line. ἐθέλουσι furnishes another surprise: the gates do not wish to keep out the woe. *LSJ* (1968) assert that οὐκ ἐθέλω is virtually equivalent to οὐ δύναμαι, but their examples do not bear out the claim;[26] and even if lexicographers frequently ignore connotation, users of a language do not. With either meaning, the sequence of thought is not quite logical. One might suppose that the gates do not wish, or are unable, to keep out the woe either because they open to let it through or because the woe jumps over them. (If the woe can jump, presumably the gates can have wishes.) But the woe jumps over the high fence. The wishes of the gates are consequently irrelevant, and it is the fence which is unable to protect its owner. As so frequently since 17, Solon is more concerned to present an emotive image than to offer reasoned exposition. He now produces another vivid picture, of the woe tracking the man down as he flees to the innermost part of his house. Note the effective repetition of sound in ὑψηλὸν δ' ὑπὲρ ἕρκος ὑπέρθορεν. The molossus word ὑψηλόν emphasizes height and therefore presumed difficulty—a difficulty immediately denied by the tripping dactyls, in which every word ends in a short syllable. The spondaic first hemiepes of 29 furnishes an effective contrast and might express the difficulty of flight before the nimble and swift-footed woe. ὑπὲρ ἕρκος ὑπέρθορεν most resembles ὑπέρθορον ἑρκίον αὐλῆς (*Iliad* 9. 476), where Bellerophon is escaping, but in general 26–29 recall the imagery of the Homeric similes in which a lion attacks domestic animals in the fold (e.g., *Iliad* 5.136–42). There is no question of allusion; but to portray the κακόν as a living creature leaping over a wall links it with the traditional and familiar. Had Solon wished to portray social injustice as a pervasive disease, 26–29 would have furnished an excellent opportunity to treat it as such in an extended metaphor.

Thus ends the more ambiguous part of Solon 4W. Those readers who grant the ambiguities but ascribe them to ineptitude are referred to Solon 9W, 11W, and 36W, where he treats similar subject matter with clarity.

30–31. The couplet begins with another vague demonstrative. ταῦτα might refer to 1–29 or to 17–29. The pronoun presumably refers back, since 1–29 are certainly concerned with διδάσκειν and Δυσνομίη. Jaeger claimed (1926, 76–77) that θυμὸς . . . με κελεύει expressed Solon's independence of divinely revealed truth of the Hesiodic or Homeric kind; but Masaracchia (1958, 266) justly observes that the words are a Homeric formula.[27] ὥς presumably means "how." Dusnomia and Eunomia have received much discussion. Ehrenberg (1930), appropriately arguing against νόμος in the sense of "law" at this period, considers the various uses of νέμω and the resulting possible senses of "Wohlregiertheit," "Wohlverteiltheit," and "Wohlgeordnetheit." He excludes "Wohlverteiltheit," but μοῖρα is a central concept of early Greek religious and moral/political thought, and μοῖραι, "shares," are the result of allocation, νέμειν.[28] In archaic and early Greece, the universe, the household, and the polis are conceived of as divided into shares, and one's position in the system is one's μοῖρα (Adkins, 1960a, 1972b, 1982a). Since "share" is equated with "due share," the value system favors the status quo. It has been noted that *eunomia* seems to be a conservative political catchword. The term does not describe any particular state of affairs: Tyrtaeus' Eunomia is very different from Solon's. It evaluates the state of affairs to which it is ascribed as one in which the shares are appropriate. And therein lies its value as a political catchword: who could possibly claim to be against Eunomia?

32-39. In these lines Solon rises to poetical, or at all events rhetorical, heights for which nothing so far has prepared us. (It should be noted that nothing very factual is said.) In 34-39, the words are carefully placed (Jaeger 1926, 82-83). παύει κόρον reverses the order (object-verb) of τραχέα λειαίνει and is followed by a further reverse in ὕβριν ἀμαυροῖ. Since each clause consists of two words only, the contrasted words are inevitably juxtaposed. The next three clauses are longer. All have the contrasted words at the beginning and end of the clause: αὐαίνει . . . φυόμενα, εὐθύνει . . . σκολιάς, ὑπερήφανα . . . πραΰνει, with less emphatic words in less prominent positions. παύει (34) is general and prosaic, ἀμαυροῖ vividly metaphorical but not the specifically appropriate verb for ὕβριν; but the other verbs and objects, as far as πραΰνει in 37, produce sustained metaphors. The clauses are skillfully positioned in the couplets and use the meter purposively. αὐαίνει in 35 (which continues the pattern of reversed word orders of 34), εὐθύνει in 36, and πραΰνει in 37 are all molossus words in first position. Each is greatly emphasized thereby, and in performance the cumulative effect of the three successive lines would be very powerful. Note that, from λειαίνει in 34 to παύει in 38, the only short syllable in any verb is the first syllable of ἀμαυροῖ, and note also that, with the exception of ἄτης (35), all the other words are dactylic in rhythm. The verbs are highlighted. εὐθύνει and πραΰνει combine identity of position in their lines with reversed word order in their clauses, and πραΰνει is not merely the third initial molossus of the sequence but is enjambed from the hexameter. When it is realized that Solon has also arranged the order of ideas in 34-39 to match the order in which they occurred in the earlier part of the poem (Halberstadt 1955), the amount of skill that he displays here can be appreciated.[29] The strain begins to be apparent in 37. Solon is running out of words and metaphors, and he repeats παύει twice (37, 38), having already used it in 34. However, as I have already noted, the ancient Greeks were less offended than the modern reader by verbal repetitions in poetry. If 39 is the end of the poem, there may be an additional reason: Greek poems frequently close on a quieter note, and possibly also Solon wished to put a little more factual content (end of stasis, end of anger and strife) into his claims concerning the good effects produced by Eunomia.

It is inappropriate to say with Linforth (1919, 205), "In the present passage Eunomia is plainly not a person, but a rhetorical personification," for the technical term "personification" ill suits a period in which Solon himself can write, in a poem of political description (36W. 3–7),

συμμαρτυροίη ταῦτ' ἂν ἐν δίκῃ Χρόνου
μήτηρ μεγίστη δαιμόνων Ὀλυμπίων
ἄριστα, γῆ μέλαινα, τῆς ἐγώ ποτε
ὅρους ἀνεῖλον πολλαχῇ πεπηγότας,
πρόσθεν δὲ δουλεύουσα, νῦν ἐλευθέρη.

The earth of Attica is spoken of as a person in 4 and as material in which markers may be placed in 6, while 7 employs adjectives appropriate in either case. Early Greeks readily see in personal terms, and treat as deities, cultural or natural phenomena which affect their well-being (Adkins, forthcoming). If the Earth, which—to us—is patently not a person, may be so regarded, why should not Eunomia, which (or whom) no one can see at all?

My concern is to discuss Solon 4W, not Solon's political thought. Here there is no clear political theory.[30] Even Vlastos (1946, 65), whose portrayal of Solon as a political thinker is the most cautious, goes too far in saying, "Certainly, Solon thinks of justice as a divine power. But he describes its operation in Fragment 4 strictly through the observable consequences of human acts within the social order" and, further, "Solon is as correct a moralist as Hesiod. But instead of turning loose upon his audience the traditional repertoire of superstitious terrors, he makes them look at history, considering cause and effect. There is no evidence that he thinks *of* a concept of social causality; but he certainly thinks *with* one" (Vlastos' emphases). Solon certainly does not threaten plague or famine as Dike's punishment for ὕβρις; but, as I have shown, the connections of thought are unclear. (οὕτω, in 26, is particularly opaque if viewed as part of an exposition.) Solon does not state in 4W how he supposes that Dike produces the ill effects mentioned. In 13W. 17–25 he says that Zeus punishes the acquisition of wealth by ὕβρις and that the punishment of θεῶν μοῖρα may not come at once, but ἦλυθε πάντως αὖτις. (Compare ἔρχεται in 4W. 17, ἦλθ' ἀποτεισομένη in 4W. 16, and Ζεὺς / πέμψῃ τεισομένην in 13W. 75–76.) This seems far from a "naturalistic" analysis (Vlastos, 1946); and Vlastos is compelled to distinguish Solon's "political justice" (in 4W) from his "acquisitive or distributive justice" (in 13W). But the punishment of Zeus falls in 13W. 11 upon men who pursue wealth ὑφ' ὕβριος, and in 13W. 12 the wealth follows ἀδίκοις ἔργμασι πειθόμενος; in 4W. 8 the punishment of Dike falls on those who are to suffer woes ὕβριος ἐκ μεγάλης and who in 4W. 11 grow wealthy ἀδίκοις ἔργμασι πειθόμενοι. Solon has one vocabulary for both political and distributive justice: there is no reason to suppose that he had distinguished realms of political and distributive justice to which different modes of causality were relevant. ὕβρις, τίνεσθαι, and μοῖρα are everywhere relevant,[31] and δυσνομίη and εὐνομίη are drawn from the same universe of discourse. (Note that many of the good results ascribed to Εὐνομίη suit the actions of a person but not the existence of a condition of "good order," in which the bad situation would not prevail at all. We readily interpret the words as "when there is good order, men place fetters[32] on the unjust, put an end to κόρος," and so on; but we possess a prosaic vocabulary of political theory, of which these lines may be taken as a metaphorical presentation. In the sixth century there was no such vocabulary in Greece.) Solon certainly perceives the danger that comes to the polis when the citizens—the rich and the poor alike—are motivated by greed; but Homer, before this, could describe in "naturalistic" terms actions which he also ascribed to the intervention of a deity or deities, and there is no reason to suppose that Homer, or Solon, did not accept both explanations. Traditionally, one may both act oneself (αὐτός) and ascribe the act to an external agent or agents, as Agamemnon does in *Iliad* 19. 86–89.[33] Solon does not explain how Dike brings about the events in 4W. 17–29, and Agamemnon does not explain how "Zeus and Moira and the Erinys that walks in darkness" brought disaster upon him. No event in the assembly of *Iliad* 1 was there ascribed to them; apart from Athena's attempt to calm Achilles (*Iliad* 1. 194–218), divine intervention is notably absent. Once again, Solon's thought is not so novel as it may appear.

In the light of my discussion, it would be inadvisable to treat Solon 4W as a source for Athenian political history. Other Solonian poems (e.g., 11W, 36W), though lacking in detail, offer rather more opportunity to the historian, so far as concerns the broad outline of Solon's actions or political events in Athens. In 4W, however, and especially in lines 17–29, Solon is exploiting the resources of Greek to poise his utterance between the particular and the general[34] and to produce a remarkably sustained series of ambiguities. We cannot draw on other poems to resolve the problem and claim that we may eliminate the ambiguity by referring a Solonian phrase to an event known to have already happened; for it is impossible to arrange the poems in chronological order. Even if we could do so, a reading of the poem which takes the ambiguities into account will quickly demonstrate that Solon's contemporaries would have been in no better case: Solon's ambiguities are pervasive and purposeful, and they are produced by linguistic skill, not linguistic ineptitude. The poem is neither good history nor bad history; it is not history at all.

Nor is Solon 4W political theory, though it makes observations which could be worked up into a political theory. The poem is a work of rhetoric, concerned throughout to persuade by emotive language, not to convey precise information. Some of the phraseology is not new,[35] but Solon uses it, and deploys it in his meter, with great skill. Much, particularly in the last fourteen lines, seems to merit the name of poetry,[36] but it is unnecessary to dispute over the term. Solon 4W is at least a fine example of what could be achieved by an Athenian orator many decades before the invention of rhetorical theory.

Solon 27W

παῖς μὲν ἄνηβος ἐὼν ἔτι νήπιος ἕρκος ὀδόντων
  φύσας ἐκβάλλει πρῶτον ἐν ἔπτ' ἔτεσιν.
τοὺς δ' ἑτέρους ὅτε δὴ τελέσῃ θεὸς ἔπτ' ἐνιαυτούς,
  ἥβης †δὲ φάνει† σήματα γεινομένης.
5 τῇ τριτάτῃ δὲ γένειον ἀεξομένων ἔτι γυίων
  λαχνοῦται, χροιῆς ἄνθος ἀμειβομένης.
τῇ δὲ τετάρτῃ πᾶς τις ἐν ἑβδομάδι μέγ' ἄριστος
  ἰσχύν, ᾗ τ' ἄνδρες πείρατ' ἔχουσ' ἀρετῆς.
πέμπτῃ δ' ὥριον ἄνδρα γάμου μεμνημένον εἶναι
10   καὶ παίδων ζητεῖν εἰσοπίσω γενεήν.
τῇ δ' ἕκτῃ περὶ πάντα καταρτύεται νόος ἀνδρός,
  οὐδ' ἔρδειν ἔθ' ὁμῶς ἔργ' ἀπάλαμνα θέλει.
ἑπτὰ δὲ νοῦν καὶ γλῶσσαν ἐν ἑβδομάσιν μέγ' ἄριστος
  ὀκτώ τ'· ἀμφοτέρων τέσσαρα καὶ δέκ' ἔτη.
15 τῇ δ' ἐνάτῃ ἔτι μὲν δύναται, μαλακώτερα δ' αὐτοῦ
  πρὸς μεγάλην ἀρετὴν γλῶσσά τε καὶ σοφίη.
τὴν δεκάτην δ' εἴ τις τελέσας κατὰ μέτρον ἵκοιτο,
  οὐκ ἂν ἄωρος ἐὼν μοῖραν ἔχοι θανάτου.

A child, having grown a hedge of teeth while yet an infant, loses them for the first time in seven years. When the god has brought to completion the next seven years(?), he manifests(?) signs of youthful prime coming to full development. In the third ⟨seven years⟩, while the limbs are still growing, the chin becomes downy, as the skin changes its bloom. In the fourth seven years everyone is by far at his best in physical strength, which men have as the bounds(?) of human excellence. In the fifth, it is time for a man to be mindful of marriage and to seek a generation of children to come after him. In the sixth, the mind of a man is being trained for everything, and it is not equally willing any longer to do lawless(?) deeds. In seven seven-year periods and in eight he is by far at his best in mind and tongue; of both, the period is fourteen years. In the ninth, he still has ability, but his tongue and wisdom are softer in relation to great excellence. If anyone were to complete the tenth and reach its limit, he would not be unseasonable in possessing the lot of death.

This poem is preserved in Greek by Philo, Anatolius, and Clement and is referred to by Censorinus, Ambrose, and Macrobius in Latin.[37] Evidently the lines were well known, and for English readers they derive an adventitious interest from their being linked with the incomparably superior "Seven Ages of Man" speech of the melancholy Jaques (*As You Like It*, 2. 7). Solon's lines have little poetic attraction. I discuss them briefly here for contrast with the other poems discussed in this book. Readers of the early elegists sometimes suppose their choice of language to be determined solely by the exigencies of meter: a supposition which this book is intended to call into question. But in 27W Solon commits himself to dividing human life into "hebdomads," seven-year periods, and to characterizing the periods in eighteen lines, one period to a couplet, save for the seventh and eighth, which receive one couplet between them. His metrical space is cramped; and in each of the periods he must include the appropriate Greek numerals, not all of which suit the elegiac meter. In this poem Solon's choice of language is often metrically determined, and the contrast with the other poems I have discussed is evident.

The lines are composed in individual couplets, each appropriately stopped with a period. The effect is monotonous. It might be argued that the schematic nature of the subject matter demands such treatment; but the schematism was Solon's choice. Shakespeare begins only one of his seven ages at the beginning of the line ("And then the whining schoolboy . . ."); he adds, "And so he plays his part" between the fifth and sixth ages to avoid beginning the sixth at the beginning of a line.

Within Solon's couplets there is variation. Three hexameters (3, 11, 17) are stopped with commas. The other six are enjambed: to the end of the pentameter in 1–2, 9–10, and 15–16; to P4 in 5–6; to P3 in 7–8; and to P3 in 13–14. The pentameters which follow end-stopped hexameters are stopped only at line end. Of the hexameters, only 15 has a stop within the line, a comma at H10 caesura. In the enjambed hexameters the sense is incomplete at the end of the line in 1, 5, 7, and 15; in 9–10 and 13–14 the pentameter merely adds a coordinate phrase.

There are some metrical curiosities. Since the second hemiepes must be dactylic, the elegiac pentameter has only four forms: the first hemiepes may be entirely dactylic or entirely spondaic or have a spondee in either first or second position. Which form appears in any pentameter is usually governed by other aesthetic decisions, so that a table of their occurrences has a random appearance. In this poem, 4 is obelized, but the number of syllables in the manuscripts—five for the first hemiepes—suggests that what Solon wrote had a spondaic rhythm. If so, the first five pentameters have spondaic first hemiepes, the next two a dactyl in the second foot, while the last two are entirely dactylic. The pentameters have a progressively lighter rhythm from the beginning of the sixth hebdomad. The result may be accidental, for its aesthetic motive is difficult to comprehend; but if it is a deliberate effect, a further constraint upon Solon's composition is revealed. The first three hexameters are entirely dactylic, so that the first three couplets are very similar. (The major caesurae are different: H7, H10, and H8 respectively.) 15 too is entirely dactylic; and no hexameter except 9 contains more than one spondee.

Solon varies the subjects of his sentences: it is παῖς in 1–2; θεός in 3; θεός or παῖς in 4 (see below, p. 128); γένειον in 5–6; πᾶς τις in 7–8; impersonal ὥριον in 9–10; νόος ἀνδρός in 11–12; "a person" in 13–15(H10); γλῶσσά τε καὶ σοφίη in 15(H11)–16; and τις in 17–18. The composition is not artless; whether the subject matter of each hebdomad is the most appropriate is another matter.

These lines as we have them have no introduction. Some indication of the structure of what is to follow seems necessary. Contrast Jaques:

> All the world's a stage,
> And all the men and women merely players.
> They have their exits and their entrances,
> And one man in his time plays many parts,
> His acts being seven ages;

A frame of reference is created, and the first age does not begin at the beginning of the line. The frame enables Shakespeare to introduce his vividly realized portraits simply: "At first the infant . . . . And then the whining schoolboy . . . . And then the lover . . . . Then a soldier . . . . And then the justice . . . ." The syntax of the first five ages depends on "His acts being seven ages." After "and so he plays his part," the grammatical subjects are "The sixth age" and "Last scene of all." Shakespeare has a general label ("scene," "age") for each unit and a noun to identify each: "the infant," "the schoolboy," "the lover." Solon has not, and no introduction could supply them to the poem as written. But the lines we have do not even establish in the first couplet that he is speaking of the whole life of man in blocks of seven years. τοὺς ἑτέρους (3) rather points the other way, since ἕτερος is used more frequently of the second of two than of the second of a longer series. (δευτέρους is impossible metrically.) An introduction could have established these facts at least. There may have been an introduction. West believes that we have neither the first nor the last line of the poem. (18 seems an effective last line.) The absence of a connecting particle in 1 proves nothing. Solon 4W four times (17, 23, 30, 34) has no connective, and 30–39 in particular, if preserved with no context, would have the air of a complete poem. On the other hand, if there were lines briefly expressing the scope of the poem, it seems strange that Philo and Clement did not quote them. (One might argue that the introduction was already lost.) The question must be deferred to the end of this discussion.

1–2. παῖς and ἄνηβος are emphasized by position in 1, φύσας ἐκβάλλει by both position and meter (the only spondees in the couplet) in 2. Given the subject of Solon's couplet, the emphasis on the verbs seems appropriate; but it seems odd to suggest that the growing and loss of the milk teeth are the most important events of the first seven years of life. πρῶτον ἐν ἕπτ' ἔτεσιν does not suggest the *first* seven years; it suggests only that teeth are grown and lost for the first time in seven years, and it implies that Solon will now describe the growth of the second set of teeth. Indeed, the first couplet suggests that *teeth* are the subject of the entire poem. ἔτι νήπιος is probably not otiose with ἄνηβος. Both terms are vague; and Achilles (*Iliad* 9. 440) is spoken of as νήπιον, οὔ πω εἰδόθ' ὁμοιίου πολέμοιο when he set off for the Trojan War. But in juxtaposition with ἄνηβος, νήπιος suggests "infant" as against "adolescent." ἕρκος ὀδόντων, as Campbell (1967, 247) notes, is a Homeric formulaic line ending, used of the teeth as "a barrier, through which a man's words or dying breath (*Iliad* 9. 409) pass out or drugs in (*Odyssey* 10. 328)." Solon seems to use it as a metrically convenient phrase. Campbell considers the possibility of humor and rejects it, since there is no evident humor elsewhere in 27W; and grandeur seems equally absent.

3–4. After the emphases of the first couplet, the audience, on hearing τοὺς δ' ἑτέρους, is likely to think of teeth, the only masculine plural noun yet mentioned; ἕτερος regularly denotes the second of two, and the milk teeth were the subject of the preceding lines. Indeed, by reading ἐκφαίνει, found in some manuscripts, for West's obelized δὲ φάνει in 4, and then punctuating with a comma before ὅτε and another comma at the end of 3, we may give some kind of sense to the resulting main clause: "[the child] shows forth his second teeth as tokens of developing youth." The subordinate clause is then unsatisfactory: "when the god has accomplished seven years." τοὺς δ' ἑτέρους seems needed to specify that these are the second seven years. But "seven years" without τοὺς δ' ἑτέρους is no more inept than πρῶτον ἐν ἕπτ' ἔτεσιν; and in the second couplet we have to choose between infelicities. If τοὺς δ' ἑτέρους is taken with "years," the second line becomes vague and unspecific: we are not told what the σήματα are.[38] Once again, Solon is evidently cramped. (Since "teeth" is not an appropriate object for τελεῖν, "when the god has accomplished the second set [of teeth] for seven years" is an unacceptable rendering; and it is no less awkward in sense.)

5–6. τῇ τριτάτῃ begins to structure the list. Even now, the constrictions of the meter are apparent. No noun is expressed: Solon can find no room for ἑβδομάς until 7. τῇ τριτάτῃ is well placed for emphasis, as are most of the subsequent ordinals. ("Fifth" presents a slight problem, "seventh" and "eighth" an insuperable one.) If γένειον is more important than γυίων as an indicator of maturity, the word order is good: γένειον is emphasized as first word in its clause, λαχνοῦται by enjambment, hyperbaton, position in its clause, and position in its line. The word order of χροιῆς . . . ἀμειβομένης is good, with the words in agreement enclosing the phrase. The word order of phrases and clauses has pleasing variation: the genitive absolute (verb . . . noun), set within the main clause (noun . . . verb), contrasts also with the second genitive absolute (noun . . . verb). However, two genitive absolutes in one couplet are perhaps excessive. As Campbell notes (1967, 247), Hesiod (*Theogony* 492–93) has γυῖα / ηὔξετο. That the reference is there to Zeus is clearly irrelevant; and Solon hardly needs Hesiod's example to combine such a noun with such a verb. Campbell also notes the use of λάχνη in *Odyssey* 11. 320; but the verb λαχνοῦσθαι is cited only from this passage and the *Palatine Anthology* (12. 178). The coinage helps to make this couplet the most aesthetically satisfying of the poem.

7–8. μέγ' ἄριστος is a Homeric line ending (*Iliad* 16. 271), as Campbell notes (1967, 247). Solon uses it in the same position in 13. The lengthening of final iota before μ is Homeric, as in *Iliad* 6. 91, ἐνὶ μεγάρῳ. Ignorance of this fact presumably accounts for the nonsensical plurals in the manuscripts of Philo and Anatolius. The enjambed ἰσχύν, with pause after initial spondaic word, has great—and appropriate—emphasis. It prepares for the contrast with νοῦν καὶ γλῶσσαν . . . μέγ' ἄριστος in 13. The reading in the remainder of the line is uncertain. For ᾗ τ' (West), Clement manuscripts have ἤν τ', Philo manuscripts have ἤ τ' or οἵ τ', Anatolius has ἤ τ', and *Anecdota Parisina* has ᾗ τ', presumably from ᾗ τ'. Sylburg emended to ἤν τ'. For πείρατα (an emendation by Stadtmüller, accepted by West), Clement and some Philo manuscripts have σήματα, while one has μνήματα. σήματα is the best-attested, and it makes sense; and a poet who writes μέγ' ἄριστος in 7 and 13 might write σήματα in both 4 and 8. With ἤν and σήματα, an interpreter who understood ἑτέρους of teeth in 3 could argue for a progression of thought: as the second teeth are an indication of developing ἥβη, so increased strength is an indication of ἀρετή. The apposition of singular ἰσχύν, ἥν with σήματα can be paralleled: Campbell (1967, 247) compares Hesiod, *Shield of Heracles* 312–13.

9–10. Though πέμπτῃ can mean "*the* fifth" in poetry, Solon would presumably have preferred to write the article, as with all the other ordinals, had space permitted. The rest of the couplet is clear, undistinguished, and reminiscent in phraseology. μεμνημένον εἶναι recalls Hesiod (*Works and Days* 616, 641); ἐξοπίσω, in the context of one's posterity, recalls *Hymn to Venus* 104, Tyrtaeus 12W. 30, and Solon 13W. 32. There is no suggestion that Solon is consciously imitating these authors or repeating himself, merely that the expressions are humdrum and lack novelty.

11–12. καταρτύω occurs first here. ἀρτύω is Homeric, however, so the novelty is not very great. As the next couplet will make clear, καταρτύεται is a continuous present: "*is being* trained or disciplined." Campbell (1967, 248) debates the meaning of ἀπάλαμνος, considering "lawless" (*Theognidea* 281W and Pindar, *Olympians* 2. 63), "stupid" (*Theognidea* 481W), and "impossible" (cited from Hesychius). The range of use of this vague term is presumably determined here by the following couplet: ἀπάλαμνα are all the acts which one who is νοῦν καὶ γλῶσσαν ... μέγ᾽ ἄριστος will not commit.

13–14. The feminine datives ἑβδόμῃ and ὀγδόῃ will stand as dactyls with correption before a vowel; but presumably Solon was unable to produce a line of this form. The lines he has written really mean "A man is best in intellect and tongue in seven sevens and in eight": not "from the ages of forty-three to fifty-six" but "for his first forty-nine and fifty-six years," which is nonsense. νοῦν καὶ γλῶσσαν derives from its position rather less emphasis than ἰσχύν does in 8, where it too is linked with μέγ᾽ ἄριστος. A poem might be written in which the repetition of μέγ᾽ ἄριστος with contrasted accusatives of respect so placed was effective: "from twenty-one to twenty-eight, strongest; from forty-three to fifty-six, wisest." In 8, ἰσχύν made its point; but the intervening lines blur the contrast, and the treatment of νόος in the preceding couplet dilutes the effect entirely. The pentameter from P4 is not mere superfluous arithmetic: that the prime of the intellect lasts through two units of seven years is a point worth making. (Indeed, Solon has little different to say of the ninth period.) But Solon's expression is awkward and unclear.

15–16. ἐνάτῃ fits readily into the verse, and Solon uses it. The hearer may be momentarily confused by ἔτι μὲν δύναται, without subject expressed; for "years" was the subject of the preceding clause. If he correctly supplies "he" from ἄριστος in 14, and "to think and speak" from νοῦν καὶ γλῶσσαν, μαλακώτερα may again puzzle him, for the word could agree with ἔτη. (Nothing suggests that Solon in 27 has any goal other than clear exposition; puzzlement here has no function.) From αὐτοῦ, however, the couplet is elegant and clear. αὐτοῦ is comparatively uncommon in elegiacs: poets rarely expend two syllables on what is usually a colorless word, and in Greek poetry γλῶσσά τε καὶ σοφίη may readily mean "his tongue and wisdom." Here, however, even the position at imperfect cadence is warranted: αὐτοῦ signals the change of subject from the person to γλῶσσά τε καὶ σοφίη and retrospectively confirms that the subject of δύναται was personal. μαλακώτερα is well juxtaposed to δύναται for contrast. The chiastic order of ideas manifested by νοῦν καὶ γλῶσσαν . . . μέγ' ἄριστος)(πρὸς μεγάλην ἀρετὴν γλῶσσά τε καὶ σοφίη is elegant and marks off the seventh, eighth, and ninth hebdomads as a subunit within the poem.

17–18. Of the tenth hebdomad Solon has nothing to say except that at the end of it one is at an appropriate age to die. Here he contradicts his reply (Solon 20W) to Mimnermus 6W; but poets are not necessarily consistent, and in 27W Solon may be using someone else's scheme of ten hebdomads as a framework for his thought. The language of 17 is Homeric: τελέω is used of completing periods of time (*Odyssey* 10. 470); and *Iliad* 11. 225 has ἥβης . . . ἵκετο μέτρον. ἄωρος, however, occurs first here in extant Greek. Solon might have coined it to provide a first hemiepes echoing that of the first line. In each there are four words of exactly corresponding metrical values, with the sound of ἄωρος recalling ἄνηβος, and ἐών identical in each. However, ἄωρος occurs in scolia (see Page 1962, 884), so the word may have been in oral use before Solon. μοῖραν ἔχοι θανάτου resembles Solon 20W. 4, μοῖρα κίχοι θανάτου, and Callinus 1W. 15, μοῖρα κίχεν θανάτου. The second half of the pentameter is metrically inflexible, and such resemblances are to be expected.

Solon 27W is not an emotional poem. It neither celebrates nor laments the length of human life. Nor is it a poem of advice: only 9–10 suggest any course of action. The rest of the poem portrays the growth, prime, and decline of a human being as a process. It gives information, or purports to do so. The first three hebdomads treat the child merely as a growing animal without social functions, and the last ascribes no functions at all. The remainder are concerned with man as an agent in society. In the fourth hebdomad the strength necessary for physical valor is at its peak, and in the fifth a man should become a husband and father; in both, one's social contribution is physical. νόος appears in the sixth, and the audience is assured that the mind is developing during that hebdomad. In the seventh and eighth, the ability both to think and to express one's thoughts is at its peak; in the ninth, this ability is somewhat diminished.

Nowhere in 27 does Solon mention the polis. But remember that one did not become a citizen of Athens until he became an ephebe, at the age of eighteen (Aristotle, *Constitution of the Athenians* 42) and that there are complaints that in old age one is no longer listened to in public life (for that is surely the implication of *Theognidea* 173–78W) or "is nothing" (Aristophanes, *Acharnians* 681). Remember that a quality is valued as an ἀρετή in the light of the contribution that it makes to the group and that the polis is the relevant group for some purposes by the early sixth century. Recall that, in the small communities of early Greece, the begetting of children is viewed as an important contribution to the well-being, not only of the household but of the polis, and that there are evident tensions in Tyrtaeus' Sparta over the question of military service. Remember also the elaborate discussions, in a more philosophical and discursive age, of the appropriate periods of life for military service and political office (e.g., Plato, *Republic* 412A–415A, Aristotle, *Politics* 1329a2–34). Recall, finally, Solon's career as a statesman and lawgiver.

If it is viewed as a rationale for actual practice in Athens and other poleis, the abstractness of Solon's poem becomes explicable. Even had he wished, Solon could not have produced the vivid particularities of Shakespeare's Jaques; but that was not his goal. If the adolescent wants to know why he is not yet a citizen, Solon has a reply: he is not yet able to perform any useful service for the city. If the young man complains that he has to fight, and possibly that no one listens to him in the assembly, Solon can explain that too (compare Aristotle, *Politics* 1329a7–11); and so on to the end. The oldest citizens "are nothing," as the last two couplets taken together hint, because their minds and tongues no longer have any contribution to make. (Aristotle allots the priesthoods to τοὺς διὰ τὸν χρόνον ἀπειρηκότας, *Politics* 1329a31–34.) That Solon does not differentiate between the seventh and eighth hebdomads is then not the result of a deficiency of imagination: his goal is not to produce ten vivid distinct pictures. Under this interpretation, ἔτι, δύναται, and the comparative μαλακώτερα have the importance that the phrasing would suggest.

If this interpretation is correct, we can only regret that Solon invented or borrowed the scheme of hebdomads and decided to allot one couplet to each hebdomad. Possibly he thought the result would remain more readily in the memory; but the scheme is not essential to his message, and the allotment of couplets drives him to absurdities and infelicities. In respect of structure, Solon 27W resembles no other poem discussed in this book.[39] Yet even here the poet struggles against his chains: not even in this poem is it quite fair to say that the meter is writing the verses.

7
"THEOGNIS"

No one doubts the existence of a historical Theognis of Megara. He proclaims his existence in lines 22–23: Θεύγνιδός ἐστιν ἔπη / τοῦ Μεγαρέως. The *Suda* gives his *floruit* as 544–541 B.C. (On the question of date, see Jacoby 1931.) But no one supposes that all the poems in the Theognis manuscripts are by the same author: "Theognis" is in reality *Theognidea*, dated by West (1972) as seventh to fifth century B.C.

The figures which can be compiled from these poems differ in several ways from those which can be compiled from the work of the other poets studied here. The material is much more copious: more than two-thirds of the 2,017 lines of the eight early elegists are drawn from "Theognis." But the *Theognidea* in fact contain lines by an indefinitely large number of poets writing at different times. However, the intention is not to prove or disprove the authorship of any poem but merely to claim that, so far as extant elegy permits us to judge, a particular poem has an unusually high or low frequency of certain phenomena; and for that purpose the average frequencies in any of the poets—in the *Theognidea*, in the complete sample of early elegists, and in the Homer sample—have some usefulness. We need not attempt to compute the statistical probability of a sequence of five pentesyllabic hexameter endings, given the frequency of words of appropriate metrical shape in Greek; we may be assured that, given that the frequency of such hexameter endings is not greater than 5 percent and that word length is a noticeable acoustic phenomenon, a sequence of five pentesyllabic endings is a very noticeable acoustic phenomenon; and we may then inquire whether there is any possible artistic motive for its occurrence in the poem we are studying.

There is no precise scholarly agreement on the number of lines in the *Theognidea*. Some lines are repeated, some are repeated with slight variations,[1] and some poems are also ascribed to other poets.[2] These facts do not seriously affect the following percentages. The number of lines is about 1,400: more than two-thirds of extant early elegiac poetry.

Of the lines printed by West, 67.8 percent are end-stopped. If the lines are taken in consecutive blocks of 100, the percentages range between 63 and 77. Many of the poems are very short.[3] (There are some 183 single couplets and 105 quatrains: 786 lines out of about 1,400.) Only five[4] exceed twenty lines. 40.63 percent of the lines have marks of punctuation within the line.[5]

Of "Theognis'" approximately 700 hexameters, 2.11 percent end in a monosyllable, 35.81 percent in disyllables, 44.52 percent in trisyllables, 13.62 percent in quadrisyllables, and 2.95 percent in pentesyllables. These figures are for lines with dactylic fifth foot. The percentages of dispondaic and molossus endings are, respectively, 0.70 and 0.28. Of the approximately 700 pentameters, 2.11 percent end in monosyllables, 33.99 percent in disyllables, 33.00 percent in trisyllables, 15.87 percent in quadrisyllables, 12.08 percent in pentesyllables, 2.80 percent in hexasyllables, and 0.14 percent in heptasyllables.

The H7 caesura occurs in 34.41 percent of Theognid hexameters, the H8 in 50.00 percent, and the H10 in 13.20 percent. In 2.39 percent of the hexameters the line could be phrased in more than one way.

That these figures should be close to those for the elegy sample as a whole is perhaps less surprising when it is remembered that the *Theognidea* comprise more than two-thirds of that sample. But it would be unwise to conclude that mere random distribution is at work, as a study of actual examples will quickly demonstrate. Compare poem 31–36W (eight stops within the line in a poem of eight lines) with poem 131–42W (one stop within the line in a poem of ten lines), and note the appropriateness of the phrase pattern to what is being said in each case. West ascribes both poems to Theognis. If the plan of each poem is not the result of the poet's conscious intentions, his muse is serving him well. (The texts are printed above, in chapter 1.)

In the circumstances, no Theognid poem can be typical; much might be learned from a detailed comparison of the poems in the manner used in this book. Of the three poems I have elected to discuss here, the first is generally agreed to be by Theognis, the authorship of the second has been disputed, and the third is probably not by Theognis.

Theognidea 183–92W

κριοὺς μὲν καὶ ὄνους διζήμεθα Κύρνε καὶ ἵππους
εὐγενέας, καί τις βούλεται ἐξ ἀγαθῶν
185 βήσεσθαι· γῆμαι δὲ κακὴν κακοῦ οὐ μελεδαίνει
ἐσθλὸς ἀνήρ, ἤν οἱ χρήματα πολλὰ διδῷ,
οὐδὲ γυνὴ κακοῦ ἀνδρὸς ἀναίνεται εἶναι ἄκοιτις
πλουσίου, ἀλλ' ἀφνεὸν βούλεται ἀντ' ἀγαθοῦ. . . .

χρήματα μὲν τιμῶσι· καὶ ἐκ κακοῦ ἐσθλὸς ἔγημε
190 καὶ κακὸς ἐξ ἀγαθοῦ· πλοῦτος ἔμειξε γένος.
οὕτω μὴ θαύμαζε γένος Πολυπαΐδη ἀστῶν
μαυροῦσθαι· σὺν γὰρ μίσγεται ἐσθλὰ κακοῖς.

Well bred, Cyrnus, are the rams, donkeys, and horses we seek out. A man wants them to mate(?) from good stock. But a "good" man feels no care at marrying the "bad" daughter of a "bad" father if the father gives him much property, nor does a woman refuse to be the wife of a "bad" man, provided he is wealthy, but wants a rich husband rather than a "good" one. It is property that they prize: a "good" man has married the child of a "bad" one, a "bad" the child of a "good." Wealth has thrown lineage into confusion. So do not be surprised, son of Polypaus, that the lineage of the citizens is being dimmed: good things are being mingled with bad.

Most scholars assume, without giving reasons, that this is an authentic poem by Theognis of Megara. For some, the reason may be no more cogent than that the poem is addressed to Cyrnus son of Polypaus. But whatever may be meant by σφρηγίς in *Theognidea* 19W, to assume that all poems so addressed are authentic is at once to overestimate the integrity and to underestimate the ingenuity of the ancient Greek and to forget the Greek practice of ascribing one's own intellectual achievements to an admired predecessor.[6] However, Carrière (1948, 100–101) argues the point on stylistic grounds, and there seems no reason to doubt the attribution.

If this be granted, the poem may throw some light on the question whether Theognis' Megara was the polis in mainland Greece or the Sicilian polis of that name. (On the problem, see Jacoby 1931, 44–51.) Set as the first word in the poem, κριούς is very emphatic. There must have been rams in most or all poleis: not all clothing, or cloth, was imported from poleis which had an export trade in woolen goods, and garments produced for sale in the polis, and homespun and homewoven garments, must have been common everywhere (Starr 1977, 66); and cheese, which requires a breeding flock, was made from sheep's milk. However, if it is supposed that such prominence for "rams" is warranted only in a city with an important wool trade, the evidence points toward the mainland Megara as Theognis' polis. Hudson-Williams (1910, 187) notes that in Stobaeus 4. 22. 99 "rams" has been replaced by "dogs," presumably to give the line wider application (Campbell 1967, 358).

This vigorous little poem, one of the small number in the *Theognidea* whose first and last lines West (1972) supposes us to possess,[7] was evidently well known. Stobaeus quotes parts of it three times: lines 183–90 in 4. 29. 53[8] and 4. 30. 11a (on εὐγένεια and δυσγένεια, respectively), and lines 183–86 in 4. 22. 99 (on marriage).

Static analysis indicates fluency of composition. All the hexameters and one pentameter (184) are enjambed. Of the other four pentameters, one (186) is stopped with a comma, two with full stops (190, 192), and one, in West's text, with ellipsis points to indicate a lacuna (188). The stops within the lines render the fluency more apparent. 183 is overrun to a comma at P4 in 184, 184 to a raised stop at H4 in 185, and 185 to a comma at P4 in 186. 186 is the first line in the poem to end with a stop. 187 is overrun to P3 in 188. 189 has a raised stop at the H8 caesura and is then overrun to the P7 diaeresis of 190. 191 is overrun to a raised stop at P4 in 192. The units of rhythm and sense demarcated by stops are all of different lengths, except that 183 and 191 are both overrun to P4. In 184 the stop is a comma and the preceding word is a choriamb, while in 192 a molossus word is followed by a raised stop, so that even here there are differences; but, as will appear, the resemblances between the first and the last couplet seem deliberate.

183–84(P4). The mandatory pause in 183 occurs at H7, followed by sense pauses before and after the vocative at H12 and H14. Most editors mark off vocatives with commas. West (1972) does not but presumably would not deny the need in performance for a pause of comparable duration to that represented by a comma. The pause at H14 is rare (see Table 1). Only 0.19 percent of the sample of elegiac hexameters have punctuation at H14 in West. (Κύρνε occurs without punctuation at the same point in the line at 333.) There follows a pause at line end, and there is a comma after εὐγενέας. The rhythm is broken and, in one respect, very unusual. (For broken rhythm, compare *Theognidea* 191–92W, 251–52W, and 731–52W, discussed below.) The broken rhythm, whose pauses demand a slower delivery, may be counterpointed against the headlong dactyls which occur in some of the following lines. διζή-μεθα is placed after the second of its three objects. The order is unusual, the common element being usually placed at beginning, end, or after the first unit; but it is neither difficult nor bathetic here. (Contrast Xenophanes 2W. 1–6.) On the contrary, ἵππους is highlighted by unusual order, unusual pause, and incompleteness of sense at line end. The poet has used the resources of the hexameter line to give greater emphasis to the spondaic rams and horses. ὄνους is metrically lighter and in a much less prominent position. The treatment of all three animals is appropriate. The ram may be essential to the prosperity of Megara, but the donkey is a comic and ugly animal in Greek eyes, as in most. Indeed, the notion of an εὐγενής donkey is rather oxymoronic. It is the horse, an expensive weapon of war, that possesses prestige and confers it upon its owner. Theognis has chosen three very disparate domesticated animals to make the point that in all cases well-bred specimens are sought for.

εὐγενέας deserves its emphasis by position and pause, for it states Theognis' theme. Campbell (1967, 358) comments, "Note the characteristic ambivalence of εὐγενής, ἀγαθός, κακός, ἐσθλός." The usage here requires careful scrutiny. From Homer onward, ἀγαθός denotes and commends a socioeconomic group and also certain kinds of behavior expected of members of that group (Adkins 1960a, passim). It is supposed that others are not capable of the behavior—reasonably enough, for the commended behavior requires the resources possessed, at the time, only by members of the group. Just behavior is neither a necessary nor a sufficient qualification for being regarded as ἀγαθός in early Greece;[9] and one may be ἀγαθός or ἐσθλός by birth, like the suitors in the *Odyssey*, even when the other valued qualities are deficient. Theognis, as will appear, has emphasized exclusively the connotations of birth in ἀγαθός, κακός, and ἐσθλός in this poem. The usage of εὐγενής is different. In Homer the spelling is εὐηγενής, and only three examples are cited: *Iliad* 11. 427, αὐτοκασίγνητον εὐηγενέος Σώκοιο; *Iliad* 23. 81, τείχει ὕπο Τρώων εὐηγενέων ἀπολέσθαι; and *Hymn to Aphrodite* 229, εὐηγενέος τε γενείου, of Tithonus. Most editors read εὐηφενής in the *Iliad* examples. εὐηγενής, if read, would not suggest more than noble birth. The word does not occur in Hesiod or in the poets in Page 1962 and 1974, in Voigt 1971, or elsewhere in West 1972 save in a doubtful reading in Hipponax (85W. 4); and, if our poem is authentic Theognis, the Hipponax may be later. Tithonus' εὐηγενές beard is the only certain predecessor of εὐγενέας in *Theognidea* 184W. In the fifth century, εὐγενής may be used to link good behavior with good birth, as does Philoctetes in addressing Neoptolemus (Sophocles, *Philoctetes* 874–76):

> ἀλλ' εὐγενὴς γὰρ ἡ φύσις κἀξ εὐγενῶν,
> ὦ τέκνον, ἡ σή, πάντα ταῦτ' ἐν εὐχερεῖ
> ἔθου.

As the son of Achilles and grandson of Peleus and Thetis, Neoptolemus was certainly of good birth, and so, says Philoctetes, he may be expected to behave well. The suggestion that just behavior will render one εὐγενής even if one's blood is insufficiently blue does occur in the late fifth century (Euripides, Frag. 495. 40–43 Nauck):

> ἐγὼ μὲν ⟨οὖν⟩ οὐκ οἶδ' ὅτῳ σκοπεῖν χρεὼν
> τὴν εὐγένειαν· τοὺς γὰρ ἀνδρείους φύσιν
> καὶ τοὺς δικαίους τῶν κενῶν δοξασμάτων,
> κἂν ὦσι δούλων, εὐγενεστέρους λέγω.

The tone of voice and the dearth of extant parallels indicate that the attitude is unusual even in the time of Euripides.

There is no evidence to suggest that εὐγενής was used to commend good behavior rather than noble birth, or even the good behavior of those of noble birth, in Theognis' day. Indeed, in the spelling εὐγενής the word may be a

Theognid coinage, and it occurs nowhere else in the *Theognidea*. The purpose of the usage is to be sought in this poem.

Theognis has carefully arranged his lines to ensure that from the beginning his audience will think not of behavior but of springing from a good bloodline, or γένος. Rams, donkeys, and horses are not termed εὐγενεῖς in consequence of any favored behavior which they all display; the characteristic which they share is that of being descended from other good specimens of their breed (ἐξ ἀγαθῶν). Within each species, there is an appropriate excellence of behavior for a ram, a donkey, or a horse. But the emphasis is elsewhere: "Pedigree bloodstock produces offspring of good quality in domestic animals and also in men" is Theognis' message. (Xenophon agrees, according to Stobaeus 4. 29. 23. On the problems associated with Stobaeus' use of Xenophon, see Harrison 1902, 73–87.)

184(P5)–186. Campbell (1967, 358) renders τις "everyone" and compares Callinus 1W. 5. τις is there used with an imperative, and Campbell's parallels (1967, 164) are all with imperatives. The use here is in some ways similar; but τις produces a different aesthetic effect from the equally metrical πᾶς. τις is light and vague, its range of usage spanning "anyone" and "someone," the latter sometimes in a dismissive sense. On encountering τις, the hearer does not know how the sentence will develop. A message of lightness and vagueness is conveyed—appropriately, since not all stockbreeders have pedigrees as good as those of their stock. τις has a wider role also. There is a chiasmus from 184(P5)–186(P4), in which γῆμαι corresponds to βήσεσθαι (similar in sense), κακὴν κακοῦ to ἐξ ἀγαθῶν (opposed in sense), οὐ μελεδαίνει to βούλεται (similar in sense), and ἐσθλὸς ἀνήρ to τις (opposed in sense). This pattern, presented sequentially in performance, reinforces the contrast between the vague τις at the beginning and the powerful ἐσθλὸς ἀνήρ at the end. καί τις, though light and vague, is rendered immediately noticeable by its position between pauses at P4 and P7 and by its being the only spondee in 184. βήσεσθαι and γῆμαι are strongly highlighted. βήσεσθαι is overrun from the pentameter and followed by a heavy stop, while γῆμαι is at the beginning of its clause and is set (with δέ) between a heavy stop and the mandatory caesura at H7. The chiasmus enhances the effect, contrasting as sharply as possible the standards used in mating animals and arranging marriages. ἐσθλὸς ἀνήρ is emphasized also by overrun and position. ἤν οἱ χρήματα πολλὰ διδῷ is a necessary qualification: aristocrats will not seek κακαί brides unless their families are wealthy.

The situation is a new and shocking one. In Homer, and in stable aristocratic societies generally, where wealth is derived predominantly from land and land remains in the possession of the same families, wealth and good breeding inevitably accompany each other, and ἀγαθοί marry women from the households of ἀγαθοί. There is no inducement to do otherwise. In Homer, κακή is used to decry the behavior of aristocratic (ἀγαθαί) women who behave badly. Clytemnestra's behavior is contrasted with Penelope's ἀρετή, and she is termed κακή both for her unchastity and for her murder of Agamemnon (*Odyssey* 24. 193; 11. 384). Here there are no such connotations: Theognis is not claiming that a man of good family will be willing to marry a Clytemnestra if her dowry is adequate. The reference is to birth alone.

The general sense of ἐξ ἀγαθῶν βήσεσθαι is clear, but scholars have disputed over the precise meaning. Hudson-Williams (1910, 188) claims that

> [t]he parallel expression γῆμαι κτλ. requires that we should take ἐξ ἀγαθῶν as the object and not the subject of βήσ.; the subject is τοὺς κριοὺς κτλ., to be supplied from the preceding line. For βήσ. ἐξ ἀγαθ., we have an exact parallel in ἐκ κακοῦ ἐσθλὸς ἔγημεν καὶ κακὸς ἐξ ἀγαθοῦ 189, 90, ... Others explain βήσ. as passive, "wishes his ewes to be mounted by rams of goodly breed"; Camerarius construes τις ἐθέλει ἐπιβήσεσθαι ἀγαθοὺς τῶν ἀρρένων (ἐξ ἀγαθῶν ὄντας) ταῖς αὐτοῦ θήλεσι. Welcker takes βήσ. as "factitivum ut βιβάζειν," "to set his horses on."

In performance, the audience cannot be aided to understand ἐξ ἀγαθῶν βήσεσθαι by γῆμαι δὲ κακὴν κακοῦ, for they have not yet heard it. All the interpretations of ἐξ ἀγαθῶν βήσεσθαι are possible, and all reinforce Theognis' point. The original audience received a powerful, complex message, of a kind very effective in the sociopolitical rhetoric of this poem. (Garzya [1958, 167–68] also regards the ambiguity as intentional, but for rather different reasons.)

187–88. These lines are entirely dactylic to 188(P3). The descriptions of misalliances—which extend from γῆμαι in 185(H5) to ἀνήρ in 186(P4), from οὐδὲ γυνή in 187 to ἀγαθοῦ in 188, and from καὶ ἐκ κακοῦ in 189(H8) to γένος in 190—contain only two spondees. The dactyls possibly suggest a headlong rush to ruin. A sense pause is needed after οὐδὲ γυνή, however, to indicate that the following is to be taken not with γυνή but with ἄκοιτις. οὐδὲ γυνή thus echoes the rhythm of ἐσθλὸς ἀνήρ (186) and hints at once that the γυνή, too, is of good family. The overrun πλουσίου is emphasized by position and following pause; and since ἀνδρός already has an attributive adjective (κακοῦ), πλουσίου is to be understood predicatively: "provided that he is wealthy." Theognis' desire is evidently to describe the distressing situation from every point of view. 185(H5)–186 portrayed the behavior of the ἐσθλὸς ἀνήρ; 187–88 portrays that of the ἐσθλὴ γυνή in two ways, characterizing both what she does not refuse and what she wants, for rhetorical effect. (Theognis will return to the subject in the next couplet.) The two clauses are once again presented in chiastic order. The choice of expression permits the use of words of similar sense in the juxtaposed parts of the chiasmus (πλουσίου, ἀφνεόν, the latter forming part of one of the two spondees mentioned above), words of opposed sense at the extremes (κακοῦ ἀνδρός, ἀγαθοῦ). ἀντ' ἀγαθοῦ is an effective echo of ἐξ ἀγαθῶν (184), contrasting yet again the standards employed in breeding human beings and in breeding other animals.

189–90. If, with West (1972), one posits a lacuna between 188 and 189, some of Theognis' poetical or rhetorical effects must have been lost. The manuscripts of the *Theognidea* have χρήματα μέν in 189, giving no connection of thought with 188. The Stobaeus manuscripts, however (4. 29. 53; 4. 30. 11a), have χρήματα γάρ. γάρ gives perfect sense: it links χρήματα in 189 (emphasized by position) with ἀφνεόν in 188 (emphasized by meter) and, more remotely, with χρήματα in 186. Stobaeus' text is on other occasions inferior to that of the *Theognidea*. Here, however, not merely does Stobaeus' text make sense, but it is difficult to imagine what could have appeared in any intervening lines that would not weaken Theognis' tirade. (The sense of 188 is complete. βούλομαι may be followed by an accusative where it is easy to supply an infinitive; see *LSJ* 1968, s.v.) χρήματα γὰρ τιμῶσι sums up 185(H5)–188 and contrasts those lines with the breeding of animals in 183–85(H4). (τιμᾶν occurs with things as object first in *Homeric Hymns* 25. 6.) The wording of 189–90 is unusually terse. 189(H8)–190(P7) suffices for a complete major unit of sense, consisting of two paratactic clauses between heavy stops; and it is preceded and followed by two other main clauses, each complete in the couplet. In this respect, 189–90 differ from Callinus 1W. 8–9; for there the preceding and following words are parts of other, longer sentences. As a consequence, the parenthetic effect is less marked in 189–90 than in Callinus. A lowering of tension from H8 to P7 is quite appropriate, however: the emphasis falls on the first three and last three words of the couplet. From H8 to P7, Theognis sums up 185(H5)–188 in a deft chiasmus, in which resemblance of meter takes precedence over exact correspondence of words: ἐσθλοῦ would scan in 190, but at the cost of a dactyl. After the chiasmus, Theognis ends his couplet with a short, damning indictment, which explicitly introduces the idea of γένος for the first time since 184 and produces a stark contrast with εὐγενέας there. (The point is made more diffusely in 189, with χρήματα and ἔγημε set at either end of the line; but πλοῦτος ἔμειξε γένος clinches it.) 189(H8)–190(P7) not merely sum up 185(H5)–188 but advance the narrative and the argument. The former lines state what the persons concerned are willing to do; the latter, that they do—or have done—it. Theognis may be exploiting the resources of the Greek aorist. After βούλεται (184), οὐ μελεδαίνει (185), οὐδέ . . . ἀναίνεται (187), and βούλεται (188), "has married" and "has mingled" suit the contexts. But to understand the aorists as gnomic would add solemnity to Theognis' complaints. For Theognis' original audience, under no necessity to translate the lines, both senses might be present. (Compare Solon 4W. 17–29, discussed in chapter 6.)

191–92. This couplet too has a broken rhythm. οὕτω does not qualify μὴ θαύμαζε but refers back to 189–90 or, more generally, to what has preceded. Some pause seems appropriate before μὴ θαύμαζε. Mandatory pause is at H8 (θαύμαζε) rather than H10, since γένος is to be taken closely with ἀστῶν, and the object of θαύμαζε is not γένος but the entire phrase γένος . . . ἀστῶν / μαυροῦσθαι. Pauses are also needed before and after the vocative, at line end, after μαυροῦσθαι, and at P7. The effect is very similar to that of 183–84. The resemblance of clause length, noted above, is part of a larger design to emphasize resemblance in form and contrast in content between the first and last couplets of the poem.

Theognis now makes his point explicit. He has pointed out that wealth has thrown γένος into confusion, mingling ἀγαθοί with κακοί. But κακοί men are so termed because they are ineffective (Adkins 1960a, passim). It might be thought that they could not harm the ἀγαθοί very much; and if simple distaste for their social inferiors does not deter the ἀγαθοί, a stronger argument is required. Theognis supplies it by claiming that wealth, in mingling γένος, mingles ἐσθλά with κακά. The use of the neuter adjectives is skillful. Since ἐσθλά are good, κακά bad, for the persons who possess them, the ἀγαθοί deteriorate when they possess κακά. (That κακοί benefit from an admixture of ἐσθλά does not interest an embittered aristocrat.) "Deteriorate" is μαυροῦσθαι, emphasized by overrun, position, and pause and by its molossus rhythm. The only other initial molossus word in this poem is βήσεσθαι (185), a fact which might again highlight the contrast in sense between the opening and closing lines. μαυροῦσθαι does not mean "become more unjust." Compare Hesiod, *Works and Days* 325–26: if anyone is unjust, the gods bring him low (ῥεῖα δέ μιν μαυροῦσι θεοί, μινύθουσι δὲ οἶκον / ἀνέρι τῷ, παῦρον δέ τ' ἐπὶ χρόνον ὄλβος ὀπηδεῖ). μίσγεται ἐσθλὰ κακοῖς resembles Hesiod, *Works and Days* 179, ἀλλ' ἔμπης καὶ τοῖσι μεμείξεται ἐσθλὰ κακοῖσιν, a line that occurs in the Myth of the Five Races (γένη). The verbal resemblance merely serves to epitomize the difference between Theognis' view of human deterioration and Hesiod's. For Hesiod, the decline, as γένος succeeds γένος, is inevitable and heaven-sent. The decline of Theognis' very different γένη results from the greed of the ἀγαθοί. It would be just as possible to practice eugenics with human beings as with other animals and thus avoid decline.

Like much of the *Theognidea*, this is a work of rhetoric rather than poetry. In the use of rhetoric and its effective deployment in the elegiac couplet, it displays great skill. Every word is a blow, and every blow reaches its mark. If its attribution is correct, this poem must have been composed decades before the composition of the first rhetorical handbooks; but it is difficult to see what our author could have learned from them.

THEOGNIDEA 237–54W

σοὶ μὲν ἐγὼ πτέρ' ἔδωκα, σὺν οἷς ἐπ' ἀπείρονα πόντον
πωτήσῃ καὶ γῆν πᾶσαν ἀειρόμενος
ῥηϊδίως· θοίνῃς δὲ καὶ εἰλαπίνῃσι παρέσσῃ
240 ἐν πάσαις, πολλῶν κείμενος ἐν στόμασιν,
καί σε σὺν αὐλίσκοισι λιγυφθόγγοις νέοι ἄνδρες
εὐκόσμως ἐρατοὶ καλά τε καὶ λιγέα
ᾄσονται. καὶ ὅταν δνοφερῆς ὑπὸ κεύθεσι γαίης
βῇς πολυκωκύτους εἰς Ἀΐδαο δόμους,
245 οὐδέποτ' οὐδὲ θανὼν ἀπολεῖς κλέος, ἀλλὰ μελήσεις
ἄφθιτον ἀνθρώποις αἰὲν ἔχων ὄνομα
Κύρνε, καθ' Ἑλλάδα γῆν στρωφώμενος ἠδ' ἀνὰ νήσους
ἰχθυόεντα περῶν πόντον ἐπ' ἀτρύγετον,
οὐχ ἵππων νώτοισιν ἐφήμενος, ἀλλά σε πέμψει
250 ἀγλαὰ Μουσάων δῶρα ἰοστεφάνων·
πᾶσι δ' ὅσοισι μέμηλε καὶ ἐσσομένοισιν ἀοιδὴ
ἔσσῃ ὁμῶς, ὄφρ' ἂν γῆ τε καὶ ἠέλιος·
αὐτὰρ ἐγὼν ὀλίγης παρὰ σεῦ οὐ τυγχάνω αἰδοῦς,
ἀλλ' ὥσπερ μικρὸν παῖδα λόγοις μ'] ἀπατᾷ [ς.

To you I have given wings, with which you shall fly over the boundless sea and(?) every land(?), soaring easily(?). You shall be present at all feasts and banquets, resting on the lips(?) of many people, and of you lovely(?) young men shall decorously sing(?) songs beautiful and clear to the music of clear-voiced pipes. And when you go beneath the depths of the dark earth to Hades' house of many lamentations, never, dead though you be, shall you lose your fame. Rather shall you be in men's minds with a name that is ever imperishable, Cyrnus, as you roam to and fro through the land of Greece and to the islands, crossing over the unharvested fishy sea, not seated on the backs of horses; the glorious gifts of the violet-garlanded Muses shall be your convoy. For all those whose minds are set on the Muses' gifts(?), those alike who are yet to be born, you shall be the subject of song, as long as earth and sun shall exist; yet I do not receive even a little regard from you, but you cheat me with words as if I were a small child.

In this poem, too, static analysis suggests fluency of composition. All but the last of the nine hexameters (253) are enjambed in West 1972, and three of the nine pentameters (238, 242, 246). Of the remainder, three are stopped with commas (240, 244, 248), two with raised stops (250, 252), and one with a full stop (254). Most editors print a comma at the end of 246, since 247 begins with a vocative. The sense certainly requires a heavier pause at the end of 246 than in an enjambed line. Even if a comma is added there, there are only sixteen stops in eighteen lines.[10]

Only eight of the stops occur at line end. Within the lines, 237 has a comma at the H8 caesura, after which there is no stop until the raised stop at H4 in 239. From H5, 239 is overrun to P4 in 240. 241 is overrun through the following pentameter to H4 in 243. From H5, 243 is overrun to the end of 244. 245 is stopped at the H12 bucolic diaeresis and is then overrun to the pause needed at the end of 246 before the vocative. After the vocative, 247 is then overrun to a comma at the end of 248. 249 has a comma at the H12 diaeresis and is then overrun to a raised stop at the end of 250. 251 is overrun to P4 in 252, which, like 253 and 254, is end-stopped.

As in poem 183–92W, there is great variety in the length of clauses and sense groups between stops. To the end of 248 all the units between stops are of different lengths. 245 and 249 are both stopped at H12, and most editors print a stop at the end of the following pentameter in 246 as well as in 250. 252, from P4 onward, has the same length between stops as 240. There is only one example (253–54) of a couplet stopped at the end of both hexameter and pentameter.

The role of these lines in the authentic works of Theognis has been much discussed. The question is not relevant to the present work. Nor is the authenticity of the lines, which some have denied, my primary concern. (For a conspectus of views, see Garzya 1958, 175.) However, some editors have doubted the unity of the poem or have rearranged the lines (Hudson-Williams 1910, 192). I shall take it as a working hypothesis that *Theognidea* 237–54W constitutes a single, probably complete poem and shall then discuss the question at the end, in the light of my analysis.

237–39(H4). Line 237 is entirely dactylic, as are two other hexameters (245, 251) and one pentameter (248). The meter here well suits the idea of wings and flight. σοί, the subject of the poem, is appropriately emphasized by its position. Campbell (1967, 361) notes the link σοὶ μέν (237), καί σε (241), and αὐτὰρ ἐγών (253). He might have included more of 237 and 253: "To you I have given wings . . . ; but from you I do not receive even a little respect." (See also Harrison 1902; Kroll 1936.) Compare σοὶ δ᾽ ἐγώ in *Theognidea* 27W, from a poem which some suppose to be the prologue to the sequence of poems to which lines 237–54 stand as epilogue. Campbell (1967,

362) labels σύν instrumental and compares *Iliad* 8. 530: σὺν τεύχεσι θωρηχθέντες. But his references to *LSJ* 1968, s.v. σύν, mngs. A4 ("of things which are attached to a person") and A7 ("of the instrument or means") recognize that simple οἷς would have a different, less subtle, meaning. If we add the basic comitative use of σύν, to which σὺν αὐλίσκοισι in 241 approximates, the preposition may convey that, metaphorically, wings have been attached to Cyrnus and that by their means he will travel everywhere in Greece, and that, literally, the name of Cyrnus will accompany the poems everywhere and that by their means he will achieve literary immortality. μεθ' ὧν would convey some of this, οἷς another part; but only σὺν οἷς conveys all of it. ἐπ' ἀπείρονα πόντον is the first of this poem's many Homeric reminiscences. Campbell (1967, 362) cites the phrase as a line ending at *Iliad* 1. 350, where it is used of Achilles ὁρόων ἐπ' ἀπείρονα πόντον. The context is evidently irrelevant. Had the poet desired an allusion, he might have drawn on *Iliad* 24. 341–42 and *Odyssey* 5. 45–46 or on *Odyssey* 1. 97–98. In the former cases Hermes, in the latter Athena, put on their immortal golden sandals, τά μιν φέρον ἠμὲν ἐφ' ὑγρὴν / ἠδ' ἐπ' ἀπείρονα γαῖαν ἅμα πνοιῇς ἀνέμοιο.

The molossus πωτήσῃ, in first position after an enjambed—and purely dactylic—hexameter, is very emphatic. In 237, πτέρα is a startling beginning. The metaphor was imitated later (see Hudson-Williams 1910, 192); but if Theognis or a poet of comparable date wrote these lines, this is its first extant appearance and might be the poet's invention. The audience will be alert to hear what follows. The Homeric phrase which closes the line may impart grandeur but does not kindle the imagination in the same way. πωτήσῃ raises the tension again. καὶ γῆν is the emendation of Bergk (1882) for the manuscripts' κατὰ γῆν. West (1972), with most modern editors, follows Bergk. γῆν is then parallel with πόντον, and ἀειρόμενος means "soaring." Campbell (1967, 362) retains κατά. He cites Aristophanes, *Birds* 1286–88: πρῶτον μὲν εὐθὺς πάντες ἐξ εὐνῆς ἅμα / ἐπέτονθ' ἕωθεν ὥσπερ ἡμεῖς ἐπὶ νόμῳ / κἄπειτ' ἂν ἅμα κατῆραν ἐς τὰ βιβλία. The parallel, which includes both flying and swooping down, is attractive; and the frequentative πωτάομαι, "fly about," gives a pleasing sense in the *Theognidea*: Cyrnus will fly about over the sea, swooping down on every land—a vivid picture, given the geography of the Greek-speaking world. But καταίρειν seems to occur first in the *Birds* (and καταείρειν not at all); and though γῆν can be construed as an accusative of the goal of motion, a Greek would have been impelled to understand κατά with γῆν. κατὰ γαῖαν occurs as a phrase already in Homer, and the P7 diaeresis here binds the words closely together and separates them from ἀειρόμενος.[11] A prefix in tmesis may be placed before a word with which it might be, but is not to be, taken (for example, ποτὶ δὲ σκῆπτρον βάλε γαίη, *Iliad* 1. 245); but the inducements to take κατά with γῆν seem too strong here. If Campbell's preferred interpretation were possible, the poetry would be greatly improved; but even Campbell's alternative rendering, "rising over the whole world," gives better poetry than Bergk's text will yield. If the phrases are parallel, πᾶσαν seems weak after ἀπείρονα, ἀειρόμενος / ῥηϊδίως is bathetic at the end without further qualification, and, as Table 3 shows, the rarity of punctuation at P9 (0.4%) indicates the elegiac poet's reluctance to begin a phrase there. (I should prefer to render the manuscripts' text "rising over every land": if the sense of swooping down is absent, it is important to insist that Cyrnus will be not merely high aloft over the whole world but present over every land.)

ῥηϊδίως in enjambment after the pentameter has appropriate emphasis: the wings are good wings, and Cyrnus will travel everywhere with ease.

239(H5)–243(H4). θοίνης is emphasized by position in its clause, by its two long syllables, and by being set (with δέ) between the stop at H4 and the mandatory caesura at H8. The word establishes the theme: feasts and honor at feasts are the subject of thought until 243(H4). θοίνη does not occur in Homer, where δαίς is used. εἰλαπίνη is "*a solemn feast or banquet*, given on a great occasion at lavish expense" (*LSJ* 1968, s.v., citing Athenaeus 362E). It is linked with marriages (*Iliad* 18. 491, *Odyssey* 1. 225–26), at which sumptuous feasting was customary. In *Iliad* 10. 217, among Nestor's inducements to persuade a Greek to volunteer for a spying expedition to the Trojan camp is αἰεὶ δ᾽ ἐν δαίτῃσι καὶ εἰλαπίνῃσι παρέσται. The word occurs in two Hesiodic fragments (274. 1 and 305. 3 Merkelbach and West) but not in Page 1962 or 1974 or in Voigt 1971. In West 1972 it occurs only here and at *Theognidea* 827W, an obelized passage. Its use gives epic grandeur to the lines. Theognis is promising Cyrnus the highest social glory: he is to be at *all* the grandest feasts (ἐν πάσαις, emphasized by overrun, spondaic rhythm, position, and pause), not merely in Megara but everywhere in Greece. No man could hope to achieve such prominence or such ubiquity in person. Theognis uses an epic term for the grand feasts; and if the echo of *Iliad* 10. 217 is taken as an allusion, he is comparing his gift to Cyrnus with the reward for heroism earned by Odysseus and Diomedes in *Iliad* 10. Great glory indeed for a boy or very young man in Megara!

ἐν πάσαις, in agreement with the initial θοίνης, demarcates its sense group. The juxtaposed πολλῶν reinforces ἐν πάσαις and completes a spondaic hemiepes, counterpointed against the dactylic second half of 239. πολλῶν . . . στόμασιν is a striking phrase, imitated in the *Palatine Anthology* (9. 62. 6): πάντων δ᾽ Ἑλλήνων κείμενος ἐν στόμασιν. The sense in which Theognis' poems "lie in the mouth" is clear; but the poet's words refer to Cyrnus, not the poems. It seems possible that the phrase will bear a literal sense too. If ἀμφιπίπτων στόμασιν can mean "kissing" (Sophocles, *Trachiniae* 930), Theognis' phrase may have erotic overtones in this context, for those who are to sing the songs are "ἐρατοί young men." (There is a play on words in *Palatine Anthology* 9. 62. 6 also. The personified city of Troy is the speaker: "Ashes of ages have devoured me ⟨and I κεῖμαι in the earth⟩, but I κεῖμαι, am situated, in Homer, and I κείσομαι in the mouths of all Greeks.") 241–43(H4) are carefully composed. In 241 καί σε (answering σοί μέν in 237) and νέοι ἄνδρες are set around a prepositional phrase which, with its polysyllabic noun and adjective, occupies most of the line. 242 consists essentially of an adverb and three adjectives—one adjective in agreement with the subject, the other two, in the accusative neuter plural, depending on a verb which is yet to be uttered. The lines lead up to the molossus verb ᾄσονται, emphasized by overrun, meter, position, and pause. The sense is unclear until the end of the sentence. σέ makes it clear that something transitive is to be done to Cyrnus. When ᾄσονται is uttered, it conveys to the audience—aware of the poet's sustained play on "Cyrnus" and "poems about Cyrnus"—two meanings: not only "will sing about you (Cyrnus)" but also "will sing you (the Cyrnus-poems)." This fact increases the likelihood that κείμενος ἐν στόμασιν has a double meaning. (The strictures of Kroll [1936, 156–57] miss some of the poetry.) εὐκόσμως is used in *Odyssey* 21. 123 to characterize Telemachus' arrangement of the axes for the Bow test, and Hesiod, *Works and Days* 628, has εὐκόσμως στολίσας νηὸς πτέρα ποντοπόροιο. (The adjective does not occur until Solon 4W. 32.) εὐκόσμως does not occur in Page 1962 or 1974, in Voigt 1971, or elsewhere in West 1972. Once again the poet has used an epic word. Its two earlier extant usages commend the neat and efficient performance of a task, a sense which well suits the dominant usages of κοσμεῖν in Homer (*LSJ* 1968, s.v.). The Hesiodic example advises Perses to store εὐκόσμως the "wings" of a ship "that travels over the sea." Cyrnus too has wings and is to travel over the sea; and now ἐρατοί young men are to do something to him—and to his wings?—εὐκόσμως. Though there is a poignant contrast between the manner in which Hesiod's father traveled over the sea (633–38) and the manner in which Cyrnus is to travel, the effect may be fortuitous. In 242, εὐκόσμως might be taken either with ἐρατοί or with the coming verb. (Even if the Homeric/Hesiodic usages of εὐκόσμως represent its earlier range, the extension to a wider sense is easy: [οὐ] κατὰ κόσμον has a wider range, and the sole occurrence of ἄκοσμος in Homer decries Thersites' lack of decorum: ὅς ῥ' ἔπεα φρεσὶν ᾗσιν ἄκοσμά τε πολλά τε ᾔδη / μάψ, ἀτὰρ οὐ κατὰ κόσμον ἐριζέμεναι βασιλεῦσιν [*Iliad* 2. 213–14]; and Solon uses εὔκοσμα of good civic order.) If the audience understands ἐρατοί as "beloved," εὐκόσμως may be taken with ἐρατοί; but if ἐρατοί is understood as "lovely," the adverb may accompany the verb. Since the context permits either meaning, the audience may apply εὐκόσμως both to what is done to Cyrnus by the young men and to what is done to the young men. As "lovely," the young men are likely to have lovers; as "beloved," they have them. Since Cyrnus is spoken of as present at all the feasts, he will presumably find the young men ἐρατοί in both senses himself. The poet has created a picture of reciprocity, in which everything is done κατὰ κόσμον. His complaint in this poem is that Cyrnus has shown him no αἰδώς and has not requited him κατὰ κόσμον.[12] Lines 241–43(H4) may already, by their contrast, implicitly reproach Cyrnus and also allude to the nature of the poet's relationship with him. They merely allude: ἐρατοί may mean no more than "lovely." Theognis does not explicitly characterize the relationship in this poem, but more hints are to follow.

ἐρατοί may have yet another function to perform. It is unclear whether the νέοι ἄνδρες are ἐρατοί in Cyrnus' eyes, the poet's, or their elders' in their own city. (The context does not suggest ἐρατοὶ γυναιξί, as in Tyrtaeus 10W. 29.) Elders they must be, for to have a "beloved" older than oneself was shocking (Dover 1978, 87), and εὐκόσμως is set next to ἐρατοί. Now the Cyrnus of the poems is certainly young: the general tone of the advice given to him indicates as much, and *Theognidea* 27–28W, σοὶ δ' ἐγὼ εὖ φρονέων ὑποθήσομαι, οἷάπερ αὐτός / Κύρν' ἀπὸ τῶν ἀγαθῶν παῖς ἔτ' ἐὼν ἔμαθον, in its context suggests that Theognis is now himself advising Cyrnus παῖδ' ἔτ' ἐόντα. It is to the young Cyrnus, the Cyrnus of the poems, that immortality is being offered. That Cyrnus will never grow old. But since the flesh-and-blood Cyrnus—who is not immortal—has been identified with the poems, there is a danger of suggesting that he will "never grow old" in a different sense, by dying young, for Theognis is about to write of Cyrnus' death. The poet cannot write "you will live on and grow old, but my poems will portray you as ever young," if his airy conceit is not to turn to leaden prose; but if there are at some time to be νέοι ἄνδρες who are εὐκόσμως ἐρατοί, "beloved in a seemly manner" by Cyrnus, then the flesh-and-blood Cyrnus, who is now a παῖς, must by that time have lived long enough to be older than they are. The hint is subtle; but anything less subtle would bring the poem to earth.

αὐλίσκος does not occur again until Sophocles' Fragment 701 (Nauck 1889, 297) and, in an emendation for λαίσκων, in Pindar, Fragment 106. 8 (Turyn 1952, 309). The word has been used to cast doubt on the authenticity of our poem, on the grounds that small *auloi* were not known in Theognis' day (Kroll 1936, 285–95; Carrière 1951). The argument is inconclusive: see Herodotus 1. 17 and Pépin 1952. Even if the small *aulos* was not known, Theognis might have used a word in -ίσκος, for these occur from the early lyric period (Buck and Petersen 1944, 637). The poet might have preferred the more polysyllabic αὐλίσκος, for the poetic/rhetorical reasons suggested above, without meaning to denote a treble instrument. If all *auloi* were the same size, αὐλίσκος could not be confusing; and even Sophocles, to whom treble *auloi* were familiar, qualifies αὐλίσκοις with σμικροῖς to make his point clear. (Alcman's κυπαιρίσκος [Page 1962, 51] is evidently not diminutive in any precise, technical sense.) λιγυφθόγγοις need not characterize a treble *aulos*. The adjective is used exclusively of κήρυκες in Homer and means "clear-voiced." There is no suggestion that the heralds have unbroken voices. All *auloi* are λιγύφθογγοι. The adjective may be used allusively here: the αὐλίσκοι, which accompanied elegiac poetry, are to be Cyrnus' heralds wherever he goes.

243(H5)–44. The remainder of 243–44 is loaded with Homeric/Hesiodic reminiscences. Homer uses δνοφερή of water (*Iliad* 9. 15 = 16.4) and night (*Odyssey* 13. 269; 15. 50). Hesiod (*Theogony* 736) couples γῆς and δνοφερῆς. (The adjective occurs only here and at *Theognidea* 672 in West 1972 and not at all in Page 1962 or 1974 or in Voigt 1971. Even were it not used in a Hesiodic phrase, it would help to contribute to the stylistic grandeur that has already been established by the poet.) At *Iliad* 22. 482–83 we find νῦν δὲ σὺ μὲν 'Αΐδαο δόμους ὑπὸ κεύθεσι γαίης / ἔρχεαι. πολυκωκύτους, however, occurs only here. Its sense is reinforced by its polysyllabic length and weight, and it leaves space for only a monosyllable at the beginning of the first hemiepes of 244. βῆς is set between two polysyllabic prepositional phrases which highlight its stark simplicity. (The effect of ἔρχεαι in *Iliad* 22. 482–83 is similar but not so intense.) Our poet's treatment of the first hemiepes of 244 shows that he does not draw on epic phrases from mere lack of skill in handling words for himself.

245–46. Campbell (1967, 363) compares these lines to *Odyssey* 24. 93–94, ὥς σὺ μὲν οὐδὲ θανὼν ὄνομ' ὤλεσας, ἀλλά τοι αἰεὶ / πάντας ἐπ' ἀνθρώπους κλέος ἔσσεται ἐσθλόν, 'Οδυσσεῦ, and *Odyssey* 9. 19–20, εἴμ' 'Οδυσεὺς Λαερτιάδης, ὃς πᾶσι δόλοισι / ἀνθρώποισι μέλω, καί μευ κλέος οὐρανὸν ἵκει. Here we have echoes, more or less close, not quotations. But *Odyssey* 24. 93–94 is spoken by Agamemnon, contrasting Achilles' glorious death with his own ignominious fate at the hands of Clytemnestra; and *Iliad* 22. 482–83, which *Theognidea* 243–44W closely resemble, is spoken by Andromache, vainly beseeching Hector to retreat into Troy to fight again another day. He will not, but will fight for the sake of his own personal glory and ἀρετή, though the destruction of Troy and the misery of Andromache are rendered inevitable (Adkins 1982c). *Odyssey* 9. 19–20 are spoken of himself by Odysseus, who was crafty and whose κλέος reached— flew?—up to heaven. In *Theognidea* 239W θοίνης δὲ καὶ εἰλαπίνῃσι παρέσσῃ could recall a reward earned by Odysseus. If these echoes could be interpreted as allusions, Theognis would be saying obliquely, "Cyrnus, I have given you a reward worthy of an Odysseus (or a Diomedes). You are behaving like the deceitful Odysseus. Your glory is secure, and my misery is assured." It would be foolish to claim these overtones as certainly intended; but we have observed many examples of what appear to be the purposive use of Homeric allusion, and only a very stupid or ignorant Greek could have missed the wealth of Homeric phraseology in this poem. If—as seems ever more likely—Homeric allusion is quite common in the culture, *Theognidea* 237–54W seems a likely place in which to find it. The suggested allusions prepare in yet another way for the theme of 253–54, whose introduction many critics have found intolerably abrupt.

247–48. Κύρνε, the only occurrence of the recipient's name in the poem, well follows ὄνομα. The couplet is rhythmically unusual, for it contains three purely dactylic hemiepe. (See above, p. 5.) The dactyls well suit the subject matter and also serve to highlight στρωφώμενος, with its two long syllables. στρωφώμενος, like πωτήσῃ (238), is frequentative; and indeed, for some tastes, 247–52 too closely resemble 237–46. Ziegler (1880) treated 247–54 as a separate poem. Hudson-Williams (1910, 192) objects, "as the explanation of 249–50 is to be sought in 237." That Theognis is responsible for Cyrnus' good fortune is needed to account for 253–54; but Hudson-Williams treats 253–54 as a separate poem. Even 247–52 cannot stand alone, for the participles in 247–49 depend not on πέμψει (249) but on μελήσεις (245). The reader must accept the fact that Theognis has to some extent repeated himself.

248, like the preceding lines, is loaded with Homeric language. Even περῶν is used with ἐπί and πόντον (*Iliad* 2. 613). ἰχθυόεντα occurs in the accusative with πόντον three times in the *Iliad* and nine times in the *Odyssey*, and ἀτρύγετον occurs in the accusative with πόντον once in the *Iliad* and seven times in the *Odyssey*; but Homer never uses both adjectives together. There need be no conscious reminiscence of any particular lines. ἰχθυόεντα in itself has the connotations of the hardships of traveling—literally, not metaphorically—over the sea in early Greece. Campbell (1967, 237–38) reminds us that in the view of Homer fish were grim creatures who ate drowned men (*Iliad* 21. 122–27; 24. 82; *Odyssey* 14. 135; 24. 291). The tone of 248 is bleak, in contrast with the glories of 245–47; or rather, it would be bleak if Cyrnus were going to travel as a mere mortal rather than in Theognis' poems. (The next couplet points the contrast.) For this reason, it is better to take ἀνὰ νήσους as parallel to καθ' Ἑλλάδα γῆν, and 248 as depending on 247, rather than to take 247–48 as two coordinate participial phrases linked by ἠδ'. To make the emotionally contrasted phrases syntactically parallel would be less effective.

249–50. Campbell (1967, 364) notes that Alcaeus (34. 5–6) addressed Castor and Pollux as οἳ κὰτ εὔρηαν χ[θόνα] καὶ θάλασσαν / παῖσαν ἔρχεσθ' ὠ[κυπό]δων ἐπ' ἵππων. If the image was associated with the Dioscuri—and unless it refers to some divine traveler, the phrase is merely grotesque[13]—οὐχ ἵππων νώτοισιν ἐφήμενος gains point. Cyrnus will travel everywhere in glory, but not in the manner of the Dioscuri. They themselves were once mortal, and the very act of denying that Cyrnus will travel as they do associates them with Cyrnus as supernatural travelers and glorifies him. The rhythm of the couplet and the choice of words enhance the splendor. Spondees pick out and contrast the backs of the horses and the Muses. The part of the sentence which tells how Cyrnus will travel begins at the H12 diaeresis, with the usual effect. The horses receive no epithet; the gifts of the Muses have two Homeric adjectives and occupy a complete pentameter. (Theognis has reserved his adjectives for the pentameter in the last three couplets, setting one grim pentameter between two glory-laden ones.) ἀγλαά . . . δῶρα is Homeric, as in *Iliad* 1. 213, but the Muses are "violet-garlanded" here only. Aphrodite is so described in *Homeric Hymns* 6. 18, possibly in *Hymn to Aphrodite* 175, and in Solon 19W. 4. Aphrodite Κυπρογενής is violet-garlanded in *Theognidea* 1304W, 1332W, and 1383W in pederastic contexts. If ἰοστέφανος was usually applied only to Aphrodite in Theognis' day, by transferring it to the Muses of his Cyrnus poems he again hints at the nature of his relationship with Cyrnus, points forward to the theme of 253–54, and indicates the manner in which that couplet is to be understood. δῶρα does not weaken σοὶ μέν . . . ἔδωκα (237), though the genitive is subjective. The belief that a god inspires an action does not in early Greece reduce the responsibility of the human agent for the action (Adkins 1960a, 10–25, 116–27); but it seems unnecessary to invoke Phemius' conjoint claim (*Odyssey* 22. 347–48) that he is self-taught and that the god set all kinds of οἴμαι in his mind. The Muses and the Homeric epithets give splendor to the line, but the phrase may now be used as a—dead—metaphor. Compare Archilochus 1W. 2, καὶ Μουσέων δῶρον ἐπιστάμενος. *LSJ* 1968 distinguishes, as meanings of ἐπίσταμαι, "I. c. inf. *to know* how to do, *to be able* to do, *capable* of doing . . . II. c. acc. *to understand* a matter, *know, be versed in* or *acquainted with* . . . . 2. after Hom. *to know* as a fact . . . ." Archilochus 1W. 2 is cited under II. 1, with *Iliad* 23. 705, πολλὰ δ' ἐπίστατο ἔργα, correctly, since Archilochus does not mean "knowing the poems of others." The usage differs from that with ἔργα, however, where an appropriate infinitive is implied by the noun. Archilochus does not mean "know how to give." Μουσέων δῶρον means "the skill of composing poetry." The syntax indicates that no act of giving is present to the mind; and in *Theognidea* 249–50W, though the meaning is "poems" rather than "skill in composing poetry," the link with any action of the Muses seems equally tenuous.

The exposition of 243(H5)–250 is very skillfully handled. To say bluntly "When you go to Hades, you will at the same time be traveling about the Greek world" would be grotesque and awkward; and the explicit "When you go to Hades, my poems about you will be traveling about the Greek world" would destroy the elegance with which the poet has used "you" in both senses in the earlier lines. 245–46 furnish a deft transition. "Even after your death, Cyrnus, people will think of you" is a prosaic paraphrase; but Cyrnus is in fact the subject of μελήσεις . . . ἀνθρώποις and ἔχων ὄνομα, and this syntax suggests his presence. The poet then addresses Cyrnus by name, reinforcing the effect of presence. He can now proceed, using "you" for both Cyrnus and the poems, as he has done throughout, without causing his audience any feeling of awkwardness.

251–52. The Homeric echoes continue. καὶ ἐσσομένοισιν ἀοιδή ends *Odyssey* 8. 580, and γῆ τε καὶ ἠέλιος begins *Iliad* 19. 259. *Odyssey* 8. 580 is spoken by Alcinous to Odysseus, who has wept on hearing Demodocus sing of the Trojan Horse. Alcinous continues (581–86):

> "ἦ τίς τοι καὶ πηὸς ἀπέφθιτο Ἰλιόθι πρὸ
> ἐσθλὸς ἐών, γαμβρὸς ἢ πενθερός, οἵ τε μάλιστα
> κήδιστοι τελέθουσι μεθ᾽ αἷμά τε καὶ γένος αὐτῶν;
> ἦ τίς που καὶ ἑταῖρος ἀνὴρ κεχαρισμένα εἰδώς,
> ἐσθλός; ἐπεὶ οὐ μέν τι κασιγνήτοιο χερείων
> γίγνεται ὅς κεν ἑταῖρος ἐὼν πεπνυμένα εἰδῇ."

There can be few lines in the Homeric poems more apposite to Theognis' message than 584–86, and they are addressed to Odysseus, with whom some earlier possible allusions would also liken Cyrnus. Hudson-Williams (1910, 193) takes ἀοιδή as both the subject of μέμηλε and the predicate of ἔσσῃ; Campbell supplies δῶρα from 250 as the subject of μέμηλε. ὁμῶς is to be taken more closely with καὶ ἐσσομένοισι than with ἀοιδὴ ἔσσῃ. Whichever noun is supplied, a pause rather more sustained than the regular mandatory pause seems needed at H8; and at H14 and P2 sense pauses seem needed. (Pause at H14 is rare, as Table 2 shows; only 0.10 percent of the elegy sample have punctuation there.) Add pauses at line end in the hexameter, at P4 and P7, and the rhythm becomes very broken. We may note also that ὄφρ᾽ ἄν may mean both "as long as" and "until." The hearer could not be immediately certain that "exist" was to be supplied, for the pentameter might have been overrun to a word meaning "perish." Other poets employ the ambiguities of Greek for their own purposes,[14] and the poet of 237–54 has shown no lack of skill. The doubt whether the sense was complete or not, combined with the broken rhythm, would well convey the effect of agitation in a sensitive performance; and if the allusion could be taken, the reason for the agitation might be divined. The theme of the final couplet is prefigured. The repetition ἐσσομένῃσι . . . ἔσσῃ is deliberate and effective, and the absence of "exist" with γῆ τε καὶ ἠέλιος also renders the existence of earth and sun less vivid than that of Cyrnus and his future admirers.

253–54. αὐτὰρ ἐγώ links the thought of the final couplet to σοὶ μὲν . . . ἔδωκα. ὀλίγης and παρὰ σεῦ could be transposed to give an equally metrical line. To do so would juxtapose ἐγώ and σεῦ more closely and produce an effect more similar to σοὶ μὲν ἐγώ; but the word order in the text includes παρὰ σεῦ in the phrase ὀλίγης . . . αἰδοῦς and sets ὀλίγης and μικρόν in analogous positions in the hexameter and pentameter, immediately before the mandatory pause. The position of ὀλίγης also makes easier the sense "even a little."

In this poem only the final couplet has both hexameter and pentameter end-stopped. After the elegant flexibility of composition of the preceding lines, this emphasis on the basic structure of the elegiac meter has the effect of a clausula, and it well mirrors the change from allusion to what is prima facie a simple statement of Theognis' complaint.

Even here, not all may be as simple as it appears. That there is a complaint is clearly stated, but its precise nature is not. αἰδώς may denote and commend an appropriate attitude of a younger man to an older from Homer onward (*Iliad* 10. 238, *Odyssey* 3. 24); and, like αἰδεῖσθαι in *Theognidea* 1331W, which may elucidate the use of αἰδώς in 1265, it may allude to the beloved's willingness to gratify his ἐραστής. These are not different meanings of αἰδώς. Theognis could have been Cyrnus' social and political mentor without being his ἐραστής, but the roles could readily be combined. In both, Cyrnus would be a παῖς in his relationship to an older man. The connotations of αἰδώς, παῖς, and other terms which members of a different culture regard as ambiguous are established by the characteristic behavior of older men toward those termed παῖδες in Greek society. In 254, Theognis likens himself to a small παῖς and claims that Cyrnus is cheating him with words. In a Greek homosexual relationship, the ἐραστής need not conceal his desire, but the ἐρώμενος was expected to display indifference and to be modest, if not chaste (Dover 1978, 52–57). Respectable young men—and it is with respectable young men we are concerned here—had to be seduced; and παῖδα λόγοις ἀπατᾶν cannot have been unknown. Theognis is complaining that he, the elder, has been treated by Cyrnus as young παῖδες are wont to be treated, and the simile readily—like αἰδώς—suggests an amorous relationship. Like the earlier lines, the last couplet does not state bluntly that Theognis is Cyrnus' lover and that Cyrnus has betrayed him, but its hints are rather stronger.[15]

The resemblances already noted between 237–38 and 253–54 in themselves virtually guarantee that these lines are all part of the same poem, and it is difficult to imagine what other lines could effectively precede or follow them. I agree with Campbell (1967, 361) in supposing 237–54 to be a complete poem and a fine one. The flexibility of composition discussed above strongly resembles that of 183–92, and identity of authorship is easy to accept. To employ Homeric language to promise immortality is entirely appropriate, and the choice of language, even without allusion, is always suited to Theognis' stated goal. The change of tone in the last couplet can be matched, as Campbell notes (1967, 361), by the change between 19–23 and 24–26. If the suggestions made above are acceptable, however, the change of tone is prepared for earlier in the poem in a very suitable manner; and if we suppose that Theognis has given clear hints in 240, 242, 250, and the final couplet that he was Cyrnus' ἐραστής as well as his social and political mentor, there need be no change of theme. Theognis has endowed Cyrnus with immortality by poems which arise from a relationship at once social and political and amorous. Cyrnus has failed to show him αἰδώς in return, and the failure may be both amorous and political. *Theognidea* 31–36W warn against a very similar relationship with the "wrong people" in politics. Cyrnus may have succumbed to their blandishments.

Poetry celebrating the relationships of men and boys, or young men, was common in early Greece, and sophistication in its composition is to be expected. *Theognidea* 237–54W is a fine example.

Theognidea 731–752W

Ζεῦ πάτερ, εἴθε γένοιτο θεοῖς φίλα τοῖς μὲν ἀλιτροῖς
ὕβριν ἁδεῖν, καί σφιν τοῦτο γένοιτο φίλον
θυμῷ, σχέτλια ἔργα· μετὰ φρεσὶ δ' ὅστις †ἀθήνης
ἐργάζοιτο, θεῶν μηδὲν ὀπιζόμενος,
735 αὐτὸν ἔπειτα πάλιν τεῖσαι κακά, μηδ' ἔτ' ὀπίσσω
πατρὸς ἀτασθαλίαι παισὶ γένοιντο κακόν·
παῖδας δ' οἵ τ' ἀδίκου πατρὸς τὰ δίκαια νοεῦντες
ποιῶσιν Κρονίδη, σὸν χόλον ἁζόμενοι,
ἐξ ἀρχῆς τὰ δίκαια μετ' ἀστοῖσιν φιλέοντες,
740 μήτιν' ὑπερβασίην ἀντιτίνειν πατέρων.
ταῦτ' εἴη μακάρεσσι θεοῖς φίλα· νῦν δ' ὁ μὲν ἔρδων
ἐκφεύγει, τὸ κακὸν δ' ἄλλος ἔπειτα φέρει.
καὶ τοῦτ' ἀθανάτων βασιλεῦ, πῶς ἐστι δίκαιον,
ἔργων ὅστις ἀνὴρ ἐκτὸς ἐὼν ἀδίκων,
745 μήτιν' ὑπερβασίην κατέχων μήθ' ὅρκον ἀλιτρόν,
ἀλλὰ δίκαιος ἐών, μὴ τὰ δίκαια πάθῃ;
τίς δή κεν βροτὸς ἄλλος ὁρῶν πρὸς τοῦτον ἔπειτα
ἅζοιτ' ἀθανάτους, καὶ τίνα θυμὸν ἔχων,
ὁππότ' ἀνὴρ ἄδικος καὶ ἀτάσθαλος, οὔτέ τευ ἀνδρὸς
750 οὔτέ τευ ἀθανάτων μῆνιν ἀλευόμενος,
ὑβρίζῃ πλούτῳ κεκορημένος, οἱ δὲ δίκαιοι
τρύχονται χαλεπῇ τειρόμενοι πενίῃ;

Father Zeus, would that it might become dear to the gods that hubris should be pleasing to the wicked, and that this, harsh deeds, might become dear to them in their heart; and that whoever, unholy(?) in his mind, committed ⟨harsh deeds⟩—recking nothing of the gods—should subsequently pay for the harm he has done, and that the wicked deeds of the father should not in later days become a source of woe to the children; and that the children of an unjust father, who, thinking just thoughts, do just deeds, O Son of Cronus, in fear of your wrath, and love justice from the beginning among their fellow citizens, should not pay for the transgressions of their fathers in their stead. Would that these things were dear to the blessed gods; but, as it is, the one man does wrong and escapes, and another suffers woe in the future. And how is *this* just, king of the immortals, that a man who is clear of unjust deeds and has committed no transgression nor wicked false oath, but is just, should not experience what is just? What other mortal, looking at this one, would then fear the immortals, and with what spirit(?), when a man who is unjust and wicked, and takes no steps to avoid the wrath of man or of the immortals, commits hubris, sated with wealth, while the just are being overwhelmed and crushed by the burden of grievous poverty?

This poem addresses a serious problem in Greek religious ethics. In Greece, justice was choiceworthy insofar as it was believed to be in one's own interest to behave justly. As Hesiod says (*Works and Days* 270–72): "Now may neither I nor my son be just among men, if the more unjust is to come off better."[16] Success and failure were ascribed to the gods. If justice was to be pursued, it rested with the gods to see to it that the unjust did not prosper; and since few Greeks of the period believed in reward and punishment after death (Adkins 1960a, 138–48), success must reward the just and disaster punish the unjust in this life. In few societies are these requirements met with regularity. If punishment must fall upon the unjust individual in this life, the problem for the moralist is insoluble. But if the relevant unit is not the individual but the kinship group, an intellectually secure theory can be advanced. Solon (13W. 25–32) states that if the unjust man is not punished, either his children or subsequent generations will suffer. The theory will explain any phenomenon: the prosperous just and unsuccessful unjust present no problem; and now, if a man is unjust and prospers, his descendants will suffer, while, if he is just and fails, he is paying for the misdeeds of an ancestor.

The theory is intellectually secure; but its acceptability depends on the willingness of the individual to regard his kinship group as more important than himself, and the period in which this theory, or belief, in postponed justice appears in extant texts is also the very period in which the individual is beginning to feel his importance. The author of this poem regards such postponed divine "justice" as manifest injustice, and he rounds in indignation upon Zeus.

731–33(H8). The rhythm of these lines is very broken. In 731, pauses are required by sense at H3, by caesura at H8 (not at H10, for θεοῖς φίλα should be taken together), and by sense at H12. In 732, sense requires a pause at P4; colon diaeresis requires one at P7. And, in 733, sense requires a pause at H3, and sense and caesura together require one at H8. Since there must be a pause also at the end even of enjambed lines (above, p. 5), there are nine pauses in nineteen words. The rhythm appropriately expresses the agitation of the speaker.

Lines 731–42, the first half of the poem, are formally a prayer; but after invoking Zeus in 731, the poet does not state his claims to be heard, in the usual Greek manner (Adkins 1969a). The poet is really uttering a wish on behalf of all just persons before complaining to Zeus and the other gods (731, 741) about their actual behavior. The invocatory Ζεῦ πάτερ (731) is appropriately placed in an emphatic position. The words of 731–33(H8), like those of the poem in general, are commonplace; but as they successively strike upon the ear, the hearer may be puzzled. τοῖς μὲν ἀλιτροῖς is well placed at the imperfect cadence of the enjambed hexameter: the hearer wishes to know what our poet is praying for the wicked. One expects "that they may be quickly punished." The actual words which follow, "that hubris should please them," are almost a tautology, for both ὕβρις and ἀλιτρός have religious connotations. Why pray that the wicked be wicked? In 732–33 the poet repeats the effect, but in such a way as to puzzle the hearer for as long as possible. σφιν (732) might refer to either the wicked or the gods. That it refers to the wicked is not clear until σχέτλια ἔργα is reached. But why does the poet pray that it should please the gods that the wicked should be wicked and should perform harsh deeds? Presumably he is trying to startle Zeus and his mortal audience. This is an excellent rhetorical beginning. I suspect that 731 is the first line of the poem.

733(H9)–736. West obelizes ἀθήνης, which could only be the genitive of Ἀθήνη, here nonsense. Bergk prints ἀθειρής, epic for ἀθερής, from a Hesychian gloss, ἀθερές· ἀνόητον, ἀνόσιον. Camerarius prints ἀπηνής, "cruel." The editors' goal is to produce an adjective, agreeing with ὅστις, with which μετὰ φρεσί may be construed, since that phrase cannot be taken with ἐργάζοιτο. But it is then necessary to supply σχέτλια ἔργα with ἐργάζοιτο, and the result seems harsh. However, there may be a progression in sense: ὕβρις (732) in early Greek usually denotes and condemns actions resulting from a state of mind rather than the state of mind itself; but to pray that ὕβρις should be pleasing to someone is not identical with praying that they should commit ὕβρις, and the same may be said of φίλον and σχέτλια ἔργα. If one reads the third clause as passing from attitude to act, the emphatic position and rhetorical weight of ἐργάζοιτο, the longest and heaviest word in the poem thus far, are explained, and the absence of the object is acceptable: "and that whoever . . . should *act*. . . ." (ἐργάζοιτο is then contrasted with θυμῷ in 733, whose emphatic position is thus also justified.) Thus interpreted, the first two and a half lines not merely startle the audience but also lead up to an emphasis on actions. The emphasis is warranted: the poem contrasts actions—the actions of the unjust, which should meet with divine punishment but do not, and the actions of the just, which are "rewarded" with failure. In 734 θεῶν is emphasized, set as it is between a sense pause (P5) and the P7 diaeresis. In 734 Hermann read μηδέν' for μηδέν; but ὀπίζομαι occurs with a genitive also at *Theognidea* 1148W. αὐτόν merits its emphatic position: it is contrasted with παῖδας in similar position in 737. 735 has a broken rhythm resembling that of 731–33. Some slight pause seems needed after αὐτόν; ἔπειτα, "in the future," is to be taken with the infinitival phrase as a whole, while πάλιν goes closely with τεῖσαι, so that a pause between ἔπειτα and πάλιν is needed; and a pause is required for major caesura at either H7 or H10. H10 seems better, for πάλιν τεῖσαι is a phrase, "pay in requital." There is then a pause both before and after κακά, which is appropriately highlighted: "that he in the future should pay in requital by suffering *woes*." Like ἔπειτα, both ἔτι and ὀπίσσω are used with vague reference to the future. Together they form a strong phrase, one which, at imperfect cadence of an enjambed hexameter, directs attention to the well-composed pentameter which follows. All the words contribute powerfully to the sense, and the two sense groups are well set, each in its own hemiepes. κακά (735) and κακόν (736) emphasize the parallelism of the contrasted clauses. That the second is longer than the first enhances the clausulaic effect of the pentameter. A strong clausula is appropriate here: this is the end of the first major unit of the poet's exposition. That the first hemiepes begins with πατρός, the second with παισί, indicates that the subject of the next major unit is to be both generations.

737–40. The emphasis of the first-foot spondaic word παῖδας is appropriate. 731–36 were concerned with the wrongdoer as an individual; his identification as a parent does not occur until 736. Now both generations are discussed, but the woes of the children are to the fore. Note the reversed order: πατρός . . . παισί in 736, παῖδας . . . πατρός in 737. The trochaic rhythm of both words in 736 is balanced by the spondaic rhythm of both words in 737. The broken rhythm of 731–35 reappears: some slight pause in performance seems desirable after παῖδας δ', since the infinitival phrase of which it is the subject does not continue until 740; and a pause is needed both before and after ἀδίκου πατρός, since the phrase is to be taken either with παῖδας (in an unusual order) or, supplying ὄντες, as a participial phrase parallel with τὰ δίκαια νοεῦντες. Note, if the line is performed in this manner, the position of ἀδίκου and τὰ δίκαια at the beginning of contiguous spoken units. (Major caesura is at H10.) In 738 a pause is needed before and after the vocative, the latter being also the mandatory pause at P7. (νοεῦντες is highlighted by imperfect cadence and enjambment, and the molossus word ποιῶσιν derives great emphasis from meter, position, and following pause. The hearer's attention is thus directed to both the attitudes and the actions of the just. This fact suggests that my interpretation of ἀδεῖν, θυμῷ, and ἐργάζοιτο, above, was correct.) 737–38 consist of seven spoken units. 739–40, on the other hand, like 736, require no pause except the major caesura, here at H8, and diaeresis at P7. (All the other words in 739 depend directly on φιλέοντες, while 740 consists of the object, the verb, and a genitive depending on the object.)

731–36 and 737–40 are the first two major units of the poem. The movement in each from a broken rhythm to a smooth one would be immediately obvious in a sensitive oral performance and would suggest a movement from problem to solution. The change of rhythm does not occur exactly at the point where the poet reaches the main infinitive phrase of his prayer. Only the second of the two clauses in 735–36 has smooth rhythm, and 739 as well as 740 has it. But the movements of sense and rhythm are parallel and seem intended. That the dactylic first hemiepes of the last pentameter of each unit (736 and 740) consists of a trochaic word followed by a pentesyllable adds a further touch. A pentesyllable in this position is not very common,[17] and the words are similar in sense: this too seems intended.

In 737 τὰ δίκαια is juxtaposed (but not grammatically linked) with ἀδίκου πατρός; in 739, with μετ' ἀστοῖσιν. The last phrase might appear superfluous; but it emphasizes that while Zeus is concerned with the just children's link with their unjust fathers, they are linked by relations of justice with their fellow citizens.

741–42. The long syllables and position of ταῦτ' εἴη immediately emphasize that this couplet is to sum up 731–40. θεοῖς φίλα occurs in 741 in the same position as in 731, but there is a subtle difference in the phrasing. In 731, θεοῖς is most closely linked with φίλα, and caesura at H8 seems most appropriate; but in 741 θεοῖς is accompanied by μακάρεσσι, and it seems better to pause at H10, leaving φίλα between major caesura at H10 and the sense pause at H12. The rhythm is unusual, but in this respect it exactly resembles 735. As in 735 αὐτόν and κακά are highlighted, so, here, are ταῦτ' and φίλα: "would that *these* things to the blessed gods were *dear*." There is an echo also of 732. There "dear" referred to (the thought of) σχέτλια ἔργα. The movement of thought is completed: would that wickedness might be dear to the wicked, and punishment dear to the gods. The remainder of 741–42 brusquely returns to the real world. Imperfect cadence, enjambment, molossus, and pause both emphasize ἐκφεύγει and highlight the preceding ἔρδων. Note the exactly similar rhythmic effect of 737–38, where the subject of thought is "the just." The contrast is heightened by the rhythmic echo. Remember also the rhythmic echo of 735 (to H12) in 741 (to H12). Even if the language is banal, this is a carefully wrought poem.

743–46. In 741(H13)–742 the poet passed from wish to statement of facts. He now turns to accusation and for a third time invokes or apostrophizes Zeus. On each occasion he addresses him in different terms: first as "father

Zeus," then as "son of Cronus," and now as "king of the immortals." In Greek poetry such variation is often used merely to avoid monotony or *metri gratia*. In this poem, however, Zeus is addressed as "father" in the passage in which the emphasis is on the individual as father; then as "son" where the poet's thoughts turn to the children; and now (relationships in the city having been mentioned in 739) as "king of the immortals." In Greek myth and belief, Zeus is both a father—in the literal and in a broader sense—and a son, and he also has "political" relationships with other deities and with men (Adkins 1982b, 64–68, and Adkins, forthcoming). In Greek belief it is always judicious to address a deity in the appropriate manner; but does the poet also wish his audience—or Zeus—to remember that Zeus was not punished for Cronus' misdeeds? And, by reminding Zeus of his political role, is the poet hinting that kings, when acting as judges, do not—or should not—punish the innocent for the crimes of the guilty? καὶ τοῦτ᾽ means "this too." The poet has been speaking of human acts of justice and injustice. He now asks Zeus whether *his* behavior is just: a striking novelty in Greek thought. The novelty is in the anger. Previous thinkers had not assumed that Zeus would always behave justly; indeed, they had taken it for granted that he would sometimes not do so (Adkins 1960a, 1972b, 1982c, and [for an author later than Theognis] 1982b. See also Adkins, forthcoming). (The success of the unjust and the misery of the just are believed to be the result of divine action.) Having used καὶ τοῦτ᾽ to point an indignant finger, the poet follows it with an invocation not only appropriate in content but, with its quadrisyllable and trisyllable, rhetorically impressive. πῶς ἐστι δίκαιον, though not the beginning of its sentence, has an effect similar to that of other sentences which begin at H11 or H13; and though 743 is stopped with a comma, the sense is incomplete and the effect is that of enjambment, for τοῦτ᾽ requires explanation. 743 consists of three units, as does 744, for a pause seems needed after ἔργων. The broken rhythm has returned. 745–46, however, flow smoothly. Each consists of two units, and one is placed before, one after, the major caesura (here at H10) and the diaeresis. 744 is well framed by the important ἔργων . . . ἀδίκων: the poet continues to emphasize that one's actions should be the criterion for reward and punishment. μῆτιν᾽ ὑπερβασίην in 745 repeats the beginning of 740. Greek poets, and presumably their audiences, are remarkably insensitive to accidental verbal repetition; but here—as of course is true of the repetitions of δίκαιος and ἄδικος—the repetition seems purposive. In 740 the emphasis is on the just person's not paying for the—actual—transgression of someone else, the father; here the emphasis is on the absence of transgressions in the person punished. In performance, the echo would strengthen the point. We have already noted several significant echoes in this poem.

The audience might gradually become aware, after 742, that the scope of the poem has been broadened. At all events, there is now no explicit mention of innocent children being punished for the misdeeds of guilty parents; our attention has been turned to the unjust who flourish while the just are impoverished. 731–42 present a specific instance of this, and the same situation may be in the poet's mind in 743–52; but his words express the matter more generally. 746 neatly expresses the broader subject in a line consisting of two completely dactylic hemiepe, with a form of δίκαιος in a corresponding position in each. The line sums up this unit of the poem.

747–52. In this six-line sentence, which ends the poem, or the lines we possess, the rhythmic pattern again varies between broken and smooth, and the syntax heightens the effect. In 747, in addition to the major caesura at H8, there is a very unusual sense pause at H14, which leaves ἔπειτα isolated at the imperfect cadence. The words are banal. It is the rhythm of the phrases that creates the rhetorical effect: "what *other* mortal, looking at *this* one, then . . . ?" The hearer's mind will be alert for what is to follow; and the banal words, when completed in sense by ἄζοιτ' ἀθανάτους, produce a sentiment shocking in the sixth or early fifth century. The spondaic rhythm adds a little more emphasis to ἄζοιτ'. In 748 West prints τίνα, Edmonds τινα (though he translates τίνα). Since accents are not canonical, either is possible. The interrogative requires a general sense of θυμόν: "in what state of mind would he revere the gods?" The indefinite gives to θυμόν the sense of "courage, spirit," as in *Iliad* 20. 174: "what mortal, looking at this one, and possessing some courage, would revere the gods?" The latter is rhetorically more powerful.

In 749–50, syntax combines with pauses, mostly in mandatory positions, to create expectation. The whole of the couplet consists of syntactical expansions of the subject, ἀνὴρ ἄδικος. After the pause at H7, another adjective is added before the sense pause at H12. There follows a genitive, at imperfect cadence, introduced by οὔτε, which promises another οὔτε and another genitive. This unit is fitted into the first hemiepes of 750; the second contains the noun on which the genitives depend, and the participle, in agreement with ἀνὴρ ἄδικος, governing the noun. The sense of the participle is startling: the man does not even take steps to avoid the wrath of the gods. The audience has been kept waiting for a finite verb throughout the preceding couplet. ὑβρίζῃ receives emphasis from that expectation and from its molossus rhythm, and it is a powerful word in its own right. The poet adds πλούτῳ κεκορημένος. The spondee added to the molossus ὑβρίζῃ produces the first sequence of five long syllables in the poem, and the pentesyllabic κεκορημένος after the caesura completes a phrase which is aurally impressive and devastating in sense. The idea that κόρος and wealth lead to ὕβρις, which is in its turn followed by ἄτη, is by this time established in Greek belief (Solon 6W. 3); but as it hears the poet's weighty description of κόρος, πλοῦτος, and ὕβρις, the audience knows that disaster has not been the result: it is the just who are suffering. The poet begins the final thought of this unit (and of his poem) at H13, a not uncommon method of producing a heightened sense of clausula. He has already used it in this poem at 735 and 741, which also mark the end of major units of his poem. The just need no more description: they were described at 744–46. The molossus τρύχονται is emphatic in itself and more so after enjambment. The word is used of the effect of the suitors upon the house of Odysseus; Mimnermus (2W. 12) uses the form τρυχοῦσθαι similarly, with the idea of poverty. χαλεπῇ and πενίῃ, set round τειρόμενοι, form an effective phrase. Since sense requires a pause after both ὑβρίζῃ and τρύχονται, both hexameter and pentameter have a break after a molossus, followed by a phrase which spans the mandatory pause for caesura and diaeresis. (Contrast 749, where the sense of the phrase is complete at the caesura, even though the phrase continues.) As has occurred so frequently in this poem, the phrases are counterpointed against the major mandatory pauses of the hexameter. In performance, the effect could not be overlooked. It might well reinforce the message of the words: the cosmos is out of joint.

The poet of *Theognidea* 731–52W has a message to convey. He conveys it effectively, not by any imaginative or creative use of language, but by a sensitive use of the rhythmic resources of his meter. Here, as in Solon 4W. 12–13, we seem almost to hear the orator's voice.

The three Theognid poems discussed here differ greatly from one another, but each is good of its kind. No confident judgment can be made about their authorship. Kroll (1936, 164) argues that 237–54 cannot be by the same poet as 19–30 (the σφρηγίς poem) on the grounds of difference of language. That argument, which rests on the implicit assumption that the poets studied in this book are in all respects unconscious of style, seems unjustified. The use of language in 237–54 is conscious and deliberate and serves an identifiable purpose; 182–90 is a poem in which such language would be inappropriate, and it does not appear. Nevertheless, the two poems have a similar flexibility of composition and may well be by the same hand. 731–52 are not usually claimed for Theognis, and the poem differs in significant ways from both 182–90 and 237–54. Yet 182–90 and 237–54 each indicate that their composer was aware of the effect of judiciously employed broken rhythms. The poet of 731–52 counterpoints broken rhythms against smooth ones as a principal device of his poem. There may be other reasons for supposing difference of authorship, but it seems difficult to deny that the poet or poets of 182–90 and 237–54 could have composed a poem which used broken rhythms to a similar extent. If we are ever to be able to distinguish poet from poet in the *Theognidea* with some confidence, much more detailed study is needed.

8
SIMONIDES

The ancient world spelled in the same way, and commonly confused, the names of the poets whom we, relying on the authority of Choeroboscus, distinguish as Semonides of Amorgos and Simonides of Ceos.[1] The *Suda* refers to "Simonides (*sic*) of Amorgos" as a poet who wrote elegiac poetry, in two books, and also iambics, and who γέγονε 490 years after the Trojan War; it adds that some credit him with the invention of iambics. Some scholars suppose that part of the *Suda*'s entry for Simmias of Rhodes also refers to Semonides. It seems to be generally agreed that he flourished in the latter half of the seventh century.

Since this book is concerned with elegiac poetry, little more will be said of Semonides of Amorgos here. Only one elegy is possibly to be ascribed to him; and though that poem will be discussed here, I shall argue that the poem is certainly not by Semonides, is certainly of later date, and is possibly by the more famous poet Simonides, the dates of whose birth and death are almost certain (556–468 B.C.).[2] Simonides wrote lyric poetry of many kinds. On this, and on his epitaphs for the dead, his fame primarily rests. If we exclude from the genre of elegiac poetry the epitaphs or other poems that were written in the elegiac meter for inscription on monuments or other works of art or craft, little remains that may be termed Simonidean elegiacs. West prints eight lines as certain, thirteen as doubtfully Simonidean, and thirteen lines and three half-lines as doubtfully elegiac. In this chapter I shall attempt both to make a stronger case for the doubtfully Simonidean fragment and to argue that West's longest Simonidean fragment, though doubtless Simonidean, is not elegy in this sense but epigram.

Simonides' poems 4W through 16W contain 37 elegiac lines and parts of lines. Including final lines of poems, 26 of them are end-stopped.[3] There are 14 stops within the lines. No statistical conclusions can be based on these small numbers; they even suggest a poet less fluent than is revealed by reading the extant lines.

162   Chapter Eight

Of the hexameters, 5 end in disyllables (23.81%), 13 in trisyllables (61.90%), and 3 in pentesyllables (14.29%). The pentameters have 4 disyllabic endings (23.53%), 7 trisyllabic (41.18%), 2 quadrisyllabic (9.52%), 3 pentesyllabic (17.65%), and 1 hexasyllabic (5.88%).

Of the 20 hexameter lines or parts of lines whose caesura can be ascertained, 6 have caesura at H7 (30%), 9 at H8 (45%), 4 at H10 (20%), and 1 which could be read with major caesura at either H7 or H10.

◫◫◫

SIMONIDES 6W

τὴν ῥά ποτ' Οὐλύμποιο περὶ πλευρὰς ἐκάλυψεν
ὠκὺς ἀπὸ Θρήκης ὀρνύμενος Βορέης,
ἀνδρῶν δ' ἀχλαίνων ἔδακεν φρένας, αὐτὰρ ἐκάμφθη
ζωὴ Πιερίην γῆν ἐπιεσσαμένη,
5   ἔν τις ἐμοὶ καὶ τῆς χείτω μέρος· οὐ γὰρ ἔοικεν
θερμὴν βαστάζειν ἀνδρὶ φίλῳ πρόποσιν.

That ⟨snow⟩ which once swift Boreas, setting out from Thrace, wrapped around the flanks of Olympus, and "bit" the minds of cloakless men, that whose life, when it had clad Pieria, rounded the turn into the final straight; of that too let someone pour a share for me; for it is not seemly to raise a hot toast to a man that is a friend.

Athenaeus (125c–d) informs us, on the authority of Callistratus, that Simonides ἀπεσχεδίασε poem 6W at a banquet on a hot day, noticing that the wine-pourers were mixing snow with the others' wine but not his. How instantaneous ἀποσχεδιάζειν must be is unclear, and, evidently, Simonides might have polished his work afterward. However, under these circumstances a mind well stocked with Homer might be expected to produce formulae and other phenomena familiar from epic.

The three couplets of 6W, which even the cautious West treats as a complete poem, contain one sentence, punctuated by two commas and a raised stop. All three hexameters are enjambed, and in each case the pentameter contains no stop before the end of the line. Two of the hexameters have the common punctuation at H12. There is no other punctuation within the lines.

◫

1–2. This couplet contains the first of three relative clauses which precede the main clause ἐν . . . μέρος (6). The relative pronoun τήν depends on the demonstrative τῆς in 6. The word "snow" is not used, but the subject of the poem is evident at the end of 2. (If the poem was improvised at a banquet, the situation would make Simonides' meaning clear.)

The relative ὅ is not uncommon in elegiacs,[4] but it occurs only here in the Simonidean poems printed by West. West's two volumes contain three other examples of ῥα: two in fragments of the *Margites*, an imitation of Homer, and one in a conjectured restoration (Mimnermus 13a. 1). ῥα is equally rare in lyric and seems to possess an epic flavor where it does occur.[5] Though neither relative ὅ nor genitive in -οιο is exclusively epic, their combination with ῥα produces a phrase with an epic ring. The snow is very grand snow, and it comes from the grandest of mountains, the abode of the gods themselves. πλευρά is an unusual word for the slopes of a mountain. In Homer it is used exclusively of the flanks of men and animals. *LSJ* 1968 cite only Theognis 513, νηός τοι πλευρῇσιν ὑπὸ ζυγὰ θήσομεν ἡμεῖς for πλευρά used of inanimate objects by writers before the early fourth century; and there the fact that ζυγόν is used of both "bench" and "yoke" might suggest some degree of personalization. Since καλύπτειν is used of covering persons with garments,[6] the juxtaposition of ἐκάλυψεν with πλευράς already suggests a mantle of snow. In 2, ὠκύς and Βορέης in agreement neatly enclose the line. ὠκύς may appear routine, but it is frequent only in epic and may be a further touch of epic grandeur. It is not used with Βορέης in Homer, though ὠκέα Ἶρις and Boreas are compared (*Iliad* 15. 168–72), and κραιπνός is used (*Odyssey* 5. 385). Boreas is the cold wind of Greece. It is associated with Thrace regularly (*Works and Days* 507–8, 553–54) and with snow in *Odyssey* 14. 475–85, where Odysseus tells how he was caught out of doors without his cloak (χλαῖνα) when Boreas was blowing. Boreas is most vividly personalized in *Iliad* 23. 192–218. ὀρνύμενος occurs in association with Boreas in *Iliad* 14. 395, but there a wave is stirred up from the sea by the blasts of Boreas.

The spondees in 1–2 highlight Οὐλύμποιο . . . πλευράς and Θρῄκης, the places mentioned, while the dactyls express the motions.

3–4. Simonides has suggested a cloak of snow, and the whole of 2 was devoted to a wind whose blasts necessitate literal cloaks. The initial spondaic hemiepes ἀνδρῶν ἀχλαίνων renders "men without cloaks" the most emphatic idea in the second couplet and serves to point up the contrast between metaphorical and literal cloaks. The second hemiepes of 4 makes more explicit the metaphorical cloak of snow. (ἐπιέννυμι is used literally only once in Homer, with χλαῖναν as object [*Odyssey* 20. 143]. It is used in more vivid metaphors with ἀναιδείην [*Iliad* 1. 149; 9. 372; *Hymn to Hermes* 156] and with ἀλκήν [*Iliad* 7. 164; 8. 262; 18. 157; *Odyssey* 9. 214, 514]. The simple verb ἕννυμι is common in Homer in the literal sense.) ἄχλαινος is not Homeric. It occurs first here, and not again until Callimachus. ἀνδρῶν followed by a molossus word in agreement begins the hexameter on a number of occasions in Homer: λικμώντων (*Iliad* 5. 500), τρεσσάντων (*Iliad* 14. 522), ἡρώων (*Odyssey* 4. 268; 11. 629; etc.), μνηστήρων (*Odyssey* 13. 396, 428; 15. 32; etc.); however, only a very broad definition of "formula" would treat ἀνδρῶν ἀχλαίνων as formulaic. δάκε φρένας occurs once in Homer (*Iliad* 5. 493): δάκε δὲ φρένας Ἕκτορι μῦθος. Sarpedon's reproachful words "bit" Hector's mind, and he took immediate action. In Hesiod, *Theogony* 567, the theft of fire bit Zeus's θυμός, and he took revenge on Prometheus. But in *Works and Days* 450–51 the voice of the crane signals the season of ploughing and bites the κραδίη of the man without oxen, who can take no effective action at all; and in a fifth-century Theognid poem (903–30W) the writer is bitten in respect of his ψυχή, since he cannot know the length of his life and so cannot make plans. In a lyric poem (Page 1962, 579) Simonides says that no one can glimpse ἀρετή whose body has not exuded sweat that bites the θυμός. To be "bitten" in a psychological function is to receive an unpleasant stimulus from one's environment or—at all events by the early fifth century— from one's own mental or physical activities, and to respond with vigorous action or—if action is not possible, as in the case of the man without oxen in Hesiod or the cloakless men of Simonides 6W—with baffled frustration. The phrase is appropriate and powerful: Simonides has not resorted to the first available formula which would fit his line. ἐκάμφθη ζωή occurs only here; but variants using βίος occur four times in later tragedy (Euripides, *Hippolytus* 87, *Electra* 956, *Helen* 1666; Sophocles, *Oedipus at Colonus* 91). The metaphor is from the racetrack. In Euripides, τέλος or τελευτᾶν accompanies κάμπτειν, and death is pictured as imminent. In Sophocles, ἐνταῦθα κάμψειν τὸν ταλαίπωρον βίον might signify that the next—and last— stretch of Oedipus' life is to be less miserable; but the audience knows that the end is near and might interpret the metaphor in the light of their knowledge. In Simonides, however, since the snow has survived the transition from Pieria to banquet hall and from mountain cloak to beverage cooler, one might render "having cloaked Pieria, its life rounded the turn into the final straight." The metaphor is somewhat mixed: one would expect swift Boreas, not the snow, to be racing. If the phrase was coined by Simonides, however, the imperfect cadence at the end of 3 would be reinforced not merely by incomplete syntax but by curiosity over what could follow ἐκάμφθη. The unexpected ζωή merits its prominence.

5–6. Simonides has written four lines with some epic coloring and has produced one phrase which is striking and novel—in extant Greek, at all events. The two couplets consist of three relative clauses, and the last pentameter contained only four words. The poem has been complex, the tone elevated. Simonides now fits a main clause of seven words into the first four feet of the hexameter. The expression is simple and direct, the tone un-epic: in place of Homer's μοῖρα or αἶσα he uses the fifth-century μέρος for his portion of snow. The long syllables καὶ τῆς χείτω highlight the snow and the pouring. οὐ γὰρ ἔοικεν is a Homeric line ending (*Iliad* 21. 379) and might restore a little epic coloring. Imperfect cadence and incomplete syntax appropriately increase the emphasis of the initial spondaic word θερμήν, counterpointed against the chill which Simonides has conveyed in the first five lines without using any word meaning "cold." βαστάζειν occurs here only in early elegy and iambus. It is not found in Hesiod or in the poets of Page 1962 or 1974. (It may occur in Lobel and Page 1955, Alcaeus F3[b]9.) It is used on two occasions in Homer, both in the *Odyssey*: of Sisyphus rolling his boulder (11. 594) and of Odysseus handling the great bow (21. 405). The previous history of the word suggests that its use conveys an idea of weight, literal or metaphorical, to anything that is raised. (Its connotations in the Alcaeus passage are not clear.) πρόποσις occurs first here. It is used both of the act of drinking a toast and—more rarely—of the beverage drunk as a toast. Here the latter sense is evidently in the foreground: one cannot βαστάζειν an act of drinking. But connotations are important in poetry, and Simonides was writing for speakers of Greek, not translators. Though θερμήν is a vague word, it seems a little strong for a beverage that, though not chilled, has not been heated: the usage attracts the reader's or hearer's attention. Now θερμός with persons or actions can mean "hasty, rash, headlong" (*LSJ* 1968, s.v., mng. II); and verbal nouns in -σις characteristically denote actions. I suggest that Simonides is playing on two senses of θερμήν and two senses of πρόποσιν, the one prepared for by the first five lines, the other revealed only by οὐ γὰρ ἔοικεν and the sixth line. The literal sense does not quite fit: even in the United States it is not unseemly to drink the health of one's friends with unchilled beverages. The audience is nudged toward a metaphorical interpretation: behavior which can be characterized as θερμήν is unseemly among friends who are drinking together. (The response of Penia to what she terms a θερμὸν ἔργον [Aristophanes, *Plutus* 415–21] illustrates the point.)

This poem is certainly an epigram in the modern sense. It is also an epigram in the sense current in later antiquity: a short poem in elegiac couplets which makes a single point in elegantly turned language. That it was extemporized seems improbable. There is no routine use of formulae. The plays on words seem unlikely to come immediately to the tip of the tongue, and the sentence structure is unparalleled in the pre-Alexandrian elegiac poets included in West's edition. Relative clauses rarely precede the word on which they depend in such poetry, and, when they do so, the clause is usually brief. Here we have a sequence of three, occupying two elegiac couplets, before the "antecedent" and the main clause are reached. The sentence has a periodic structure uncommon in poetry and, if we take Homer as our exemplar of ἀποσχεδιάζειν, very uncommon in extemporized poetry, even in the hands of its finest practitioners.⁷ The poem seems carefully polished. Can it be an example of an ἐπίγραμμα in the more precise sense: a poem made to be inscribed on an artifact—here, presumably, a mixing bowl? Callistratus makes a different claim; but what additional evidence had Callistratus? ἐμοί (5) might well refer to the mixing bowl; the position of καί in 5 suggests not "pour in some snow for me too" but "pour in some snow too for me"; and why should the wine-pourers have discriminated against Simonides in the distribution of snow? If the mixing bowl is speaking,⁸ the lines are a general admonition to all users of the bowl. The remainder of the poem can readily be interpreted as "for it is unseemly for *anyone* to lift a θερμὴν πρόποσιν to a man who is his friend."

Simonides 8W

ἓν δὲ τὸ κάλλιστον Χῖος ἔειπεν ἀνήρ·
"οἵη περ φύλλων γενεή, τοίη δὲ καὶ ἀνδρῶν"·
παῦροί μιν θνητῶν οὔασι δεξάμενοι
στέρνοις ἐγκατέθεντο· πάρεστι γὰρ ἐλπὶς ἑκάστῳ
5   ἀνδρῶν, ἥ τε νέων στήθεσιν ἐμφύεται.
θνητῶν δ' ὄφρά τις ἄνθος ἔχῃ πολυήρατον ἥβης,
κοῦφον ἔχων θυμὸν πόλλ' ἀτέλεστα νοεῖ·
οὔτε γὰρ ἐλπίδ' ἔχει γηρασέμεν οὔτε θανεῖσθαι,
οὐδ', ὑγιὴς ὅταν ᾖ, φροντίδ' ἔχει καμάτου.
10 νήπιοι, οἷς ταύτῃ κεῖται νόος, οὐδὲ ἴσασιν
ὡς χρόνος ἔσθ' ἥβης καὶ βιότου ὀλίγος
θνητοῖς. ἀλλὰ σὺ ταῦτα μαθὼν βιότου ποτὶ τέρμα
ψυχῇ τῶν ἀγαθῶν τλῆθι χαριζόμενος.

One thing that is very fine(?) the man from Chios said: "As is the generation of leaves, so is that of men too." Few of mortals receiving it in their ears deposited it in their chests; for hope, which grows in the breasts of the young, is present to each of men. So long as any of mortals possesses the much-loved flower of youth, with a mind that is featherbrained he thinks many thoughts that are not to be fulfilled(?); for he has no expectation that he will grow old or die, nor, when he is healthy, has he any anxiety(?) about toil(?). Fools are they whose mind is so inclined, nor do they know that the time of youth and life(?) is brief for mortals. But do you, learning these things, to the end of your life endure, gratifying your soul with good things.

This poem may have been written by neither Simonides nor Semonides. Victor Steffen (1973, 1:88–93) argues for Mimnerman authorship, while West (1974) treats it as "a product of about the time of Simonides, preserved under his name, but probably not by him," since "the simplicity of thought and the absence of distinctive language do not remind us of Simonides. As far as the thought goes, there is nothing that could not have been said in the seventh or early sixth century." (Lloyd-Jones [1975] also doubts Semonidean authorship without ascribing the poem to Simonides.) West is echoing Bergk; but he does not join Bergk in ascribing the poem to Semonides, for he argues that some of the linguistic usages it contains, and the practice of quoting and commenting on a previous writer, seem to belong to the fifth century. (West regards Solon's comments on Mimnermus as different.) The linguistic indications will be discussed below; the thought may be less simple than it appears to be. Here it is especially important to remember that the poem was composed for performance.

West marks the last line of Simonides 8W as the end of the poem. It would be difficult to disagree. At least a hexameter must have preceded the first line, since only the Delphic Oracle and Dionysius Chalcus are credited with elegies beginning with a pentameter (above, p. 6, and below, p. 209, n. 4).

Of the thirteen lines we have, eight are end-stopped by West, and the hexameter which preceded 1 would have required a comma. Three hexameters (4, 10, 12) and two pentameters (3, 11) are enjambed: 3–5 and 10–13 are composed less by the line than is the remainder of the poem. Of the enjambed hexameters, 4 is overrun to a comma after the first spondee (P3) in the pentameter, 10 to a full stop after an enjambed pentameter, at the end of the first spondee in the following hexameter (12 [H3]). Of the stops within the line, three occur at the major or mandatory pause: at the H10 caesura in 2 (the Homeric line), at the H8 caesura in 4, at colon diaeresis P7 in 9. Line 9 also has a comma at P1. In 10 there are commas at H3 and H12, to produce a line with three pauses. The overall effect is one of fluency in composition.

1–2. It is difficult to guess the content of the line or lines that preceded 1. The suggestion οὐδὲν ἐν ἀνθρώποισι μένει χρῆμ' ἔμπεδον αἰεί is not even plausible: as Steffen (1973) noted, the poet's theme is in fact rather the folly of mankind in failing to follow the advice of 12–13. The initial οὐδέν also sets up an implied opposition with ἕν which is irrelevant to the sense. To read adverbial ἐν, as suggested in West's apparatus, would permit a preceding line concerned with other themes in Homer. The poet evidently believes that Homer composed at least the *Iliad* and that he was a Chian. The latter is an inference from the "Homeric" *Hymn to Apollo* 172, whose author, referring to himself, writes τυφλὸς ἀνήρ, οἰκεῖ δὲ Χίῳ ἐνὶ παιπαλοέσσῃ: "the author of the *Hymn to Apollo* was a Chian, but Homer wrote the *Hymn to Apollo*; therefore Homer was a Chian." The inference is valid, but the conclusion is false, since the second premise is false. Whatever one means by "Homer," the "Homeric" hymns are of later date than the *Iliad* and *Odyssey*. κάλλιστον, emphasized by its long syllables, does not mean, unequivocally, "aesthetically beautiful." Recall Odysseus' "ξεῖν', οὐ καλὸν ἔειπες," uttered to Euryalus (*Odyssey* 8. 166) when he taunted Odysseus with being a merchant and no athlete. Here χαρίεντα in the following line suggests that οὐ καλόν decries the offensive content of Euryalus' speech. But καλόν is also used in contexts where translators use "beautiful" or "noble" as equivalents. Simonides uses κάλλιστον before quoting the line. Had Tyrtaeus written line 1 and continued by quoting *Iliad* 12. 243, εἷς οἰωνὸς ἄριστος, ἀμύνεσθαι περὶ πάτρης, translators would render κάλλιστον by "noblest"; but the Greek of line 1 would be unchanged. On hearing 1, the audience would not be certain of the subject matter of 2. The poetry of 2 is clearly Homer's responsibility, not Simonides'; but its function in the economy of Simonides' poem may display his skill.

3–4(H8). The enjambment here occurs at the end of a sense group, but the sentence is not complete until the main verb is reached. οὔασι, immediately after the mandatory word break and pause at P7, balances στέρνοις at the beginning of 4, and the following verbs produce two parallel two-word phrases. But their positions in the couplet give each phrase a different effect. οὔασι δεξάμενοι ends at the perfect cadence and reflects the actual reception of the message; στέρνοις ἐγκατέθεντο ends at the trochaic caesura, a mandatory but temporary pause, which leaves the audience expecting an explanation. The rhythm produces a similar effect. The spondaic hemiepes παῦροί μιν θνητῶν is solemn. The only other spondee in lines 4–5 emphasizes στέρνοις, the abode in which Homer's message should rest, while the following dactyls reflect the ease with which the message is forgotten. The contrast between ears and mind may suggest a fifth-century date; it recalls the words of the Guard in Sophocles' *Antigone* 317, 319: ἐν τοῖσιν ὠσὶν ἢ 'πὶ τῇ ψυχῇ δάκνῃ; and ὁ δρῶν σ' ἀνιᾷ τὰς φρένας, τὰ δ' ὦτ' ἐγώ. Simonides' phrases seem novel, but the raw material for the idea exists already in Homer. In any language, the distinction between hearing and understanding or remembering will be drawn only when relevant; at other times "hearing" may stand for "hear, understand, and remember," even when "ears" are mentioned. οἱ δ' οὔασι πάντες ἄκουον (*Iliad* 12. 442) has no implication of "but did not understand." But in *Iliad* 15. 128–29 Athena says to Ares "μαινόμενε, φρένας ἠλέ, διέφθορας· ἦ νύ τοι αὔτως / οὔατ' ἀκουέμεν ἐστί, νόος δ' ἀπόλωλε καὶ αἰδώς." δέχεσθαι of a speech is Homeric (*Odyssey* 20. 271), and ἄλλο δέ τοι ἐρέω, σὺ δ' ἐν φρεσὶ βάλλεο σῇσιν is a Homeric formula (*Odyssey* 11. 454, etc.). Theoclymenus (*Odyssey* 20. 365–66) enumerates: "εἰσί μοι ὀφθαλμοί τε καὶ οὔατα καὶ πόδες ἄμφω / καὶ νόος ἐν στήθεσσι." The explicit distinction between words reaching the ears and reaching the mind is not drawn in Homer or in any extant poem which can with confidence be dated earlier than the death of Simonides. The explicitness may be the work of our poet; the parallel phrases, and their neat positioning in the couplet, certainly are.

But what is the poet's message? How will Simonides develop his poem? The audience does not yet know; and I suggest that Simonides' goal in this poem is to be enigmatic to the last line of the poem. To remember the context of Homer's line will not help, for Homer's message is unclear; and, insofar as it is clear, it is not Simonides' message. In *Iliad* 6, Diomedes asks Glaucus about his lineage, to establish that he is not a god; if he is a mortal, Diomedes will fight him. Glaucus' reply includes the line quoted in Simonides 8W; and after their conversation the heroes do not fight each other. The reason is not that the brevity of human life renders war a folly: the two discover that they are guest-friends as a result of a compact entered into by their grandfathers, and so they will not engage in combat with each other, since there is no lack of other Greeks and Trojans to fight (*Iliad* 6. 224–29). The brevity of human life is explicitly linked with war elsewhere: Sarpedon says to Glaucus (*Iliad* 12. 322–28) that if those who were not killed in war would be ageless and deathless otherwise, he would not fight, nor would he urge Glaucus to do so; but since death is inevitable, let them fight the foe and win glory if they can. Here, in our poem, κάλλιστον, in 1, may suggest the martial excellences. 2 carries no nonmartial implications in Homer. The audience cannot yet know the subject of Simonides' poem.

4(H9)–5. Here many editors punctuate after ἑκάστῳ, including ἀνδρῶν in the relative clause and eliminating the emphasis derived from enjambment. West has a great sensitivity for punctuation, but in this instance his comma after ἀνδρῶν gives inferior sense. In 2, ἀνδρῶν, though uttered in the context of battle and possibly with only men in mind, is equally relevant to women: in poetry, unemphatic ἀνήρ may be equivalent in sense to ἄνθρωπος. ἀνδρῶν in 2 is equivalent to θνητῶν in 3, 6, and 12, and it is Homer's word, not Simonides'. Elsewhere in the poem, Simonides uses θνητῶν; and had he simply wanted to say clearly that every member of the human race feels hope, θνητῶν is a much better word than ἀνδρῶν. To include ἀνδρῶν in the relative clause—young *men*—maintains the possibility that Simonides is concerned with the martial excellences: all hope (ἑκάστῳ), but the theme of Simonides' poem is the young warrior, such as Glaucus in *Iliad* 6. ἐμφύεται is used elsewhere of mental contents: "the god" ἐνέφυσεν Phemius' songs in his mind (*Odyssey* 22. 347–48), and *Theognidea* 396W has ἰθεῖα γνώμη στήθεσιν ἐμπεφύη. The word may not be metaphorical. The concept of the nonmaterial cannot be shown to exist clearly before Plato (or Socrates); and the growth of the hope may be pictured as in a quite literal sense preventing, by its material presence (πάρεστι), the storage of the Homeric line. ἐμφύεται, πάρεστι, and ἐγκατέθεντο may be more than a sustained metaphor. (ἐγκατατίθεμαι is Homeric with ἀτήν [*Odyssey* 23. 223]; with a personalized Μῆτις [Hesiod, *Theogony* 890]; and with ταῦτα [*Works and Days* 27].) But for what is the ἐλπίς? And to what action or inaction does it lead?

6–7. θνητῶν, spondaic first word in an otherwise dactylic line, emphatically restates the theme of 2. In 3 the word needed no such emphasis: the whole sentence was contrasted with the adjacent 2. ἄνθος . . . ἥβης is also Mimnerman, and in his poetry it denotes primarily beauty and the pleasures of love (above, p. 100). In Mimnermus 1. 4W and 2. 3W the context makes the meaning clear. But in Homer (*Iliad* 13. 484, *Hymn to Hermes* 375) the word denotes the strength and prowess of the young warrior. πολυήρατον does not restrict the range of ἄνθος: πολυήρατον is used in sexual contexts, as in *Odyssey* 15. 126 (γάμος) and Hesiod, *Theogony* 404 (εὐνή). But with εὐνή in Mimnermus 12W. 5 there are no evident sexual connotations, and it is used of ὕδωρ in Hesiod, *Works and Days* 739, of Thebes in *Odyssey* 11. 275, and of Athens in Solon 4W.21. The young man may find his own youth πολυήρατον; and even if the amorous desire of others is denoted, it may be felt for the warrior as a fighting man. κοῦφος in Homer is used only adverbially, in a literal sense. Its meaning here is indicated by Solon 13W.36: χάσκοντες κούφαις ἐλπίσι τερπόμεθα. (*Theognidea* 497–98W and 579–80 are similar.) The phrase is pejorative: "featherbrained," not "lighthearted." πολλὰ νοεῖν could mean "have many thoughts that are not to be accomplished" or "have many plans that are not to be fulfilled."[9] In the first case, the young man presumably supposes that he will live forever; in the second, he makes plans which would be sensible only if he were going to live forever. In the first case, the young man might do nothing, thinking he had plenty of time: he has forgotten what Sarpedon said to Glaucus. In the second, he might be very strenuous, not reflecting—one would suppose—that he will be old or dead before his efforts meet with their reward. The second is closer to Simonides' message, when that is revealed; but κοῦφον ἔχων θυμόν rather suggests the other interpretation.

8–9. The light dactylic rhythm reflects the frame of mind of the young. ἐλπίς now occurs in a sense different from that of 4: clumsy, if Simonides is writing a straightforward expository poem, purposeful if he is playing off meaning against meaning throughout. οὔτε . . . γηρασέμεν οὔτε θανεῖσθαι recalls Sarpedon's "if we would be ἀγήρω τ' ἀθανάτω τε should we not be killed in war" (*Iliad* 12. 323). I claim no allusion, merely that a train of thought based on the most powerful of Greek values leads from facing the fact of one's mortality to active valor in war. Simonides might be blaming the young for letting the chance of glory pass them by. In 9, φροντίς is a fifth-century word. This may be its first extant appearance. *LSJ* 1968 lists among its meanings "thought, care, attention, anxiety." The usual rendering here is "nor, when he is healthy, is he anxious about illness." The commentators do note that κάματος is very rare in the sense of "illness"[10] (though the verb κάμνω is fairly common in this sense in writers from Herodotus onward), but they fail to draw the conclusion that unless the sense "illness" is the only one possible in the context created by the preceding lines of the poem, the hearer will understand the word in one of its more common senses: "toil" (*Odyssey* 7. 325, etc.), "weariness" (*Iliad* 4. 230), or even "hard-earned wages" (*Odyssey* 14. 417). The last is ruled out by the context. But in combination with the new and somewhat vague word φροντίς, the clause might mean "he takes no thought of toil," i.e., he does not toil, or "he is not anxious about weariness or toil," i.e., he does toil. Nothing as yet written in Simonides 8W helps the audience to decide in favor of either interpretation. Neither is quite correct. If the line had been preserved without context, commentators would almost certainly accept "work" as the sense of κάματος. ὑγιής and καμάτου are neatly arranged at opposite ends of a wholly dactylic line each of whose phrases occupies one dactylic hemiepes; but that does not suffice to establish the sense of κάματος.

10–12(H3). νήπιοι, οἷς ταύτῃ κεῖται νόος sums up without clarifying, for it is unclear whether νόος refers to φροντίς, the nearer word, or to νοεῖ, the more similar one. Since the sense of neither νοεῖ nor φροντίς is clear, the audience is still receiving more than one message, none of which is Simonides' actual message. οὐδὲ ἴσασιν . . . θνητοῖς says quite clearly that the time of youth and life is short for mortals; but the inference to be drawn from the statement is as unclear as it was in 2. Even here Simonides has left some vagueness in his language: both βίος and βίοτος may mean "life" or "livelihood," but βίοτος seems more strongly established in the latter sense.[11] Simonides could easily have written βίου: ἠδὲ βίου produces a line not inferior to the line he wrote. The word must denote "life" in 11; but the connotation "livelihood" will be in the hearer's mind.

12(H4)–13. Thus far Simonides has delivered no clear message. The design of the last couplet suggests that the unclarity is not an accident. ἀλλὰ σὺ ταῦτα μαθών, like οὐδὲ ἴσασιν . . . θνητοῖς, is clear in itself, but the meaning of ταῦτα depends on one's understanding of the advice in the preceding lines. For βιότου West suggests θανάτου, apparently to avoid the repetition. But βιότου ποτὶ τέρμα continues Simonides' word plays. "To the limit of one's life" and "to the limit of one's livelihood" are both possible meanings, and indeed both are relevant. If Simonides is exhorting to a life of exertions, "life" will be more in the foreground; and the audience does not yet know the nature of his exhortation. ψυχῇ τῶν ἀγαθῶν τλῆθι: until the very last word, the sense is unclear. The audience cannot know whether τῶν ἀγαθῶν is the genitive of τὰ ἀγαθά or of οἱ ἀγαθοί. The latter is much more common in early Greek. (The neuter occurs in *Theognidea* 999–1000W, δείπνου δὲ λήγοιμεν . . . παντοίων ἀγαθῶν γαστρὶ χαριζόμενοι, where the preceding words leave no doubt as to the sense.) The singular ψυχῇ debars taking the sense as "the ψυχή of brave men"; but one might interpret ψυχῇ with τλῆθι and expect a phrase meaning "emulating the valor of brave men" to follow. τλῆναι is followed by an infinitive, not a participle (*Odyssey* 20. 311 is a possible exception). When a participle appears in the same clause, the sense is usually concessive, as in *Iliad* 1. 586, τέτλαθι . . . καὶ ἀνάσχεο κηδομένη περ. A word like χαριζόμενος is unusual in accompaniment to τλῆναι; and Simonides has spent the earlier part of his poem in confusing the expectations of his audience.

There seems to be no doubt that this poem is not by Semonides or by Mimnermus. Semonides' use of language is simple: contrast Simonides 8W with the superficially similar sentiments of Semonides 1W. The presence of words which occur next in fifth-century writers does not disprove Mimnerman authorship. In addition to *hapax legomena* (ἀτίμαστος, 1W. 9; χαλεπήρης, 11W. 3; φερεμμελίην, 14W. 4), Mimnermus has πήχυιος (2W. 3), which occurs next in Apollonius Rhodius; τρυχόω for the Homeric τρύχω (2W. 12), next in Thucydides and medical writers; ὀλιγοχρόνιος (5W. 4), next in Herodotus 1. 38; ἄμορφον (5W. 5), next in Herodotus 1. 196; ὑπερκρεμμάννυμι (5W. 6), next in Pindar, *Olympians* 1. 91; ἑξηκονταέτης (6W. 2), next in *Hippocratic Corpus* 1149D; ἀνά- (ἄμ-) παυσις (12W. 2), next in Pindar, *Nemeans* 7. 52; and ὑπόπτερος (12W. 7), next in Pindar, *Olympians* 9. 36, *Pythians* 8. 130, and Aeschylus, *Choephori* 603. But all these words are quite rare, and their coinage and use require no conceptual innovation. West, citing *IG* 12(9). 287, argues that the use of the comparatively common ψυχή as something capable of gratification does not antedate the fifth century. In fact, Hipponax (39. 1) writes κακοῖσι δώσω τὴν πολύστονον ψυχήν, and Anacreon (Page 1962, 360) has a ψυχή under the influence of love. Either could presumably have written of gratifying the ψυχή, but we are still far from the lifetime of Mimnermus.

More significantly, though Mimnermus may keep his audience in suspense for a few lines,[12] no extant Mimnerman poem possesses the sustained ambiguity of Simonides 8W; and Mimnermus neither recommends τλῆναι nor supposes that any gratification could alleviate the horrors of old age.

The simplicity of the thought need not exclude Simonidean authorship; for the thought is not simple. If Simonides 6W is by Simonides of Ceos—and no one doubts it—then 8W is not unworthy of that poet. 8W displays to an even higher degree a capability for wordplay; and whereas 6W reveals its point only in the last line, 8W does so only in the last word.[13]

9
XENOPHANES

Like Simonides, Xenophanes lived a long life that extended into the earlier fifth century. The dates of his birth and death are less certain: about 570 to 478. He informs us in 8W that he is already ninety-two years of age and has spent all but the first twenty-five years away from his native city of Colophon. The statements that have been made by some modern scholars about Xenophanes' mode of life and social status seem unjustified by the evidence; they will be discussed in the context of the poem.

Of our eight elegists, Xenophanes is the only one whose extant works appear also in Diels-Kranz (1951, 1:113–39). Those in elegiac couplets fall under the definition of elegy, and West duly prints them; but it is on his philosophical achievements that Xenophanes' fame must rest, and it may appear fruitless to discuss his work as poetry. Nevertheless, though there was in Xenophanes' day an established tradition of writing philosophy in prose, Xenophanes chose to write in verse;[1] and his extant elegiacs have some characteristics, not all of them defects, which distinguish him from the other elegists discussed. As a poet, he is probably the least well equipped technically of the eight,[2] but he has an imagination with some poetic qualities.

Of Xenophanes' elegiacs, 35 hexameters and 34 pentameters are extant. There are ten poems, or fragments, ranging in length from one that is twenty-four lines long (1W), to single hexameters (7W) or pentameters (9W). Including final lines, 49 of the 69[3] are end-stopped, and there are only 20 stops within the lines. These figures—appropriately—do not suggest a fluent composer.

Of the 35 hexameters, 1 ends in a monosyllable (2.86%), 7 end in disyllables (20%), 17 in trisyllables (48.57%), 8 in quadrisyllables (22.86%), and 2 in pentesyllables (5.71%). As Table 6 shows, Xenophanes' proportion of disyllabic endings in these lines is much lower than that of Homer (30.87%) or the elegists of this book (36.87%), that of quadrisyllables much higher than Homer (11.01%) or elegy (12.49%).

174

Xenophanes' 34 extant pentameters have 2 monosyllabic endings (5.88%), 7 disyllabic (20.59%), 17 trisyllabic (50%), 4 quadrisyllabic (11.76%), and 4 pentesyllabic (11.76%). In these lines, Xenophanes shows a marked preference for trisyllabic over disyllabic endings that is not characteristic of elegy in general (see Table 7).

Of Xenophanes' caesurae, 10 occur at H7 (28.57%), 11 at H8 (31.43%), and 14 at H10 (40%). As Table 4 shows, only 13.96 percent of the hexameters of the elegists discussed here have caesura at H10; a figure of 40 percent thus gives an individual character to the movement of Xenophanes' extant lines.

XENOPHANES 1W

νῦν γὰρ δὴ ζάπεδον καθαρὸν καὶ χεῖρες ἁπάντων
καὶ κύλικες· πλεκτοὺς δ' ἀμφιτιθεῖ στεφάνους,
ἄλλος δ' εὐῶδες μύρον ἐν φιάλῃ παρατείνει·
κρητὴρ δ' ἕστηκεν μεστὸς εὐφροσύνης·
5 ἄλλος δ' οἶνος ἑτοῖμος, ὃς οὔποτέ φησι προδώσειν,
μείλιχος ἐν κεράμοις, ἄνθεος ὀζόμενος·
ἐν δὲ μέσοις ἁγνὴν ὀδμὴν λιβανωτὸς ἵησιν,
ψυχρὸν δ' ἐστὶν ὕδωρ καὶ γλυκὺ καὶ καθαρόν·
παρκέαται δ' ἄρτοι ξανθοὶ γεραρή τε τράπεζα
10 τυροῦ καὶ μέλιτος πίονος ἀχθομένη·
βωμὸς δ' ἄνθεσιν ἂν τὸ μέσον πάντῃ πεπύκασται,
μολπὴ δ' ἀμφὶς ἔχει δώματα καὶ θαλίη.
χρὴ δὲ πρῶτον μὲν θεὸν ὑμνεῖν εὔφρονας ἄνδρας
εὐφήμοις μύθοις καὶ καθαροῖσι λόγοις,
15 σπείσαντάς τε καὶ εὐξαμένους τὰ δίκαια δύνασθαι
πρήσσειν· ταῦτα γὰρ ὦν ἐστι προχειρότερον,
οὐχ ὕβρεις· πίνειν δ' ὁπόσον κεν ἔχων ἀφίκοιο
οἴκαδ' ἄνευ προπόλου μὴ πάνυ γηραλέος.
ἀνδρῶν δ' αἰνεῖν †τοῦτον ὃς ἐσθλὰ πιὼν ἀναφαίνει,
20 ὡς ᾖ μνημοσύνη καὶ τόνος ἀμφ' ἀρετῆς,
οὔ τι μάχας διέπειν Τιτήνων οὐδὲ Γιγάντων
οὐδὲ ⟨ ⟩ Κενταύρων, πλάσμα⟨τα⟩ τῶν προτέρων,
ἢ στάσιας σφεδανάς· τοῖς οὐδὲν χρηστὸν ἔνεστιν·
θεῶν ⟨δὲ⟩ προμηθείην αἰὲν ἔχειν ἀγαθήν.

For now the floor(?) is clean, and the hands of all, and the cups; and ⟨one slave⟩ puts plaited garlands ⟨on the heads of the guests⟩, while another holds sweet-smelling perfume near them in a bowl. A mixing bowl stands there full of good cheer. Another wine, which says it will never play the traitor, is ready in jars, gentle, smelling of flowers. In the midst the frankincense puts forth its pure(?) scent, and there is(?) cold, sweet, clear water. Nearby are lying yellow loaves and a lordly(?) table, laden with cheese and rich(?) honey. An altar is all shaded with flowers in the midst, and singing and feasting possess the house all about.

Men of good cheer(?) should first hymn the god with pious(?) stories and pure(?) themes, having poured libations and prayed to be able to do what is just. For ⟨to do⟩ these things, not acts of violence, is easier(?). One should drink as much as would enable one to reach home without an attendant, unless one is very old. One should commend that man who, having drunk what is good(?), manifests(?) what is good, that there may be remembrance of excellence(?) and pursuit of it. One should not(?) handle(?) battles of Titans or Giants or . . . Centaurs, the inventions of our elders, nor violent civic(?) discords. In them there is nothing useful; and of the gods one should always take good heed(?).

The text of Xenophanes 1W is disputed at a number of important points, and interpretations of Xenophanes' message have varied widely. Bowra (1938b) regards the poem as innovating within a framework of familiar ideas; Defradas (1962) thinks it is much more radical. It will be best to discuss the work line by line before attempting any general conclusions.

This poem exhibits a marked preference for trisyllabic words in final position in the hexameter. Seven lines end thus (1, 5, 7, 9, 15, 21, 23); only one (13) has a disyllabic ending, and four (3, 11, 17, 19) end in a quadrisyllable. The figures for the pentameters are similar: six endings are trisyllabic (2, 8, 12, 20, 22, 24), one is disyllabic (14), three are quadrisyllabic (6, 10, 18), and two are pentesyllabic (4, 16). The numbers are too small to be statistically significant; but 2W, Xenophanes' only other extant poem of more than twenty lines, displays a similar pattern, which is shared by the work of no other extant elegiac poet. In Xenophanes 1W and 2W, twenty-six lines (fourteen hexameters, twelve pentameters) out of forty-six end in trisyllabic words.

In West's edition, six of the hexameters (1, 9, 13, 15, 17, 21) are enjambed, four (5, 7, 11, 19) are stopped with commas, and two (3, 23) with raised stops. No sentence ends at the end of a hexameter. Every pentameter is stopped with at least a comma. Five (2, 14, 16, 20, 22) have commas at line end, four (4, 6, 8, 10) have raised stops, and three (12, 18, 24) have full stops. Only three hexameters have stops within the line, two of them at major caesura: at H8 in 5, at H7 in 23. The third occurs at H4 in 17. All are raised stops. Four pentameters are thus stopped: 6 and 22 have commas at P7, the colon diaeresis, while 2 and 16 have raised stops, at P4 and P3, respectively.

Static analysis suggests a poet composing couplet by couplet: no pentameter is enjambed. The sentences are long: there are only three of them in the twenty-four lines (1–12, 13–18, 19–24). But the sentences do not flow smoothly: West prints ten raised stops in twenty-four lines in 1W. In comparison, there are five in Xenophanes 2W (22 lines, 2 sentences), four in Tyrtaeus 12W (44 lines, 7 sentences), and eight in Solon 4W (39 lines, 3 sentences). These poets possessed no marks of punctuation, and no version is canonical; but West is sensitive to nuances of punctuation, and these figures serve a purpose in a preliminary survey.

1–2. The first line of 1W cannot be the first line of Xenophanes' poem if the text as printed by West is correct. The γάρ is connective and explanatory. It must be, for, with the exception of the relative clause after the H8 caesura in 5, the twelve lines of Xenophanes' sentence consist of coordinate main clauses. If, following the epitomator and Eustathius, one omitted δ' in 2, some case could be made for treating νῦν . . . κύλικες as an anticipatory γάρ-clause:[4] "Since the floor is clean . . . , someone is . . . ." But the cleanliness of the floor, hands, and cups seems an inappropriate reason to give for the statements which follow. One might expect such a clause to be followed by one or more commands or exhortations: "Let our drinking begin."[5] Presumably the sense of the missing couplet or couplets was "Let us begin our drinking party. We have what we need; for . . . ."

The first clause must be supplemented with the appropriate part of εἶναι. However, when the performer reaches καθαρόν, the hearer cannot be certain that ζάπεδον καθαρόν is not the subject or object of a verb. If it were the object, καὶ χεῖρες ἀπάντων might be the first of two or more coordinate subjects. Again, the hearer might supply ἐστι with ζάπεδον καθαρόν and await a different verb with χεῖρες. These possibilities may serve to keep the hearer's mind more alert than that of the reader, whose eye takes in the structure of νῦν . . . κύλικες at a glance. But καὶ κύλικες seems not to warrant its emphatic position: γάρ (1) suggests that Xenophanes has already established that this is to be a drinking party, so that the presence of wine cups hardly needs emphasis. The first clause has a common order, with the shared element (καθαρόν) at the end of the first unit of the list.[6] Modern readers may regard such lists as rather unpoetic, but better early Greek poets than Xenophanes do not avoid them.[7] In the first line, a noun and an adjective are set together immediately before the hephthemimeral caesura at H10. Xenophanes seems to favor this caesura (above, p. 175). There are ten or eleven occurrences in 1W and 2W (1W. 1, 7, 9, 11, 15; 2W. 1, 7, 11, 15, 17, and perhaps 21);[8] and, of these, five (1W. 1, 7, 9; 2W. 7, 15) have noun and adjective so placed. In each of the five, though the major caesura is clearly at H10, there is caesura also at H7, between the noun and the adjective. In comparison, Solon places noun and adjective in this position only twice (36, 38) in 4W, once (59) in 13W; and Tyrtaeus has no examples in 10W, none in 11W, and one (21) in 12W (10W. 5 and 12W. 17 are similar but have an additional caesura at H8, not H7). In other words, Xenophanes has five examples in twenty-three hexameters, Solon has three in fifty-seven hexameters, and Tyrtaeus has one in fifty-seven hexameters.

In 2, the subject is not expressed, but it is different from that of 1. ἄλλος μέν must be supplied from ἄλλος δ' in 3. The effect seems awkward and clumsy. πλεκτούς . . . στεφάνους furnishes a neatly enclosed phrase. πλεκτούς, at the beginning of its clause and given increased prominence by the following pause at P7, may seem not to merit such emphasis: garlands are of their nature πλεκτοί. But the effect is intended: it highlights a visual detail.

3–4. ἄλλος seems unnecessarily emphatic. It is unimportant that different slaves are performing different tasks. Possibly Xenophanes thought that ἄλλος so placed would render 2 less clumsy. There is no metrical constraint: εὐῶδες δ' ἄλλος is equally acceptable meter. ἄλλος and εὐῶδες are highlighted by their meter: the first sequence of five long syllables in the poem. 4 also begins with a spondaic hemiepes: κρητὴρ δ' ἕστηκεν. The emphasis is merited. ἕστηκεν is not otiose, nor is it a waste of three long syllables to express something quite unemphatic. Xenophanes is taking pains to indicate spatial relationships. He begins with the floor or the earth.[9] ἀμφιτιθεῖ (2) introduces an encircling motion, παρατείνει (3) a motion alongside. In 4, the mixing bowl stands firm and upright, a contrast enhanced by the change from dactyls to spondees. The spatial indications continue: ἐν φιάλῃ (3), ἐν κεράμοις (6), ἐν δὲ μέσοις (7), παρκέαται (9), ἀν τὸ μέσον (11), πάντῃ (11), ἀμφίς (12).

5–6. West's text imputes clumsiness to Xenophanes. ἄλλος δ' of wine (5) is awkward after ἄλλος δ' used of a slave (3). One slave garlands the guests (3), another offers an unguent (4). ἄλλος δ' (5) suggests either that another slave is to do something or that another mixing bowl is to be mentioned. (The fact that ἄλλος δ' is the only spondee in a dactylic couplet increases its emphasis.) However, the correct reading is doubtful. The manuscripts have the unmetrical ἄλλος δ' οἶνός ἐστιν ἑτοῖμος. Hermann (1837, 323) proposed οἶνος δ' ἐστὶν ἑτοῖμος. There remains a clumsiness, for nothing now indicates that this is a different wine, and "⟨the⟩ wine is ready" might mean "mixed, ready for drinking." Not until 6 do we discover that this wine is still in the jars. Whatever Xenophanes wrote before ἑτοῖμος in 5, the words are prosaic. The novel personification of wine in the second half of 5 stands in sharp contrast.[10] μείλιχος continues the personification. The word is always used of persons in the *Iliad* and also in the *Odyssey*, except in 15. 374, where it is used of the words of Penelope. It is used of words again in Hesiod, *Theogony* 84, and of gifts in *Homeric Hymns* 10. 2. In these cases the adjective is transferred from the speaker or giver, who is himself μείλιχος. No such transference is relevant in this case: the wine itself is personified and pictured as friendly. Since it is the wine which sets the mood of the drinking party, Xenophanes may be preparing for the advice of 15, 17, and 20–23. For this reason, despite Herodotus' use of προδιδόναι of rivers in the sense "run dry" (7. 187; discussed in Marcovich 1978, 5), I interpret οὔποτε . . . προδώσειν as "will not betray us by provoking drunken brawls." ἐν κεράμοις must be taken with ⟨ἐστιν⟩ ἑτοῖμος: the wine does not cease to be μείλιχος when not in the jars. The hyperbaton is clumsy,[11] but it enables Xenophanes to include another spatial expression.

The personification of wine in this couplet is a literary device, to be distinguished sharply from the personalization of what we regard as abstractions and natural phenomena, which is a common mode of early Greek thought (Hesiod, *Theogony*, passim).

7–8. Xenophanes begins with another spatial expression: in the midst, frankincense is pouring out its sacred, pure scent. The hexameter is contrasted with the pentameter. Frankincense must be burnt; its scent is pungent; it produces a cloud of smoke, which moves, as Xenophanes indicates (ἵησι). In contrast, there is cold, sweet, clear water. (In the context, this seems preferable to "the water is cold, sweet, and clear.") Long syllables highlight ἁγνὴν ὀδμήν in 7, ψυχρόν in 8. Since the scent is accompanied by warm smoke, the phrase is contrasted with ψυχρόν, which is emphasized also by position. If the water is for mixing with the wine—the most probable interpretation—it is also still, in contrast with the smoke.

9–10. The manuscripts have πάρκεινται, corrected by Wackernagel (1916, 97) to παρκέαται. West, printing παρκέαται, suggests πάρκειται (*schema Pindaricum*) in his apparatus. πάρκειται, like the manuscript reading, gives a line entirely spondaic to the caesura at H10, a rhythm which would serve to emphasize that the objects mentioned are at rest. With παρκέαται, the rhythm of 9–10 is identical with that of 7–8. ἄρτοι . . . τράπεζα is presumably a hendiadys, since the bread, like the cheese and honey, is on the table. The expression as a whole seems a little quaint and suggests difficulties with the meter. γεραρή is a surprising adjective with τράπεζα. In Homer it is used of Agamemnon in *Iliad* 3. 170, and a few lines later (3. 211) it serves to contrast Odysseus, as γεραρώτερος, with Menelaus, who was bigger. *LSJ* 1968 suggests "majestic" as a general meaning; Hesychius has ἔντιμος or, better, μεγαλοπρεπής. For this passage *LSJ* had "a table of honor." The *Supplement* corrects this to "lordly, splendid," which is evidently better but perhaps fails to convey the novelty of using γεραρός of an artifact. πίων too seems to be a novel adjective to apply to honey. In Homer it is used of animals, or the fat of animals, and of rich soil or crops. ξανθός seems not to be used with ἄρτος elsewhere. It is used of Demeter (*Hymn to Demeter* 302). Though used of Demeter personalized, the adjective might be derived from the color of ripe wheat; but echo or allusion seems unlikely. Xenophanes is enriching his couplet with adjectives which are striking in their own right. His determination to use precisely these adjectives may have necessitated the quaint form of expression.

11-12. Xenophanes could have arranged the words of 11 in several ways: βωμός and πάντῃ are interchangeable, and ἄνθεσι δ' ἂν τὸ μέσον could stand as the first hemiepes, followed by either βωμὸς πάντῃ or πάντῃ βωμός. Each order would create different nuances. Xenophanes' order appropriately highlights βωμός as spondaic first word. The table was the subject of thought, and one of the grammatical subjects, of 9-10; and initial βωμός leads the hearer smoothly from a table laden with food to an altar covered with flowers. The perfect tenses of 9 and 11, set at either end of the description of the table and altar, present states of affairs to the mind, and the effect of 12 is similar. Xenophanes could have written "and they are singing and making merry," using present tenses to describe activities. μολπή and θαλίη with ἔχει present the singing and merrymaking rather as prevailing conditions. Consider 1-12 as a whole: 1-2(P4) are concerned with rest, 2(P5)-3 with motion, 4-6 with rest, 7 with motion, and 8-12 with rest (unless ἀχθομένη is regarded as a kind of motion), though 12 could readily have been presented as activity. Amid all the static description, only the unnamed slaves and the smoke and scent of the frankincense move. Save for the anonymous subjects of ἀμφιτιθεῖ and παρατείνει, the account is impersonal; and the wine is more vividly personalized than they are. In setting the scene, Xenophanes appeals to all the senses: sight (καθαρόν in 1, πλεκτούς in 2, ξανθοί in 9, and ἄνθεσιν in 11, the last of which also evokes the idea of scent, made explicit in 6); hearing (μολπή in 12); taste (γλυκύ in 8 and perhaps πίονος in 10); scent (εὐῶδες μύρον in 3, ἄνθεος ὀζόμενος in 6, ἁγνὴν ὀδμήν in 7); and touch (ψυχρόν in 8).

If Xenophanes' description is less evocative than my analysis would suggest, the fault lies with his skill in handling the meter and deploying his ideas effectively within it. Xenophanes' craft as a versifier falls short of his aspiration as a poet.

13-16(P3). The remainder of Xenophanes 1W is direct personal advice to εὔφρονας ἄνδρας. χρή and εὔφρονας ἄνδρας, the first and last words of

13, set the keynote for what follows. In 4, εὐφροσύνη clearly meant "good cheer." For εὔφρονας LSJ have "of sound mind, reasonable," but cite no parallel; the word usually means "cheerful," "cheering" (of things), or "kindly." Defradas (1962, 357) supposes a play on "cheerful" and "of sound mind"; but εὔφρων is not attested in the sense of σώφρων,[12] and to advise drinkers who are εὔφρονες in the usual sense to behave piously and decorously is perfectly comprehensible. In 14 there must be some distinction between μῦθοι and λόγοι, though at this period μῦθος does not denote fiction, as it does for Plato. Bowra (1936, 357) well observes that when Pindar twice (*Olympians* 1. 29, *Nemeans* 7. 24) uses μῦθος of false stories, other words in the context establish their falsity. Plato's usage (*Protagoras* 320C, etc.) cannot be read into Xenophanes. Bowra's suggestion that μῦθοι means "stories" and λόγοι "themes" seems reasonable. This may be the first occurrence of εὔφημος in any sense. εὐφημεῖν in the sense "keep a religious silence" occurs as early as *Iliad* 9. 171, but in the sense "shout in honor" it does not occur before Aeschylus, *Agamemnon* 596. Xenophanes' use of εὔφημος may have surprised his audience. The interpretation of καθαροῖσι is linked with that of the poem as a whole. The heavy spondaic rhythm of 13–14 gives appropriate weight to Xenophanes' advice; but πρῶτον μέν suggests that something rhetorically fuller than δ' (17, 19) will follow. To write three consecutive two-word phrases (εὔφρονας ἄνδρας, εὐφήμοις μύθοις, καθαροῖσι λόγοις) in which an adjective precedes the noun with which it stands in agreement is unpleasing. 13 is comprehensible in itself, so that 14, a line consisting exclusively of instrumental datives, appears both inelegant and bathetic; but if one or both of the adjectives was novel and surprising, Xenophanes' audience must have been affected differently. The distance between σπείσαντας and ἄνδρας is awkward. σπείσαντας is bound together with εὐξαμένους not only by τε καὶ but also by the H10 major caesura; but τὰ δίκαια . . . πρήσσειν depends only on the second participle. Spondaic rhythm, position, and punctuation endow πρήσσειν (16) with a prominence which suggests a contrast, most probably with merely δίκαια φρονεῖν. In the context of a symposium, Ion of Chios (26W. 15–16) prays to Dionysus δίδου δ' αἰῶνα . . . πίνειν καὶ παίζειν καὶ τὰ δίκαια φρονεῖν, to which τὰ δίκαια δύνασθαι / πρήσσειν might be a rejoinder. But Ion can have been no more than ten years old when Xenophanes died. If we supposed that Ion was expressing a traditional sympotic prayer, we could interpret Xenophanes as commenting on an earlier poet, now lost to us.

16(P4)–18. Interpreters usually do not comment on ταῦτα . . . προχειρότερον, but the clause is one of the most difficult in the poem. πρόχειρον means "close at hand" or "easy." With West's punctuation, ταῦτα, presumably "just behavior," is explicitly contrasted with ὕβρεις. But it is not plausible to say that justice is *easier* than ὕβρις, and προχειρότερον cannot mean "preferable." προτιμότερον or προτιμότερα would make sense. The word is rare but occurs in Xenophanes 2W. 17. However, the manuscript tradition of 16 is unanimous. Many editors punctuate after προχειρότερον and take οὐχ ὕβρις (Musurus, for ὕβρεις) πίνειν δ' together. ὕβρις with an infinitive is rare; but Euripides, *Hippolytus* 474–75, has ὕβρις / τάδ' ἐστι, κρείσσω δαιμόνων εἶναι θέλειν. However, as West observes (1974, 189), Xenophanes would then have written οὐδ' ὕβρις πίνειν. Defradas (1962, 357–58), punctuating at the end of 16, claims that προχειρότερον contrasts being able to act justly with achieving success, the usual object of prayer to Greek gods. He speaks of the gods granting "une grâce efficace" to act justly. The contrast between god-given strength or success and the cooperative actions of the agent is as old as *Iliad* 9. 254–56. In normal circumstances the Greeks of this period assume that justice is within their power while success depends on deity (Adkins 1960, chaps. 2 and 6). Xenophanes does not mention success and suggests that divine aid is needed if one is to be just. Since his hearers already suppose that divine aid is needed if one is to be successful, how are they to infer from Xenophanes' words that he is maintaining that justice is easier than success? Bergk (1882) read δέ for τε in 15, making σπείσαντας ... πρήσσειν ... πίνειν parallel to πρῶτον μέν ... λόγοις. This emendation improves the structure of Xenophanes' sentence. In West's text the whole of 14–16(P3) is dependent on 13, and the sentence is running away into the sand. With δέ, τὰ δίκαια δύνασθαι depends on εὐξαμένους, πρήσσειν on χρή: "and having poured libations and prayed to be able ⟨to perform⟩ just acts, one should perform them." δύνασθαι is found without a dependent infinitive expressed as early as *Odyssey* 4. 237, δύναται γὰρ ἅπαντα (*LSJ* 1968, mng. 1), where, as here, an infinitive can readily be supplied from the context. τὰ δίκαια may be understood with πρήσσειν. This interpretation explains the prominence of πρήσσειν rather better and is no more Procrustean than that required by West's text in 19. But Bergk (1882) does not solve the problem of προχειρότερον. With West's text in 17, πίνειν is appropriately emphasized. It stands at the beginning of its clause and is marked off from the remainder by the H7 caesura; and it is the subject of thought of its couplet. ὁπόσον κεν ἔχων, with the relative governed by the participle, seems prosaic; but the word order highlights ἀφίκοιο: one would actually arrive. 18 qualifies ἀφίκοιο in three ways: (1) οἴκαδ', (2) ἄνευ προπόλου, (3) μὴ πάνυ γηραλέος. The colon diaeresis separates (2) from (3) by a mandatory pause; and sense requires a slight pause between (1) and (2). The line contains three demarcated units of gradually increasing length (two, five, and seven syllables): a pleasing effect. In 16, the pentesyllabic ending προχειρότερον highlights an important word. The spondaic first hemiepes of 17 contrasts well with the otherwise dactylic couplet, in which the light rhythm suits the sense. The sense groups are unusually placed in the couplet: they end at πίνειν, ἔχων, οἴκαδ', προπόλου, and γηραλέος. Suitable performance might suggest a rather unsteady progress.

19–20. ἀνδρῶν, a first-foot spondaic word at the beginning of a new sentence, has great emphasis, which seems undeserved unless Xenophanes is contrasting it with θεόν in 13. Had he written αἰνεῖν δ' ἀνδρῶν, αἰνεῖν would stand in an analogous position in its clause to πίνειν (17). Since the phrases are metrically identical, Xenophanes presumably preferred ἀνδρῶν δ' αἰνεῖν. To begin a dactylic hexameter with two disyllabic spondaic words is unusual but is less unpleasing in Greek than in the stress-accented Latin language. For πιών Fränkel read εἰπών (1951, 422), Untersteiner ἐπιών (1955, 104). ἐσθλά should be construed with both πιών and ἀναφαίνει. The wine should be good, beneficial, as the wine presently at hand is (5–6); then the drinker will ἀναφαίνειν what is good, beneficial. ἀναφαίνειν can be used of both action (*Iliad* 20. 411, etc.) and speech (*Iliad* 1. 87; Pindar, *Pythians* 4. 110). ἐσθλά merits the emphasis derived from its position as first word in its clause after the relative pronoun.[13] In 20, the general sense is clear, but the text is very doubtful. It is impossible to be confident that any of the suggestions best represents what Xenophanes wrote. Unless one accepts σύντονος (Stadtmüller), μνημοσύνη is linked with another noun by καί. ἀρετή seems relevant to both nouns: for μνημοσύνη, compare the Homeric μνήσασθε δὲ θούριδος ἀλκῆς (*Iliad* 6. 112, 8. 174, etc.) and λελάσμεθα θούριδος ἀλκῆς (*Iliad* 11. 313). It is perhaps easier to understand ἀρετή with μνημοσύνη if the genitive is read after ἀμφί rather than the dative or accusative. Of the nouns which have been suggested for the manuscripts' τὸν ὅς, τόνος is evidently closest and makes sense. The meaning of ἀρετή is unclear. The Berlin papyrus (West, 1972, *Adespota elegiaca* 27), quoted by Wilamowitz (1926), Bowra (1938b), and Defradas (1962), ἡ δὲ σπουδὴ ἐπέσθω ἀκούωμέν τε λεγόντων / ἐμ μέρει· ἥδ' ἀρετὴ συμποσίου λέγεται, is not evidence for Xenophanes if the poem indeed belongs to the late fourth century, for much thought about ἀρετή had occurred in the intervening years (Adkins, 1960a, chaps. 8–16). There is a contrast with the mythical battles and the στάσιας σφεδανάς of 21–23; but the meaning of these is also unclear. Alliteration and assonance seem rarer effects in Greek than in Latin poetry; but here the sequence of α- and ν-sounds and of π̲ι̲ώ̲ν̲ and ἀναφαίνει, might be deliberate. ο̲ἶ̲ν̲ο̲ς̲ ἑ̲τ̲ο̲ῖ̲μ̲ο̲ς̲ (if the text is correct) and οὔ̲π̲οτέ φ̲η̲σι π̲ροδώσειν in 5 and the interplay of αν and π in ἄ̲ν̲θ̲ε̲σ̲ι̲ν̲ ἄ̲ν̲ τὸ μέσον π̲ά̲ν̲τ̲η̲ π̲ε̲π̲ύ̲κ̲α̲σ̲τ̲α̲ι̲ ... ἀ̲μ̲φ̲ί̲ς̲ in 11–12 might be similar effects. Where coincidence is so possible, any claim must be very tentative;[14] but if Xenophanes includes alliteration and assonance among his poetic goals, the quest for these effects places a further constraint upon his strangely unfluent verses.

21–24. West prints οὔ τι μάχας in his text but expresses a preference for οὐδέ, so that διέπειν may be appropriately coordinated with αἰνεῖν. Fränkel (1951) suggested διέπων, continuing the relative clause of 19(H9)–20. (The long sequence of infinitives depends on χρή, so that μή is the expected negative. Either Xenophanes has forgotten or he rather awkwardly expects the hearer to supply χρή after οὐ.) Defradas (1962, 349), reading διέπει with the epitomator, renders "il ne construit pas de Titanomachies." But διέπειν means "handle, order, arrange." It is used of battles. Achilles says (*Iliad* 1. 165–66) ἀλλὰ τὸ μὲν πλεῖον πολυάϊκος πολέμοιο / χεῖρες ἐμαὶ διέπουσ'. In *Theognidea* 893W it is used of administering a city: οἱ δ' ἀγαθοὶ φεύγουσι, πόλιν δὲ κακοὶ διέπουσιν. διέπειν is not a verb of saying, and οὔ τι μάχας διέπειν does not readily mean "not arrange stories about battles": Xenophanes is urging the guests primarily not to bring about battles and stasis. In this sense the battles would be *like* those of the Titans, Giants, and Centaurs. But πλάσματα τῶν προτέρων directs the hearers' thoughts to myth, and they may interpret Xenophanes as adjuring them neither to tell of these—in every sense—mythical battles nor to emulate them. Since ἀναφαίνει (19) may similarly refer to either speech or action of a beneficial kind, we may infer that Xenophanes is producing the effect deliberately. Did he, like Plato later (*Republic* 383B–392A), suppose that violent and immoral myths would produce similar behavior in those who heard and believed them? (It is only toward the end of the fifth century that we find anyone explicitly arguing that "it must be all right. The gods do it" [Aristophanes, *Clouds* 1079–82].) τοῖς (23) could refer to πλάσματα, to πλάσματα combined with μάχας and στάσιας, or to the Titans, Giants, and Centaurs. The vagueness adds scope to Xenophanes' condemnation. "There is nothing useful or beneficial in any of that, whether"—we may add, if we accept the play on διέπειν—"narrated or emulated." As Bowra points out (1938, 363), χρηστός is a fifth-century, not an archaic Greek, word; but the use of χρηστός of persons to denote and commend good citizens does not entail that χρηστόν, when not used of a person, means "useful for the city."[15] In 24, Franke suggested ἀγαθόν for ἀγαθήν, to contrast with οὐδὲν χρηστόν; but ἀγαθήν makes good sense.[16] If not the last line of the poem, 24 seems to be the last line of the paragraph which began with χρή; and Xenophanes may well have sustained the sequence of infinitives after χρή to the end of his paragraph. As Defradas notes (1962, 362), προμηθείην is a new word. In the context, προμηθείη urges the hearer to follow the advice of 21–23. The position of θεῶν δέ corresponds with ἀνδρῶν δ' in 19, but the functions of the words in their clauses are not similar, and the word order adds nothing to the poem.

This is a difficult poem and, at first sight, a rather crabbed and unattractive one. Detailed analysis has shown that Xenophanes has aesthetic and expository goals which seem different from those of any other poet studied here. When every allowance has been made for the corrupt state of the text, readers may well conclude that Xenophanes' poetic technique was simply inadequate to his aspirations. Nevertheless, an individual sensibility, not merely a philosophic intellect, is discernible in these verses.

There remains the general interpretation of the poem, which has been bedeviled by unnecessary assumptions. There is no evidence that Xenophanes was a rhapsode in the usual sense [17] or a person of low birth. In this poem, as Campbell notes (1967, 332–33), Xenophanes' language is quite un-Homeric. We may not argue that Xenophanes could not have presided at a symposium of aristocrats.[18] Nor does this poem portray him as so doing. The Berlin papyrus, quoted above (p. 183), continues τοῦ δὲ ποταρχοῦντος πειθώμεθα. Pace Wilamowitz (1926) and Bowra (1938b), it is clear that the writer is *not* himself the "ruler of the symposium." In Plato's *Symposium* the rules of the occasion are arrived at by friendly discussion, to which Socrates contributes his share. There is no reason to suppose that Xenophanes is of lower social or economic status than Socrates. But we may go further. No word in 1W necessitates that the poet is even present or that the occasion is actual and particular rather than vividly imagined. Dover's observations on oral poetry (above, p. 33) remain valid for such poems as this: we are not told, and cannot guess, the circumstances for which 1W was composed. Even if it was subsequently performed at symposia, it need not have been written for a particular occasion.

Any interpretation must rest solely on the words of the poem. Defradas (1962, 353) points out that archeologists have discovered no altars in Greek houses, and he argues that the symposium is a reunion around an altar, a "réunion d'un thiase dont les préoccupations réligieuses sont probables." Defradas might have gone further. He insists (1962, 350–51) that Xenophanes is describing, as no other Greek does, the period between the end of dinner and the beginning of drinking, and he maintains that the poet's motive is to emphasize "ce qui'il y a de plus serein et de plus réligieux." But there is no mention of dinner, and Athenaeus' words (462c) do not necessitate that Xenophanes is describing a symposium after dinner: ὁρῶν οὖν ὑμῶν καὶ αὐτὸς τὸ συμπόσιον κατὰ τὸν Κολοφώνιον Ξενοφάνη πλῆρες ὂν πάσης θυμηδίας. συμπόσιον refers to Athenaeus' work; and while Xenophanes' poem certainly precedes a "drinking together," that it occurred after dinner is an inference. We know little of Greek social customs outside Athens; we do not know the location of this festivity. There is a group of potential drinkers, an altar covered with flowers, and what Defradas himself grants are the customary trappings of a drinking party. But since ζάπεδον (1) may mean "earth" as well as "floor," and the water (7) might be a stream, the drinkers might be gathered around a rural altar in the open air. (There is at least one building present but not necessarily more than one; for δώματα, which occurs here in line 12, can be used of a single building as early as *Odyssey* 2. 259. And ἀμφὶς ἔχει does not necessarily mean that the singers and dancers are in the building; compare *Odyssey* 8. 340, δεσμοὶ . . . ἀμφὶς ἔχοιεν.) The identity of the god cannot be guessed. There is no need to postulate Pythagoreanism (Defradas 1962, 365), and the problem of Xenophanes' attitude to Pythagoreanism does not arise.

καθαρός (1, 8, 14) and δίκαια (15) have been held to express new ideas. Where a phrase can be understood in its customary sense, it will be so understood unless the writer makes it plain that the sense is different. No Greek of Xenophanes' day could have supposed him to be innovating in writing τὰ δίκαια δύνασθαι πρήσσειν: behavior appropriate to a symposium is the obvious meaning. καθαρόν (1) seems to mean "clean" in a mundane sense; but, since we do not know the nature of the occasion, it is possible that a ritual purification had taken place. καθαρόν (8) also may mean "pure, clear"; but the occurrence of ἁγνήν, its virtual synonym in a ritual sense, in 7 might well evoke religious overtones in 8. Used with λόγοις, καθαροῖσι (14) cannot mean either "*ritually* pure" or "*morally* good." It denotes a state of affairs which, like ritual purity, is pleasing to deity. Just as Xenophanes uses εὔφημος to denote not ritual silence but words pleasing to deity, so καθαρός denotes not merely the absence of stain but a positive quality; and the use of both εὔφημος and καθαρός in this way appears novel. Xenophanes apparently believes that the gods are, or wish to be portrayed as, cooperative and unquarrelsome among themselves; and it is εὔφημον and καθαρόν so to portray them. The moral implications of the situation derive from Xenophanes' belief that peaceful myths will bring about good behavior among mortals. (That Xenophanes, *qua* metaphysician, tended toward monotheism and did not believe in anthropomorphic deities is immaterial. Aristotle's references to deity in the *Ethics*, where he is discussing and clarifying the beliefs of his contemporaries, sometimes bear no resemblance to the deities of the *Metaphysics*.)[19] Defradas (1962, 354–55) discusses γεραρὴ τράπεζα, arguing that, though the phrase in itself proves nothing, in the neighborhood of an altar and incense a table thus characterized must contain offerings to the gods.

Bowra's conclusion, that Xenophanes was introducing some innovations against a background of traditional values and beliefs, seems justified.

Xenophanes 2W

ἀλλ᾽ εἰ μὲν ταχυτῆτι ποδῶν νίκην τις ἄροιτο
ἢ πενταθλεύων, ἔνθα Διὸς τέμενος
πὰρ Πίσαο ῥοῆς ἐν Ὀλυμπίῃ, εἴτε παλαίων
ἢ καὶ πυκτοσύνην ἀλγινόεσσαν ἔχων
5 εἴτε τὸ δεινὸν ἄεθλον ὃ παγκράτιον καλέουσιν,
ἀστοῖσίν κ᾽ εἴη κυδρότερος προσορᾶν,

```
       καί κε προεδρίην φανερὴν ἐν ἀγῶσιν ἄροιτο,
       καί κεν σῖτ' εἴη δημοσίων κτεάνων
       ἐκ πόλεως, καὶ δῶρον ὅ οἱ κειμήλιον εἴη—
10     εἴτε καὶ ἵπποισιν· ταῦτά κε πάντα λάχοι,
       οὐκ ἐὼν ἄξιος ὥσπερ ἐγώ· ῥώμης γὰρ ἀμείνων
       ἀνδρῶν ἠδ' ἵππων ἡμετέρη σοφίη.
       ἀλλ' εἰκῇ μάλα τοῦτο νομίζεται, οὐδὲ δίκαιον
       προκρίνειν ῥώμην τῆς ἀγαθῆς σοφίης·
15     οὔτε γὰρ εἰ πύκτης ἀγαθὸς λαοῖσι μετείη
       οὔτ' εἰ πενταθλεῖν οὔτε παλαισμοσύνην,
       οὐδὲ μὲν εἰ ταχυτῆτι ποδῶν, τόπερ ἐστὶ πρότιμον,
       ῥώμης ὅσσ' ἀνδρῶν ἔργ' ἐν ἀγῶνι πέλει,
       τοὔνεκεν ἂν δὴ μᾶλλον ἐν εὐνομίῃ πόλις εἴη·
20     σμικρὸν δ' ἄν τι πόλει χάρμα γένοιτ' ἐπὶ τῷ,
       εἴ τις ἀεθλεύων νικῷ Πίσαο παρ' ὄχθας·
       οὐ γὰρ πιαίνει ταῦτα μυχοὺς πόλεως.
```

But(?) if a man were to win a victory by the fleetness of his feet, or competing in the pentathlon, where the precinct of Zeus is by the streams of the river of Pisa(?) at Olympia, or wrestling, or even(?) engaging in grievous boxing or the terrible contest which they call the pancration, he would be more awesome for his citizens to look upon, and would win a conspicuous front seat at the contests, and there would be food consisting of public possessions from the city, and a gift which would be a treasured heirloom for him—or if (he won) by means of horses. All these things would fall to his lot, though he is not worthy of it, as am I; for better than the strength of men and of horses is my wisdom. But custom is all awry in this, and it is not just to give strength precedence over good wisdom; for neither if there is a good boxer among the people, or (a man good at) the pentathlon, or at wrestling, or because of the fleetness of his feet, which is most highly esteemed of all the deeds of men that there are in the contest, would the polis be more in a condition of good government(?) for that reason. Small would be the joy to the polis over that man, if one were to compete and win a victory by the banks of the river of Pisa; for these things do not fatten the storehouses of the polis.

As was stated above, this poem shares with Xenophanes 1W an unusual preference for trisyllabic words in final position in the hexameter. Seven of the eleven hexameters of 2W end thus (1, 3, 7, 11, 13, 15, 17), as do seven of the twelve hexameters of 1W. 2W has three disyllabic endings (9, 19, 21) and one quadrisyllabic (5), compared with one disyllabic and four quadrisyllabic endings in 1W. Trisyllabic endings preponderate in the pentameter too: as in 1W, there are six (2, 6, 8, 12, 14, 22). Three pentameters end in disyllables (4, 10, and 18; only one does in 1W); none ends in a quadrisyllable (three do in 1W); one ends in a pentesyllable (16; none does in 1W); and one (20), very unusually, ends in a monosyllable (of this there are only nineteen examples in the extant lines of the eight elegists [see Table 7]).

In West's edition, five hexameters (1, 3, 11, 13, 15) and three pentameters (2, 4, 8) are enjambed. The figures for 1W are six hexameters and no pentameters. The first nine lines of 2W are more flexibly composed than 1W. Of the stopped hexameters, three (5, 7, 17) have commas, two (19, 21) have raised stops, and one (9) has a dash, with which West marks the awkward hyperbaton in 10. Of the stopped pentameters, five (6, 10, 16, 18, 20) have commas, one (14) has a raised stop, and two (12, 22) have full stops. West punctuates 2W as two sentences, 1W as three. All the sentences end at the end of pentameters.

Five hexameters have stops within the line, two at major caesura: at H10 in 11 (raised stop) and 17 (comma). There is a comma at the H12 diaeresis in 3 and 13 and a comma at H4 in 9. Two pentameters are thus stopped, both at the P7 diaeresis: in 2 with a comma, in 10 with a raised stop.

Xenophanes 1W has twenty-five stops in twenty-four lines, while 2W has twenty-one stops in twenty-two lines. The greater feeling of lightness in 2W results less from the—very slightly—smaller number of stops than from the greater flexibility of lines 1–9 and from the nature of the stops: 1W has ten raised stops and three full stops in twenty-four lines; 2W has only five raised stops, two full stops, and a dash in twenty-two lines.

1. This may be the first line of Xenophanes' poem. Both Campbell (1967, 337) and Marcovich (1978, 18) adduce examples of poems apparently introduced by ἀλλά or δέ. Caution is needed, for, as Campbell (1967, 140) grants, it is usually uncertain whether the alleged parallels are themselves the first lines of poems. The ring composition formed by the echo of πὰρ Πίσαο ῥοῆς (3) in Πίσαο παρ' ὄχθας (21) undoubtedly binds the lines together as a unit (Marcovich 1978, 18); but the unit might be less than a complete poem, and there are possible hints of a larger ring. ἀλλ' εἰ μὲν ταχυτῆτι ποδῶν, demarcated by the H10 caesura, is an appropriate first phrase. With the second half of the line it establishes the subject matter of the lines; and footracing is well placed at the beginning, since Xenophanes supposes it to be most highly esteemed by the Greeks in general (17).[20] Observe the order of events in 1–4 (*footrace*, pentathlon, wrestling, *boxing*) and in 15–17 (*boxing*, pentathlon, wrestling, *footrace*). This too produces the effect of ring composition: a smaller ring, in the first part of which πὰρ Πίσαο ῥοῆς is embedded. The last line of the poem falls outside both rings, and it introduces a theme, the prosperity of the city, which has not been explicitly mentioned before; for εὐνομίη (19) denotes, in part, the correct distribution of goods in the polis, but it does not require that the city be wealthy (above, p. 122). Possibly the themes of σοφίη and prosperity were introduced before line 1, forming a larger ring.

2. Though 1 is not end-stopped, the sense is complete at ἄροιτο. ἢ πενταθλεύων is parallel to ταχυτῆτι ποδῶν. The position of νίκην τις ἄροιτο with respect to its dependent phrases is a frequent one in all styles and periods. Where one element is common to two or more sense groups, that element is frequently placed at the end of the first of the units to which it is common, just before the beginning of the second. νίκην τις ἄροιτο has that position here with respect to ταχυτῆτι ποδῶν and the parallel sequence of participles πενταθλεύων (2) . . . παλαίων (3) . . . ἔχων (4). ἔχων itself is thus placed in relation to its two objects (4, 5). (Compare καθαρόν in Xenophanes 1W. 1, above.) πενταθλεύειν and πενταθλεῖν (16) are used *metri gratia* for the Ionic πενταεθλεύειν and πενταεθλεῖν, which are not found. (πενταθλεύειν occurs only here, πενταθλεῖν also in Pausanias 6. 14. 13 and Artemidorus of Daldis 1. 57.) The five long syllables of ἢ πενταθλεύων well contrast with the dactylic ταχυτῆτι ποδῶν. That each phrase ends at the mandatory pause in its line enhances the effect.

3. The sense is not complete at the end of the pentameter: the audience needs to know which τέμενος of Zeus is meant. πὰρ . . . Ὀλυμπίῃ is essential to the sense. It merits the emphasis derived from its position at the beginning of a hexameter following an enjambed pentameter: victory at the Olympic Games is the most important. εἴτε παλαίων, however, is complete in sense and must appear rather bathetic. Xenophanes may have misled his audience's ears. ἔνθα . . . Ὀλυμπίῃ is to be taken with all the contests. But whenever authors do not follow the tendency, noted above, to place the common element in a sequence at the end of the first unit, they are inclined to place it at the beginning or end of the whole sequence. The position of ἔνθα . . . Ὀλυμπίῃ suggests that ταχυτῆτι ποδῶν and πενταθλεύων constitute a set of two. The sentence cannot be complete at Ὀλυμπίῃ: an apodosis is needed. But the protasis seems complete. To continue it from the H12 bucolic diaeresis, end the phrase at the end of the line, and follow it with two more phrases of greater, and increasing, length, leaves εἴτε παλαίων as a very weak and unemphatic phrase with respect both to what precedes and to what follows: an effect which is certainly not sought by Xenophanes.

4. The quadrisyllabic noun and pentesyllabic adjective which occupy most of the line provide a heaviness that suits the sense. Of ἢ καί Denniston (1954, 306) says, "In this combination ἤ separates two ideas objectively, in point of fact, while καί denotes that, subjectively, both must be kept before the mind.

Render often 'or again': but sometimes καί means 'also' or marks a climax, 'even.'" Denniston adds, "usually in the second clause of a disjunction," and lists this passage. But εἴτε παλαίων (3) and line 4 are not more closely bound together than lines 4 and 5, since ἔχων must be understood with 5. Denniston's account of ἢ καί is not in dispute, but one may suspect that its occurrence with boxing rather than the pentathlon, wrestling, or the pancration is the result of Xenophanes' difficulties with the meter. ἀλγινόεσσαν is a powerful adjective, used by Hesiod of personalized Woe, Ὀιζύς, a daughter of Night, and of personalized Toil, Πόνος, a child of Strife (*Theogony* 214, 226), and by Mimnermus (11W. 2) of Jason's homeward journey with the Golden Fleece. It is a word drawn from mythological and epic contexts. (Homer has πυγμαχίης ἀλεγεινῆς, *Iliad* 23. 653.) The line is not end-stopped, but, as in 1 and 3, the sense is complete at the end of the verse.

5. The first line, concerned with running, contained two spondees. We have observed on many occasions that a simple equation of dactyls with speed and joyfulness, spondees with slowness and gloom, is inappropriate: the alternation between dactyls and spondees has many tasks to perform. Yet the rhythm of 5, which is entirely dactylic, seems remarkable in a line concerned with the "terrible" pancration. (The only other completely dactylic line in the poem is 17, whose subject is running.) With ὃ παγκράτιον καλέουσιν compare *Iliad* 24. 316, of the eagle, μόρφνον θηρητῆρ', ὃν καὶ περκνὸν καλέουσιν (and 18. 487; 22. 506). In the manuscripts, 5 begins εἴτε τι, which Wakefield, followed by most recent editors, emended to εἴτε τό. Campbell (1967, 338), reading τι, suggests that τι and the Homeric reminiscence are intended as sarcasm. (He might have adduced the meter as additional evidence.) But Campbell quotes no parallel, and ironic/sarcastic τις seems to depend for its effect on a studied vagueness. Here Xenophanes immediately renders his words specific with ὃ παγκράτιον καλέουσιν. Granted, the line could be read as sarcastic even if τό is read. Campbell presumably so reads Xenophanes 32. 1 (Diels/Kranz 1951), which he cites (1967, 338): ἥν τ' Ἶριν καλέουσι, νέφος καὶ τοῦτο πέφυκε. But sarcasm there is equally uncertain, and in 2W. 5 its point would be unclear. The pancration was in fact a δεινὸν ἄεθλον,[21] and to single it out for scorn seems incomprehensible. But the description of boxing in 4 appears serious and grand, and 1–3 can hardly be ironic or sarcastic. Again, sarcasm will not serve Xenophanes' goal in the poem. In 11–12, he makes the novel claim that he is more worthy than the athlete and possesses something better than the athlete. Therefore, the higher the value set on athletes in 1–10, and the less their claims are challenged, the greater is the effect of 11–12.

6. ἀστοῖσιν is emphasized, both as first word in its line and as first word of the long-awaited apodosis. Its prominence is merited, for it introduces the relationship between the individual and the polis, which is a major theme of the

poem. The athlete does the polis no good and is honored and rewarded; Xenophanes benefits the polis and is neither honored nor rewarded. κυδρός is a very powerful word. Indeed, it may be more powerful in the positive and—rare—comparative than in the form assigned as its superlative by *LSJ* 1968. κύδιστος is in fact formed directly from κῦδος, not κυδρός, and may have been felt to be a different word. κύδιστος is used twelve times of Agamemnon in Homer (ten times in the *Iliad*, two in the *Odyssey*) and twice of Anchises (*Hymn to Aphrodite* 108, 192); there are fewer uses with gods (six of Zeus, one of Athena, one of Leto, and one of Hera). κυδρός, however, which appears only in the feminine in the *Iliad* and *Odyssey*, is almost entirely confined there and in the *Homeric Hymns* to major goddesses closely linked with Zeus. Hera (*Iliad* 18. 184, *Hymns* 12. 4) is Zeus's sister and consort, as is Demeter (*Hymn to Demeter* 179, 292); Leto (*Odyssey* 11. 580) is his consort; Persephone (*Hymn to Demeter* 66) is his daughter, as is Athena (*Hymn to Hermes* 461 and *Hymns* 28. 1). Hesiod also uses it of Hera (*Theogony* 328), of Dike, another daughter of Zeus (*Works and Days* 257), and of the great goddess Hecate (*Theogony* 442), τὴν περὶ πάντων Ζεύς . . . τίμησε (*Theogony* 411–12). The masculine first occurs in *Hymn to Hermes* 461: Apollo says that he will render Hermes, another child of Zeus, κυδρὸν ἐν ἀθανάτοισι καὶ ὄλβιον in return for his invention of the lyre. Alcman 2 (iv) 7 (Page 1962, 11) uses κυδρός of Polydeuces, also a child of Zeus. This is the sole use of κυδρός in Page 1962 and 1974; in Voigt 1971, 374 there is a doubtful occurrence in a fragment of uncertain authorship; and besides Xenophanes 2. 6 only the comparative adverb (Ion 27. 10, certainly later than Xenophanes) and the superlative adjective (*Theognidea* 904) are found in West 1972. The feminine is used only once of a mortal woman in Homer. Athena thus flatteringly refers, not to a named individual, but to the wife whom Telemachus will one day marry (*Odyssey* 15. 26). Apart from this passage, Xenophanes 2W. 6 is the first extant positive or comparative of κυδρός used of a mortal; and the superlative is confined to Agamemnon and to Anchises, the latter in the hymn in which he appears as the consort of Aphrodite. Few adjectives confer more status: Xenophanes is building up the stature of the athlete, in preparation for his own startling claim. Campbell (1967, 338) interprets κυδρότερος as "either more glorious than his fellows or more glorious than the poet"; but "more glorious than he was before" suits the situation very well. (Compare Telemachus' words in *Odyssey* 1. 392–93: οὐ μὲν γάρ τι κακὸν βασιλευέμεν· αἶψά τέ οἱ δῶ / ἀφνειὸν πέλεται καὶ τιμηέστερος αὐτός. Telemachus is speaking of one who *becomes* a king.) The use of προσορᾶν is similar to the use of ὁρᾶν in Callinus 1W. 20. Grandeur is given to Xenophanes' line both by the five long syllables of the first hemiepes and by the two heavy polysyllables of the second.

7. προεδρίην occurs first here. Bowra (1938c, 273–74) cites Herodotus to show that a front seat at the games was "an ancient and prized honour, for the

most part given to persons of high rank or to families and even to cities as a reward for services rendered" (Herodotus 1. 54, 4. 88, 5. 57, 9. 73). The effect of φανερήν is difficult to evaluate. It does not occur in Homer or Hesiod, in Page 1962 or 1974, or elsewhere in West 1972 except for the undatable *Adespota elegiaca* 23. 2 (with καιρός). The only certainly earlier example is Alcaeus 67(26). 4–5 (Voigt 1971, 205): μή τις τῶν κακοπατρίδαν ἔσσεται φανερ[ὸς] τ[οῖ]σιν ἀπ ἀρχαῳ[. The word might be common in everyday speech, and prosaic; but if its use in Alcaeus and Xenophanes were typical, and if it denoted and commended prominence and success in the polis, it would carry a powerful emotive charge and be well fitted to make Xenophanes' point.

8. Being fed at public expense is also an ancient privilege, as Bowra demonstrates at length (1938, 274–76). He notes that Olympic victors were feasted in the prytaneum at Olympia but supposes it more likely that Xenophanes is referring to their feasting in the prytaneum of their own polis. This seems certain. The ἀστοί of 6 are the athlete's own fellow citizens, in whose eyes he becomes κυδρότερος on his return. The reference cannot be to Olympia and the moment of victory; the inhabitants of Olympia were a tiny minority among the spectators, and "citizens of any city present" is pointless in the context of the poem as a whole. Like ἀστοῖσι, every mention of the πόλις (9, 19, 22) refers to the athlete's own city. For σῖτ᾽ εἴη Kaibel suggested σίτησιν, the regular term in prose for the custom, presumably to avoid the echo of 6. But, like the echo of ἄροιτο (1 and 7), the effect may be deliberate. 6 and 8 have the same rhythm, a spondaic first hemiepes; and not merely does each have εἴη in the same position, but the second hemiepes of each consists of a quadrisyllable followed by a trisyllable. The quadrisyllables are both adjectives, the only adjectives in their lines; and the only adjective in the intervening hexameter has its first syllable at H8, just as the adjectives in 6 and 8 begin at P8. Xenophanes has situated the three adjectives as similarly as the different structures of the hexameter and pentameter permit. (The major caesura, however, falls after φανερήν.) Xenophanes seems to be striving for similarity and echo in these lines. The effect of each adjective is enhanced by the similarity of position.

9. Run on from an enjambed pentameter and followed by a stop at H4, ἐκ πόλεως has great emphasis. In sense, it is strictly redundant after δημοσίων, but its prominence is fully merited. Xenophanes is highlighting the public response, an important part of his case: the successful athlete is admired by his fellow citizens and publicly rewarded; but, as will appear, he confers no public good. δῶρον ὅ οἱ κειμήλιον εἴη is evidently intended to recall δῶρον . . . ὅ τοι κειμήλιον ἔσται in *Odyssey* 1. 311–12. The context is irrelevant. The purpose of using this Homeric language, like that of ὅ παγκράτιον καλέουσιν (5), seems to be to increase the athlete's status, a goal which Xenophanes pursues in these lines in a variety of ways.

10. The hyperbaton of εἴτε καὶ ἵπποισιν is intolerably harsh. The hearer or reader must link these three words with the sequence of protases which ended at 5; indeed, he must go back to 1 for a similar construction and then proceed with the interrupted sequence of apodoses which began at 6. The effect is much harsher and clumsier than in Xenophanes 1W. 5–6 or Tyrtaeus 10W. 25–27, where the hyperbaton is of one line only. Tyrtaeus' goal was to begin a new sentence after the caesura (Adkins 1977, 82). Xenophanes needs ἵπποισιν for 12, for there has been as yet no mention of chariot racing. The hearer or reader is given an impression not merely of clumsy technique but of absentmindedness. However, the remainder of 10–11 is very successful. ταὐτά κε πάντα λάχοι (linked by no connecting particle to the earlier lines) sums up, in a colorless manner, what has preceded. The prosaic words, placed in the second hemiepes of the pentameter, lower the emotional pitch. Since the sentence cannot end there, the mind is alert for what will follow. Should anything striking in form or content follow, its effect will be increased by these quiet words.

11–12. Xenophanes does not disappoint his hearers' expectations. Having given a vivid account of the glories and rewards of the athlete's life, followed by a brief respite, he makes his own remarkable claim. Though there is no formal enjambment, the necessary continuation of the thought of 10 to a strong pause at the H10 caesura in the following hexameter gives great prominence to οὐκ ἐών . . . ἐγώ, while ῥώμης γὰρ ἀμείνων possesses the usual enhanced upswing and imperfect cadence of clauses which begin at H11 or H13. As we have observed elsewhere (for example, *Theognidea* 735W, 741W, 751W), sentences or clauses beginning at H11 or H13 and continuing to the end of the pentameter are frequently used, as here, to close a paragraph of thought. The spondees here distinguish οὐκ ἐών, ῥώμης, and ἀνδρῶν ἠδ' ἵππων from the dactylic ἄξιος, ὥσπερ ἐγώ, γὰρ ἀμείνων, and ἡμετέρη σοφίη. The athletes are spondaic (heavy?), Xenophanes dactylic (nimbler?): an effect which would readily strike the ear in performance. The emphatic and particular ἐγώ well contrasts with the vague and general τις of 1 and 21. It is true that, unless particular athletes are used as types, any reference to athletes as a class inevitably precludes the use of names. But Xenophanes has used this situation for aesthetic effect. If Tyrtaeus 12W. 1–14 and *Theognidea* 699–718W are compared with this poem, Xenophanes' achievement becomes clear. Tyrtaeus lists the different excellences that a man might possess. He endows the characteristics with vividly particularized color, and he contrasts them, not with his own qualities and achievements, but with the military valor and exploits of another equally unnamed person. Theognis writes of the possible qualities, again linked with mythological characters, of another unnamed and unparticularized person and sourly proclaims that all are inferior to the possession of money. Tyrtaeus and Theognis are judging others. Xenophanes throws his own claims and qualities into the balance, and the counterpoint of 10(P8)–12 against what has preceded enables him to do so with great panache.

13. The sequence of thought seems odd. If ἀλλ' is understood in its common adversative sense (Denniston 1954, 1), one would expect it to contrast 13–14 with 11–12. In fact, ἀλλ' . . . νομίζεται is a comment not on 11–12 but on 1–10. If the poem were performed with a significant pause after 12, however, and if 13–14 were uttered as an indignant outburst against the general state of affairs revealed by 1–12, the strict illogicality of the sequence of thought might pass unnoticed. The use of ἀλλ' would then be inceptive, or, alternatively, its use to express opposition (Denniston 1954, 7, 20). Were the goal simply to produce a neat logical argument, the deletion of 11–12 would serve. But there is no reason to suspect the lines: the echo ἡμετέρη σοφίη . . . τῆς ἀγαθῆς σοφίης is characteristic (compare the repeated ἄροιτο in 1 and 7 and the echo of the first hemiepes of 6 in 8 and the first half of 1 in 17); moreover, 11–12 are among the most effective lines of the poem. In 13, οὐδὲ δίκαιον produces an enhanced effect of upswing and imperfect cadence similar to that in 11 and gives additional indication of the parallelism between the two couplets. The couplets are the contiguous parts of a larger mirror image. Xenophanes begins, as we have seen, with a sequence of athletic events contained in protases. He ends this part of the poem with a claim about his σοφίη, introduced by γάρ. He then makes another claim about σοφίη and introduces by γάρ a further sequence of protases, containing four of the same list of contests—in reverse order, as has been noted already. In the remoter parts of the mirror image are also the two mentions of Pisa. Marcovich (1978, 23) notes that the order in which the contests are mentioned in the first half of the poem is the historical order of their introduction at Olympia. It seems unlikely that these features of the poem are the result of chance, for they reveal the same type of sensibility as does Xenophanes 1W. It is not surprising that the verses of a poet who composes in this manner are rarely fluent or that clumsinesses, like the hyperbaton of 10, sometimes result.

σοφίη in 12 and 14 has been much discussed (Jaeger 1939, 172; Bowra 1938c, 258–61; Marcovich 1978, 21–22). In early Greek the word does not denote abstract philosophical wisdom, for none exists; instead, it is widely applied to practical skills. In *Iliad* 15. 412 there is reference in a simile to a shipwright's σοφίη, and Hesiod (Frag. 306 Merkelbach and West) refers to the σοφίη of the musician Linus. Solon (13W. 51–52) writes ἄλλος Ὀλυμπιάδων Μουσέων πάρα δῶρα διδαχθείς, / ἱμερτῆς σοφίης μέτρον ἐπιστάμενος. Solon is often taken to mean the skill of writing poetry rather than the knowledge needed to produce a poem filled with sage advice; but it is doubtful whether the distinction was drawn in early Greece and even more doubtful whether a poet such as Solon would draw it. Solon 27W. 15 provides a clearer example. (For the text, see above, chap. 6.) There, γλῶσσά τε καὶ σοφίη are related to great ἀρετή, to producing good advice for the city. σοφίη means "wise advice"; the advice is not poetically expressed. Similarly here, Xenophanes is claiming that his σοφίη will produce εὐνομίη and fatten the storehouses of the city. Even if his σοφίη was always expressed in verse, the content of that verse is evidently as much before his mind as its form. προκρίνειν is possibly coined by Xenophanes. It is not in Homer or Hesiod, elsewhere in West 1972, or in Page 1962 or 1974. Homer has προβέβουλα in a similar sense in *Iliad* 1. 113. ἀγαθῆς is not "moral," in the sense of "just," but "effective," as in 15. (So also Bowra 1938c, 260.) Xenophanes' skill is effective in benefiting the city, as the boxer's skill is not.

15–19. As noted above, Xenophanes now refers again to four of the six events mentioned earlier, with the last in first position, the first in last. (He omits the pancration and the chariot race.) The footrace had pride of place in 1 and is the climax of the sequence in 15. The climax is emphasized by placing οὐδέ, and indeed οὐδὲ μέν, after οὔτε . . . οὔτε . . . οὔτε (Denniston 1954, 193, 362). In this structure there is not merely ingenuity but some elegance, and the use of ἀγαθός in four different constructions for the four events also strives for elegance. (It is not dictated by the meter: παλαισμοσύνην would scan equally well in the dative, ταχυτῆτι in the accusative.) The fact that ἀγαθός is to be employed four times raises a problem of performance. With πύκτης, ἀγαθός is an attributive adjective, so that caesura at H10 might seem appropriate, to emphasize the unity of the phrase; but caesura at H7, giving greater isolation to ἀγαθός, might make the lines easier to understand. Whichever is treated as the caesura, a sense pause at the other seems desirable also. (There may be no satisfactory phrasing: as in 1W, Xenophanes' aspirations may have outrun his technique.) The placing of the next three events in units demarcated by the mandatory pauses of their lines doubtless aims at clarity. λαοῖσι (15) may, but need not, refer to the athlete's own citizens. The word is vague and might refer to the competitors and crowds at the Olympic Games.[22] This interpretation gives a good contrast with πόλις, the athlete's own city, at the climax in 19.

ἔργα, strictly the antecedent of ὅσσα, is drawn within the relative clause, while ῥώμης, which depends on ἔργα, is separated from it and set in a prominent position—appropriately, since ῥώμη (11, 14, 18) is a key word of this part of the poem (Marcovich 1978, 19).

The four protases—the last ornamented with two subordinate clauses— have ended at the end of a pentameter. There is no enjambment at 18; but the mind is awaiting the apodosis, and the subsequent hexameter is highlighted in the same way as a hexameter following an enjambed pentameter. Xenophanes uses the highlighted line to express rather more clearly why his σοφίη is "better." (He will not be fully explicit until 22.) Athletes do not bring about εὐνομίη for their polis. τοὔνεκεν is emphatic and is to be taken with the four preceding negatives: not for any of these reasons would the polis enjoy εὐνομίη. The mind is led to inquire what reason there might be for a polis' enjoying εὐνομίη, and the ideas of the earlier lines then fall into place. Athletes are splendidly honored for their victories, but those victories do not produce εὐνομίη. Xenophanes is more worthy of honor, for his σοφίη is better than their strength: his must produce εὐνομίη, and any other good things which he may subsequently claim are not the fruit of athletic success.

20–22. Xenophanes now clinches his point. σμικρόν, the only spondee in its line, is highlighted by meter and position, while the athlete, a mere monosyllable, whose brevity is emphasized by its unusual position, is much diminished. (As is shown in Table 7, only 1.88 percent of the pentameters of the eight elegists end in monosyllables. Xenophanes' other example, γῆν in 8W. 2, has no obvious aesthetic motivation.) The effect of the monosyllabic τῷ is reinforced by another vague τις in 21. As at the beginning of 2W, the activities of the unemphatic τις are endowed with grandeur. Three very strong sense units follow. Here too the line might be phrased with the mandatory pause in either of two places: at H7 or H10, before or after νικῷ. A pause in both places would give a measured stateliness to the achievement, befitting its customary evaluation: "competing—won a victory—at Olympia." To compete at all is to partake in an esteemed activity; to win in competition is glorious; to win in competition at Olympia, more glorious still.

Lines 20–21, like 15–19, have a rhythm counter to the usual rhythm of the elegiac, for they end with a hexameter. The prominence of 21 is thereby increased yet more. But whereas the apodosis of 19 was the resolution of its sentence, the contents of 20–21 do not fully satisfy the mind, which eagerly awaits the pentameter. Xenophanes well exploits the eagerness by expressing in the final pentameter of his poem, or of the lines we possess, the sum of his message for the first time: athletes do not—and Xenophanes does—"fatten the storehouses of the city."

This poem differs in some ways from 1W. Though the second half of 1W contains general advice, like 2W, the first half is descriptive and depends for its effect in great part on the choice of adjectives and on Xenophanes' appealing to the impressions of different senses. 1W has twenty-five adjectives in twenty-four lines; 2W, thirteen adjectives in twenty-two lines. In both, however, the adjectives are chosen and deployed with care, and some may have been coined by Xenophanes. Xenophanes shows more skill than in 1W in composing his sentences in the elegiac couplet (10H8–12, 19–22), though not uniformly (εἴτε παλαιῶν [3]; εἴτε καὶ ἵπποισιν [10]). Nevertheless, there is a general resemblance with 1W, in which we may discern the poet's cast of mind. Once again Xenophanes aims high, this time to produce a poem with a very complex formal structure and numerous verbal echoes. Once again we may conclude that the poet's reach exceeds his grasp. But in both poems Xenophanes is far from the merely prosaic writer, content if only his verses scan, that he is sometimes imagined to be.

In 2W as in 1W, Xenophanes' standpoint has been much discussed. Jaeger (1939, 1:168–73) argues that Xenophanes' work was "an invasion of poetry by the spirit of philosophy." He maintains that nature philosophy "had a potent influence on state and society" and claims that Xenophanes in his elegies "popularized the enlightened doctrines of the Ionian physicists and took up the cudgels for them against the prevailing ideals of culture." These ideals are in general carried by the poetry of Homer and Hesiod; in 2W the particular opposition is between sport, the ideal of aristocratic society, and "spirit," represented by Xenophanes.

Jaeger's claims are too sweeping and too vague. How nature philosophy influenced society is not explained; and Bowra (1938c) maintains in reply that 2W is not concerned with Xenophanes' philosophy, that Xenophanes' status cannot be proved to be humble, and that admiration for athletic prowess is not confined to aristocrats. Of Xenophanes' σοφίη Bowra says (1938c, 260): "He meant simply the philosophical and didactic poetry which he himself wrote and which he believed to be worthy of better rewards than it got." Bowra makes a good case but then produces a positive theory of his own which is not convincing. He argues that victors in the great games were held to be more than human. Some of his examples will not withstand scrutiny; but, certainly, victory in the games led to great public prominence, which could be translated into political power and, sometimes, into tyranny. Bowra supposes that Xenophanes evaluates the prominence and power as ὕβρις and for that reason uses οὐδὲ δίκαιον in 13 and εὐνομίη in 19. Bowra also quotes *Works and Days* 236–37, where Hesiod says that just government makes a land rich and is rewarded by the prosperity of its people, and he adds (1938c, 273): "If he had this, or a similar passage, in mind, Xenophanes' meaning is clear. He criticizes the rewards given to athletes, because they do not enrich the city, that is, they have not the true sign of a just government in making the country prosperous, and are in fact ὕβρις."

Bowra imputes to Xenophanes either a simple logical error or an unusual view of justice, far from the traditional values which Bowra in general claims to be present. That just government produces prosperity entails neither that whatever produces prosperity is just nor that whatever fails to produce prosperity is unjust. (The claim that whatever does not produce prosperity is hybristic is even less plausible.) Xenophanes himself says nothing of the kind. Nor does he say that athletes cause δυσνομίη. The natural interpretation of 19 is that the strength of athletes does not—and Xenophanes' σοφίη does—produce εὐνομίη, possibly out of a prevailing δυσνομίη. Again, if Xenophanes was really worried that the rewards and honors given to athletes engendered ὕβρις in them, his own claim to greater rewards and honors, if met, would render him even more liable to ὕβρις. If Xenophanes believed that he could receive the rewards and honors without behaving with ὕβρις, so important a step in his argument could not be omitted; but there is no more mention of it than of ὕβρις itself.

In general I agree with Marcovich on the interpretation of Xenophanes' message in 2W: "In short, the message of the whole poem boils down to this: 'Only a useful wisdom (such a one as my own) can bring about good government (on which the well-being of the city depends): no athlete's strength can'" (Marcovich 1978, 19). Of Xenophanes' σοφίη he says (1978, 22), "The practical wisdom of a sage may be meant." Noting that Xenophanes does not wish to abolish the athlete's honors but only to diminish them, relative to his own, he notes (1978, 25), "Xenophanes shared this social need for *moderate* reform with Solon." Solon, too, termed the reformed state of affairs εὐνομίη; but this fact need not be emphasized, since the value of εὐνομίη to the moralist and reformer lies in its combination of vague denotation with a high emotive charge (above, p. 122).

10
RETROSPECT AND PROSPECT

In my first chapter I presented the results of some quantitative analyses and made some observations about the character of the Greek elegiac couplet. On the basis of these I formulated some hypotheses about the resources offered to a Greek elegist by his meter. In subsequent chapters I have analyzed in detail the skill, greater or less, with which a number of early Greek elegists employed those resources in individual poems. In each of these chapters I have offered an evaluation of the poems discussed.

Overarching my other hypotheses is evidently a very broad one: that one can discover at least part of an artist's or author's intentions. This, like other hypotheses, must be tested by the results it gives, and gives in a particular case; for nothing prevents different arts and genres from posing different problems.

All artistic media have definite characteristics; they are in some ways tractable, in other intractable. One cannot produce the same effects in watercolors as in oils. A meter is an artistic medium, and a strict quantitative meter is a medium with very evident tractabilities and intractabilities, as one can readily discover by attempting to compose in it. The opportunities offered by the elegiac couplet are not those offered by the iambic trimeter, and those offered by the Greek elegiac couplet are not those offered by its Latin counterpart. To endeavor to write poetry in the media of Sophocles, Virgil, or Archilochus is to feel the grain and texture of the verse; to write badly, or—as can be guaranteed—less well than Sophocles, Virgil, and Archilochus, may induce the thoughtful to try to identify the characteristics in virtue of which these lines are a limping botch, those a masterpiece. Not all the differences are to be ascribed to *callida iunctura* or, if Horace smacks too much of craft, to the tropes of genius; some arise directly from the poet's working with, rather than against, the grain of his meter, which is a constant, as the striking trope is not. Comparison of what succeeds in a medium with what one has discovered, by personal experience, does not may be very informative and a fruitful source of hypotheses. The hypotheses remain hypotheses; but if one is aware of the means that can be employed to produce certain results in a given material, and if an artist consistently so organizes his material as to produce appropriate results, the likelihood that the results were also intended is at least increased. I shall accordingly continue to use words such as "skill" in this chapter. Determined reductionists may translate sentences containing these words, here and earlier, into others concerned solely with the arrangement which the words chance to have on the page.

I shall not attempt here a detailed comparison of all the poets or poems studied in this book. The number of relevant criteria is so high, and their distribution among the poets and poems is so varied, that only a careful comparison of individual poems will suffice. The reader must return to the relevant earlier chapters. Nor shall I offer a ranked order of poems or poets; there are more ways than one of being a good, or an interesting, poet. My goal in this book has been to enable the reader, after having considered the data supplied and other relevant data that I may have overlooked, to agree or disagree with my judgments and evaluations and, in either case, to come to appreciate not merely the manifold differences between the poetry of Xenophanes and Archilochus, of Xenophanes and Tyrtaeus, or Tyrtaeus and Theognis, and all the other possible combinations, but also the differences between one poem and another by the same author, so as to perceive and evaluate the individual poem in its individuality. In addition, this book proposes a method, or a set of relevant considerations, for the discussion and evaluation of Greek poetry; and my hope is to persuade others to approach Greek poetry—and, *mutatis mutandis*, Greek prose—in a similar manner. To that end, it is much more appropriate to recapitulate the hypotheses which this study has attempted to test and then to summarize the arguments for their plausibility.

That there exists in these authors a discernible poetic craft which can be studied was itself a hypothesis, and one whose wording needs clarification. I have not assumed a sharp distinction between art and craft, both of which the Greeks termed τέχνη, or attempted to reduce art, however defined, to craft, however defined. But the art of the early elegists, of Greek poetry, of classic artists in general, is a conscious, indeed self-conscious, one, resting on carefully acquired skills. Its practitioners do not utter native woodnotes wild or rely solely on the white heat of inspiration. Even if Simonides 6W was improvised, which is very doubtful, the ability to compose the poem rested on years of development of a craft. To speak of "craft" does not demean the artist; the psychological processes which render A a better craftsman with words, or in any other medium, than B are no less mysterious than those dignified by the term "inspiration." On the other hand, as my detailed studies have shown, all the early elegists do aspire at least to craft; not even Tyrtaeus, Xenophanes, or the Solon of 27W is content with any collocation of words which will fit the meter of the elegiac couplet, and they bring other skills to the crafting of their poems. Every poem studied in this book exhibits poetic craft.

I now turn to the considerations that have proved relevant. The first is factual, not hypothetical. The modern poet writes primarily for a readership rather than an audience, and his readers do not customarily read aloud. Greek poets—and prose writers—after Homer are literate, as are some members of their society; but they write for audiences, to stimulate by means of the ear rather than the eye, and they live in a culture in which readers read aloud from books that were quite difficult to decipher.

That these facts are relevant to the composition and appreciation of Greek elegiac poetry was a hypothesis. In my first chapter I proposed a number of hypotheses concerning the characteristic aural rhythm and music of the elegiac couplet and the opportunities these afforded to the composer in elegiacs. The hypotheses were in part based on a quantitative survey, in part on individual observations. Detailed study of particular poems has established that all the elegists are aware of, and can use in their poetry, at least some of the resources whose existence was there posited, while some elegantly employ all of them. Any poem or poet will supply examples of the effective counterpoint of spondees against dactyls, whether his purpose is to give added emphasis to evidently important words, to highlight words over which the eye of the reader passes quickly, or to match sound and rhythm to sense. No poet is unaware of the possibilities of word position. Several skillfully exploit the opportunities available in a meter with a double movement and mandatory, if in part flexible, pauses. Poems such as Solon 4W and *Theognidea* 731–52W effectively contrast broken with smooth rhythm. Frequent effective use is made of the complete control which, in a poem destined for performance, a poet enjoys over the order in which information reaches the audience. It would be difficult to deny that the elegists, as a group, are aware of all the opportunities offered to them by oral performance of their poems.

It has also proved relevant to consider the connotations of words. That words have connotations is a fact overlooked at their peril by the readers of languages not their own. Even when confronting the simplest prose, the reader is well advised to remember that the words he is reading may have a different range of usage, and hence connotations, from the words with which he is translating them. Where connotations exist, the poet, by skillful composition of phrases, may use them as a poetic resource. That the early elegists so used them was a hypothesis; but already in Archilochus and Callinus we observed the poets creating new phrases which derived their effect from the connotations which the words possessed in Homer. Connotative effects are produced not only by the range of denotation of a word but also by the style and genre to which it usually belongs. At least the later elegists, like the author of *Theog-*

nidea 237–54W, can obtain grandeur by using individual Homeric words in their own un-Homeric verses; the earlier elegists, most of whose vocabulary is shared with Homer, must use Homeric phrases to produce similar effects.

The elegists have also demonstrated that different languages offer different opportunities to the poet through their grammar and syntax. For example, though instances of the definite article occur in Homer, the article is in the early stages of its development: context for the most part determines whether ναῦς means "a ship" or "the ship." Later poets retain the freedom to use language in this way; and, like Homer, they may allow pronominal adjectives to be understood too. These observations are commonplace; but it is less commonplace to observe the shrewd use which Archilochus makes of these opportunities in 5W. The Greek aorist indicative may be used either as a past tense or timelessly and gnomically. Solon in 4W makes skilled rhetorical use of this fact of language, and the author of *Theognidea* 183–92W may do so. It seems likely that other Greek poets similarly exploit the grammatical and syntactical resources of their language.

That Homeric phrases occur in many early elegiac poems is a fact. That some of these phrases are employed as purposive allusions is a hypothesis; but in the light of the evidence presented it seems a more plausible hypothesis than to suppose that our poets drew on Homeric phrases because they could think of no other way of expressing themselves. (They use Homeric phrases also to confer Homeric grandeur on appropriate contexts; we may recall Archilochus 13W. 3, where πολυφλοίσβοιο θαλάσσης not only performs this function but possibly points to other phrases that are allusively intended.)

To claim the possibility of allusion is to propose a hypothesis not only about the poets but about their audiences. In the culture which they share, it must be possible for the allusions to be taken. The practice of using Homer allusively in ordinary conversation would be a virtually necessary prerequisite for the use of allusion in the more formal diction of art. The Homeric poems and Hesiod possessed the cultural preeminence needed by a source of allusions, but evidence of their use outside written texts is not to be expected.

However, uses of Homer which seem allusive may be sought in other writers. Plato, in addition to quoting Homer in order to criticize him, also introduces Homeric lines and shorter sequences of Homeric words into his dialogues. Some of these enrich their contexts if understood allusively. In *Crito* 44A–B, Socrates narrates his dream of a white-robed woman, who said to him: ἤματί κεν τριτάτῳ Φθίην ἐρίβωλον ἵκοιο. It is evident both that the Socrates and Crito of the dialogue recognize the quotation and that Plato expected his readers or audience to recognize it. The line (*Iliad* 9. 363) is drawn from one of Achilles' speeches in reply to the embassy sent by Agamemnon. Adam comments (1896, 27): "It is possible (as Cron suggests) that the meaning of the line for Socrates lay partly in the fact that Phthia was the *home* of Achilles; but I feel sure that (rightly or wrongly) Socrates associated Φθίην with φθίω and φθίσις, and derived comfort from the epithet ἐρίβωλον." Editors in general seem to hold similar views. They may be correct; but perhaps more can be said. Phthia is in Thessaly. Crito is urging Socrates to escape and go to Thessaly (45c). The Laws of Athens (53E) later speak contemptuously of Socrates' possible escape as going off to carouse in Thessaly. Socrates and Crito are in no doubt that the quotation prophesies Socrates' death, not his departure for Thessaly in a literal sense. May it not also hint that by dying Socrates will be going to a more real "Thessaly," with more real rejoicing? The white-clad figure is not in mourning garb. Again, the line is spoken by Achilles, who considers that his ἀρετή, his contribution to his fellows' well-being, has been undervalued and consequently chooses to leave them. (See *Iliad* 1. 163–71, which end with Achilles' statement that he intends to return to Phthia.) The Socrates of the *Apology* also claimed to have been undervalued by his fellows and to deserve a conspicuous reward rather than punishment (36c–d); and he associated himself with Achilles, though in a rather different manner (28b–c). Achilles claimed to be ἄριστος Ἀχαιῶν (*Iliad* 1. 412); the closing words of the *Phaedo* (118A) assert that Socrates was ἄριστος of all men whom the speaker had met. The theme of the *Crito* is a choice which Socrates must make; and Crito, like Agamemnon's embassy, appears bearing offers of money to affect Socrates' choice. The allusion associates the situation of Socrates with that of Achilles in a complex manner. Socrates, in the eyes of most of his contemporaries, had behaved and was behaving like a κακός (Adkins 1960a, 259); the association with the ἄριστος Ἀχαιῶν reflects Plato's very different evaluation. (Plato's Socrates compares his situation explicitly in *Apology* 41B with that of other Homeric heroes, Ajax and Palamedes.)

In *Protagoras* 315B Socrates, describing the sophists at the house of Callias, says τὸν δὲ μετ' εἰσενόησα, ἔφη Ὅμηρος, Ἱππίαν τὸν Ἠλεῖον; and he adds, a few lines later, καὶ μὲν δὴ καὶ Τάνταλόν γε εἰσεῖδον· ἐπεδήμει γὰρ ἄρα καὶ Πρόδικος ὁ Κεῖος. Now, τὸν δὲ μετ' εἰσενόησα is not a striking phrase in itself; but since it occurs only once in Homer, at *Odyssey* 11. 601, it can serve as a trigger for an allusion, and Socrates evidently expects his hearers to recognize it. To continue with "and I saw Tantalus too" presupposes that his audience has identified the reference of τὸν δὲ μετ' εἰσενόησα, which continues βίην Ἡρακληείην / εἴδωλον. Lamb (1924, 114–15) comments: "A touch of epic dignity is given to the two sophists, Hippias and Prodicus." I suspect that the reverse is intended. If the quotation is taken allusively, the sophists are compared with the shades of the dead; and the shadowiness of Heracles' shade is particularly emphasized, for it is contrasted with the real Heracles, who leads a very different life as a god on Olympus. The line referring to Tantalus continues χαλέπ' ἄλγε' ἔχοντα; and Socrates immediately describes Prodicus as lying luxuriously, in ironic contrast, ἐγκεκαλυμμένος ἐν κῳδίοις τισὶν καὶ στρώμασιν καὶ μάλα πολλοῖς. The lines seem carefully selected for allusion; and τὸν δὲ μέτ' εἰσενόησα is a "trigger" less striking than virtually any of those in the elegiac poets. (Possibly for this reason Plato adds ἔφη Ὅμηρος; but his evident confidence that the allusion will be taken indicates a remarkable knowledge of Homer among his intended audience.)

Plato writes in this manner not because he is a great philosopher but because he is deeply imbued with Greek literary culture and is himself a great literary artist. Being also a more complex personality in a more developed world of thought and literature, he uses his allusions in more complex ways than do his elegiac predecessors. Verbal irony abounds in the dialogues; it may well have pleased him that, though the manner in which both Socrates and Crito understand *Iliad* 9. 363 is evident, the literal and the figurative interpretations of the words give Socrates contradictory advice. I have argued elsewhere that the portrayal of the sophists as ghosts is not merely a *jeu d'esprit* but a rejoinder to Aristophanes' portrayal of Socrates and his pupils as ghosts in the *Clouds* (Adkins 1970). If the culture furnishes a context in which allusions may be made and taken, the use to which the allusions are put will vary from writer to writer. We have observed differences among the elegists: Mimnermus' motives in using allusions to Homer are very different from those of Tyrtaeus.

Other aspects of the historical and cultural context may prove relevant. Any poem, even if unique, is at the same time embedded in its culture. If, like many early elegiac poems, it is a *pièce d'occasion*, the circumstances in which it was composed are important. Tyrtaeus 4W cannot be understood unless the historical circumstances, the rhetoric, and the possibilities afforded by oral performance are all taken into account. All affected its reception by its original audience. One cannot hope to understand its significance as a document in isolation from the poetry and rhetoric, nor can the poetry and rhetoric be understood in isolation from the historical situation in which they were employed. Solon 4W is in many respects similar: the modern reader who ignores Solon's rhetoric and poetry and treats the poem as an—irritatingly vague—document of history or political theory is likely to misunderstand what Solon has written.

The goal of every line of comment in this book is to furnish data by means of which perceptions of elegiac poetry may be sharpened and evaluations made. My studies of meter endeavor to reconstruct the experience of rhythm directly present to the poets as they composed in elegiacs, with a view to establishing which poets made more successful use of their opportunities; my studies of word use, of connotation, of allusion, have a similar intent.

Little Greek poetry has been studied in this manner. This book discusses in detail a comparatively small proportion of extant early elegiacs. Many other poets in West 1972 are not even mentioned. Later elegy, and epigram of all periods, remain. The characteristics of many poets, and of individual poems, await analysis. (By these means it might be possible to identify more accurately different poetic "hands" in the *Theognidea*.)

Nor is the method of approach relevant to elegy alone. In the first instance, only stichic meters of which a sufficient quantity is extant seem likely to be capable of rhythmic analysis. At all events, it would be prudent to begin with these. The dactylic hexameter and the iambic trimeter certainly, the anapaestic dimeter and the trochaic tetrameter probably, furnish sufficient material. The dactylic hexameter was used for many purposes, by epic poets both oral and literate, by didactic poets, by bucolic poets, by philosophers; the iambic trimeter by writers of *iamboi* and by tragic and comic dramatists. Some very interesting quantitative work on the iambic trimeter has already been done (Schein 1979; Devine and Stephens 1977, 1978, 1980, 1982); but more is needed, and little attempt has been made to draw on the quantitative to make qualitative judgments, though my preliminary investigations of both the stichic hexameter and the iambic trimeter give promise of fruitful results. Much work in the manner of this book is needed: first, studies of individual works and poets; then, comparison of different poets in the same genre; then, of poets in different genres; and, finally, when the resources of each meter are more fully understood, of poets in different meters. There is good reason to expect that such studies would lead to a more informed appreciation of Greek poetry than is possible today.

APPENDIX
SOLON 4W. 12-13

The rhythm produced by the choriambic δημοσίων at the end of the enjambed pentameter 12, followed by the choriambic φειδόμενοι at the beginning of 13, marked off by a pause (above, p. 115), is very unusual. The nearest approximations are:

(a) Mimnermus 2W. 4–5   εἰδότες οὔτε κακὸν οὔτ' ἀγαθόν·
(b) Mimnermus 11aW. 2–3   κεῖαται ἐν θαλάμῳ Ὠκεανοῦ παρὰ χεῖλος,
(c) Solon 13W. 12–13   ἔργμασι πειθόμενος οὐκ ἐθέλων ἔπεται,
(d) Tyrtaeus 5W. 4–5   ἐννέα καὶ δέκ' ἔτη νωλεμέως αἰεί . . .
(e) Tyrtaeus 11W. 36–37   βάλλετε χερμαδίοις δούρασί τε ξεστοῖσιν . . .
(f) Theognidea 862–63W   ἀλλ' ἐγὼ αὐτομάτη ἑσπερίη τ' ἔξειμι καὶ ὀρθρίη . . .
(g) Theognidea 1250–51W   ἤλυθες ἡμετέρους ἡνίοχόν τε ποθῶν ἀγαθὸν . . .

Solon 4W. 12–13 is marked by the need for a pause after each of the choriambic words. Of the lines quoted above, only (f) and (g) have two choriambic words in these positions; the others have a choriambic phrase in one or both. In (f) and (g) no pause is required after the choriamb in the hexameter, and (b) through (e) are in this respect similar. In (a) the parallelism of the phrases gives point to the similar rhythm. None of these produces an effect similar to Solon 4W. 12–13.

NOTES

Notes to Chapter 1

1. We are consequently dependent on what native speakers have chanced to tell us. See, e.g., Aristotle's remarks on poetic diction, *Poetics* 1458a18–1459a16, and Dionysius of Halicarnassus, cited below, n. 12.

2. Maas (1962, 60) evidently uses this method, for he reckons about one hephthemimeral caesura to 100 lines of Homer. The method used in this book gives at least five—in lines 3, 7, 10, 19, and 20—in the first twenty lines of *Iliad* 1. See also Adkins 1977a, 62, n. 9, for the ways in which the term "caesura" has been used. Fränkel (1926, 197–229) argued for a four-colon hexameter. (See also Porter 1951.) Kirk (1966, 73–152) offers other plausible grounds for the phenomena.

3. Except for enclitics, which are pronounced with the preceding word. Proclitics are more debatable, and generalization is more difficult.

4. Athenaeus (602b–c) ascribes to the Pythian oracle one couplet in which the pentameter precedes the hexameter, "in the manner later used by Dionysius Chalcus in his elegies." The expression suggests that Dionysius alone composed elegies of this kind.

5. Such enjambment is characteristic of oral poetry; but other types occur in Homer. See below, p. 23.

6. Punctuation at H16 does occur, e.g. in *Odyssey* 1. 62: τί νύ οἱ τόσον ὠδύσαο, Ζεῦ;

7. Similarly, a natural phrasing of *Iliad* 1. 53, ἐννῆμαρ μὲν ἀνὰ στρατὸν ᾤχετο κῆλα θεοῖο, gives diaeresis after στρατόν.

8. Word end at H11 contravenes "Hermann's Bridge" (Hermann 1816, 338–39). Such lines are very rare, but Xenophanes writes two consecutive hexameters of this kind, 1W. 17 and 1W. 19.

9. The precise manner in which a more emphatic pause differs from a less emphatic one is irrelevant to my argument here.

10. West (1974), using the definition of "caesura" noted above (p. 4 and n. 2), comes to quite different conclusions. Noting the argument of Edmonds (1931, 11) that the ratio of caesura at H7 rises markedly between the seventh century and the end of the fifth, he computes these percentages of hexameters with H7 caesura, dividing the

poets into three groups as indicated: "Ar. 27, Ca. 23, Mi. 35, Ty. 33; Th. 44, Sol. 42, X. 44, Sim. 43, Dion. Ch. 42, Anonymous pieces in Book 2 of the Theognidea, 40; Ion 61, Eue. 58, Crit. 63." West expresses the caveats appropriate where the number of lines is so small but concludes: "Nevertheless, the grouping seems significant." If major caesura is identified in the manner suggested in the text, however, the percentages become: Ar. 25, Ca. 25, Ty. 23, Mi. 34, Sol. 36, Th. 34, X. 29, Sim. 30, Dion. Ch. 36, Ion 39, Eue. 30, Crit. 37; and it is difficult to argue for any trend. (Critias 7W. 1 is an excellent example of the effect of phrasing on meaning and vice versa. Can one believe that a performer who supposed that ἦν Λακεδαιμόνιος Χίλων σοφός, ὃς τάδ' ἔλεξε meant "Wise Chilon' was a Lacedaemonian" [or "There was a Lacedaemonian, wise Chilon"] would phrase the line in the same way as one who interpreted it as "Chilon the Lacedaemonian was wise"? The first sense gives H7 caesura, the second H10.)

11. In the eight elegists as a whole, 9.31 percent of all pentameters are enjambed. For the individual poets, the percentages are: Archilochus 25, Callinus 27.3, Tyrtaeus 8.1, Mimnermus 22.5, Solon 8.18, *Theognidea* 5.5, Simonides 22.2, Xenophanes 11.8.

12. See Dionysius of Halicarnassus, *De Compositione Verborum* 6. 20. 8 ff.

13. That is to say, pitch is the predominant element. See, e.g., Dionysius of Halicarnassus, *De Compositione Verborum* 6. 11. 15–17.

14. See Adkins 1977b, 145–58, and the extensive bibliography there (in note 4, p. 146).

15. For example Πεισηνορίδαο, *Odyssey* 1. 429; ὑπερηνορέοντες, *Odyssey* 2. 266.

16. See, e.g., Solon 4W. 12–13, discussed in chapter six, below.

17. Dionysius (above, n. 12) pertinently asks (6. 20. 12): καὶ παρὰ τί γέγονε τούτων ἕκαστον; οὐ γὰρ εἰκῇ οὐδ' ἀπὸ ταὐτομάτου.

18. Once again, writers such as Dionysius of Halicarnassus record the response of a native speaker. The reader of *De Compositione Verborum* should particularly note that to the ancient Greek both prose and poetry are experienced primarily as sounds, not as marks on papyrus. My "sense group" approximates to Dionysius' κῶλον (*De Comp. Verb.* 6. 17. 15); but his use of κῶλον lays more emphasis on sound, though it remains a unit of sense shorter than (any but the simplest) sentence.

19. In prose, too, the counterpoint of short sentences against long, periodic sentences is a frequent rhetorical device; in Demosthenes *Philippic* 1. 4–10, note the effect of the abrupt questions of 10 in contrast with the long sentences which precede them. For an extended discussion of Greek prose style, see Denniston, 1952.

20. Mimnermus too acknowledges Homer, but in a different way. See below, chapter five.

21. The ancient world ascribed other epics to Homer, for example the *Cypria* and the *Epigoni*. Herodotus (2. 117) argues against Homer's authorship of the *Cypria* and (4. 32) expresses doubts about his authorship of the *Epigoni*.

22. Homer knows two towns of this name. This one occurs also at *Iliad* 21. 87, at the beginning of the line, followed by αἰπήεσσαν, which next occurs in Apollonius Rhodius and is evidently a variant to give a formula with H8 caesura. (The other Pedasus is ἀμπελόεσσαν on both occasions, *Iliad* 9. 152 and 294.)

23. As shown in Table 1, 13.70 percent of all punctuation within the line in the epic

sample occurred at H3. Many examples have dactylic first foot, and many, like ὡς φάτο (*Iliad* 1. 188, etc.), are routine. There are three in four lines, *Iliad* 1. 334–36. Spondaic examples may be equally routine, e.g., *Iliad* 1. 468; but *Iliad* 1. 521 and 526 are not without effect. For pause at H1 as effective as φεύγοντ', see *Iliad* 1. 52.

24. The dialect is not simply Homeric: see below, p. 34.

25. More may be attempted. In selecting *Dear Brutus* as the title of one of his plays, J. M. Barrie (1922) at least expected his audience to remember the rest of the sentence. (That Cassius speaks the sentence is entirely irrelevant to Barrie's purposes.)

26. "The Exiles' Line," to be found in Kipling 1948, 163–65.

27. Contrast Gelett Burgess, "Extracts from the Rubaiyat of Omar Cayenne" (Wells 1947, 512–14) or Kipling's "The Rupaiyat of Omar Kal'vin" (Kipling 1948, 25–26).

28. Stanza 46 of Fitzgerald 1859 (retranslated as stanza 68 of Fitzgerald 1889).

29. Stanza 9 of Fitzgerald 1868 and subsequent editions. The version of Fitzgerald 1859 (stanza 8) is much less close. Comparison with the previous note suggests that Kipling was drawing on his memory of the poem, not on a particular edition.

30. Compare stanza 13 with stanza 70 of Fitzgerald 1859, which is identical with stanza 94 of Fitzgerald 1890.

31. "Exit, Pursued by a Bear," stanza 5. The poem may be found in Nash 1959.

32. Stanza 17 of Fitzgerald 1859; stanza 18 of Fitzgerald 1889.

33. The King James Bible once enjoyed a similar cultural supremacy and could be used in purposive allusion. Kipling ends his short story "The Gardener" (Kipling 1926, 433–50) with "and she went away, supposing him to be the gardener." The allusion retrospectively affects the whole story, which is narrated in a very different style.

34. In some cases the poet's communication is far from straightforward, e.g., Solon in 4W, Simonides in 8W; but irony seems absent.

35. Note, as one example, the repeated anaphora of εὖ in *Iliad* 2. 382–84 (a tetracolon, in which the last two elements are longer than the first two), followed by the anaphora of ἰδρώσει in 388–90.

36. For Archilochus, see Lefkowitz 1976, 181–89; 1981, 25–31. To reply that Lefkowitz's skepticism is extreme is not to demonstrate that it is unjustified.

37. The text printed here differs in that it employs subscript iotas.

Notes to Chapter 2

1. Invention of the elegiac couplet, and many other meters, was ascribed to Archilochus by Plutarch (*De Musica* 28), but ancient scholars knew no more than we of the early history of meters and certainly knew nothing of any oral predecessors.

2. Later antiquity unduly restricted his emotional and poetic range, representing him as solely a poet of invective; see, e.g., Pindar, *Pythians* 2. 99–101; Diogenianus, *Proverbs* 2. 95; Horace, *Epodes* 6. 13–16 and schol. ad loc.; Horace, *Epistles* 1. 19. 23–31; Horace, *Ars Poetica* 79; etc. Invective is absent from Archilochus' extant elegies, but emotion is not.

3. Archilochus 1W, 2W, 5W, and 13W may be complete poems, but none is certainly so.

4. Page (in Hardt 1964, 119–63) argues that Archilochus himself could not write.

On the question of nonliteracy in ancient Greece, see Havelock 1963, 1978, etc. It is not necessary to agree with Havelock's answers to appreciate the importance of the questions he has raised.

5. Lefkowitz (1976, 181–89; 1981, 25–31) is comprehensively skeptical. Rankin (1977) argues that one can usually believe Archilochus, and he constructs a careful account. Tarditi (1968, 1) holds that Archilochus' poetry is "intessuta di elementi biografici." Neither he nor any other of those who approach Archilochus biographically really meets Dover's arguments.

6. Many of the *Homeric Hymns* may be later in date than Archilochus. See R. Wunsch, *RE*, s.v. "Hymnos."

7. That Shakespeare is a better poet than Chatterton is a quite distinct question. Merely using the vernacular does not render a poet better—or worse—than a poet who uses an art language. Skill in using the resources is the decisive factor.

8. In Homer, too, the proportion of words shared by the art language and the vernacular would affect the "flavor" of the verse. Here, however, formulae would also have some effect: the regular concatenation of vernacular words in metrical expressions produces an effect quite different from prose, no matter what the poetic quality of the expressions.

9. Page and Dover briefly discuss the question (in Hardt 1964, 164–65). For the language of Archilochus in general, see Hoffmann 1898, 182; Hauvette 1905, 232–45; Scherer, in Hardt 1964, 89–107, and the works there cited and listed. Merone (1960) discusses the aesthetic effect of certain Archilochan usages.

10. Dover (in Hardt 1964, 183) argues that "[Archilochus' elegiacs and ἴαμβοι], like archaic epitaphs and dedicatory poems, give an epic colouring to a predominantly vernacular phonology and morphology." This in itself affects the "flavor," but vocabulary is an additional factor.

11. There are also some spurious elegiacs: 325W, 326W, 331W.

12. Notopoulos (1966, 311–15) adduces the available evidence and argues that Archilochus was in fact an epic poet—indeed, an oral epic poet. (Since the ancient world had forgotten about oral poetry, there is no suggestion of orality in the passages cited by Notopoulos.)

13. See chapter 1, n. 10, above, and West 1974, 112.

14. Fränkel (1951, 196–97) and Croiset (1914, 189) argue that even if 13W and 11W are not part of the same poem, 13W must have continued in the manner of 11W. Kamerbeek (1961, 1–15) merely argues that it is possible that 11W and 13W are part of the same poem. Van Groningen (1958, 139) supposes that 8, 12, and 16W might be part of the same poem as 13W but doubts that 11W could be.

15. Among extant poems and fragments, 212W, ἴστη κατ' ἤκην κύματός τε κἀνέμου seems equally suitable. 213W, ψυχὰς ἔχοντες κυμάτων ἐν ἀγκάλαις, is quoted by Aristophanes, *Frogs* 704, in a metaphor referring to the woes of Athens. The phrase need not have been metaphorical in Archilochus. One might reject it as part of a shipwreck poem, nevertheless, since κυμάτων ἐν ἀγκάλαις need not refer to a *rough* sea; but Aristophanes' use of the phrase suggests that the original context associated it with stormy weather. 105W is certainly metaphorical: Heraclitus (*Homeric Allegories* 5. 2) quotes the lines as an example of *allegoria*.

16. Even the cautious West writes (ad loc.), "*fortasse carmen integrum.*"

17. Nor is this surprising. See above, p. 18.

18. Each of the five contributes to the poem by highlighting appropriately the word in which it occurs, and this is an effective use of spondees. (See p. 19, above).

19. See above, chapter 1, p. 13, n. 10, and Table 4. By my method of identifying major caesura, of the elegists in note 10 only Critias has a higher proportion of caesurae at H7 than at H8.

20. I take 13W. 1 to be the first line of Archilochus' poem. The absence of a connecting particle does not prove the point (see, e.g., Mimnermus 2W. 15, 12W. 11); but it is difficult to imagine what could have effectively preceded it.

21. For a sensitive treatment of the adjectives in this poem, see Merone 1960, 9–11.

22. Contrast Johnson's epitaph on Garrick, "His death eclipsed the gaiety of nations"; for there the nations may be merely the sum of their inhabitants.

23. See p. 43. The genitive phrase occurs with κῦμα, *Iliad* 2. 209, 6. 347, *Odyssey* 13. 85 (κῦμα in previous line); with κύματα, *Iliad* 13. 798; with θῖνα or θινί, *Iliad* 1. 34, 9. 182, 23. 59, *Odyssey* 13. 220, *Hymn to Hermes* 341. In *Homeric Hymns* 6. 4 κῦμα π. θ. is preceded by κατά, but the syntax is different. Hesiod uses the phrase in *Works and Days* 648.

24. Compare Shakespeare's "And should the multitudinous seas incarnadine" (also counterpointed against short words in the next line, but for a different purpose). The effect of the rolling sea is given by the formula; but to choose that formula and counterpoint it against ἔκλυσεν shows Archilochus' own art. Homer and Hesiod attempt nothing similar with the phrase in the passages cited in note 23.

25. Of the pentameters of the poets under discussion, 9.3 percent are enjambed. The percentage varies widely from poet to poet, ranging from 5.5 in the *Theognidea* to 27.3 in Callinus. (The remainder are: 25% in Archilochus, 8.1% in Tyrtaeus, 22.5% in Mimnermus, 8.18% in Solon, 22.2% in Simonides, and 11.8% in Xenophanes.) These results have no statistical significance. Those for the *Theognidea* are skewed by the large number of one-couplet poems, in which no enjambment of the pentameter is possible, and the sample of the other poets' elegiacs is too small. Nevertheless, a careful study of the poets' versification will suggest that the percentages reflect a qualitative difference in methods of composition of elegiac couplets.

26. Compare Mimnermus 1W. 5 and 5W. 5, discussed below in chapter 5, and Mimnermus 2W. 5 and Tyrtaeus 10W. 27, which I discuss in Adkins 1977a.

27. Surprisingly, Denniston (1954, 98–108) does not consider the emphasis given to a word so placed, but many of his examples illustrate the point. (See my discussion of Tyrtaeus 11W. 1 in note 30 of chapter 5.) This usage of ἀλλά . . . γάρ seems to contrast 1–5(H3) with the more important pronouncement of 5(H4)–7 (Denniston 1954, 101, noted by Campbell 1967 ad loc.).

28. Though the matter is not quite clear in Homer. See Adkins 1960a, chapter 2.

29. μένος may be imparted by a deity to the hero, but, once imparted, it is actively expressed.

30. The emendation κρατερόν for κρατερήν (Reeve 1971, 324–29) produces poetry inferior to the manuscript text.

31. So West 1972. The MS tradition of Stobaeus has (nonsensical) τἆλλος, to avoid hiatus after a short syllable.

32. Compare Callinus 1W. 3–4, discussed below in chapter 3.

33. Compare its use at Archilochus 5W. 4, the only other occurrence of the word in pre–Alexandrian elegy. Homer uses it more routinely, as at *Iliad* 1. 223.

34. Individual words, as opposed to phrases, need not for that reason have been experienced as peculiarly Homeric; many of them are also the words of ordinary speech. See Dover's comments (cited on p. 34, above). Of words in this poem not found in the Homeric poems, Homer has ἐπιμέμφομαι (e.g., *Iliad* 1. 65, *Odyssey* 16. 97) but not μέμφομαι (2); and πλεύμων, not πνεύμων (5), is the Homeric spelling. οἰδαλέος (4) occurs first in this poem in extant Greek; and ἀναστένω is not Homeric, though στένω occurs (e.g., *Iliad* 10. 16). τλημοσύνας (acc. plural) is found in *Hymn to Apollo* 191 (which may be later than Archilochus).

35. Indeed, Kamerbeek (1961) and Koster (cited and discussed by Kamerbeek [1961, 2]) have to strain syntax or the meanings of words in order to produce a sense acceptable to them.

36. Homer's characters do display fortitude. (They also exhort themselves to do so, as in *Odyssey* 20. 18.) But they are more emotional than later Greeks were or, at all events, more than some later Greeks thought that they should be, as Plato eloquently shows (*Republic* 386A–389A). See also my discussion of Tyrtaeus in chapter 4 (pp. 78–92).

37. In particular, there can be no allusion to Helen wishing that she had been drowned at birth (*Iliad* 6. 345–48).

38. Schwartz, as Solmsen (1970) notes ad loc., deleted lines 602–12. Those who follow him may doubt whether they had been composed when Archilochus wrote 13W.

39. Homer (*Iliad* 2. 542) calls the Abantes ὄπιθεν κομόωντες but assigns no reason for the practice.

40. δουρικλυτοί seems likely to be the last word of its sentence. Note the position of ξιφέων at the beginning of this sentence, and πολλὰ . . . τόξα at the beginning of the first sentence.

41. The effect of the comma at H12 in 1 is quite different from that of the (probable) full stop at H12 in 5, particularly in combination with the enjambed 4.

42. Page (in Hardt 1964, 182) notes that μάχης ἀδαήμονι occurs at *Iliad* 5. 634, μάχης ἀδαήμονες at *Iliad* 13. 811. He comments, "δαίμονές εἰσι μάχης is obviously an adaptation."

43. As an example of fluidity of pronunciation in elegiacs, see Mimnermus 1W. 4, where in the same line the poet writes ἄνθεα and ἁρπαλέᾰ. Scherer (in Hardt 1964, 93) offers several Ionic parallels (e.g., Δανᾷ for Δανάῃ in Hecataeus) for δάμων = δαήμων.

44. For example, ἀειρείτην for ἀρετήν in a dialogue one of whose participants is the Heraclitean Cratylus (415D; and cf. the derivations of ἵμερος and ἔρως in 420A–B). There is no such obvious motivation for δαίμων as "knower"; and indeed Socrates appeals to "the old form of our language," not to some hypothetical earlier form of the word, for corroboration (398B7).

45. Homer, *Iliad* 5 and 20. After Homer, gods are said to "fight together with" (συμμαχεῖν, more vivid than "be ally of") their worshiper (e.g., Aeschylus, *Septem* 266, 586; Euripides, *Supplices* 630), but in what sense they are believed to be present at the battle is unclear.

46. Page (in Hardt 1964, 132) prefers ἄορι κλυτοί, which produces a tautology. (δουρικλυτός does not occur in Hesiod, but δουρικλειτός is used of Menelaus in Hesiod, Frag. 175. 1 Merkelbach and West.)

47. The fragment as we have it is very different from the exhortations of Callinus and Tyrtaeus; but presumably Archilochus also adduced reasons why his fellow sol-

diers should be sanguine about ultimate victory over the Euboeans, δαίμονες or no, and exhorted them to make every effort.

48. δεσπότης is not, though δέσποινα occurs in the *Odyssey*.

49. ξιφέων . . . πολύστονον . . . ἔργον resembles Homeric/Hesiodic phraseology: the Homeric ἔργον Ἄρηος (*Iliad* 11. 734), πολέμοιο . . . ἔργον (*Iliad* 8. 453), and Hesiod's οἷσιν Ἄρηος / ἔργ᾽ ἔμελε στονόεντα (*Works and Days* 145–46); but it need not be a conscious adaptation.

50. Contrast Page's remarks in Hardt 1964, 132.

51. At least the prepositional phrases precede the verb. Contrast Tyrtaeus 10W. 3–6, where the last two lines of a four-line sentence consist exclusively of prepositional phrases. (See Adkins 1977a, 77–78.) There may be a point in Archilochus' low-key writing here; see below, p. 50.

52. Page (in Hardt 1964, 129–30) denies this; but the word seems to retain the idea of repeated or sustained movement in all its uses. *Odyssey* 12. 420 is closest to Archilochus' phrase.

53. Compare Archilochus 13W. 9.

54. The papyrus has νηφέμεν (with the accent). The manuscripts of Athenaeus have νήφειν μέν. Musurus conjectured νήφειν ἐν; Bergk (1882) νηφέμεναι.

55. Merone (1960, 16–17) argues that even these adjectives give new appropriateness to Homeric formulae.

56. The manuscripts of Strabo have ἀγείλετο, ἀνείλετο, ἀνείλατο, and ἀφείλατο with ἀσπίδα and τήν to avoid hiatus. All give inferior sense or nonsense.

57. So that Achilles' lack of spare armor presumably reflects the situation with which Homer was familiar in life. His years of combat before Troy should have furnished him with armor by the shipload from this source. ἐναρίζειν is used even in *Iliad* 1. 191, when Achilles is about to kill Agamemnon at the assembly.

58. An increased supply of metal seems a necessary prerequisite for the existence of hoplites in significant numbers.

59. See Euripides, *Supplices* 528–30; Herodotus 1. 128, 6. 45; Thucydides 5. 9. 9.

60. See Tyrtaeus 11. 11–14, and Plato, *Symp.* 220E7-221c1 (Socrates at Delium). Though Delium was a defeat for the Athenians, they had earlier broken the Boeotian left wing (Thucydides 4. 96. 3). Yet the Athenians lost almost twice as many hoplites as the Boeotians, in consequence of their own subsequent rout (Thucydides 4. 101). In the rout and panic at Amphipolis, the Athenians lost about six hundred men, the Spartans only seven (Thucydides 5. 11). Plato gives a graphic account of the retreat from Delium (*Symposium* 221E).

61. *P. Oxy.* 2313, fr. 5. 5. Since ἔντεα is solely epic, lyric, and (once) tragic, the choice of the word may dignify the lost weapon in the same way as does ἀμώμητος, so that it might be held even more shameful to lose it.

62. The Greeks in fact accepted no excuses for such behavior. Even to be defeated while fighting bravely was αἰσχρόν. Cf. the passages cited in note 59 above.

63. The δέ is Hoffmann's emendation (1898). For the text of 3 in general, see note 65 below.

64. A Freudian interpretation would be possible. Even while brazenly admitting that he has run away, Archilochus distances himself from the event by using a pronoun which is usually third-person.

65. Of the other transmitted versions of the third line, none gives such satisfactory poetry. Sextus' αὐτὸς δ᾽ ἐξέφυγον θανάτου τέλος, a reminiscence of two Homeric

phrases, has the longer stride of epic rather than the compression of the rest of this poem, reduces the last three vigorous and staccato expressions to two, and destroys the balanced oppositions mentioned in the previous paragraph. The sense of ψυχήν has been objected to, on the general grounds that the word means only "ghost" in Homer; but if Achilles (*Iliad* 9. 322) can speak of staking his ψυχή when he fights, presumably Archilochus can save his when he runs away. Again, Aristophanes is by far our earliest evidence for the line. Yet αὐτόν, particularly in archaic Greek, is much more personal than ψυχή: note the contrast of ψυχάς and αὐτούς in *Iliad* 1. 3–4. Those who read some form of αὐτός have made efforts to include both με and δέ. με is dispensable: cf. *Iliad* 24. 503, where the context indicates the sense of αὐτόν as it does here. αὐτὸν δ' occurs in no text: the Neoplatonists who quote the lines have αὐτόν μ' ἐξεσάωσα (Elias) or αὐτὸν μέν μ' ἐσάωσα (Olympiodorus); but δέ seems necessary, for reasons discussed in the text, and it occurs in Sextus and Aristophanes. Gigante (1956, 196–200) argues for αὐτός μ' ἐξεσάωσα; but both αὐτόν and δέ are necessary to furnish a train of thought: "I lost my shield, but I saved *myself*. I can get another shield." Compared with that, "I lost my shield. I *myself* saved me. I can get another shield" is obscure: αὐτός lays emphasis on Archilochus' activity—presumably, running away; and one might then expect, as line 4, "Who needs a shield at all if his legs are nimble enough?" The text that is printed in Diehl 1949 and West 1972 is derived from the tradition, and in the circumstances it seems reasonable to suppose that the best poetry preserved is what Archilochus wrote: those who misquote from memory, or miscopy, rarely improve aesthetically on their original. (Diehl's suggestion of a pun between Σαίων and ἐξεσάωσα seems doubtful; but the pun would not be feebler, or aurally or visually less close, than some of Aristophanes' puns in circumstances where the line is pointless if no pun is intended, e.g., *Frogs* 970, despite the editors' efforts.)

66. West's index contains four elegiac examples. The disyllabic κεῖνος is a little more common: there are eleven elegiac examples.

67. κάλλιπον is one of Archilochus' Aeolic forms. See Scherer, in Hardt 1964, 91. (It occurs in Homer, *Iliad* 9. 364.) In general, see p. 34, above, and note 9 of this chapter.

68. *Iliad* 4. 300 would be a suitable allusion for contrast: there the inferior fighters are compelled to fight καὶ οὐκ ἐθέλων, whereas Archilochus has fled καὶ οὐκ ἐθέλων; but allusion is not possible with so ordinary and common a phrase.

69. It occurs three times in Hesiod: of Iolaus in the *Shield of Heracles* 102, of female companions in Frag. 185. 13, and of Ajax in Frag. 204. 44 Merkelbach and West. There is no question of allusion.

70. It occurs once in Hesiod, Frag. 23a22 Merkelbach and West. There is no allusion.

71. It is the most likely position for a word with the metrical shape ∪–∪∪.

72. Page's opinion (in Hardt 1964, 133) is diametrically opposed. Archilochus "composes in this manner because he has no choice; his technique is wholly that of the oral Epic."

Notes to Chapter 3

1. For the figures, see Table 4.
2. Since Callinus 2W is the first half of a hexameter, twelve caesurae are known.
3. For the figures, see Table 6.

4. Since Callinus 4W is—probably—the second hemiepes of a pentameter, thirteen pentameter endings are known.

5. He seems less concerned to vary his hexameter endings (though more so than Tyrtaeus in Tyrtaeus 10W; see Adkins 1977a, 75); but contrast, e.g., *Iliad* 6. 80–87, where eight consecutive lines end in a trisyllabic word.

6. For the tense of κατακεῖσθε, see Campbell (1967), ad loc.

7. See Tyrtaeus 10W. 15–32.

8. I doubt, however, whether Bergk (1882) is correct in supposing that in the missing verses Callinus "descripserat calamitates, quibus terra tunc premebatur, bello ut videtur contra Magnetas adversa fortuna gesto." I suspect the disappearance of a striking extended figure of speech rather than a résumé of the course of the war or a mere description of present woes.

9. The effect would be acoustically similar to chiasmus, which places contrasted ideas at opposite ends of an utterance.

10. Cf. my comments on 9(P8)–11, 12–13, and 14–15.

11. See also my comments on 14–16.

12. For discussion of the effectiveness of beginning a new sentence after the major caesura of the hexameter, see Adkins 1977a, 82, on Tyrtaeus 10W. 27.

13. The light dactylic line 10 is not particularly appropriate to the sense in itself, but the contrast with ἔλσας is undeniably effective. For the general point, see chapter 1, p. 18.

14. Notably found in *Iliad* 6. 487–89.

15. Cf. the use of ἀνδρεῖος in Greek and contrast the positioning of the word in Hector's μοῖραν δ' οὔ τινά φημι πεφυγμένον ἔμμεναι ἀνδρῶν (*Iliad* 6. 488), where the emphasis is on μοῖραν and οὔ τινα.

16. So Higham (1938, 183): "Many from war and ringing lance have sheltered, / Homeward fled: at home death finds them out."

17. "Returneth safe from the war" (Edmonds 1931) is evidently incorrect.

18. Cf. also 19, ζώων δ' ἄξιος ἡμιθέων.

19. Below, p. 64. Hudson-Williams (1926) observes that ἔρχεσθαι is the regular word for the homecoming of Odysseus (e.g., *Odyssey* 14. 382 ff.) and is accordingly appropriate here with ἐν δ' οἴκῳ.

20. E.g., Bergk 1882, Edmonds 1931, Campbell 1967.

21. On the tense, see Bergk 1882, ad loc.

22. See, e.g., Campbell 1967, 162.

23. *Iliad* 17. 677; 24. 10, 523, 527; *Odyssey* 10. 532; 11. 45; 19. 439; *Hymn to Hermes* 254, 324, 358.

24. *Iliad* 24. 10; 17. 677; *Odyssey* 19. 439; *Hymn to Hermes* 254.

25. It occurs seven times if we include *Iliad* 21. 571 (where ἄλκιμον occurs in the next line). The others are *Iliad* 5. 529; 16. 209, 264; 17. 111; 20. 169; and *Homeric Hymns* 27. 9. The phrase occurs also in Callinus 1W. 10.

26. It may well have been coined by Callinus, to supply a word to fill the entire second hemiepes.

27. Even in the circumstances described in *Iliad* 10. 121–23.

28. *Iliad* 1. 213; 4. 97; 16. 86; 24. 447, 534; *Odyssey* 11. 357; 16. 230; 19. 413, 460; 24. 314; *Hymn to Hermes* 462, 470.

29. On εὖχος, see Adkins 1969a.

30. Callinus emphasizes the glory of victory and the shame of cowardice rather than

the disaster of utter defeat, as does Tyrtaeus in his 10W. 3–6; the impression given is that the crisis is somewhat less severe than at Sparta.

31. It occurs nine times, of which *Iliad* 1. 114 refers to Clytemnestra, 7. 392 and 13. 626 to Helen, of whom Callinus presumably did not wish to remind his audience.

32. Campbell (1967, 162) points out that ἀλλά τις αὐτὸς ἴτω (*Iliad* 17. 254) is the beginning of a Homeric line, slightly varied by Callinus. (But it seems not impossible that Callinus could have composed so ordinary a phrase for himself.)

33. For μένος and μενεαίνειν, see Adkins 1969b, 7 ff.

34. This is presumably the point of τὸ πρῶτον. The metaphor is unlikely to be drawn from winds (*Odyssey* 5. 317), for the winds are plural: one cannot μείγνυσθαι one wind.

35. Gods are portrayed in art as larger than mortals, e.g., in *Iliad* 18. 516 ff.

36. Cf. the use of παχύς in Herodotus 5. 30, 77; 6. 91.

37. It occurs at *Odyssey* 4. 333 and 17. 124.

38. In *Iliad* 4. 334, 347, πύργος is interpreted as "column, battalion." This usage occurs only in these passages in extant Greek; but if it was an established usage in the Greek known to Callinus, this too would enrich the meaning of Callinus 1W. 20.

39. *Iliad* 7. 219; 11. 485; 17. 128. This is a whole-line formula and is likely to have occurred also in many contexts now lost.

40. The allusion in ἀνδράσι μαρνάμενοι in Tyrtaeus 10W. 18 (discussed in Adkins 1977a, 91) is to Achilles and his mighty deeds. The Homeric original occurs in a speech where Achilles is declining to fight; the audience is evidently to remember the immediately adjacent lines but not the wider context.

41. Plutarch, *De Musica* 28; Marius Victorinus, *Ars Grammatica* 6. 1, pp. 81, 85, 104 K.

Notes to Chapter 4

1. Archaic Sparta down to 550 B.C. compares well with other Greek cities for artistic achievements, whether in poetry (Alcman, Terpander, Tyrtaeus) or the other arts (e.g., the Arcesilaus cup, of which there is a good illustration in Charbonneaux 1971, 79, fig. 84). Even if none of the artists was Spartan (and Terpander was not), their work was evidently appreciated in Sparta. See, e.g., Forrest 1968, 57, for the visual arts.

2. See Wyatt 1966, 617–43. Wyatt argues that such scansions as δημότᾱς (Tyrtaeus 4W. 5) are not colloquial Doric but result from Hesiod's analogies from Homeric short-vowel nominatives of the ἵππότα type.

3. Acceptance of this view does not render allusion less possible, for the Ionic phrase and the epic phrase will sometimes be identical and always similar; but non-Ionic epicisms will be more marked and thus even better triggers for allusion.

4. These figures are based on Tyrtaeus 1W through 14W and exclude the restorations in 19W. In 4W. 8 the restoration σκολιόν seems certain.

5. I have not included 13W or 14W (one-line fragments) for this purpose.

6. Contrast Andrewes 1938, 97.

7. He is said to have been Charillus' guardian (*Politics* 1271b25), and Charillus reigned about 776.

8. See above, n. 1.

9. The texts preserved by Plutarch and Diodorus are not chance variants. Plutarch's version, by omitting line 8 in particular, seems to give the *demos* more freedom of action. Diodorus' version, by ascribing the whole to the Delphic oracle, gives Apollo's sanction to the more restrictive version.

10. In 10W, for example, there are nine in a poem of thirty-two lines, but there is only one in the first fourteen lines.

11. The effective rhythmical contrast of 5 and 6 should still be reckoned to Tyrtaeus' credit.

12. Kings are successful and prosperous. The gods give prosperity. Status-enhancing material goods are *time* (Adkins 1960b). Kings must be θεοτίμητοι, given *time* by the gods.

13. Hesiod, Frag. 43a62 Merkelbach and West, has (apparently) ἱμερόεντα πόλιν. West (1972) supplies ἱμερόεσσα πόλις at Tyrtaeus 21. 15. Thucydides' Pericles (2. 43) exhorts the Athenians to become ἐραστάς of Athens.

14. The heptasyllable is rare in this position, but cf. Callinus 1W. 2 and [Demodocus] 5W. 4. (The effect is different in each case.)

15. If Tyrtaeus in fact began with the hexameter oracle (lines 3, 5, 7, and 9) as a datum, note once again his skill in composing.

16. Edmonds (1931) in fact has "answering back" and "forthright ordinances" (εὐθείαις ῥήτραις), which quite misses the subtlety of the Greek.

17. The poet sometimes seems to postulate the presence of many well-armed soldiers, but in his detailed description of battles it is evident that such armor is rare. See, e.g., Greenhalgh 1972, 532–33.

18. Homer displays little knowledge of the use of massed chariots in battle. Nestor (*Iliad* 4. 293–309) is the exception, and he speaks of it as the practice of earlier generations. See, e.g., Wace and Stubbings 1962, 521–22. However, the Homeric use of chariots to ensure that heavily armed warriors arrive fresh and unweary on the battlefield, and can retreat rapidly if need be, is not a tactical absurdity. (Homeric warriors do sometimes fight from their chariots: cf. Euphorbus, below, p. 91).

19. Athens could apparently put some 30,000 hoplites into the field at the beginning of the Peloponnesian War (Thuc. 2. 13; see Gomme 1945, ad loc., for discussion). Aristotle claims that Sparta had enough land to support 30,000 hoplites and 1,000 cavalry; that she did not do so was due to her inheritance laws, which brought the land into the hands of a few (*Politics* 1270a29–32). In the seventh century Athens certainly had fewer hoplites and Sparta possibly more. Smaller cities possessed much smaller forces but, nevertheless, considerably more than the twelve ἄριστοι mentioned by Nestor (*Iliad* 11. 691) as the effective fighters of Pylos in his youth.

20. It also required a greatly increased supply of metal. The dearth of metal in the period of composition of the Homeric poems is reflected in the eagerness with which the victor strips his foe of his armor. (ἐξ)εναρίζειν, indeed, may be used of killing (see p. 51, above).

21. Even though the bards confuse the armor of different periods, the elements of the Homeric panoply are not a product of the bardic imagination. On this topic, and on the question of the armor of the Tyrtaean hoplite, see Snodgrass 1964.

22. For illustrations of hoplite armor of different dates, see Snodgrass 1964.

23. See chapter 2, n. 60.

24. The whole phalanx tended to drift off to the right because each man moved his

unprotected sword-arm as close as possible to the shield of the man stationed on his right (Thucydides 5. 71).

25. See, e.g., Aristotle, *Nicomachean Ethics* 1115a28–31, where courage in other fields is hardly rated as courage at all.

26. In poem 12W Tyrtaeus redefines ἀρετή by excluding many aspects which were ἀρεταί in Homer in favor of martial courage displayed in the phalanx. Whether or not Sparta was more threatened than Troy, Tyrtaeus supposed a change in values to be necessary. See Adkins 1960a, 73.

27. Though West (1972) prints no stop at the end of 9, there must have been a pause before the vocative ὦ νέοι at the beginning of 10, as in Callinus 1. 1–12, where West prints a comma.

28. There are 50 in 38 lines in 11W, 178 in 139 lines in all extant Tyrtaeus. Archilochus has 32 in 38 lines, Callinus 25 in 23.

29. Certainty on this point seems unattainable. Most scholars suppose that 11W. 1 is not the first line of Tyrtaeus' poem. ἀλλά with an imperative can begin a speech in tragedy (e.g., Sophocles, *Electra* 431, *Oedipus at Colonus* 238). Denniston (1954, 14) characterizes such speeches as "an objection in the form of a command." The speeches are rejoinders to another character's words; but one might view Tyrtaeus' poem as a rejoinder to defeatist talk in Sparta or even to the general situation. Dover's remarks on the context of performance (in Hardt 1964, 199–212) are relevant not only to oral verse.

30. Denniston (1954) does not discuss possible emphasis by position; but it is noteworthy how frequently in negative sentences οὐ is placed between ἀλλά and γάρ (e.g., Homer, *Odyssey* 14. 355, Aristophanes, *Clouds* 798, Herodotus 8. 8. 1, Plato, *Protagoras* 336A). In Denniston's "complex" use (where ἀλλά and γάρ retain their separate meanings, and there are two clauses expressed, as in Tyrtaeus 11W. 1), the following examples show the tendency to place the most emphatic word in the γάρ-clause between ἀλλά and γάρ: Aeschylus, *Choephori* 375–76, ἀλλὰ διπλῆς γὰρ τῆσδε μαραγνῆς δοῦπος ἱκνεῖται, where διπλῆς is followed by μέν and δέ to detail the alternatives; Sophocles, *Philoctetes* 81, ἀλλ' ἡδὺ γάρ τι κτῆμα τῆς νίκης λαβεῖν, τόλμα, where ἡδύ is the motive for the action; Euripides, *Iphigenia in Tauris* 118, ἀλλ' εὖ γὰρ εἶπας, πειστέον, where εὖ gives the reason for obeying; and Euripides, *Electra* 1245, ἀλλ' ἄναξ γάρ ἐστ' ἐμός, σιγῶ, where the status of Apollo supplies the reason for Castor's silence.

31. Evans (1962, 182–83) argues that the line means "Zeus is not yet afraid." He compares Horace, *Satires* 2. 5. 92, *stes capite obstipo, multum similis metuenti*, and Apollonius of Rhodes 2. 581–82, οἱ δ' ἐσιδόντες / ἤμυσαν λοξοῖσι καρήασι. But with Zeus as subject, "afraid" seems to make little sense, except as an ἀδύνατον; and then "yet" is difficult. One could construct an argument: "Zeus is not yet afraid of the Messenians (and never could be): you are descended from Zeus (who will therefore take good care of you); so do not you fear the Messenians either." But this would require ὑμεῖς to be expressed, to emphasize the parallelism.

32. Cf. *Iliad* 13. 1–9, where Zeus turns his head away from Troy (πάλιν τρέπεν ὄσσε φαεινώ, 3) and does not notice Poseidon's help to the Greeks; the deception of Zeus in *Iliad* 14; and Poseidon's ignorance of the other gods' plan to bring Odysseus home, *Odyssey* 1. 19–79; 5. 286–90.

33. In Homer, φόβος and φοβεῖσθαι regularly mean "flight" and "flee," not merely "fear." φοβεῖσθε need not be otiose here: in conjunction with δειμαίνετε,

"flee" is likely to be brought to mind. Conversely, in Tyrtaeus 10W. 16 φόβου set next to φυγῆς seems likely to have suggested "fear." On the latter line, see Adkins 1977a, 80.

34. Cf. Sophocles, *Ajax* 1122–23, where 1123 indicates that "having a shield" signifies ὡπλισμένος. For this reason I cannot agree with Campbell (1967, 176) that the ἀσπίς of Tyrtaeus 11W. 35 belongs to the light-armed. See also note 45 of this chapter.

35. In a military context νέος means "of military age," not "tyro." Cf. Tyrtaeus 10W. 15 ff.

36. Tyrtaeus is capable of coining new and effective poetic phrases. See Adkins 1977a, 83–84, 90–91.

37. Unfortunately, Denniston (1954) does not discuss this passage.

38. λαός seems to be used of the less effective fighters, as in *Iliad* 2. 365, 13. 108. I discuss the word further, above, p. 61.

39. Lines 15–20 elaborate 14; but the sentence ends at 14, and the following lines are not linked to 11–14 by a connecting particle.

40. West (1972) supports μάθῃ by comparing it with διδασκέσθω πολεμίζειν (27), with *Iliad* 6. 444, ἐπεὶ μάθον ἔμμεναι ἐσθλός, and with *Odyssey* 17. 226, ἔργα κάκ' ἔμμαθεν. Certainly μάθῃ makes sense, and, if the manuscripts made none, it would be an acceptable emendation; but though αἰσχρὰ πάσχειν does not occur in Homer, it is good Greek (e.g., Herodotus 3. 36. 5), and in *Iliad* 18. 73 ff. παθεῖν τ' ἀεκήλια ἔργα is used of an analogous situation. Again, if one πάσχει something, it γίγνεται αὐτῷ (cf. Hesiod, *Theogony* 512, *Works and Days* 88). κακὰ πάσχειν is a common phrase in Homer (e.g., *Odyssey* 2. 370); Tyrtaeus is saying that if one suffers (experiences) what is dishonorable by fleeing in battle one also suffers (experiences) what is harmful. The MSS reading ἀργαλέον (17) seems to make no sense. 17–18 may be rendered in two ways: (*a*) taking ἀνδρὸς φεύγοντος as a possessive genitive, "It is difficult to pierce from behind the back of a man who is running away . . ."; (*b*) taking the genitive as absolute, "It is difficult to . . . when one is running away." Alternative (*b*) would be said in a sarcastic or ironic tone of voice, which seems to be alien to Tyrtaeus. Alternative (*a*) seems to be simply untrue. It is certainly un-Homeric. In Homer, ἀργαλέον is used, in the context of fighting, when heroes fight against superior numbers (*Iliad* 20. 355 ff., *Odyssey* 2. 243 ff.) or reflect on the difficulty of fighting against gods (*Iliad* 20. 366 ff.). It is not used when a hero is pursuing a defeated foe. Nor would one expect Tyrtaeus to use it when he is trying to encourage the young men of Sparta to fight bravely against an as yet undefeated foe. Emendation seems needed, and Ahrens' ἁρπαλέον (1841) is easy and appropriate.

41. For a similarly placed φεύγοντ' in Homer, cf. *Iliad* 6. 36, discussed above, p. 23.

42. Contrast the language and situation in Hesiod, *Shield of Heracles* 365. (But even though Ares fought bravely, he would have been λωβητὸς ἐν ἀθανάτοισι as a result of his defeat [366–67].)

43. The words of Lycurgus (*In Leocratem* 107) suggest that, in the fourth century, τὰ Τυρταίου ποιήματα—a phrase which could denote the whole corpus of his war poems—were performed before the Spartans went into battle.

44. Similar lists of weapons (but not in participial phrases) occur in Homer, *Iliad* 13. 130–31; 16. 215.

45. For the social and emotional connotations of ἀσπίς, cf. Sophocles, *Ajax* 1120–

25, discussed in Adkins 1972a, 63–67. For its effectiveness as a weapon, see Blyth 1977, 1982.

46. An ear accustomed to Homer would certainly not be offended.

47. Cf. Callinus 1W. 16.

48. West (1972) cites *Iliad* 16. 734, 21. 393, and Tyrtaeus 11. 4. The last is an imperfect parallel: ἰθύς and ἐς προμάχους affect the sense of ἔχειν.

49. That these soldiers each had both sword and spear is suggested by line 25 and by later Greek practice. The development of the hoplite panoply required time. See Snodgrass 1964, passim.

50. See, e.g., Kühner-Gerth 1898, 2(1):189.

51. In Homer, the word is used of locusts (*Iliad* 21. 14); of small birds fleeing vultures (*Odyssey* 22. 304); of beggars—strictly, of their cringing attitude (*Odyssey* 17. 227), but also of the act of asking for alms (*Odyssey* 18. 363); and of warriors at a disadvantage (*Iliad* 4. 371; 5. 634; etc.).

52. The disadvantage of the light-armed is related both to social status and to military effectiveness. (See, e.g., Sophocles, *Ajax* 1120–25, cited in note 34, above.) Where the citizen buys his own armor and weapons, the wealthier will be better armed or, at all events, more fully and expensively armed; and light-armed troops *were* less effective. Though the mountainous terrain of much of Greece favors quick-moving guerilla warfare, as has been demonstrated many times, in ancient Greece the necessity to defend one's fields and the growing crops demanded that the enemy be met on the level plain, where his heavy infantry must be met by a similar ponderous and slow-moving force. The point should not be overstated. Light-armed troops could not defend the crops of the polis by themselves; but in the later fifth century, at all events, it was realized that hoplites without a screen of light-armed of their own were very vulnerable to light-armed attack. Note Demosthenes' debacle in Aetolia (Thucydides 3. 97–98) and his subsequent use of similar tactics against the Spartan hoplites on Sphacteria (Thucydides 4. 29–40). In Tyrtaeus' Sparta the fact that the γυμνῆτες mingled on the battlefield with the heavy-armed troops—more closely than would have been possible later, in the days of the developed phalanx—doubtless indicates that their contribution was not negligible; but Tyrtaeus expects them to know their place and keep to it.

53. West (1972), a cautious editor, marks a last line in only a few elegiac poems: *Theognidea* 38, 52, 100, 192, 232 (= Solon 13 ad fin.), 260, 266, 400, 456, 496, 522, 682, 756, 764, 768, 830, 864, 962, 978, 1164d (= 100); *Adespota Elegiaca* 7, 27; Demodocus 2, [3], [4], [5]; Ion 26; Simonides 6, 8; Solon 13; and Sophocles (I)4. He acknowledges no examples from Archilochus, Callinus, Tyrtaeus, Mimnermus, or Xenophanes.

54. None of the "Homeric" hymns can be accurately dated.

55. "Do not merely not fear the πληθύς, but go straight for the πρόμαχοι" would preserve the Homeric balance of terror; but it seems impossible to read Tyrtaeus' Greek in this way. (Could ἰθύς . . . ἐχέτω mean "exert pressure with your shield against the front rank of the foe"? But possibly the phalanx was less like a rugby scrum than is sometimes supposed, at least in countries where rugby is played.)

56. *Iliad* 16. 188. "To see the light of the sun" is more common: e.g., *Iliad* 5. 120; 18. 61, 442; 24. 558. See Snell 1969, 13.

57. It occurs in Hesiod, *Works and Days* 304.

58. It seems certain that Polemos was never a personal deity, as Ares was. Polemos had no cult. (See G. Herzog-Hauser, *RE* s.v.) For close juxtaposition of what we should distinguish as personal and nonpersonal, see Solon 36W. 4–7.

59. The κακόν differs in some respects from what Tyrtaeus has in mind. Odysseus is not defending his own land. See also Tyrtaeus 10W. 1 ff.

60. It appears in *Iliad* 17. 721 and *Odyssey* 5. 227 in the plural and in *Iliad* 5. 572 and *Odyssey* 23. 211 in the dual (*Odyssey* 5. 227 refers to the relationship between Odysseus and Calypso, 23. 211 to that between Odysseus and Penelope).

61. It may be argued that such "allusions" are not deliberate but result from the subconscious processes of composition of Tyrtaeus' mind, which was evidently steeped in Homer. Granted; but it must also be granted that Tyrtaeus' Muse is then performing her task with greater deftness and grace than she would usually be credited with.

62. τινάσσειν seems more appropriate to a Homeric throwing spear than to the thrusting spear of the hoplite.

63. The priamel, Tyrtaeus 12W. 1–14, rejects those aspects of Homeric ἀρετή that Tyrtaeus regards as irrelevant in the present circumstances. See Adkins 1960a, 73.

64. Cf. Hesiod, *Theogony* 996, on which Hofinger (1977 s.v.) observes; "Dans ce passage, comme en *Il.* xxii 418, l'adjectif tire du contexte une valeur péjorative qu'il n'a pas par lui-même." But to speak of a man as "mighty and wicked" does not render "mighty" pejorative, even in the particular context.

NOTES TO CHAPTER 5

1. Contrast the figures for Tyrtaeus, above, p. 67.

2. For complete figures, see Table 6.

3. For complete figures, see Table 7.

4. That is to say, acceptable sense groups are produced by phrasing the line in either manner.

5. Campbell (1967, ad loc.) believes Mimnermus 1W to be a complete poem. West (1972, ad loc.) is not confident that we have either the first or the last line. Bowra (1938a, 17, 18) speaks both of "some famous lines" and of "this poem." He makes some sensitive comments (19) on Mimnermus 1W.

6. In, e.g., Archilochus 13W (see above, chapter 2).

7. Mimnermus 2W has nine of sixteen end-stopped, Mimnermus 5W has five of eight. Callinus 1W has ten of twenty-one; Tyrtaeus 11W has nine of thirty-eight.

8. For example, 11W. 4, 8 (but not 12), 22, 28, 30.

9. For other examples, see pp. 104 and 225, n. 32.

10. He employs it also at 2W. 5, 2W. 7, and 5W. 5. Indeed, if one considers only the first eight lines of 2W, οὔτ' ἀγαθόν in 2W. 5 has exactly the same function as ἥβη τιμήεσσα in 5W. 5 and occurs at the same point in the eight lines. Mimnermus evidently employs the device in units of composition smaller than complete poems.

11. Van Groningen (1960, 124) emphasizes the division at this point. See also Fränkel 1962, 240.

12. Tyrtaeus 11W. 17 is an emendation, but a very probable one. See p. 83, above.

13. See Dover, in Hardt 1964, 199–212; and recall Propertius 1. 9. 9–10: "plus in amore viget Mimnermi versus Homero; carmina mansuetus lenia quaerit Amor."

14. Compare Archilochus 13W. 4–5, discussed above, p. 38.

15. Campbell (1967, ad loc.) writes "κακόν will here have its moral sense." It certainly denotes and decries the absence of the most-valued Greek qualities, but to render it "immoral" or "unjust" would be to misinterpret Mimnermus' meaning: he is lamenting the absence of opportunity for illicit love in old age. κακός denotes and decries the inferior and unvalued. Compare *Theognidea* 173–78W.

16. Somewhat different analyses are offered by Fränkel (1962, 240) and Schmiel (1974, 284).

17. Consider the closing lines of the *Iliad* and *Odyssey*.

18. Mimnermus knows that the loss is inevitable, and in early Greece what is inevitable is ascribed to deity.

19. Compare Tyrtaeus 4W, discussed above, p. 69. Schmiel (1974, 284) argues for a similar effect in 6 and 10: γῆρας/γῆρας, αἰσχρόν/ἀργαλέον, τιθεῖ/ἔθηκε. These, however, are verbal echoes, not parallels: γῆρας is the subject of ἐπέλθῃ, the object of ἔθηκε, and the sense is quite different.

20. The usual reading is τέρπειν.

21. Alcibiades' days as reigning beauty are evidently numbered in Plato, *Protagoras* 309A. On the question of the age of ἐρώμενοι, see Dover 1978, 84–87, 141, 171, and 195 n. 20.

22. The reference may be to beauty too, as Hector's speech to Paris shows; but one concerns oneself (μέλει, 2) with activities, so that beauty is not primarily in mind in Mimnermus 2W. 3.

23. εὐνή, too, is Homeric in this sense; see, e.g., *Iliad* 3. 445.

24. The phrase occurs in its usual sense in Tyrtaeus 10W. 28. It has amatory connotations in Solon 25W. 1, and in *Theognidea* 994W, 1305W, and 1348W. Mimnermus uses it again twice (2W. 3 and 5W. 2). In Solon and the *Theognidea* the love is homosexual, and the ἄνθος is that of the adolescent beloved—in *Theognidea* 1348W, of Ganymede in particular; but the usage must be less restricted in Mimnermus.

25. Homeric warriors prefer life to death at any age. Nestor may term old age λυγρόν (*Iliad* 23. 644), but he has a place of honor in Agamemnon's army, even if (*Iliad* 4. 313–16) he is no longer the warrior he once was.

26. Compare the allusions in Archilochus 13W, discussed above, pp. 41–43.

27. Campbell (1967) prints only 4–8. Edmonds (1931) brackets the first three lines, as does Bergk (1882), but with the note "cum v. 4–6 legantur in Theognideis v. 1020–1022, recte Brunck fragmento, quod servavit Stobaeus, tres versus praemisit . . . qui praecedunt apud Th. 1017–1019." Gaisford (1814) prints all eight lines.

28. Sappho has ἐπτόαισεν in 31. 6, ἴδρως ψῦχρος in 31. 13. (See, e.g., Voigt 1971, 57–58.)

29. Not that his nature, or that of his poetic persona, was unwarlike. As Campbell (1967) notes, his poetry appeared in other chapters of Stobaeus' anthology as well: 14W in the chapter on courage, 1W in the chapter labeled 'Aphrodite,' 2W in the one on the brevity of life, and 5W in the one on complaints against old age.

30. In Aristophanes' *Clouds*, it is used, in adjacent lines, of the skin of the healthy athlete (1012) and the unhealthy intellectual (1017).

31. Homeric dreams seem to exist objectively. The dream which Zeus sends to Agamemnon in *Iliad* 2. 6–34 may visit Agamemnon only briefly, but its visit does not

constitute its entire existence. (A more familiar view of dreams appears at *Iliad* 22. 199–201.)

32. Compare Archilochus 13W. 5, 7 and Callinus 1W. 8, discussed above.

33. This seems to be the idea which links the various uses of ποικίλος.

34. ἀργαλέον (5) is a minor exception.

35. See, e.g., *Iliad* 5. 776; 8. 50; 17. 270; *Odyssey* 13. 189. Homer has no word for "invisible" in the sense of "directly before the unimpeded eyes but unable to be seen." Hades (if the name is from α privative + ἰδεῖν) is invisible because he is under the earth.

36. As—notoriously—is Anaxagoras' Nous, in the later years of the fifth century. It is doubtful whether there is a concept of the nonmaterial before Plato.

37. The other interpretation is possible. See *Iliad* 15. 724, *Odyssey* 14. 178 (φρένας βλάπτειν), and *Theognidea* 705W (βλάπτειν νόοιο). But it is less appropriate in this context.

Notes to Chapter 6

1. The literature is too abundant to discuss comprehensively in a work whose primary concerns are different, particularly since I argue here that Solon 4W is not a document of either history or political theory. Linforth 1919, 194–206, will serve as a good example of interpretation in terms of both history and political theory, for he gives a detailed commentary on the poem (which he numbers XII). Ehrenberg (1921, 83 ff.; 1930, 16–29), Jaeger (1926, 69 ff.), and Vlastos (1946, 65–83) interpret Solon as a political thinker in very abstract terms. Masaracchia (1958, 246–72) comments shrewdly on their interpretations but does not question the aim of Solon's work, which he terms (246) the "testimonianza piu esauriente dell' ideologia politica del legislatore" and (272) "questo mediocre trattato di teoria politica."

2. S and L, the two best Demosthenes manuscripts, do not have the poem, and A has only a few verses. In the other manuscripts no lacunae are indicated.

3. Lines 10 and 11 cannot be counted.

4. So Campbell 1967, ad loc.; Masaracchia 1958, 248; and Voemel 1862. Voemel's parallel from Xenophon (*Anabasis* 5. 5. 13) will stand; but the fit with *P. Oxy.* 2824 shows that Tyrtaeus 2D. 1 (= 2W. 12–15) is not the first line of that poem, as Masaracchia (1958) claims.

5. Solon's hearers might recall *Iliad* 4. 25–84.

6. Wilamowitz (1893, 306) suggested a different version of the preceding lines.

7. And not only rhetorically. Bianchi (1953), while correctly emphasizing the absence of any idea of fatalism, overestimates Zeus's control over αἶσα and μοῖρα. To translate Διὸς αἶσα by "il decreto di Zeus" (Masaracchia 1958, 248) inappropriately suggests an utterance of Zeus to establish what is αἶσα. The relationship between Zeus and αἶσα is rather that between the player of a game and the rules of the game. See also Adkins 1972b.

8. There is no reason to suppose χεῖρας not to be literal. Sixth-century Athenians, accustomed to the physical help ascribed to Athena and other deities in the Homeric poems, would certainly understand Solon's words in this way. In *Iliad* 9. 419–20

Achilles advises the Greeks to return home, since Zeus has held his hand (χεῖρα ἑὴν ὑπερέσχε) over Troy in protection.

9. Compare Aeschylus, *Seven against Thebes* 78–180, discussed in Adkins, 1982b, 42–43.

10. Approximately 12 percent of the extant pentameters of the authors discussed in this book have pentesyllabic endings.

11. Even in Athens in the later fifth century this attitude remained prevalent. See Adkins 1960a, Index, s.v. *oikos*.

12. Linforth (1919, 196–98) denies that ἀστοί could at this period denote a smaller group than the whole citizen body. But in *Theognidea* 191–92W the γένος of the ἀστοί can be dimmed by unsuitable marriages only if it was distinguished before. The effect of the rhetoric depends not on ἀστοί clearly denoting the prominent citizens but on the possibility of its doing so.

13. Most interpreters agree. See, e.g., Linforth 1919, 198. Bergk (1882), citing Herodotus 5. 71, held that the ἡγέμονες were the πρυτάνεις τῶν ναυκράρων, but nothing so precise is intended.

14. Inaction, e.g., *Iliad* 19. 221; ὕβρις, e.g., Solon 6W. 3–4.

15. Pindar, *Pythians* 8. 1, on which see Burton 1962, 175–80, and Bowra, 1964, 85.

16. Bergk (1882), however, took δαιτός with ἐν ἡσυχίῃ, in the sense "in the peace of the feast."

17. "The trachea, or windpipe, . . . extends from the lower part of the larynx, on a level with the sixth cervical vertebra, to opposite the fourth, or sometimes the fifth, dorsal vertebra" (Gray 1977, 965).

18. I avoid the word "personified." See below, p. 123.

19. Of the 1,010 extant pentameters of the authors studied in this book, 2.48 percent have hexasyllabic endings, as is shown in Table 7.

20. They occur in Aristotle, *Constitution of the Athenians*, 2. 2; Plutarch, *Solon* 13.

21. "Sore," Linforth (1919, 201); "Krankheit," Jaeger (1926, 79). For other counterarguments see Masaracchia 1958, 260–63, and the other scholars there cited.

22. See Solon 9W. 4, 11W. 4. That δουλοσύνη in those poems means "servitude under a tyrant" does not necessitate understanding it thus in 4W. 18.

23. West (1974) makes no comments on Solon 4.

24. I have not counted elided τε. Even if one does not count words without syllabic value, four-word hexameters are very rare. Cf. *Theognidea* 821W, οἵ γ' ἀπογηράσκοντας ἀτιμάζωσι τοκῆας and Xenophanes 3W. 5 (corrupt, but the text and some emendations give four words). An example from Homer is *Odyssey* 11. 594, λᾶαν βαστάζοντα πελώριον ἀμφοτέρῃσιν (Sisyphus), where, as in Solon, the weighty line is evidently a deliberate effect.

25. There is no archeological evidence for the houses of the poor (or the rich) in Solonian Athens. Our best evidence for Hellenic houses, drawn from Olynthus, is deficient in three ways: it is too late (430–348 B.C.), the houses are on the grid plan, and their owners were not poor. See D. M. Robinson, *RE*, s.v. Olynthos.

26. The best example in *LSJ* 1968 is from *Hymn to Demeter* 45, since virtually no one knew where Persephone was; but οὐκ ἐθέλειν with nonpersonal subjects seems always to suggest personification (which is explicit in *Iliad* 21. 366); and connotation gives a charm to τὰ δένδρα οὐδέν μ' ἐθέλει διδάσκειν (Plato, *Phaedrus* 230D), which is utterly lost if ἐθέλει is replaced by δύναται.

27. The formula occurs at *Iliad* 7. 68, 349, 369; 8. 6; and 19. 102; at *Odyssey* 7. 187; 8. 27; 17. 469; 18. 352; and [21. 276].

28. Zeus νέμει ὄλβον in *Odyssey* 6. 188, and νέμειν μοίρας is used of human characters in *Odyssey* 8. 470 and 15. 140.

29. Jaeger's comparison of the style with Hesiod, *Works and Days* 3–8, does not significantly affect this judgment. Solon's verses are not an imitation of Hesiod's.

30. Unlike most interpreters, Masaracchia (1958) regards the poem as "mediocre" political theory; but it is not political theory at all.

31. Vlastos (1946, 78–82) attempts to restrict the range of μοῖρα to distributive justice; but μοῖρα is relevant where ὕβρις and νέμειν are relevant. Cf. Masaracchia 1958, 262, and Adkins 1972a, 44–45, 50–54, 69–70, 84–93.

32. "Fetters" is the usual rendering; but on its one occurrence in Homer (*Iliad* 13. 36) πέδαι denotes foot-hobbles for horses.

33. He ascribes his act to the three deities in *Iliad* 19. 87, to himself in *Iliad* 19. 89. See Dodds 1951, chapter 1; Adkins 1972a, 22–57.

34. If some Athenians sold into slavery had been away long enough to forget how to speak Attic (see Solon 36W. 11–12), presumably 4W. 24 refers in part to a past event. But Solon's ἱκνέονται presents it as either a generalization ("arrive") or as present continuous ("are now arriving").

35. For Homeric vocabulary in the poem, see Linforth 1919, Masaracchia 1958, and Campbell 1967. Solon seems not to attempt purposive allusion, but at least in 27–29 Homeric echoes seem to be used for grandeur.

36. *Pace* Masaracchia 1958; but he underestimates the effect of, e.g., the language of 32–39 on those who believe what Solon is saying in a literal sense.

37. Philo, *De opificio mundi* 104; Anatolius, Περὶ δεκάδος, p. 37 Heiberg; Clement, *Stromateis* 6. 144. 3; Censorinus, *De die natali* 14. 7; Ambrose, *Epistulae* 31 (44). 13; Macrobius, *In Somnium Scipionis* 1. 6. 70–76.

38. Philo (103) comments "beginning to produce seed"; but the content of Philo's hebdomads does not always match Solon's.

39. Tyrtaeus' priamel (12W. 1–12) shows evidence of some similar constraints.

Notes to Chapter 7

1. Compare *Theognidea* 1164a–dW with 97–100W (exact repetition), 1164e–hW with 415–18W (variations).

2. For example, 153–54W (= Solon 6W. 3–4), 227–32W (= Solon 13W. 71–76), 467–96W (= Euenus[?] 8aW), and 1017–22W (= Mimnermus 5W. 1–6).

3. Steffen (1968) attempts to construct larger poems. West (1974, 40–41) has some very apposite comments.

4. *Theognidea* 373–400W, 467–96W, 697–718W, 903–30W, none of which is ascribed to Theognis by West.

5. The percentage would be higher in other editions. West is reluctant to place marks of punctuation around vocatives.

6. For example, Pythagoreans and Orphics ascribed their discoveries or compositions to Pythagoras and Orpheus. The practice was not disinterested: anything so ascribed gained in status, a consideration not irrelevant to the hortatory poet.

7. The others are 39–52W, 257–60W, 263–66W, 373–400W, 467–96W, 511–22W, 667–82W, 861–64W, and 959–62W. In 373–400W, as in 183–92W, West (1972) supposes that we possess the first and last lines but not the whole poem.

8. Stobaeus here refers to a book by Xenophon on Theognis, which is mentioned nowhere else. See Campbell 1967, 358. If Stobaeus' text is indeed derived from Xenophon's book, the lacuna which West supposes to exist after 188 presumably existed already in Xenophon's day.

9. *Theognidea* 147–48W is a startling exception. See Adkins 1960a, 78.

10. The average—0.89 marks of punctuation per line—coincides almost exactly with that for extant Xenophanes, who is at the other end of the range of variation from the *Theognidea* (1.084 marks per line). (See above, p. 14.) There could be no clearer demonstration that averages are the result of a large number of individual aesthetic decisions, which they inadequately represent; the lines are utterly unlike Xenophanes' poetry and are almost certainly authentic Theognis.

11. κατὰ γαῖαν is usually accompanied in Homer by an adjective referring to a particular place, as is γῆν in 247 of this poem; but κατ' ἀπείρονα γαῖαν (*Odyssey* 17. 418; cf. *Homeric Hymns* 15. 4) and κατὰ γαῖαν unqualified (*Hymn to Apollo* 215) both occur.

12. For the relation between αἰδώς and κατὰ κόσμον, see Adkins 1972c, 13.

13. It would resemble *Odyssey* 1. 170–73, but there the tone and context are different.

14. See my discussion of Solon 4W and Simonides 6W and 8W.

15. Explicit erotic poetry in the *Theognidea* is confined to "Book 2" (1231–1389W). Dover (1978, 57) notes that since much of the language is equally applicable to sexual attachment, friendship, and political alliance, some poems in Book 2 may have no sexual reference. Conversely, some of the poems in 1–1230W may be covertly erotic.

16. See Adkins 1960a, passim, on this topic.

17. Some sixteen in the *Theognidea* (including repeated lines), Mimnermus 14W. 8, and Solon 22aW. 2: 1.8 percent of the 1,010 pentameters of the eight elegists.

Notes to Chapter 8

1. Both are to be found under "Simonides" (1) and (2) in *RE*. There is a good brief discussion of the question in West 1974, 179–80.

2. See *RE*, Simonides 2. 2. If the Marmor Parium's date for Simonides' death is doubted, the dates become less precise.

3. It seems very likely that 15 too should be end-stopped.

4. West's index contains nineteen certain and two doubtful examples drawn from the elegists discussed in this book.

5. See Page 1962, 181. 2, the only example cited in the index. The lines are from Stesichorus' *Geryoneis*.

6. *Iliad* 10. 29, etc. περικαλύπτω is used in Hippocrates, *Aphorisms* 5. 59, Xenophon, *Cyropaedia* 7. 3. 14.

7. Homer rarely has a sentence even as periodic as *Iliad* 6. 87–92 (cf. 271–73).

8. Cf. *Palatine Anthology* 6. 127, where the speaker is a shield.

9. Lines such as *Odyssey* 2. 122 show the range of νοεῖν followed by an accusative.

10. *LSJ* 1968 cites this passage and Dionysius of Halicarnassus 10. 53. 2, οὔτε τῶν ἰατρῶν ἀρκούντων ἔτι βοηθεῖν τοῖς καμάτοις. Even here, the connotation is different from that of νόσοι, which occurs a few lines later: κάματος emphasizes the exhaustion caused by serious illness.

11. Mere counting of heads is inconclusive; but "livelihood" is about three times more common than "life" in Homer; and even when we translate "life," the connotation of "livelihood" will be present wherever it is possible.

12. As in Mimnermus 5W. 1–3, for which see p. 102, above.

13. An unpublished Oxyrhynchus papyrus overlaps Simonides 8W and 11W (basic statement by E. Lobel in Parsons and Rea 1981, 21–23); and Plutarch's ascription of 11W to Simonides seems to be generally accepted. The conjunction in the papyrus does not prove Simonidean authorship of 8W but tends to confirm it. (For this information I am indebted to Dr. P. J. Parsons and the anonymous reader of the University of Chicago Press.)

NOTES TO CHAPTER 9

1. For his possible motives, see Jaeger 1939, 1:168.

2. Cicero speaks of his *minus bonis . . . versibus* (than those of Empedocles), *Academica* 2. 23. 74.

3. B14.1 (Diels-Kranz 1951, Vol. 1) is an iambic trimeter.

4. Verdenius (1969, 337–55) thus explains γάρ in Tyrtaeus 10W. 1, comparing *Odyssey* 17. 78–83. δή emphasizes γάρ (see Denniston 1954, 243).

5. One might interpret δέ (13) as apodotic and argue that the advice is contained in 13–24. But (*a*) Denniston (1954, 177–81) quotes no examples of apodotic δέ after γάρ and few after ἐπεί, and (*b*) the singing of 12 is then a reason for the singing of 13.

6. Common already in Homer, e.g., *Iliad* 1. 61 (δαμᾷ), 62–63 (ἐρείομεν), 65 (ἐπιμέμφεται), and 66 (κνίσης), and equally common in prose, e.g., Plato's *Crito* 50B1 (ἀπολέσαι); 50C1 (ἡ πόλις), 50D3 (ὁ πατήρ), and 51A9 (πατρίς).

7. Cf. Callinus 1W. 7, Mimnermus 1W. 3.

8. Line 21 could be phrased with the pause for major caesura after either ἀεθλεύων or νικῷ.

9. Not necessarily the floor of a room: see *Odyssey* 11. 577; Aristophanes, *Plutus* 515.

10. ἕτοιμος does not suggest personification. The first examples of ἕτοιμος with persons cited by *LSJ* 1968 are Aeschylus, *Agamemnon* 842 and Pindar, *Olympians* 4. 18.

11. Compare Xenophanes 2W. 10 for an even clumsier example: εἴτε καὶ ἵπποισιν (10) continues the sequence of protases in 1–5, which has been interrupted by a sequence of main clauses in 6–9.

12. εὖ φρονεῖν is so used, as in Aeschylus, *Prometheus Bound* 385, Euripides, *Bacchae* 851, and Aristophanes, *Clouds* 817.

13. With word end at H11, both 17 and 19 violate Hermann's Bridge. The emendations in 19 "correct" the meter at the expense of the meaning.

14. But for an ancient Greek attitude to the sounds of vowels and consonants, see Dionysius of Halicarnassus, *De compositione verborum* 6. 14. 1–16. 1.

15. The argument would be similarly unsound in the case of ἀγαθός. See Adkins 1960a, passim.

16. See also Wilamowitz 1926, 279.

17. Diogenes Laertius 9. 19, after referring to Xenophanes' criticisms of Homer and Hesiod, adds ἀλλὰ καὶ αὐτὸς ἐρραψῴδει τὰ ἑαυτοῦ. But both the meaning of the statement and Diogenes' evidence for making it are unclear. It seems unlikely that Xenophanes could have made a living by performing his own verses; and 8W. 2 tells us no more than that Xenophanes was a wandering intellectual.

18. As does Defradas (1962, 347), referring to Jaeger 1936, 1:233 (= Jaeger 1939, 1:171).

19. Contrast *Nicomachean Ethics* 1145a20–25; *Metaphysics* 1072a19–1075a10. We have no grounds for supposing that Xenophanes was more consistent in poems with different types of subject matter, and εἷς θεός, ἔν τε θεοῖσι καὶ ἀνθρώποισι μέγιστος (Xenophanes B23, Diels-Kranz 1951, 1) is not the clearest statement of monotheism that could be desired.

20. τόπερ ἐστὶ πρότιμον can hardly mean "which I, Xenophanes, esteem most highly, even if other Greeks rank athletic contests in a different order." Xenophanes may not wish to deprive athletes of public esteem altogether, but he clearly does not value any of them himself.

21. Gardiner (1910, 437) cites Pausanias 6. 6. 5; 15. 5; and Artemidorus, *Oneirocritica* 1. 64 (in fact, 1. 62) as evidence that the pancration was less dangerous than boxing. Neither Pausanias passage proves his point, and Artemidorus is concerned with the significance of dreaming about the pancration.

22. Contrast ἀστοῖσι (6), which explicitly associates the people denoted with a city, presumably the athlete's own.

BIBLIOGRAPHY

Adam, J.
    1896   *Platonis Crito*. Cambridge: Cambridge University Press.

Adkins, A. W. H.
    1960a   *Merit and Responsibility: A Study in Greek Values*. Oxford: Clarendon Press.
    1960b   "Honour" and "Punishment" in the Homeric Poems. *Bulletin of the Institute for Classical Studies* 7:23–32.
    1969a   εὔχομαι, εὐχωλή and εὖχος in Homer. *Classical Quarterly* 19: 20–33.
    1969b   Threatening, Abusing and Feeling Angry in the Homeric Poems. *Journal of Hellenic Studies* 89:7–21.
    1970   Clouds, Mysteries, Socrates, and Plato. *Antichthon* 4:13–24.
    1972a   *Moral Values and Political Behaviour in Ancient Greece*. London: Chatto & Windus; Toronto: Clarke, Irwin.
    1972b   Homeric Gods and the Values of Greek Society. *Journal of Hellenic Studies* 92:1–19.
    1972c   Truth, κόσμος and ἀρετή in the Homeric Poems. *Classical Quarterly* 22:5–18.
    1975   Art, Beliefs, and Values in the Later Books of the *Iliad*. *Classical Philology* 70:239–54.
    1977a   Callinus 1 and Tyrtaeus 10 as Poetry. *Harvard Studies in Classical Philology* 81:59–97.
    1977b   Lucretius 1. 136–139 and the Problems of Writing *Versus Latini*. *Phoenix* 31:145–58.
    1982a   Laws versus Claims in Early Greek Religious Ethics. *History of Religions* 21:222–39.
    1982b   Divine and Human Values in Aeschylus' *Seven against Thebes*. Antike und Abendland 28:32–68.

1982c Values, Goals, and Emotions in the *Iliad*. *Classical Philology* 77:292–326.

Forthcoming Cosmogony and Order in Ancient Greece. In *Cosmogony and Ethical Order*, edited by F. Reynolds and R. Lovin. Chicago: University of Chicago Press.

Ahrens, H. L.
1841 Meletemata in elegiacos Graecos. *Zeitschrift für Altertumswissenschaft* 8:1214–24; 9:1012–18.

Allen, T. W.
1905 Theognis. *Classical Review* 19:386–95.

Andrewes, A.
1938 Eunomia. *Classical Quarterly* 32:89–102.

Barrie, J. M.
1922 *Dear Brutus: A Comedy in Three Acts*. New York: Scribner's.

Bergk, Th.
1882 *Poetae Elegiaci et Iambographi*. 4th ed. Leipzig: Teubner.

Bianchi, U.
1953 ΔΙΟΣ 'ΑΙΣΑ. Rome: Signorelli.

Blyth, P. H.
1977 *The Effectiveness of Greek Armour against Arrows in the Persian War (490–479 B.C.): An Interdisciplinary Inquiry*. University of Reading dissertation.
1982 The Structure of an Homeric Shield in the Museo Gregoriano Etrusco. *Bolletino dei Musei e Gallerie Pontificie* 3:5–21.

Bowra, C. M.
1938a *Early Greek Elegists*. Cambridge, Mass.: Harvard University Press.
1938b Xenophanes, fragment 1. *Classical Philology* 33:353–67.
1938c Xenophanes and the Olympic Games. *American Journal of Philology* 59:257–79.
1964 *Pindar*. Oxford: Clarendon Press.

Buck, C. D., and W. Petersen
1944 *A Reverse Index of Greek Nouns and Adjectives*. Chicago: University of Chicago Press.

Burton, R. W. B.
1962 *Pindar's Pythian Odes*. Oxford: Clarendon Press.

Campbell, D. A.
1967 *Greek Lyric Poetry*. Basingstoke and London: Macmillan.

Carrière, J.
1948 *Théognis: Poèmes élégiaques*. Paris: Les belles Lettres.

1949   *Théognis de Mégare*. Paris: Bordas.
1951   Controverse sur Théognis. *Revue des études anciennes* 52:11–17.

Charbonneaux, J.; R. Martin; and F. Villard
1971   *Archaic Greek Art*. New York: Braziller.

Croiset, A.
1914   *Histoire de la littérature grecque*. Paris: Thorin.

Defradas, J.
1962   Le Banquet de Xénophane. *Revue des études grecques* 75:344–65.

Denniston, J. D.
1952   *Greek Prose Style*. Oxford: Clarendon Press.
1954   *Greek Particles*. 2d ed., revised by K. J. Dover. Oxford: Clarendon Press.

Devine, A. M., and L. D. Stephens
1977   Preliminaries to an Explicit Theory of Greek Metrics. *Transactions of the American Philological Association* 107:103–29.
1978   The Greek Appositives: Toward a Linguistically Adequate Definition of Caesura and Bridge. *Classical Philology* 73:314–28.
1980   Rules for Resolution: The Ziclinskian Canon. *Transactions of the American Philological Association* 110:63–79.
1982   Towards a New Theory of Greek Prosody: The Suprasyllabic Rules. *Transactions of the American Philological Association* 112:33–63.

Diehl, E.
1949–   *Anthologia Lyrica Graeca*. Vol. 1: *Poetae Elegiaci*. 3d ed. Leipzig: Teubner.
1952

Diels, H., and W. Kranz
1951   *Die Fragmente der Vorsokratiker*. 6th ed. 3 vols. Berlin-Grunewald: Weidmann.

Dodds, E. R.
1951   *The Greeks and the Irrational*. Berkeley: University of California Press.

Dover, K. J.
1960   *Greek Word Order*. Cambridge: Cambridge University Press.
1978   *Greek Homosexuality*. Cambridge, Mass.: Harvard University Press.

Ebeling, H.
1885   *Lexicon Homericum*. Leipzig: Teubner.

Edmonds, J. M.
1931   *Greek Elegy and Iambus*. 2 vols. Cambridge, Mass.: Harvard University Press; London: Heinemann.

Ehrenberg, V.
1921   *Die Rechtsidee im frühen Griechentum.* Leipzig: Hirzel.
1930   Eunomia. Pp. 16–29 in *Charisteria Alois Rzach,* presented by Die Deutsche Gesellschaft für Altertumskunde in Prag. Reichenberg: Stiepel.

Evans, J. A. S.
1962   Tyrtaeus fr. 8, 1–2. *Glotta* 40:182–83.

Fitzgerald, Edward
1859   *The Rubaiyat of Omar Khayyam.* 1st ed. London: Quaritch.
1868   *The Rubaiyat of Omar Khayyam.* 2d ed. London: Quaritch.
1890   *The Rubaiyat of Omar Khayyam.* 5th (final) ed. New York: Burt.

Forrest, W. G. G.
1968   *A History of Sparta, 950–192 B.C.* London: Hutchinson.

Fränkel, H.
1926   Der kallimachische und der homerische Hexameter. Pp. 197–229 in *Nachrichten von der Gesellschaft der Wissenschaft zu Göttingen.*
1962   *Dichtung und Philosophie des frühen Griechentums.* 2d ed. Munich: Beck.

Fritz, K. von
1943   Noos and noein in the Homeric Poems. *Classical Philology* 38: 79–93.

Gaisford, A. M.
1814   *Poetae Minores Graeci.* Oxford: Clarendon Press.

Gardiner, E. A.
1910   *Greek Athletic Sports and Festivals.* London: Macmillan.

Garzya, A.
1958   *Teognide: Elegie.* Florence: Sansoni.

Gentili, B., and C. Prato.
1979   *Poetae Elegiaci, Testimonia et Fragmenta.* Leipzig: Teubner.

Gigante, M.
1956   Il testo del fr. 6.3 di Archiloco. *La Parola del Passato* 11: 196–200.

Gomme, A. W.; A. Andrewes; and K. J. Dover.
1945–1981   *A Historical Commentary on Thucydides.* 5 vols. Oxford: Clarendon Press.

Gray, H.
1977   *Anatomy, Descriptive and Surgical.* 15th ed. New York: Bounty Books.

Greenhalgh, B. A. L.
  1972   Patriotism in the Homeric World. *Historia* 21:528–37.

Groningen, B. A. van
  1958   La Composition littéraire archaïque grecque. *Verhandelingen der Koninklijke Nederlandse Academie van Wetenschappen, Afdeeling Letterkunde*, n.s. 65:2.

Halberstadt, M.
  1955   On Solon's Eunomia (frg. 3D). *Classical Weekly* 48:197–203.

Hardt, Fondation.
  1964   *Entretiens sur l'antiquité classique* no. 10. Vandoeuvres-Geneva.

Harrison, E.
  1902   *Studies in Theognis*. Cambridge: Cambridge University Press.

Hauvette, A.
  1905   *Archiloque: Sa vie et ses poésies*. Paris: Fontemoing.

Havelock, E. A.
  1963   *Preface to Plato*. Cambridge, Mass.: Harvard University Press.
  1978   *The Greek Concept of Justice from Its Shadow in Homer to Its Substance in Plato*. Cambridge, Mass.: Harvard University Press.

Hermann, G.
  1816   *Elementa doctrinae metricae*. Leipzig: Fleischer.
  1837   Extemporalia. *Zeitschrift für Altertumswissenschaft* 39:323.

Higham, T. F.
  1938   *Oxford Book of Greek Verse in Translation*. Oxford: Clarendon Press.

Hoffmann, O.
  1898   *Die griechischen Dialekte*. Vol. 3. Göttingen: Vandenhoeck & Ruprecht.

Hofinger, M.
  1977   *Lexicon Hesiodeum cum Indice Inverso*. Leiden: Brill.

Hudson-Williams, T.
  1910   *The Elegies of Theognis*. London: Bell.
  1926   *Early Greek Elegy*. Cardiff: University of Wales Press.

Jacoby, F.
  1931   *Theognis*. Berlin: de Gruyter, for the Akademie der Wissenschaften.
  1941   The Date of Archilochus. *Classical Quarterly* 35:97–109.

Jaeger, W.
  1926   Solons Eunomie. *Sitzungsberichte der Preussischen Akademie der Wissenschaften* 25:69–85.

1936   *Paideia*. 3 vols. 2d ed. Berlin and Leipzig: de Gruyter.
1939   *Paideia*. Translated by G. Highet. 3 vols. New York: Oxford University Press.

Kamerbeek, J. C.
1961   Archilochea. *Mnemosyne* 4th ser. 14:1–15.

Kipling, R.
1926   *Debits and Credits*. New York: Doubleday, Page.
1948   *The Definitive Edition of Rudyard Kipling's Verse*. London: Hodder & Stoughton.

Kirk, G. S.
1966   Studies in Some Technical Aspects of Homeric Style. *Yale Classical Studies* 20:73–152.

Kroll, J.
1936   Theognis-Interpretationen. *Philologus* Supplementband 29, Heft 1.

Kühner, R., and B. Gerth.
1898   *Ausführliche Grammatik der griechischen Sprache*. 3d ed. 4 vols. Hanover and Leipzig: Hahnsche Buchhandlung.

Lamb, W. R. M.
1924   *Plato*. English translation, vol. 4. London: Heinemann.

Leaf, W., and M. A. Bayfield.
1895   *The Iliad of Homer*. London: Macmillan.

Lefkowitz, M. R.
1976   Fictions in Literary Biography: The New Poem and the Archilochus Legend. *Arethusa* 9:181–89.
1981   *The Lives of the Greek Poets*. Baltimore: Johns Hopkins University Press.

LSJ [Liddell, H. G.; R. Scott; and H. S. Jones]
1968   *A Greek-English Lexicon*. Revised by Sir Henry Stuart Jones, with a supplement by E. A. Barber and others. Oxford: Clarendon Press.

Linforth, I.
1919   *Solon the Athenian*. University of California Publications in Classical Philology no. 6. Berkeley: University of California Press.

Lloyd-Jones, H.
1978   *Females of the Species*. Park Ridge, N.J.: Noyes Press.

Lobel, E., and D. Page
1955   *Poetarum Lesbiorum Fragmenta*. Oxford: Clarendon Press.

Maas, P.
1962   *Greek Metre*. Translated by H. Lloyd-Jones. Oxford: Clarendon Press.

Marcovich, M.
1978 Xenophanes on Drinking-Parties and the Olympic Games. *Illinois Classical Studies* 3:1–26.

Masaracchia, A.
1958 *Solone*. Florence: La Nuova Italia Editrice.

Méautis, G.
1950 Théognis (vv. 237–254). *Revue des études anciennes* 51:16–25.

Merone, E.
1960 *Aggettivazione, sintassi e figure di stile in Archiloco*. Naples: Armanni.

Monro, D. B.
1890 *Homer, "The Iliad."* 3d ed. 2 vols. Oxford: Clarendon Press.

Nagy, G.
1974 *Comparative Studies in Greek and Indic Meter*. Cambridge, Mass.: Harvard University Press.

Nash, O.
1959 *Verses from 1929 On*. Boston: Little, Brown.

Nauck, A.
1889 *Tragicorum Graecorum Fragmenta*. 2d ed. Leipzig: Teubner.

Notopoulos, J. A.
1966 Archilochus, the Aoidos. *Transactions of the American Philological Association* 97:311–15.

Page, D.
1962 *Papyri Melicae Graecae*. Oxford: Clarendon Press.
1974 *Supplementum Lyricis Graecis*. Oxford: Clarendon Press.

Parsons, P. J., and J. R. Rea
1981 *Papyri, Greek and Egyptian, Edited in Honour of Eric Gardner Turner*. London: Egypt Exploration Society.

Pépin, A.
1952 A propos d'une controverse sur Théognis (237–254). *Revue des études anciennes* 53:107.

Porter, H. N.
1951 The Early Greek Hexameter. *Yale Classical Studies* 12:1–63.

Rankin, H. D.
1977 *Archilochus of Paros*. Park Ridge, N.J.: Noyes Press.

RE
1894– *Paulys Realencyclopädie der classischen Altertumswissenschaft*.
1963 Revised edition, begun by G. Wissowa, continued by W. Kroll and K. Mittelhaus.

Reeve, M.
1971   Eleven Notes. *Classical Review* 21:324–29.
Schein, S. L.
1979   *The Iambic Trimeter in Aeschylus and Sophocles: A Study in Metrical Form.* Leiden: Brill.
Schmiel, R.
1974   Youth and Age: Mimnermus 1 and 2. *Rivista di Filologia e di Istruzione Classica* 102:283–89.
Snell, B.
1969   *Tyrtaeus und die Sprache des Epos.* Hypomnemata no. 22. Göttingen: Vandenhoeck & Ruprecht.
Snodgrass, A.
1964   *Early Greek Armour and Weapons from the End of the Bronze Age to 600 B.C.* Edinburgh: Edinburgh University Press.
Solmsen, F.
1970   *Hesiodi Theogonia, Opera et Dies, Scutum.* Oxford: Clarendon Press.
Starr, C.
1977   *The Economic and Social Growth of Early Greece.* New York: Oxford University Press.
Steffen, V.
1968   Die Kyrnos-Gedichte des Theognis. Wrocław: Zakład Narodowy im Ossolińskich. (*Archiwum filologiczne* 16.)
1973   *Scripta Minora Selecta.* 2 vols. Wrocław: Zakład Narodowy im Ossolińskich.
Tarditi, G.
1968   *Archilochus.* Rome: Edizioni dell' Ateneo.
Turyn, A.
1952   *Pindari Carmina cum Fragmentis.* Cambridge, Mass.: Harvard University Press.
Untersteiner, M.
1955   *Senofane: Testimonianze e Frammenti.* Florence: la Nuova Italia.
Verdenius, W. J.
1969   Tyrtaeus 6–7D. *Mnemosyne* 4th ser. 22:337–55.
Vlastos, G.
1946   Solonian Justice. *Classical Philology* 41:65–83.
Voemel, J. T.
1862   *Demosthenis Orationes contra Aeschinem de Corona et de Falsa Legatione.* Leipzig: Teubner.

Voigt, E. M.
  1971   *Sappho et Alcaeus*. Amsterdam: Polack & Van Gennep.
Wace, A. J. B., and F. Stubbings
  1962   *A Companion to Homer*. London: Macmillan.
Wackernagel, J.
  1916   *Sprachliche Untersuchungen zu Homer*. Göttingen: Vandenhoeck & Ruprecht.
Wade-Gery, H. T.
  1943   The Spartan Rhetra in Plutarch, *Lycurgus* VI. *Classical Quarterly* 36:62–72.
  1944   The Εὐνομία of Tyrtaeus. *Classical Quarterly* 37:1–9, 115–26.
Wells, C.
  1947   *The Book of Humorous Verse*. Compiled by Carolyn Wells. Rev. and enl. ed. Garden City, N.Y.: Garden City Publishing Co.
West, M. L.
  1972   *Iambi et Elegi Graeci ante Alexandrum Cantati*. 2 vols. Oxford: Clarendon Press.
  1974   *Studies in Greek Elegy and Iambus*. Berlin and New York: de Gruyter.
  1982   *Greek Metre*. Oxford: Clarendon Press.
Wilamowitz-Moellendorf, U. von
  1893   *Aristoteles und Athen*. 2 vols. Berlin: Weidmann.
  1926   Lesefrüchte. *Hermes* 61:277–303.
Woodhouse, W. J.
  1938   *Solon the Liberator*. London: Oxford University Press.
Wyatt, W. F., Jr.
  1966   Short Accusative Plurals in Greek. *Transactions of the American Philological Association* 97:617–43.
Young, D.
  1961   *Theognis*. Leipzig: Teubner.

GENERAL INDEX

Adam, J., 202
Adjectives: in Archilochus, 50; in Callinus, 62–63; in Mimnermus, 104–5; in Xenophanes, 196–97
Ahrens, H. L., 82, 221 n.40
Alliteration: in Solon, 121; in Xenophanes, 183
Allusion, 202, 218 n.3, 223 n.61; in Archilochus, 42–43; in Callinus, 65–66; and Fitzgerald, 25–27; and King James Bible, 211 n.33; in Kipling, 25–27; in Mimnermus, 99–101; in Ogden Nash, 27, 42; in Plato, 202–4; in Simonides, 169; in *Theognidea*, 145, 148–49, 151; in Tyrtaeus, 28, 87–91, 92; in Xenophanes, 190
Ambiguity: in Simonides, 169–72; in Solon, 118, 119, 122, 124–25; in *Theognidea*, 139, 152–53
Andrewes, A., 218 n.6
Aorist: in Solon, 118; in *Theognidea*, 140–41
Archilochus: adjectives in, 50; allusions in, 41–43, 54; and "art language," 34; and cadences, 49; first lines in, 51; and Homeric phrases, 49–50; and Homeric values, 51; and hoplite warfare, 46, 51, 215 n.58; and ring composition, 41; textual variants in, 215 n.65; variations of intensity in, 41, 50
Artistic media, 199
Authorial intention, 28, 199

Barrie, J. M., 211 n.25
Bergk, Th., 119, 144–45, 155, 167, 217 n.8, 217 nn.20, 21, 224 n.27, 226 nn.13, 16
Bianchi, U., 225 n.7
Biography of Greek poets, 31
Blyth, P. H., 225 n.7
Bowra, C. M., 98, 176, 181, 183, 184, 185, 191, 192, 195, 197
Buck, C. D., and W. Petersen, 147
Bucolic diaeresis, 13 and *passim*

Cadence, perfect and imperfect, 14; in Archilochus, 38, 40, 49; in Callinus, 58, 61; in Mimnermus, 96–97, 98, 103; in Simonides, 168; in Solon, 114; in *Theognidea*, 155, 156, 157, 159; in Tyrtaeus, 73, 80; in Xenophanes, 194
Caesura, *passim*; acoustic demand for, 4; hephthemimeral (H10), 4; major, distinguished from mandatory, 3–5; and M. L. West, 4, 209 nn.2, 10; penthemimeral (H7), 3; and P. Maas, 4, 209 n.2; trochaic (H8), 3
Callinus: and allusion, 61, 66; and ca-

241

Callinus (*continued*)
dences, 58, 61; creative use of Homeric language in, 63; and enjambment of pentameter, 58, 59; and epic formulae, 62; first lines in, 57; lacuna in, 58; poetry and rhetoric in, 57, 63, 65; polysyllables in, 58; and repetitions, 61; and reversed movement of couplet, 61; variations of intensity in, 58, 59, 64

Campbell, D. A., *passim*

Carrière, J., 147

Catalexis and brachycatalexis, 6

Charbonneaux, J., 218 n.1

Chiasmus: in *Theognidea*, 138, 139–40; in Tyrtaeus, 83

Choriambs, 115–16, Appendix

Clumsiness in Xenophanes, 178, 180, 193, 194; not merely prosaic, 197

Coinage of words : in Archilochus, 44; in Callinus, 217 n.26; in Mimnermus, 104, 172; in Solon, 131

Connotations, 1, 201, 226 n.26; in Callinus, 62–63; in Mimnermus, 106; in Simonides, 165

Courage, in Homer and Tyrtaeus, 78

Croiset, A., 212 n.14

Dactylic hemiepes (D): in Maas (1962), 2; in West (1982), 2

Dactylic hexameter: and anapaests, 6; of four words, 120; mandatory features of, 3

Dactyls: and broken rhythm in *Theognidea*, 136; and words ending in long syllable, 116

Definite article, omitted in poetry, 52, 118, 202

Defradas, J., 176, 181, 183, 184, 185, 186, 230 n.18

Demosthenes, and word order in Greek prose, 19–20

Denniston, J. D., 38, 120, 189–90, 194, 195, 213 n.27, 220 nn.29, 30, 221 n.37, 229 nn.4, 5

Devine, A. M., and L. D. Stephens, 205

Dicolon, 98

Diehl, E., 53, 215 n.65

Dionysius Chalcus, 209 n.4

Dionysius of Halicarnassus, 210 nn.12, 17, 18, 229 n.14

Dodds, E. R., 227 n.33

Dover, K. J., 19, 33, 34, 67, 74, 147, 152, 185, 212 n.10, 214 n.34, 223 n.13, 224 n.21, 228 n.15

Early Greek elegists: defined, 2; and Homer, 1

Edmonds, J. M., 114, 159, 217 n.20, 219 n.16, 224 n.27

Ehrenberg, V., 122, 225 n.1

Elegiac couplet: acoustic features of, 3; analyzed, 2–17; dynamics of, 103; flexibility of, 3, 5, 17–18; rhythm reversed in, 46, 61, 82, 85, 96–97, 116, 158

Elegiac pentameter as clausula, 6

Elision in elegiacs: at major caesurae and diaeresis, 5; not at line end, 5

Emotions, Greek vocabulary of, 104

Enclitics and proclitics, 209 n.3

Enjambment: in Archilochus, 36, 40, 41, 45, 48, 49; in Callinus, 57, 58, 59, 60, 61; and change of theme, 39, 51, 97, 104, 213 n.26; in Homer, 22–23; in Mimnermus, 97, 98, 103, 104–5; of molossus, 61, 71, 82, 84, 120, 122, 129, 141, 144, 146, 157, 160; of pentameters, 58, 59, 210 n.11, 213 n.25; and prepositional phrases, 45; in Simonides, 168; in Solon, 114, 115, 120, 129; in *Theognidea*, 136, 138, 139, 141, 144, 145–46, 151, 155, 156, 157, 159, 160; three types distinguished, 7, 209 n.5; in Tyrtaeus, 71, 73, 80, 82, 83, 85; in Xenophanes, 177, 189, 190, 192, 193, 194, 195–96. *See also* Cadences *and introductions to individual poets and poems*

Epic language: in Archilochus, 34, 41–43, 49–50, 53–54; in Callinus, 61–66; in Mimnermus, 99–101, 102–6; in Simonides, 163–64; in

Theognidea, 148, 152–53; in Tyrtaeus, 87–92; in Xenophanes, 190, 192–93. *See also* Allusion; Homeric language
Epigram, in Simonides, 161
Eunomia: in Solon, 122; in Tyrtaeus, 122; in Xenophanes, 196–98
Evans, J. A. S., 220 n.31
Exhortation in elegiac poetry, 30, 44–45

Final word of hexameter, 15–16 and Table 6; monosyllable, 209 n.6; pentesyllable, 113. *See also introductions to individual poets and poems*
Final word of pentameter, 15–16 and Table 7; heptasyllable, 58, 73; hexasyllable, 117; monosyllable, 196; pentesyllable, 49, 104. *See also introductions to individual poets and poems*
First and last lines of poems, 57, 111, 128, 135, 220 n.29
Fitzgerald, E., 25–28, 89
Formulae, and appreciation of novelty, 47
Fränkel, H., 183, 212 n.14, 224 n.16
Freudian interpretation, 215 n.64
Fritz, K. von, 106

Gaisford, A. M., 224 n.27
Gardiner, E. A., 230 n.21
Garzya, A., 143
Genos, in Hesiod and *Theognidea*, 141
Gigante, M., 216 n.25
Gods: favor their own, 79–80; irascible and not omniscient, 79
Greek alphabet, date of introduction of, 70
Greek poetry: and everyday speech, 34, 212 n.19; meant for performance, 1; problems of, for modern reader, 1
Greek poets and autobiography, 33
Greek word order: flexible but not arbitrary, 19; and sense groups, 19
Greenhalgh, B. A. L., 219 n.17

Groningen, B. A. van, 212 n.14, 223 n.11

Harrison, E., 138
Hearing and understanding, 168–69
Hermann, G., 156, 209 n.8
Hermann's Bridge, 209 n.8, 229 n.13
Hiatus, common at line end, 5
Higham, T. F., 217 n.16
Hoffmann, O., 215 n.63
Hofinger, M., 223 n.64
Homer and the early elegists, 1, 21–29
Homeric formulae, 90. *See also* Allusion; Epic language; Homeric language
Homeric hymns, date of, 212 n.6
Homeric language: creative use of, 63; how defined, 34
Homeric values: and Archilochus, 42–43, 51; and Mimnermus, 99–100; and Tyrtaeus, 90
Homeric vocabulary, 202, 214 n.34, 227 n.35. *See also* Epic language; Homeric language
Hoplites, numbers of, 219 n.19
Hoplite warfare: and Archilochus, 46, 51; casualties in, 215 n.60; and metal supply, 215 n.58; and Tyrtaeus, 90
Hudson-Williams, T., 135, 139, 143, 144, 149, 151, 217 n.19

Intensity, levels of: in Archilochus, 41, 50; in Callinus, 58, 59, 64; in Mimnermus, 103; in *Theognidea*, 140; in Xenophanes, 193

Jacoby, F., 33, 135
Jaeger, W., 117, 225 n.1, 226 n.21, 227 n.29, 230 n.18
Justice: and deity, 154; types of, 124

Kamerbeek, J. C., 212 n.14, 214 n.35
Kipling, R., 25–28, 211 n.33
Kirk, G. S., 22, 209 n.2
Kroll, J., 143, 146, 147, 160

Lacunae: in Callinus, 58; in Solon, 111; in *Theognidea*, 140

Last lines, 222 n.53
Leaf, W., and M. A. Bayfield, 65
Lefkowitz, M. R., 107, 211 n.36, 212 n.5
Life and death, in Homer and Tyrtaeus, 87–88
Light-armed troops, 86–87, 222 n.52
Linforth, I., 115, 118, 119, 120, 123, 225 n.1, 226 nn.13, 21, 227 n.35
Lists, in Greek poetry, 177
Lloyd-Jones, H., 167
Lobel, E., and D. L. Page, 165
Lycurgus: Attic orator, 86, 221 n.43; Spartan king, 70

Maas, P., 2, 4, 209 n.2
Marcovich, M., 179, 188, 194, 195, 198
Masaracchia, A., 116, 117, 225 nn.1, 4, 7, 226 n.21, 227 nn.30, 31, 35, 36
Merone, E., 215 n.55
Metaphor, sustained, 122
Meter constraining language, 126–32
Mimnermus: allusions in, 99–101, 106; balanced phrases in, 105; and cadences, 96–97, 98; and change of theme, 97, 104; coinage of words by, 172; and dynamics of the elegiac couplet, 103; and fifth-century usage of words, 172; and Homeric connotations, 106; and Homeric values, 99; quoted by Solon, 108; and reversed movement of couplet, 96–97; and rhetoric, 98–100; ring composition in, 99; spondees and dactyls in, 102; and tensions of couplet, 104; textual problems in, 101–2; and varied intensity, 103; and word length, 104
Monosyllabic ending, 196
Monro, D. B., 8
Myth, and Xenophanes, 184, 186

Nagy, G., 34
Nanno, 93–94, 102
Nash, O., 27–28, 89
Native speakers, 1, 15; and sound of verses, 17; and word length, 17
Notopoulos, J. A., 212 n.12

Page, D. L., 43–44, 49, 137, 146, 147, 148, 191, 195, 211 n.4, 214 nn.42, 46, 215 nn.50, 52, 216 n.72, 228 n.5
Papyri: of Archilochus, 48; of Simonides, 229 n.13
Parallel phrases in Tyrtaeus, 71
Parry, M., and the aesthetics of oral poetry, 44
Parsons, P. J., and J. R. Rea, 229 n.13
Particles, absence of, 82, 213 n.20
Pentameter: and dying fall, 53, 81, 82; of three words, 73
Pépin, A., 147
Performance: and Greek poetry, 1, 3, 10, 14; and Greek prose, 19–20; and the rhythm of the elegiac couplet, *passim*; and the sequence of ideas, *passim*; and short spondaic words, 98; and Simonides 8W, 167
Personalization, 88, 123
Personification, 123, 179
Plato, and allusion, 202–4
Poem as hierarchy of interacting systems, 17
Poetic craft, ix, 200–201
Poetry: and history, 69–71, 77, 110; in nonliterate cultures, 33; and political theory, 110–11, 113, 117–19, 123–25; and rhetoric, 29–31, 57, 63, 65, 71–74, 79–92, 98, 111–25, 141–42
Political theory, 110, 113, 114, 117–19, 123–25
Polysyllables: in Archilochus, 38, 43, 49; in Callinus, 58; in Mimnermus, 104; in Solon, 117; in *Theognidea*, 133, 148; in Tyrtaeus, 73; in Xenophanes, 189, 191, 192
Porter, H. N., 209 n.2
Procedure used in this book, 31–32
Pronunciation, fluid, 214 n.23
Punctuation: different frequencies of, in different poets, 14; effect of, 11–13; at H16, 209 n.6; less frequent in pentameter, 13; none canonical, 7; not at H6, H9, or H11, 10; and pause, 7; and poetry, 60; positions in hexameter and pentameter, 7–17 and Tables 1,

2, 3; relatively infrequent, 14; in Xenophanes, 177

Quantitative data and qualitative judgments, 35

Rankin, H. D., 212 n.5
Reeve, M., 213 n.30
Repetition of words, in Greek poetry, 65, 85, 158
Rhetoric: in Mimnermus, 98, 100; and poetry, 29–31; in Solon, 111–25; in *Theognidea*, 141–42; in Tyrtaeus, 31, 71–74, 79–92
Rhetorical figures, 31; already in Homer, 31, 211 n.35
Rhythm: broken, 115–16, 136, 151, 154, 156–60, 201; of elegiac couplet, 2–17, 201; and sense, 136, 151, 182, 201
Ring composition: in Archilochus, 41; in Mimnermus, 99; in Tyrtaeus, 69

Schein, S. L., 205
Schmiel, R., 224 nn.16, 19
Semonides, not author of Simonides 8W, 161, 167, 173
"Seven Ages of Man," and Solon, 126–27
Shakespeare: and Solon, 126; as source for allusions, 24
Shield, defines hoplite, 80, 85
Simonides: ambiguity in, 169–72; author of Simonides 8W, 161; cadences in, 168; and connotations, 165; enjambment in, 168; epic language in, 163, 164; epigram in, 161; and formulae, 162; on hearing and understanding, 168–69; and performance, 167; spondees and dactyls in, 165, 170
Snell, B., 91
Snodgrass, A., 77, 219 nn.21, 22, 222 n.49
Solmsen, F., 214 n.38
Solon: alliteration in, 121; ambiguity in, 113, 118, 119, 121, 122, 124–25, 129; broken rhythm in, 115–16; cadences in, 114; enjambment in, 114, 115, 120, 129; and *eunomia*, 122; first and last lines in, 111, 128; Homeric vocabulary in, 227 n.35; meter constraining language in, 126–32; and performance of 4W, 111; and personification, 123; poetry and history in, 110; poetry and political theory in, 110–11, 113, 117, 118, 119, 123–25; poetry and rhetoric in, 119, 122; and political theory, 110, 113, 114; polysyllables in, 113, 117; and purpose of 27W, 132; reversed rhythm in, 116; rhetoric in, 112, 113, 114; and "Seven Ages of Man," 126–27; spondees and dactyls in, 113, 117; unusual rhythm in, 115–16, Appendix; wounds not diseases in, 118
Sparta: and the arts, 218 n.1; constitution of, 69–71, 74–75
Spartan constitution, and Tyrtaeus, 70
Spondees and dactyls, 3, 18–19, 213 n.18; in Archilochus, 37, 45, 48, 52; effective use of, by all eight poets, 201 and *passim*; in Mimnermus, 96, 97, 102; in Simonides, 163, 165, 170; in Solon, 113, 117, 127; in *Theognidea*, 139, 145, 149, 150, 153; in Tyrtaeus, 72, 79, 80, 81, 82, 83; in Xenophanes, 178, 179, 181–83, 189–90, 192–93, 196
Statistical significance and limited data, 35. *See also introductory discussion of each poet and poem*
Steffen, V., 167, 227 n.3
Syllaba anceps in elegiacs: frequent at line end, 5; rare at caesura and diaeresis, 5
Syllables, system of numbering, 3
Synizesis, 46–47, 97–98
Syntax and poetry, 202

Tarditi, G., 212 n.6
Tensions and verbal patterns, 104
Textual variants: in Archilochus, 46–47, 53, 214 n.46, 215 n.65; in Homer,

Textual variants (*continued*) 224 n.20; in Mimnermus, 101–2, 103; in Solon, 120; in Tyrtaeus, 69, 82–83, 221 n.40; in Xenophanes, 179, 182

Theme change, not at line end, 97, 104

Theognidea: allusions in, 148–49, 151; ambiguity in, 139, 152–53; broken and smooth rhythm in, 136, 151, 154, 156–57, 158, 159, 160; cadences in, 155, 159; chiasmus in, 138, 139–40; enjambment in, 136, 138, 139, 141, 144, 145–46, 151, 155, 156, 157, 159, 160; epic language in, 148, 152–53; first and last lines of poems in, 135; justice and deity in, 154; polysyllables in, 133, 148; as proportion of extant early elegy, 133; repetitions in, 133, 158; rhetoric and poetry in, 141–42; spondees and dactyls in, 139, 149; and Theognis, 133; variations of tension in, 140

Theognis' Megara, identity of, 135

Tmesis, 144

Transvaluation of values, 81

Tricolon, 100

Tyrtaeus: allusions in, 11, 87–92; ambiguity in, 73–74; and cadences, 73; courage in, 78; Homeric courage in, 78; Homeric formulae in, 90; and Homeric values, 90; and hoplite armor, 77; life and death in, 87–88; parallel phrases in, 71; and personalization, 88; reversed rhythm in, 82, 85; rhetoric in, 72, 74, 80, 82, 92; ring composition in, 69; and the Spartan constitution, 70; spondees and dactyls in, 72, 79, 81, 82, 83; and transvaluation of values, 81; variant readings in, 221 n.40

Untersteiner, M., 183

Variant readings. *See* Textual variants
Variety as possible poetic goal, 18
Verdenius, W. J., 229 n.4
Vlastos, G., 123, 124, 225 n.1, 227 n.31
Voemel, J. T., 225 n.4
Voigt, E. M., 137, 145, 146, 148, 191, 192

Wackernagel, J., 179
Wade-Gery, H. T., 69, 75
West, M. L., *passim*
Wilamowitz-Moellendorf, U. von, 183, 185, 225 n.6, 230 n.16
Woodhouse, W. J., 110
Word divisions, graded, 11
Word end, permitted positions for, 8–10
Word length, 133; in final position, Tables 6 and 7
Word order, *passim*
Wounds not diseases, 118
Wyatt, W. F., Jr., 218 n.2

Xenophanes: adjectives in, 196–97; alliteration in, 183; and cadences, 194; clumsiness in, 178, 180, 193, 194; epic language in, 190, 192–93; and *eunomia*, 196–98; and Hermann's Bridge, 229 n.13; and lists in Greek poetry, 177; monosyllabic ending in, 196; and myth, 184, 186; personification in, 179; polysyllables in, 189, 191, 192; punctuation in, 177; rhythm and sense in, 182; social status of, 185; *sophia* and poetry in, 194–95; spondees and dactyls in, 183, 190, 192, 193, 196; varied tensions in, 193; and word order, 178, 189

Zeus, addressed by appropriate titles, 157–58

GREEK INDEX

WORDS AND PHRASES DISCUSSED AS POSSIBLE SOURCES OF ALLUSION

ἀγάλλεται, 54
αἰεὶ δ' ἐν δαίτῃσι καὶ εἰλαπίνῃσι παρέσται, 145
ἀμώμητον, 54
ἀνδρῶν τρεσσάντων, 89
ἀνήκεστον κακόν, 43

διδασκόμενος πολέμοιο, 91

ἐξεσάωσα[ε], 54
ἐπιθήσει / φάρμαχ', 41
ἔργ' ἀΐδηλα, 88
ἐρρέτω, 54

ἥβης ἄνθος, 100
ἤματί κεν τριτάτῳ Φθίην ἐρίβωλον ἵκοιο, 202

θοῆς ἐπὶ νηός, 51

ἰοστέφανος, 150

καὶ ἐσσομένοισιν ἀοιδή, 151
καί μευ κλέος οὐρανὸν ἵκει, 148
καὶ μὴν Τάνταλον εἰσεῖδον, 203
κατακεῖσθαι, 62
κήδεα . . . στονόεντα, 41

κρατερόφρονος ἀνδρός, 65
κρυπταδίη φιλότης, 99
κῦμα πολυφλοίσβοιο θαλάσσης, 43

μεθιέναι, 62
μείλιχα δῶρα, 99

ὀβριμόεργος, 90
οἵη περ φύλλων γενέη, τοίη δὲ καὶ ἀνδρῶν, 166
οἶνον ἐρυθρόν, 50
ὃν καὶ περκνὸν καλέουσιν, 190
ὃς πᾶσι δόλοισιν / ἀνθρώποισι μέλω, 148
οὐδὲ θανὼν ὄνομ' ὤλεσας, 148
οὐκ ἐθέλων, 53

παρ' ἀλλήλοισι μένοντες, 89
πολύδακρυν Ἄρηα, 88
πύργος, 65–66

ταλασίφρων, 28
τέρπεται ἐν θαλίῃσι, 41
τὸν δὲ μέτ' εἰσενόησα, 203

χρυσῆς Ἀφροδίτης, 99

Other Important Words Discussed in the Text

ἀγαθός, in lines 183–92 of the *Theognidea*, 135, 137–41; in Xenophanes, 195
ἀγλαός, and creative use of Homeric words, 63–64
αἰδώς, and Cyrnus, 152
αἰσχρός, -όν: and defeat while fighting bravely, 215 n.62; and Homer, 78; spans "shameful" and "ugly," 83
ἀμφιπερικτίονας, probably coined as heptasyllabic hemiepes, 58. *See also* ἀνταπαμειβομένους
ἀναφαίνειν, of both words and deeds, 184
ἀνδράσιν ἠδὲ γυναιξίν, not otiose in Mimnermus 5W, 97
ἀνήρ: and ἄνθρωπος, 169; puzzling emphasis of, 183; "warrior," 59, 79
ἄνθεα, pronounced as disyllable, 97
ἀνταγορία, and the Spartan constitution, 74–75
ἀνταπαμειβομένους, probably coined as heptasyllabic hemiepes, 73. *See also* ἀμφιπερικτίονας
ἄρχειν, ambiguous in Tyrtaeus 4W, 72
ἄσπετος, use of, in Homer and Mimnermus, 102
ἀστοῖσιν, emphatic in Xenophanes 2W, 190
ἄτη, hybristic persons not punished with, 159
αὐλίσκοι, not necessarily treble, 147
ἄωρος, possibly coined by Solon, 131

βλάπτειν, meaning of, in Mimnermus 5W, 105, 225 n.37
βούλεσθαι, distinguished from μέλλειν, 113

δαήμονες, sound and spelling of, 46
δαιτὸς ἐν ἡσυχίη, phrasing of, 115
δήμου . . . ἡγεμόνων, not a technical usage, 114
δῆμος, δημόσιος, ambiguous in Solon 4W, 120

δνοφερός, and epic usage, 148
δουλοσύνη, ambiguous in Solon 4W, 118
δουρικλυτοί, not otiose in Archilochus 3W, 45–47
δυσμενέσιν, and change of theme, 59
δώματα, used of single building, 185

εἴτε καὶ ἵπποισιν, harsh hyperbaton of, in Xenophanes 2W, 193
εἴτε παλαίων, bathetic in Xenophanes 2W, 189
ἕλκος, not "disease," 118
ἐλπίς, and Simonides' goal in 8W, 170
ἑλών, more vivid than ἔχων in Tyrtaeus 11W, 86
ἐντός, rare in singular, 52
ἐξ ἀγαθῶν βήσεσθαι, ambiguous in *Theognidea* 185W, 139
[ἐξ]εναρίζειν, in sense of "kill," 51
ἐπιτιθέναι, of drugs, 39
ἐρατός, spans "lovely" and "beloved," 147
ἕρκος ὀδόντων, and metrical convenience, 128
ἐσθλός, and good pedigree, 135, 137–41
ἕτοιμος, not of persons before fifth century, 229
εὐγενής, εὐηγενής, used strictly of birth in the *Theognidea*, 136, 137–38
εὔφημος, new usage in Xenophanes, 181
εὔφρων, not attested in sense of σώφρων, 181

ζάπεδον, both "earth" and "floor," 185
ζυγόν, of animals and ships, 163

ἥβης ἄνθος: in Homer and Mimnermus, 100; in Simonides, 166
ἥβη τιμήεσσα, youth as status-conferring gift, 104

Index   249

θέμεθλα δίκης, not "foundations of justice," 116–17
θερμός, ambiguous in Simonides 6W, 165

ἱμερόεις, use before Tyrtaeus, 72–73
ἰοστέφανος, of Aphrodite and the Muses, 150
ἵππota and short-vowel accusative plurals, 218 n.2

καθαρός, and the interpretation of Xenophanes 1W, 181, 186
κακός, -όν: of birth, in lines 183–92 of the *Theognidea*, 135, 137–41; in Homer, 78; in Tyrtaeus, 78
κάλλιπον: ambiguity of, 53; one of Archilochus' Aeolic forms, 216 n.67
κάλλιστον, ambiguity of, in Simonides 8W, 168
κάματος, ambiguity of, in Simonides 8W, 171
κατὰ γῆν, and tmesis, 144, 288 n.11
κείμενος ἐν στόμασιν, possibly erotic, 145
κινεῖν, more terrible than νεύειν in Tyrtaeus 11W, 90
κοσμεῖν, and discipline, in Solon 4W, 115
κρατερός, and active and passive states of mind, 40
κριούς, replaced by "dogs" in Stobaeus, 135
κύδιστος, possibly stronger than κυδρός, 191

λαχνοῦσθαι, possibly coined by Solon, 129
λιγύφθογγος, means "clear-voiced," 142

μάθη, emendation for πάθη in Tyrtaeus 11W, 82, 221 n.40
μέγας, possibly Ephesian use of, 65
μείγνυμι, metaphorical use of, 64
μείλιχος, and personification of wine, 179

μέρος, fifth-century usage in Simonides 6W, 162
μοῖρα, and Solon's thought, 122
μῶλος, and the depersonalization of war, 46

νέοι, not necessarily tyros in war, 80-81

ὄβριμος, and repetition of words in Greek poetry, 85
οἰδαλέους: and D. L. Page, 43–44; first in Archilochus, 39
ὀλίγος, possibly Ephesian use of, 65
ὀλιγοχρόνιος, possibly coined by Mimnermus, 104
ὁμηλικίη, as bond of association, 103
ὀργή, and personalization of πόλεμος, 88
οὐκ ἐθέλω, not synonymous with οὐ δύναμαι, 121, 226 n.26

πάσῃ πόλει, ambiguous in Solon 4W, 118
πλεκτός, not otiose in Xenophanes 1W, 178
πλέον εἶναι, not Greek for "last longer," 103
προδιδόναι, of wine, 179
προεδρίη, an ancient privilege, 191–92
προκρίνειν, possibly coined by Xenophanes in 2W, 195
πρόμαχοι, in Homer and Tyrtaeus, contrasted, 87
πρόποσις, ambiguous in Simonides 6W, 165
προχειρότερον, puzzling in Xenophanes 1W, 182
πτέρα διδόναι, novel metaphor in line 237 of the *Theognidea*, 144
πτοιῶμαι, in Homer and Mimnermus, 102–3
πτώσσοντες, of light-armed, pejorative, 86

σκολιόν: contrasted with εὐθείαις, 73; virtually certain in Tyrtaeus 4W, 73

Σμυρνηῖς, possible name for a woman, 94

τέχνη, spans "art" and "craft," 1, 200
τιμήεις, and creative use of Homeric words, 63–64
τοίους, and emphasis of spondees in elegy, 38
τρύχεσθαι, does not suggest "disease" in Solon 4W, 119

ὕβρις: not relevant in Xenophanes 2W, 197; in Solon's political thought, 124; in *Theognidea*, 155; in Xenophanes 1W, 182

φανερός, possible political overtones of, in Xenophanes 2W, 192
φειδόμενοι, and the rhythm of line 13 in Solon 4W, 115–16
φιλοψυχεῖν, elaborated in lines 5–6 of Tyrtaeus 11W, 87
φοβεῖσθε, not necessarily otiose with δειμαίνετε, 220 n.33
φοιτᾶν, of repeated motion, 49

χρήμασι πειθόμενοι, and Solon's political rhetoric, 113